THE

FATAL HARVEST
—— READER ——

THE TRAGEDY OF INDUSTRIAL AGRICULTURE

EDITED BY
ANDREW KIMBRELL

ISLAND PRESS

WASHINGTON ❖ COVELO ❖ LONDON

DEDICATION

*To the agrarian mind, which is the
only mind capable of rebuilding the
culture of healthy soils, water cycles,
richness, and diversity. May it multiply
in future generations so they can
recoup what has been lost and create
farms and economies that are
sustainable, humane, and beautiful.*

*And to wildness, that essential quality
whereby nature in all her wisdom
unfolds with a genius that can only
be manifested by undomesticated,
unhumanized, and unmanaged large
portions of the landscape.*

LIBRARY OF CONGRESS CATALOGING-IN-PUBLICATION DATA
   The Fatal harvest reader: the tragedy of industrial agriculture /
edited by Andrew Kimbrell.
      p. cm.
   Includes bibliographical references (p.   ) and index.
   ISBN 1-55963-944-X (paperback : alk. paper)
   1. Agriculture—Environmental aspects. 2. Agricultural ecology.
   3. Organic farming. 4. Agriculture—Environmental aspects—United States.
   5. Agricultural ecology—United States. 6. Organic farming—United States.
   I. Kimbrell, Andrew.
   S589.75 .F39 2002
   630'.2'77—dc21   2002002661

Published by the Foundation for Deep Ecology in collaboration with Island Press.

Printed in the United States on acid-free recycled paper, of which 30 percent is post-consumer waste.

Cover and book design by Daniela Sklan
Front cover photograph by Ken Hammond, USDA
Back cover photograph by Miguel Altieri

Foundation for Deep Ecology
Building 1062, Fort Cronkhite
Sausalito, California 94965

10 9 8 7 6 5 4 3

CONTENTS

AFTERWORD

*Essays that do not carry an author's name were written
by the editors.*

PROLOGUE

DOUGLAS TOMPKINS

We are currently in the midst of a crisis of culture and agriculture. This dual crisis, first described by Wendell Berry 25 years ago in *The Unsettling of America*, has now become tragically apparent. The cultural crisis is rooted in the transformation of America from an essentially agrarian culture to one that is now almost completely industrialized.

Our conversion from agrarian, local, fully integrated food systems to industrialized, monocultured agricultural production has brought a staggering number of negative side effects, many of them unanticipated. Throughout the entire food system, we can trace this crisis as it manifests itself in soil erosion, poisoned ground waters, food-borne illnesses, loss of biodiversity, inequitable social consequences, toxic chemicals in foods and fiber, loss of beauty, loss of species and wildlife habitat, and myriad other environmental and social problems. To make the crisis even worse, we continue to export this destructive industrial system of food production around the world.

The essays in this book provide a comprehensive and integrated portrait of the current cultural and agricultural crisis. They also analyze the pathology of the transformation we have witnessed in food production. The book's subject matter reaches into virtually every facet of our daily lives, beyond the obviousness of the meals we eat each day and the cotton clothes we wear. Agriculture, with its related processes, one discovers, is the largest and most important industry in our economy. And as this book amply documents, it is also a primary contributor to our environmental woes as it has created massive monocultures which have replaced our small and diverse family farms, poisoned our waters, air, and food, and biologically and aesthetically degraded our landscapes. In the implacable march of agriculture across our continent we have lost vast areas that should have been left to wildlife habitat; we have displaced wild species with domesticated animals and oceans of monocultures. Clearly, if one wants to be an "environmentalist," the study of agriculture and its catastrophic impacts is absolutely essential. There is great wisdom in the old dictum "environmentalism begins at the breakfast table."

A primary purpose of this book is to give the public and activists a compelling textbook with which to understand the interconnections, the mind-set, and the economic and political power interests involved in our globalized food production system. This in-depth understanding is essential if we are to strategically confront the powers controlling our food supply and reverse the crisis in which we find ourselves ensnared. There are also numerous essays which describe very real sustainable alternatives to our current disastrous course. You will read of the work of farmers, activists, and organizations who vividly demonstrate that there is hope, despite the seemingly overwhelming odds against reversing the crisis of culture and of agriculture. Their message is that we must inform ourselves, and join in solidarity with the countless activists all around the world to fight the threat of globalization, industrial agriculture, industrial forestry, aquaculture, toxics, and megatechnologies.

Ultimately, this book is a call to arms — arms to hug with, arms to dig and plant with, and arms to link together to confront the juggernaut of industrialism, especially its tragic takeover of our agriculture. We cannot rest until we have regained a culture and agriculture that is local, family-scale, and fully integrated with the richness and diversity of creation.

ACKNOWLEDGEMENTS

Creating this book required an unusually committed and talented team. Leading the editorial staff were associate editors Rebecca Spector and Amy Bricker, whose tireless efforts are reflected on virtually every page of this book. We also wish to acknowledge the invaluable contributions of designer Daniela Goff-Sklan; writer Mark Briscoe; researchers Miyoko Sakashita and Stephanie Welch; copyeditor Ellen Smith; proofreader Vicki Botnick; indexer Ellen Davenport; and Island Press for their invaluable assistance in bringing this book to the public. This book would not have been possible without their work and contributions.

Two organizations, The Foundation for Deep Ecology (FDE) and the Center for Food Safety (CFS) were also key collaborators in the making of this book. Special thanks go to FDE for its unflagging vision and support, and to FDE staff, including publishing manager Sharon Donovan who artfully negotiated the book's publication; agriculture program officer Melanie Adcock whose supervisory oversight was essential; and Quincey Imhoff for her continued guidance. We also wish to acknowledge the vital research and writing support of CFS staff including contributions from legal director Joseph Mendelson III, Sheila Knoploh-Odole, and Juliana Jones.

The most significant contributors to the *The Fatal Harvest Reader* are of course the writers whose work fill the book's pages. These prominent thinkers and activists contributed their work with enthusiasm and often with little or no remuneration. We therefore extend our deepest thanks and appreciation to them.

Finally, we are indebted to Douglas Tompkins, whose unflagging vision, support, and effort made possible this book, and its companion volume *Fatal Harvest: The Tragedy of Industrial Agriculture*.

— Andrew Kimbrell, Editor

INTRODUCTION

ANDREW KIMBRELL

As were other Americans of my generation, I was brought up inundated with such corporate bromides as "better living through chemistry," "progress is our middle name," and even "DDT is good for me." As for food, the future was clear. It was epitomized by the culinary habits of TV's futuristic Jetson family, who met their daily nutritional requirements by eating various tablets rather than food. And emulating the astronauts, our future beverage of choice would be Tang. Behind all the jingles, ads, and media mantras of that time was the unquestioned message that the more we industrialized our food production, the more "modern" and desirable the food. Agribusiness and the food industry tirelessly promoted industrial food — food that depends on massive chemical and biological inputs, huge monocultures, and factory-like farms and that results in huge corporate profits. Over the years the media strategies have become more clever and the technology has grown more sophisticated, but the decades-old "artificial is better" worldview still dominates today's agribusiness. The corporations continue to foist this industrial food model on us by strong-arming our elected officials and government agencies, buying out our educational institutions, suing recalcitrant farmers, and, of course, flooding the media.

For several decades, our indoctrination into this industrial food mind-set went without widespread challenge. Our highly urbanized society is far removed from the sources and origins of its daily bread. Over the last century we have been transformed from a nation of farmers, with our hands and minds linked to the soil, to consumers lined up in supermarkets to buy an array of slickly packaged food products about which we know very little. This great physical and psychological distance between consumer and food production creates a tragic disconnect between the general public and the social and environmental consequences of the food being grown and eaten. This disconnect between us and our agricultural system was, and remains, essential "cover" that allows the corporations to hide the real and terrible impacts of the industrialization of our food supply. The disconnect is fostered by cynical ads and media images which continue to portray farmers in the old agrarian tradition — overalls, family farms, and regional dialects intact — and the average American is lulled into thinking his food production is still localized and done on a human scale. Meanwhile, crimes against nature, biodiversity, and farmers are being perpetrated with little or no public awareness, as the industrialized agriculture revolution continues to transform America's farmlands and food supply. We eat our daily bread without being conscious of the massive loss of topsoil, diversity, and farm communities involved in its production. We happily munch on hamburgers without a thought to the forest and prairie being destroyed for cattle grazing or the immense cruelty in the raising and slaughtering of the animals. Mothers continue to prod their youngsters to eat their vegetables, unaware of the pesticide poisoning of our waters, farmworkers, and wildlife that is involved in their production, not to mention the new human health and ecological risks of genetic engineering. This distancing and ignorance make us all unintentionally complicit in the eco-crimes and social devastation caused by current agriculture. In this way industrial food creates a moral as well as an environmental crisis.

Remarkably, in recent years, something happened on the way to the corporate-planned industrialized food future — something that the agribusiness proponents did not see coming. Despite untold billions spent in advertising and disinformation campaigns, people started making the connections between industrial food and ecological and social havoc. Perhaps this revolution really began in earnest when Rachel Carson forcefully described how the death of the nation's birds, a "silent spring," was being caused by the use of DDT and other pesticides. It soon became evident that a number of our most urgent environmental problems — whether water and air pollution, topsoil loss, or wilderness and habitat destruction — were direct results of our food production system. Some of those suffering from or treating cancer began to realize that one major cause of the epidemic was the chemicals in our food. Others witnessed the devastation of farms and farm communities under the heel of corporate takeovers and said "enough." Now, across the country numerous organizations fight the misuse of pesticides and against the genetic engineering and irradiation of our foods. Many others struggle for the protection of farmers and their communities. What's worse for the proponents of agribusiness is that this movement has had an effect. Millions of Americans have decided to vote day after day with their food dollars for a different vision of agriculture. Through their food choices they have begun to demonstrate new attitudes about maintaining their health, healing the earth, and protecting farm communities and animal welfare. As a result, more of us are eating organic than ever before, and organic food production, though still small, is the fastest growing segment in U.S. agriculture today. Ambitious projects are underway for "beyond organic" farming that is humane and ecologically sound and that comports with wilderness protection.

We therefore find ourselves in the midst of a historic battle over two very different visions of the future of food in the 21st century. A grassroots public movement for organic, ecological, and humane food is now challenging the decades-long hegemony of the corporate, industrial model. *The Fatal Harvest Reader* is designed to be an aid in this critical battle, a timely treasure trove of ammunition for the growing public movement of activists, farmers, and policy makers against industrial agriculture. It will also be useful to all consumers as an antidote to corporate indoctrination about industrialized foods. For example, even as it finally admits to the considerable social and ecological costs of industrial food, agribusiness claims that, whatever the impacts, this system of agriculture is the only way to feed the world's ever-growing population. Part One of this book specifically identifies the seven most popular and egregious "lies" of agribusiness and fully debunks these myths, an invaluable contribution to any activist working on these issues.

The fight against industrial agriculture cannot be fought solely on an issue by issue basis. Even as we continue to work on various industrial food issues, whether pesticides, farm loss, or genetic engineering, we must also devote ourselves to becoming "paradigm" warriors against the industrial worldview and for a revived agrarian consciousness. Our ultimate goals must include nothing less than altering the thinking and very habits of perception of the public and policy makers. In Part Two, *The Fatal Harvest Reader* provides this kind of paradigm analysis by some of the world's leading agrarian thinkers. These high-ground essays provide ample arguments and food for thought as we come to a new understanding of industrial consciousness and its impacts.

Part Three of this book describes the tremendous environmental costs of industrial agriculture. The first wave of industrialization, including the widespread use of pesticides, synthetic fertilizers, and mechanization, has resulted in water, air, and food pollution. Wildlife, fisheries, biodiversity, topsoil, and many other natural resources have been decimated. The second wave of industrialization in food production, led by biotechnology, now threatens to create even more environmental and human health havoc.

Part Four of *The Fatal Harvest Reader* outlines a specific alternative vision for the future of agriculture. The essays in this section, called "Organic & Beyond," describe how organic agriculture is only the beginning of the evolution of a food system that respects farmers, communities, the land, biodiversity, and the wild. Hopefully, this section provides a blueprint for our collective efforts to fundamentally transform agriculture.

There can be no healing without relationship, and ultimately, the new agrarian consciousness advocated in this book seeks to heal and restore our relationship with nature, the farmer, and the land. Clearly, we cannot heal the wounds caused by industrial agriculture if we remain mere "consumers." The word "consume" means to destroy (as in a consuming fire) or waste. We can no longer be food "consumers," destroying and wasting our lands and farm communities. This book urges each of us to be "creators," not consumers. It lets us truly understand that each action we take in deciding which foods to buy, grow, or eat creates a very different future for ourselves and the earth. Please read this book carefully and become a creator of the new food future.

Part One

CORPORATE LIES

BUSTING THE MYTHS OF
INDUSTRIAL AGRICULTURE

SEVEN DEADLY MYTHS OF
INDUSTRIAL AGRICULTURE

Industrial agriculture is devastating our land, water, and air, and is now threatening the sustainability of the biosphere. Its massive chemical and biological inputs cause widespread environmental havoc as well as human disease and death. Its monoculturing reduces the diversity of our plants and animals. Its habitat destruction endangers wildlife. Its factory farming practices cause untold animal suffering. Its centralized corporate ownership destroys farm communities around the world, leading to mass poverty and hunger. The industrial agriculture system is clearly unsustainable. It has truly become a fatal harvest.

However, despite these devastating impacts, the industrial paradigm in agriculture still gets a free ride from our media and policy makers. It is rare to hear questioning, much less a call for the overthrow, of this increasingly catastrophic food production system. This troubling quiescence can be attributed, in part, to the enormous success that agribusiness has had in utilizing the "big lie," a technique familiar to all purveyors of propaganda. Corporate agriculture has flooded, and continues to inundate, the public with self-serving myths about modern food production. For decades, the industry has effectively countered virtually every critique of industrial agriculture with the "big lie" strategy.

These agribusiness myths have become all too familiar. Most farmers, activists, and policy makers who question the industrial food paradigm know the litany of lies by heart: industrial agriculture is necessary to feed the world, to provide us with safe, nutritious, cheap food, to produce food more efficiently, to offer us more choices, and, of all things, to save the environment. Additionally, when confronted with the indisputable environmental and health impacts of industrial agriculture, the industry immediately points to technological advances, especially recent achievements in biotechnology, as the panacea that will solve all problems. These claims are broadcast far and wide by way of industry lobbying efforts, product promotions, and multimillion-dollar advertising campaigns, including television, newspaper, magazine, farm journal, and radio ads. Moreover, as the industry becomes more consolidated — with biotech companies owning the seed and chemical businesses and a handful of companies controlling a majority of seeds and food brands — the strategies for promulgating these myths become ever more concerted and the messages ever more honed. Archer Daniels Midland is now known to us all as the "supermarket to the world," while Monsanto offers us "Food, Health, Hope."

These myths about industrial agriculture have been, and are being, repeated so often that they are taken as virtually unassailable. A central goal of this book is to debunk the myths that have for too long been used to promote and defend industrial agriculture. This myth busting is an essential step in exposing the impacts of current agriculture practices and educating the public about the realities of the food they are consuming.

Many people in the sustainable agriculture community have been instrumental in publishing and disseminating factual information to counter these myths. In particular, Peter Rosset and Frances Moore Lappé of the Institute for Food and Development Policy/Food First have taken the lead on dispelling myths about hunger by publishing numerous reports and the latest edition of their groundbreaking book, *World Hunger: Twelve Myths*; Pat Mooney, Hope Shand, and others at the Rural Advancement Foundation International have played an essential role in cataloging the loss of genetic diversity in agriculture; David Pimentel has conducted unprecedented research on the true ecological costs of industrial agriculture; and Margaret Mellon and Jane Rissler of the Union of Concerned Scientists, as well as Miguel Altieri at the University of California, Berkeley, have been invaluable in dispelling many of the myths currently being spread by the biotech industry.

In this section, we identify the seven central myths of industrial agriculture, note their assumptions and dangers, and provide direct and clear refutations. This myth-busting section is specifically designed to provide consumers, activists, and policy makers with clear, compact, and concise answers to counter the industry's well-funded misinformation campaigns about the benefits of industrial agriculture. We encourage you to utilize these seven short essays whenever you are faced with the "big lies" being used by corporate agribusiness to hide the true effects of their fatal harvest.

INDUSTRIAL AGRICULTURE
WILL FEED THE WORLD

T H E   T R U T H

*World hunger is not created by lack of food but by poverty and
landlessness, which deny people access to food. Industrial agriculture actually increases hunger by raising the cost of farming, by
forcing tens of millions of farmers off the land, and by growing primarily high-profit export and luxury crops.*

▼

There is no myth about the existence of hunger. It is estimated that
nearly 800 million people go hungry each day. And millions live
on the brink of disaster, as malnutrition and related illnesses kill as
many as 12 million children per year. Famine continues in the 21st
century, though few of us are aware of the truly global nature of the
problem. In Brazil, 70 million people cannot afford enough to eat,
and in India, 200 million go hungry every day. Even in the United
States, the world's number one exporter of food, 33 million men,
women, and children are considered among the world's hungry.

There is, however, a myth about what is causing this tragic
hunger epidemic and what it will take to alleviate it. Industrial agriculture proponents spend millions on advertising campaigns each
year claiming that people are starving because there is not enough
food to feed the current population, much less a continually growing
one. "Guess Who's Coming to Dinner? 10 billion by 2030" proclaimed
an old headline on Monsanto's Web page. The company warns of the
"growing pressures on the Earth's natural resources to feed more people" and claims that low-technology agriculture "will not produce
sufficient crop yield increases to feed the world's burgeoning population." Their answer is pesticide- and technology-intensive agriculture
that will produce the maximum output from the land in the shortest
amount of time. Global food corporations, they say, will have to serve
as "saviors" of the world's hungry.

HUNGER IN A WORLD OF ABUNDANCE

A deeper look at the root causes of hunger will reveal that any claim that world hunger is caused by a lack of food is simply a self-serving agribusiness myth. In reality, food production has kept pace with population growth. Studies conducted by the U.N. Food and Agriculture Organization (FAO) clearly indicate that it is abundance, not scarcity, that best describes the world's food supply. Every year, enough wheat, rice, and other grains are produced to provide every human with 3,500 daily calories. In fact, enough food is grown worldwide to provide 4.3 pounds of food per person per day, which would include two and a half pounds of grain, beans, and nuts, a pound of fruits and vegetables, and nearly another pound of meat, milk, and eggs.

What about the pace of population growth in the future? Although many argue that we should curtail population growth for ecological and socioeconomic reasons, history has not yet borne out the Malthusian concept that population growth equals hunger. Indeed, during the last 35 years per capita food production has actually grown 16 percent faster than the world's population. Moreover, as Peter Rosset of Food First states, "We now have more food per person available on this planet than ever before in human history."

THE REAL CAUSE OF HUNGER

If we have plenty of food to feed today's population and to support population growth for the foreseeable future, why do 800 million people still go hungry every day? One basic cause is food dependence. The industrial system has, over centuries and in virtually every area of the globe, "enclosed" farmland, forcing subsistence peasants off the land, so that it can be used for growing high-priced export crops rather than diverse crops for local populations. The result of enclosure was, and continues to be, that untold millions of peasants lose their land, community, traditions, and most directly their ability to grow their own food — their food independence. Removed from their land and means of survival, the new "landless" then flock to the newly industrialized cities where they quickly become a class of urban poor competing for low-paying jobs and doomed to long-term hunger or starvation. The victims of enclosure are becoming ever more numerous. Just 50 years ago, only 18 percent of the population of developing countries resided in cities; by the year 2000 the figure jumped to 40 percent. Unless current policies change, by 2030 it is estimated that 56 percent of the developing world will be urban dwellers. A United Nations report has found that close to 50 percent of this urban population growth is due to migration, much of it forced, from rural to urban communities.

After enclosure, both the urban and rural poor are completely food dependent. Their access to food is solely by purchase. Very often they simply do not have enough money to buy food, so they starve. Increasing agricultural output has little effect on the hungry because it fails to address the key issues of access to land and purchasing power that are at the root of hunger. As summarized in a Food First report, "If you don't have land on which to grow food or the money to buy it, you go hungry no matter how dramatically technology pushes up food production."

FARMERS WHO CAN'T BUY FOOD

Industrial agriculture causes mass starvation not only among the urban poor but also in the world's farming communities. Over the last decades the chemical and technological inputs and patented seeds brought to farmers in the third world by agribusiness have dramatically increased the costs of farming. Even as the farmer must pay more and more to farm "industrially," higher yields and worldwide competition lower prices paid to the farmer (but because of high middleman costs, the prices of food are not generally lower for the consumer).

Advances in industrial agriculture have therefore put millions of the world's farmers in a fatal bind, as they spend ever more in production costs, yet receive ever less income. The cruel irony is that even as these farmers grow the world's food, they cannot afford food for themselves or their families. This has resulted in mass starvation in the rural communities, epidemics of farmer suicides, and the annihilation of farm communities throughout the globe. Currently, more than half a billion rural people in the third world have become landless or do not have either sufficient land to grow their own food or money to buy that food.

EXPORTS DEVOUR PEOPLE

Yet another way that industrial agriculture increases hunger is by what it grows. The problem is that corporate-driven agriculture, after it "encloses" land and evicts the farm communities from these lands, does not grow staple foods for the hungry. Global corporations favor luxury high-profit items like flowers, sugarcane, beef, shrimp, cotton, coffee, and soybeans for export to wealthy countries. Local people are often left with nothing. In Africa, where severe famines have occurred in the past decade, industrialized agriculture has not produced foods for the people, but rather record crops of cotton and sugarcane. As export crops and livestock use up available land, small farmers are forced to use marginal, less fertile lands. Staple food production for local use plummets and hunger increases. In fact, one could classify the world's population into three groups: about 1.2 billion "overconsumers" who eat the equivalent of 850 kilograms of grain each year, mostly in the form of animal products or other "luxury" foods; 3.5 billion "sustainers" who consume the equivalent of 350 kilograms of grain in a mixed diet; and 1.2 billion who are surviving on only 150 kilograms or less each year. With this understanding, it is not surprising that during industrial agriculture's prime years (1970–90), the number of hungry people in every country except China actually increased by more than 11 percent.

Currently, most government and private efforts to reduce world hunger are focused on the technological quest to produce ever higher yields on agricultural land. This misguided approach is actually increasing the hunger crisis and is causing environmental and social devastation. Equally troubling is that the myth that more food will cure hunger diverts attention from the urgent need for economic reforms, land redistribution, and sustainable and affordable farm practices. We need a major shift in efforts to feed the world, where the focus is on supporting local agriculture, where people live close to (or on) the land, grow food to feed their own communities, and use ecologically sustainable techniques. In other words, hunger can only be solved by an agricultural system that promotes food independence.

INDUSTRIAL FOOD IS SAFE, HEALTHY, AND NUTRITIOUS

THE TRUTH

Industrial agriculture contaminates our vegetables and fruits with pesticides, slips dangerous bacteria into our lettuce, and puts genetically engineered growth hormones into our milk. It is not surprising that cancer, food-borne illnesses, and obesity are at an all-time high.

▼

A modern supermarket produce aisle presents a perfect illusion of food safety. Consistency is a hallmark. Dozens of apples are on display, waxed and polished to a uniform luster, few if any bearing a bruise or dent or other distinguishing characteristics. Nearby sit stacked pyramids of oranges dyed an exact hue to connote ripeness. Perhaps we find a shopper comparing two perfectly similar cellophane-wrapped heads of lettuce, as if trying to distinguish between a set of identical twins. Elsewhere, throughout the store, processed foods sit front and center on perfectly spaced shelves, their bright, attractive cans, jars, and boxes bearing colorful photographs of exquisitely prepared and presented foods. They all look unthreatening, perfectly safe, even good for you. And for decades, agribusiness, the U.S. Department of Agriculture (USDA) and the Food and Drug Administration (FDA) have proclaimed boldly that the United States has the safest food supply in the world.

As with all the myths of industrial agriculture, things are not exactly as they appear. The Centers for Disease Control (CDC) report that between 1970 and 1999, food-borne illnesses increased more than tenfold. And according to the FDA, at least 53 pesticides classified as carcinogenic are presently applied in massive amounts to our major food crops. While the industrialization of the food supply progresses, we are witnessing an explosion in human health risks and a significant decrease in the nutritional value of our meals.

INCREASED CANCER RISK

A central component of the industrialized food system is the large-scale introduction of toxic chemicals. This toxic contamination of our food shows no signs of decreasing. Since 1989, overall pesticide use has risen by about 8 percent, or 60 million pounds. The use of pesticides that leave residues on food has increased even more. Additionally, the Environmental Protection Agency (EPA) reports that more than 1 million Americans drink water laced with pesticide runoff from industrial farms. Our increasing use of these chemicals has been paralleled by an exponential growth in health risks, to both farmers and consumers.

The primary concern associated with this toxic dependency is cancer. The EPA has already identified more than 165 pesticides as potentially carcinogenic, with numerous chemical mixtures remaining untested. Residues from potentially carcinogenic pesticides are left behind on some of our favorite fruits and vegetables — in 1998, the FDA found pesticide residues in over 35 percent of the food tested. Many U.S. products have tested as being more toxic than those from other countries. What's worse, current standards for pesticides in food do not yet include specific protections for fetuses, infants, or young children, despite major changes to federal pesticide laws in 1996 requiring such reforms. Many scientists believe that pesticides play a major role in the current cancer "epidemic" among children. And the cancer risk does not just affect consumers; it also imperils tens of thousands of farmers, field hands, and migrant laborers. A National Cancer Institute study found that farmers who used industrial herbicides were six times more likely than non-farmers to develop non-Hodgkin's lymphoma, a type of cancer. Along with their cancer risk, pesticides can cause myriad other health problems, especially for young people. For example, exposure to neurotoxic compounds like PCBs and organophosphate insecticides during critical periods of development can cause permanent, long-term damage to the brain, nervous, and reproductive systems.

INCREASE IN FOOD-BORNE ILLNESSES

In addition to increased health risks associated with our current pesticide dependency, industrialized food production has also brought with it a rise in food-borne illnesses. Researchers from the CDC estimate that food-borne pathogens now infect up to 80 million people a year and cause over 9,000 deaths in the United States alone.

This increase is largely attributed to the industrialization of poultry and livestock production. Most meat products now begin in "animal factories," where food animals are confined in shockingly inhumane and overly crowded conditions, leading to widespread disease among animals and the creation of food-borne illnesses. According to the CDC, reported cases of disease from salmonella and *E. coli* pathogens are ten times greater than they were two decades ago, and cases of campylobacter have more than doubled. The CDC saw none of these pathogens in meat until the late 1970s when "animal factories" became the dominant means of meat production. Even our fruits and vegetables get contaminated by these pathogens through exposure to tainted fertilizers and sewage sludge. Contamination can also occur during industrialized processing and long-distance shipment.

The use of antibiotics in farm animal production may also be accelerating the alarming growth of antibiotic resistance exhibited by dangerous pathogens. Residues of these veterinary antibiotics that make their way into our food supply may confer resistance upon bacteria responsible for a wide variety of human maladies. Infections resistant to antibiotics are now the 11th leading cause of death in the United States. Guided by popular media reports, we may hastily conclude that doctors, by overprescribing antibiotics for people, are solely to blame for growing resistance. This assessment, however, ignores the fact that nearly 50 percent of U.S. antibiotics are given to animals, not people.

KILLER FOODS

The introduction of fast, processed, and frozen foods in the 1950s has forever changed our dietary habits. At least 175,000 fast-food restaurants have sprouted among the gas stations, strip malls, and convenience stores of America's ever creeping suburban sprawl. Frozen dinners, prepackaged meals, and take-out burgers have, for many people, replaced the home-cooked meal. Consequently, people are consuming more calories, preservatives, and sugar than ever in history, while reducing their intake of fresh whole fruits and vegetables. It is no mystery that these changes have led to overwhelming increases in obesity, Type II diabetes, high blood pressure, and heart disease among Americans. About one in three Americans is overweight, and obesity is now at epidemic levels in the United States. According to a joint New York University/Center for Science in the Public Interest report "added sugars — found largely in junk foods such as soft drinks, cakes, and cookies — squeeze healthier foods out of the diet. That sugar now accounts for 16 percent of the calories consumed by the average American and 20 percent of teenagers' calories. Twenty years ago, teens consumed almost twice as much milk as soda; today they consume almost twice as much soda as milk." The Surgeon General has determined that two out of every three premature deaths is related to diet.

NEW TECHNOLOGIES: A CLEANER CURSE

The purveyors of industrial food, when confronted with the health crisis that their food has caused, respond by assuring us that new industrial technologies will be a quick fix. For example, in response to the huge increase in food-borne illnesses, the industry promotes the use of irradiation to sanitize our foods. Through this technology, the average hamburger, for example, may receive the equivalent of millions of chest X rays in an attempt to temporarily remove any potential bacterial contaminants. However, as the meat continues to flow through the industrial food supply, it loses its "protection" and is quickly subject to additional contamination. Meanwhile, numerous reputable studies have shown that consuming irradiated meat can cause DNA damage, resulting in abnormalities in laboratory animals and their offspring. Moreover, irradiation can destroy essential vitamins and nutrients that are naturally present in foods and can make food taste and smell rancid.

Contrary to our government's pronouncement, industrial food is not safe. It is, in fact, becoming increasingly deadly and devoid of nutrition. Ultimately, we cannot achieve food safety through simple political fiat or technological quick fixes. Increased dependence on chemical, nuclear, or genetically engineered inputs will only intensify the problem. The real solution is a return to sound organic agricultural practices. It turns out that food production that is safe for the environment, humane to animals, and based in community and independence is also a food supply that is safe and nutritious for humans.

INDUSTRIAL FOOD IS CHEAP

THE TRUTH

If you added the real cost of industrial food — its health, environmental, and social costs — to the current supermarket price, not even our wealthiest citizens could afford to buy it.

▼

In America, politicians, business leaders, and the media continue to reassure us that our food is the cheapest in the world. They repeat their mantra that the more we apply chemicals and technology to agriculture, the more food will be produced and the lower the price will be to the consumer. This myth of cheap food is routinely used by agribusiness as a kind of economic blackmail against any who point out the devastating impacts of modern food production. Get rid of the industrial system, we are told, and you won't be able to afford food. Using this "big lie," the industry has even succeeded in portraying supporters of organic food production as wealthy elitists who don't care about how much the poor will have to pay for food.

Under closer analysis, our supposedly cheap food supply becomes monumentally expensive. The myth of cheapness completely ignores the staggering externalized costs of our food, costs that do not appear on our grocery checkout receipts. Conventional analyses of the cost of food completely ignore the exponentially increasing social and environmental costs customers are currently paying and will have to pay in the future. We expend tens of billions of dollars in taxes, medical expenses, toxic clean-ups, insurance premiums, and other pass-along costs to subsidize industrial food producers. Given the ever-increasing health, environmental, and social destruction involved in industrial agriculture, the real price of this food production for future generations is incalculable.

ENVIRONMENTAL COSTS

Industrial agriculture's most significant external cost is its widespread destruction of the environment. Intensive use of pesticides and fertilizers seriously pollutes our water, soil, and air. This pollution problem grows worse over time, as pests become immune to the chemicals and more and more poisons are required. Meanwhile, our animal factories produce 1.3 billion tons of manure each year. Laden with chemicals, antibiotics, and hormones, the manure leaches into rivers and water tables, polluting drinking supplies and causing fish kills in the tens of millions.

The overuse of chemicals and machines on industrial farms erodes away the topsoil — the fertile earth from which all food is grown. The United States has lost half of its topsoil since 1960, and we continue losing topsoil 17 times faster than nature can create it. Biodiversity is also a victim of industrial agriculture's onslaught. The U.N. Food and Agriculture Organization reports that 75 percent of genetic diversity in agriculture disappeared in this past century. The resulting monocultured crops are genetically limited and far more susceptible to insects, blights, diseases, and bad weather than are diverse crops.

There is also large-scale downstream pollution caused by long-distance transport of industrial food. The food on an average American's plate now travels at least 1,300 miles from the field to the dinner table. Vehicles moving food around the world burn massive amounts of fossil fuels, exacerbating air and water pollution problems. Currently, consumers pay billions of dollars annually in environmental costs directly attributed to industrial food production, not including the loss of irreplaceable and priceless biodiversity and topsoil, and the incalculable costs of problems such as global warming and ozone depletion.

HEALTH COSTS

Conventional analyses also ignore the human health costs of consuming industrial foods, including the contribution of pesticides, hormones, and other chemical inputs to our current cancer epidemic. Also uncalculated are the expenses and lost workdays of 80 million Americans who contract food-borne illnesses each year. Moreover, industrial food's health price tag should reflect the expense, pain, and suffering of the tens of millions who are victims of such diseases as obesity and heart disease caused by industrial fast-food diets. Taken together these medical health costs are clearly in the hundreds of billions of dollars annually.

According to the U.S. Department of Agriculture, farming is among the most accident-prone industries in the United States. Whereas the occupational fatality rate for all private sector industries is 4.3 per 100,000 full-time employees, the rate for agriculture, forestry, and fishing occupations was 24 per 100,000 — or nearly six times the national average. For migrant farmworkers, health conditions are even worse. Migrant workers, who now account for more than half of all food production in the United States, are 15 times more likely to manifest symptoms of pesticide exposure than non-migrant farm employees in California, according to Sandra Archibald of the Humphrey Institute. The Environmental Protection Agency estimates that 300,000 farm workers suffer acute pesticide poisoning each year.

LOSS OF FARMS AND COMMUNITIES

Industrial agriculture's dislocation of millions of farmers and thousands of farm communities also does not appear in usual food cost calculations. Seventy years ago there were nearly 7 million American farmers. Today, after the onslaught of industrial agriculture, there are only about 2 million, even though the U.S. population has doubled. Between 1987 and 1992, America lost an average of 32,500 farms per year, about 80 percent of which were family-run. A mere 50,000 farming operations now account for 75 percent of U.S. food production. Meanwhile, at supermarkets our purportedly cheap food is getting more expensive as industrial agriculture passes along the high costs of wasteful processing and packaging techniques. But the money isn't going to the farmers. The vast majority of the profits go to corporate middlemen who squeeze farmers both when selling them seed and when purchasing their crops for processing.

The loss of farmers also means the loss of farm communities and culture, along with the businesses those communities supported. Current costs associated with industrial food and agriculture do not include welfare and other government payments to ex-farmers and farmworkers driven into poverty. The U.S. Office of Technology Assessment studied 200 communities and discovered that as farm size increases, so does poverty. As farm size and absentee ownership increase (both endemic to industrial agriculture), social conditions in the local community deteriorate. Businesses close and crime increases. It is difficult to put a dollar value on the loss of farmers and communities; clearly much of what is lost is priceless. However, numerous studies have put the costs of such dislocation since World War II in the tens of billions of dollars.

TAX SUBSIDIES

Taxpayers cover billions of dollars in government subsidies to industrial agriculture. Price supports, price "fixing," tax credits, and product promotion are all forms of "welfare" for agribusiness. Among the most outrageous subsidies is the $659 million of taxpayer money spent each year to promote the products of industrial agriculture, including $1.6 million to McDonald's to help market Chicken McNuggets in Singapore from 1986 to 1994 and $11 million to Pillsbury to promote the Doughboy in foreign countries. Taken together these subsidies add almost $3 billion to the "hidden" cost of foods to consumers.

The powerful myth that industrial food is cheap and affordable only survives because all of these environmental, health, and social costs are not added to the price of industrial food. When we calculate the real price, it is clear that far from being cheap, our current food production system is imposing staggering monetary burdens on us and future generations. By contrast, non-industrial food production significantly reduces and can even eliminate most of these costs. Additionally, organic practices reduce or eliminate the use of many chemicals on food, substantially decreasing the threat of cancer and other diseases and thus cutting health-care costs. Finally, small-scale sustainable agriculture restores rural communities and creates farm jobs. If the public could only see the real price tag of the food we buy, purchasing decisions would be easy. Compared to industrial food, organic alternatives are the bargains of a lifetime.

INDUSTRIAL AGRICULTURE
IS EFFICIENT

THE TRUTH

Small farms produce more agricultural output per unit area than large farms. Moreover, larger, less diverse farms require far more mechanical and chemical inputs. These ever increasing inputs are devastating to the environment and make these farms far less efficient than smaller, more sustainable farms.

▼

Proponents of industrial agriculture claim that "bigger is better" when it comes to food production. They argue that the larger the farm, the more efficient it is. They admit that these huge corporate farms mean the loss of family farms and rural communities, but they maintain that this is simply the inevitable cost of efficient food production. And agribusiness advocates don't just promote big farms; they also push big technology. They typically ridicule small-scale farm technology as grossly inefficient, while heralding intensive use of chemicals, massive machinery, computerization, and genetic engineering — whose affordability and implementation are only feasible on large farms. The marriage of huge farms with "mega-technology" is sold to the public as the basic requirement for efficient food production. Argue against size and technology — the two staples of modern agriculture — and, they insist, you're undermining production efficiency and endangering the world's food supply.

IS BIGGER BETTER?

While the "bigger is better" myth is generally accepted, it is a fallacy. Numerous reports have found that smaller farms are actually more efficient than larger "industrial" farms. These studies demonstrate that when farms get larger, the costs of production per unit often increase, because larger acreage requires more expensive machinery and more chemicals to protect crops. In particular, a 1989 study by the U.S. National Research Council assessed the efficiency of large industrial food production systems compared with alternative methods. The conclusion was exactly contrary to the "bigger is better" myth: "Well-managed alternative farming systems nearly always use less synthetic chemical pesticides, fertilizers, and antibiotics per unit of production than conventional farms. Reduced use of these inputs lowers production costs and lessens agriculture's potential for adverse environmental and health effects without decreasing — and in some cases increasing — per acre crop yields and the productivity of livestock management systems."

Moreover, the large monocultures used in industrial farming undermine the genetic integrity of crops, making them more susceptible to diseases and pests. A majority of our food biodiversity has already been lost. This genetic weakening of our crops makes future food productivity using the industrial model far less predictable and undermines any future efficiency claims of modern agriculture. Moreover, as these crops become ever more susceptible to pests, they require ever greater use of pesticides to produce equal amounts of food — a classic case of the law of diminishing returns. This increasing use of chemicals and fertilizers in our food production results in serious health and environmental impacts.

With all this evidence against it, how does the "bigger is better" myth survive? In part, it survives because of a deeply flawed method of measuring farm "productivity" which has falsely boosted the efficiency claims of industrial agriculture while discounting the productivity advantages of small-scale agriculture.

OUTPUT VERSUS YIELD

Agribusiness and economists alike tend to use "yield" measurements when calculating the productivity of farms. Yield can be defined as the production per unit of a single crop. For example, a corn farm will be judged by how many metric tons of corn are produced per acre. More often than not, the highest yield of a single crop like corn can be best achieved by planting it alone on an industrial scale in the fields of corporate farms. These large "monocultures" have become endemic to modern agriculture for the simple reason that they are the easiest to manage with heavy machinery and intensive chemical use. It is the single-crop yields of these farms that are used as the basis for the "bigger is better" myth, and it is true that the highest yield of a single crop is often achieved through industrial monocultures.

Smaller farms rarely can compete with this "monoculture" single-crop yield. They tend to plant crop mixtures, a method known as "intercropping." Additionally, where single-crop monocultures have empty "weed" spaces, small farms use these spaces for crop planting. They are also more likely to rotate or combine crops and livestock, with the resulting manure performing the important function of replenishing soil fertility. These small-scale integrated farms produce far more per unit area than large farms. Though the yield per unit area of one crop — corn, for example — may be lower, the total output per unit area for small farms, often composed of more than a dozen crops and numerous animal products, is virtually always higher than that of larger farms.

Clearly, if we are to compare accurately the productivity of small and large farms, we should use total agricultural output, balanced against total farm inputs and "externalities," rather than single-crop yield as our measurement principle. Total output is defined as the sum of everything a small farmer produces — various grains, fruits, vegetables, fodder, and animal products — and is the real benchmark of efficiency in farming. Moreover, productivity measurements should also take into account total input costs, including large-machinery and chemical use, which often are left out of the equation in the yield efficiency claims. Perhaps most important, however, is the inclusion of the cost of externalities such as environmental and human health impacts for which industrial scale monocultured farms allow society to pay. Continuing to measure farm efficiency through single-crop "yield" in agricultural economics represents an unacceptable bias against diversification and reflects the bizarre conviction that producing one food crop on a large scale is more important than producing many crops (and higher productivity) on a small scale.

Once the flawed yield measurement system is discarded, the "bigger is better" myth is shattered. As summarized by the food policy expert Peter Rosset, "Surveying the data, we indeed find that small farms almost always produce far more agricultural output per unit area than larger farms. This is now widely recognized by agricultural economists across the political spectrum, as the 'inverse relationship between farm size and output.'" He notes that even the World Bank now advocates redistributing land to small farmers in the third world as a step toward increasing overall agricultural productivity.

Government studies underscore this "inverse relationship." According to a 1992 U.S. Agricultural Census report, relatively smaller farm sizes are 2 to 10 times more productive per unit acre than larger ones. The smallest farms surveyed in the study, those of 27 acres or less, are more than ten times as productive (in dollar output per acre) than large farms (6,000 acres or more), and extremely small farms (4 acres or less) can be over a hundred times as productive.

In a last-gasp effort to save their efficiency myth, agribusinesses will claim that at least larger farms are able to make more efficient use of farm labor and modern technology than are smaller farms. Even this claim cannot be maintained. There is virtual consensus that larger farms do not make as good use of even these production factors because of management and labor problems inherent in large operations. Mid-sized and many smaller farms come far closer to peak efficiency when these factors are calculated.

It is generally agreed that an efficient farming system would be immensely beneficial for society and our environment. It would use the fewest resources for the maximum sustainable food productivity. Heavily influenced by the "bigger is better" myth, we have converted to industrial agriculture in the hopes of creating a more efficient system. We have allowed transnational corporations to run a food system that eliminates livelihoods, destroys communities, poisons the earth, undermines biodiversity, and doesn't even feed the people. All in the name of efficiency. It is indisputable that this highly touted modern system of food production is actually less efficient, less productive than small-scale alternative farming. It is time to reembrace the virtues of small farming, with its intimate knowledge of how to breed for local soils and climates; its use of generations of knowledge and techniques like intercropping, cover cropping, and seasonal rotations; its saving of seeds to preserve genetic diversity; and its better integration of farms with forest, woody shrubs, and wild plant and animal species. In other words, it's time to get efficient.

INDUSTRIAL FOOD
OFFERS MORE CHOICES

THE TRUTH

The supermarket is an illusion of choice. Food labeling does not even tell us what pesticides are on our food or what products have been genetically engineered. Most importantly, the myth of choice masks the tragic loss of tens of thousands of crop varieties caused by industrial agriculture.

▼

A persistent myth created and sustained by food manufacturers is that only industrial production could provide consumers with the wide variety of food choices available today. Industrial farming and processing, so the myth goes, have broken down limitations on food choices imposed by growing seasons, plants' geographical ranges, and crop failures. Wandering the aisles of a 40,000-square-foot supermarket, we may be readily taken in by the myth. The breakfast cereal section, for example, may contain upwards of 50 different brand names, each one uniquely packaged and presented. Take a minute, however, and try to find a variety made primarily of a grain other than corn, rice, wheat, or oats. For an equally daunting challenge, try to find a box that does not list sugar and salt among the leading ingredients.

With one simple test, the myth of industrial food variety begins to break down. We begin to see that despite clever packaging and constant advertising blitzes, much of what is presented to us as variety is actually little more than the repackaging of extremely similar products. Meanwhile, most of the vastly diverse foods available to humanity since the beginning of agricultural history have been virtually eradicated, never making their way to modern supermarket shelves.

THE LOSS OF DIVERSITY

A seldom-mentioned impact of industrial agriculture is that it deprives consumers of real choice by favoring only a few varieties of crops that allow efficient harvesting, processing, and packaging. Consider the apple. It is true that without industrial processes we might not be able to eat a "fresh" Red Delicious apple 365 days a year. However, we would be able to enjoy many of the thousands of varieties grown in this country during the last century that have now all but disappeared. Because of the industrial agriculture system, the majority of those varieties are extinct today; two varieties alone account for more than 50 percent of the current apple market. Similarly, in 2000, 73 percent of all the lettuce grown in the United States was iceberg. This relatively bland variety is often the only choice consumers have. Meanwhile, we have lost hundreds of varieties of lettuce with flavors ranging from bitter to sweet and colors from dark purple to light green. The monoculture of industrial agriculture has similarly reduced the natural diversity of nearly every major food crop in terms of varieties grown, color, size, and flavor.

By growing all of our crops in monocultures, industrial agriculture not only limits what we can eat today, but also reduces the choices of future generations. The U.N. Food and Agriculture Organization (FAO) estimates more than three-quarters of agricultural genetic diversity was lost in this past century. As agribusiness utilizes only high-yield, high-profit varieties, we fail to save the seed stock of thousands of other varieties. The Rural Advancement Foundation International (RAFI) conducted a study of seed stock readily available in 1903 versus the inventory of the U.S. National Seed Storage Laboratory (NSSL) in 1983. RAFI found an astounding decline in diversity: we have lost nearly 93 percent of lettuce, over 96 percent of sweet corn, about 91 percent of field corn, more than 95 percent of tomato, and almost 98 percent of asparagus varieties. This represents not only an environmental disaster but also a staggering reduction in food choices available to us and future generations.

UNLABELED AND UNTESTED

Even as we are robbed of our right to choose many desirable, diverse foods, we are also deprived of the right to reject those we do not wish to eat. Food labels often do not provide enough information to allow consumers to know what is in our food and how and where it is produced. The government, bending under pressure from agribusiness, has never required labels that inform consumers about the pesticides and other chemicals used on crops or the residues still left on those foods at time of purchase. Similarly there is no mandatory labeling of the geographic origin of foods, despite the wishes of a growing number of consumers who prefer to choose local produce.

The use of potentially hazardous nuclear and genetic technologies on foods is also hidden from consumers. While a major consumer lobbying effort forced the government to mandate labeling of irradiated whole foods, similarly "nuked" processed foods are not labeled. Food processors and distributors are now fighting to repeal the label requirement for irradiated whole foods. In a similar vein, the U.S. Food and Drug Administration (FDA), under pressure from the biotechnology industry, has decided not to require genetically engineered foods to be independently safety tested or labeled. This decision represents a particularly egregious affront to food choice, as up to 60 percent of processed foods already have some genetically engineered ingredients that many consumers would like to avoid. The FDA's no labeling and no testing policy was made even though the agency was aware that the genetic engineering of foods can make safe foods toxic, create new allergens, lower food nutrition, and create antibiotic resistance.

Agribusiness not only uses its political muscle to prevent food labeling, it also has pushed through laws to stop critics from getting important information about foods to consumers. The industry has pressured 13 states to pass "food disparagement" legislation — laws that can be used against those trying to expose any of the harmful effects of the industrial food system. While many believe these laws are clearly unconstitutional, until they are struck down, they serve to intimidate people and groups who want to provide truthful information on food safety. These laws also may stop potential whistle-blowers from coming forward with crucial information that the public needs to make informed food choices.

THE ILLUSION OF THE PACKAGE

Each year more than 15,000 new food products come to market in the United States. Clever marketing ploys and millions of dollars spent on packaging create a variety of images, graphics, and materials to display these products in stores. However, these introductions rarely represent an increase in food choices for consumers. The packages attempt to hide the fact that we are essentially eating the same set of ingredients over and over, even though they go by different names. Rarely do their ingredients contain anything out of the ordinary. Astonishingly, a full 95 percent of the calories we eat come from only 30 varieties of plants, according to the FAO.

Moreover, for all the different brands and food names on the market, only a handful of companies dominate the industry. For instance, Philip Morris, known to the public primarily for its tobacco products, owns hundreds of food brands. Two of the largest are Kraft and Nabisco, whose products include Post cereals, Ritz, Triscuit, Waverly, SnackWell's, Honey Maid, Premium Saltines, Planters, Nutter Butter, ChipsAhoy!, Newtons, Oreo, Cool Whip, Jell-O, Kool-Aid, Capri Sun, Miracle Whip, Philadelphia cheeses, Velveeta, Cracker Barrel, Maxwell House coffee, Starbucks, Grey Poupon, A-1, Oscar Mayer, and Tombstone Pizza. Do consumers really have a wide variety of food choices if one tobacco company controls the processing, packaging, and ingredients of all these top-selling foods?

A highly consolidated distribution process encourages large supermarket chains and many restaurants to feature industrial monocultured products over more diverse foods produced by small-scale sustainable growers. Just a few food distributors dominate this process. These massive distributors deal almost exclusively with equally massive food producers and pass along their lack of choice to the consumer. As a result, small-scale growers, who may produce a greater variety of crops and ingredients, must use other means of distributing their products. They rely on farmers' markets, community supported agriculture, and organic retail outlets to get their products into the hands of consumers.

Clearly the way to create real choice for food consumers is to promote local, small-scale organic farming. By choosing these growing techniques instead of the industrial model, we could not only give ourselves the choice of safe and healthy food and a cleaner environment, but we could also incorporate literally thousands of different varieties and tastes into our diets.

INDUSTRIAL AGRICULTURE BENEFITS THE ENVIRONMENT AND WILDLIFE

THE TRUTH

Industrial agriculture is the largest single threat to the earth's bio-diversity. Fence-row-to-fence-row plowing, planting, and harvesting techniques decimate wildlife habitats, while massive chemical use poisons the soil and water, and kills off countless plant and animal communities.

▼

Industrial agriculture's mythmakers have been so successful in their efforts to shape opinion that they must believe we'll swallow just about anything. They now assure us that intensive farming methods that rely on chemicals and biotechnology somehow protect the environment. This myth, as illogical as it may sound to an informed reader, is increasingly widespread in America today and is increasingly accepted as valid. What's worse, agribusiness is saturating the media with misleading reports of the purported ecological risks of organic and other environmentally sustainable agricultural practices.

A typical claim of the industrial apologists is that the industrial style of agriculture has prevented some 15 million square miles of wildlands from being plowed under for "low-yield" food production. They continuously assert that the biggest challenge of the 21st century is to increase food yields through modern advances in agricultural science, which include the genetic engineering of commercial food crops. They also claim that if the world does not fully embrace industrial agriculture, hundreds of thousands of wildlife species will be lost to low-yield crops and ranging livestock.

There is a plethora of evidence that busts this myth. At the outset, the idea that sustainable agriculture is low-yield and would result in plowing under millions of square miles of wildlands is simply wrong. Relatively smaller farm sizes are much more productive per unit acre — in fact 2 to 10 times more productive — than larger ones, according to numerous government studies. In fact, the smallest farms, those of 27 acres or less, are more than ten times as productive (in terms of dollar output per acre) than large farms (6,000 acres or more), and extremely small farms (4 acres or less) can be over a hundred times as productive.

Additionally, in contrast to industrial agriculture, sustainable or alternative agriculture minimizes the environmental impacts of farming on plants and animals, as well as the air, water, and soil, often without added economic costs. The simple use of composted organic manures is a cost-effective alternative to chemical fertilizers, and increases soil microbiology and fertility, decreases erosion, and over the long term helps preserve wildlife habitats. Organic and diversified farming practices increase the prevalence of birds and mammals on farmlands and ensure biological diversity for the planet. In sum, in terms of preserving and augmenting soil productivity and the biodiversity of the planet, small-scale sustainable agriculture is far more beneficial and efficient than its industrial counterpart.

Moreover, instead of being a boon to the environment as the myth proclaims, industrial agriculture is currently the largest single threat to the earth's biodiversity. There are two primary reasons for this: the devastation of wild species caused by chemical use, and the destruction of wildlife habitat from industrial agriculture's inefficient fence-row-to-fence-row plowing, planting, and harvesting techniques.

CHEMICALS AND THE ENVIRONMENT

Pesticide use — endemic to industrial agriculture — has been clearly identified as a principal driving force behind the drastic reduction of biodiversity on America's farmlands. According to Tracy Hewitt and Katherine Smith of the Henry Wallace Institute, there are no fewer than 50 scientific studies that have documented adverse environmental effects of pesticide use on bird, mammal, and amphibian populations across the United States and Canada. The Virginia Department of Game and Inland Fisheries, for example, found that at least 6 percent of the breeding population of bald eagles along the James River were killed annually by insecticide poisonings. Professor David

Pimentel estimates that 672 million birds are affected by pesticide use on farmlands and 10 percent of these — 67 million — die each year. In Texas, where some 15 million acres of croplands are treated with pesticides, tens of thousands of migratory waterfowl come in direct contact with the treated grains, risking sickness and ultimately death. Between 1977 and 1984, half of all the fish kills off the coast of South Carolina were attributed to pesticide contamination. These are only a few of the many tragic examples of wildlife destruction in the United States alone.

Chemical fertilizers — which are also a key component of industrial agriculture — pose an even greater risk to soil and water quality, threatening biodiversity and wildlife populations around the globe. Aquatic and marine life are especially vulnerable to the tons of residues from chemically treated croplands that find their way into our major estuaries each year. In the Chesapeake Bay, native sea grasses, fish, and shellfish populations have declined dramatically in number in the last few decades due to extremely high nitrogen and phosphorous levels caused by the excessive use of chemical fertilizers. According to Kelley R. Tucker of the American Bird Conservancy, use of inorganic fertilizers also tends to reduce overall plant species diversity on farmlands, allowing farm edges to be dominated by only one or a few types of plants. Bird populations suffer as a result because they are highly dependent upon the variety of insects that are supported by diverse, native landscapes.

HABITAT DESTRUCTION

In addition to the environmental damage caused by chemical pesticides and fertilizers, the huge, monocultured fields characteristic of industrial agriculture have dramatically reduced a number of wildlife populations by transforming habitats, displacing populations of native species, and introducing non-native species. Planting thousand-acre fields of corn, for example, leaves virtually no room for the propagation of other species. Among countless other wild plants and animals, important game species such as prairie chickens, bobwhite quail, cottontail rabbits, and ring-necked pheasants have been greatly reduced or eliminated in areas of industrial agriculture. Diversified farming techniques, on the other hand, incorporate numerous varieties of plants, flowers, and weeds, and encourage the proliferation of various wildlife, insect, and plant species.

No myth can hide the fact that decades of industrial agriculture have been a disaster for the environment. Its chemical poisoning has caused eco-cide among countless species. And it has resulted in irreversible soil loss, reduction in soil and water quality, and the proliferation of non-native species that choke out indigenous varieties. Without question, the tilling, mowing, and harvesting operations of industrial agriculture have affected, and continue to catastrophically destroy, wildlife and soil and water quality. By contrast, sustainable and organic farming methods result in the reduction of land under the plow and the increase of biodiversity and wildlife on farmlands and beyond.

BIOTECHNOLOGY WILL SOLVE THE PROBLEMS OF INDUSTRIAL AGRICULTURE

THE TRUTH

New biotech crops will not solve industrial agriculture's problems, but will compound them and consolidate control of the world's food supply in the hands of a few large corporations. Biotechnology will destroy biodiversity and food security, and drive self-sufficient farmers off their land.

▼

The myths of industrial agriculture share one underlying and interwoven concept — they demand that we accept that technology always equals progress. This blind belief has often shielded us from the consequences of many farming technologies. Now, however, many are asking the logical questions of technology: A given technology may be progress, but progress toward what? What future will that technology bring us? We see that pesticide technology is bringing us a future of cancer epidemics, toxic water and air, and the widespread destruction of biodiversity. We see that nuclear technology, made part of our food through irradiation, is bringing us a future of undisposable nuclear waste, massive clean-up expenses, and again multiple threats to human and environmental health. As a growing portion of society realizes that pesticides, fertilizers, monoculturing, and factory farming are little more than a fatal harvest, even the major agribusiness corporations are starting to admit that some problems exist. Their solution to the damage caused by the previous generation of agricultural technologies is — you guessed it — more technology. "Better" technology, biotechnology, a technology that will fix the problems caused by chemically intensive agriculture. In short, the mythmakers are back at work. But looking past the rhetoric, a careful examination of the new claims about genetic engineering reveals that instead of solving the problems of modern agriculture, biotechnology only makes them worse.

WILL BIOTECHNOLOGY FEED THE WORLD?

In an attempt to convince consumers to accept food biotechnology, the industry has relentlessly pushed the myth that biotechnology will conquer world hunger. This claim rests on two fallacies: first that people are hungry because there is not enough food produced in the world, and second that genetic engineering increases food productivity.

In reality, the world produces more than enough to feed the current population. The hunger problem lies not with the amount of food being produced, but rather with how this food is distributed. Too many people are simply too poor to buy the food that is available, and too few people have the land or the financial capability to grow food for themselves. The result is starvation. If biotech corporations really wanted to feed the hungry, they would encourage land reform, which puts farmers back on the land, and push for wealth redistribution, which would allow the poor to buy food.

The second fallacy is that genetic engineering boosts food production. Currently there are two principal types of biotechnology seeds in production: herbicide resistant and "pest" resistant. Monsanto makes "Roundup Ready" seeds, which are engineered to withstand its herbicide, Roundup. The seeds — usually soybeans, cotton, or canola — allow farmers to apply this herbicide in ever greater amounts without killing the crops. Monsanto and other companies also produce "Bt" seeds — usually corn, potatoes, and cotton — that are engineered so that each plant produces its own insecticide.

Independent research shows that these genetically engineered (GE) types of seed do not actually increase overall crop yields. A two-year study by University of Nebraska researchers showed that growing herbicide-resistant soybeans actually resulted in lower productivity than that achieved with conventional soybeans. These results confirmed the findings of Dr. Charles Benbrook, the former director of the Board on Agriculture at the National Academy of Sciences. His work looked at more than 8,200 field trials and showed that Round-

up Ready seed produced fewer bushels of soybeans than similar natural varieties.

Far from being an answer to world hunger, genetic engineering
could be a major contributor to starvation. There are currently more
than a dozen patents on genetically engineered "terminator" technology. These seeds are genetically engineered by biotech companies to
produce a sterile seed after a single growing season, insuring that the
world's farmers cannot save their seed and instead will have to buy
from corporations every season. Does anyone believe that the solution
to world hunger is to make the crops of the world sterile? With more
than half of the world's farmers relying on saved seeds for their harvest, imagine the mass starvation that would result should the sterility
genes escape from the engineered crops and contaminate non–genetically
engineered local crops, unintentionally sterilizing them. According to
a study by Martha Crouch of Indiana University, such a chilling scenario is a very real possibility.

WILL BIOTECHNOLOGY PROTECT THE EARTH?

The idea that biotechnology is beneficial to the environment centers
on the myth that it will reduce pesticide use by creating plants resistant to insects and other pests. In actuality the government's own
independent research has disproved this claim. A study by the U.S.
Department of Agriculture in 2000 revealed that there is no overall
reduction in pesticide use with genetically engineered crops.

Even as it does nothing to alleviate the chemical pollution crisis,
biotech food brings its own very different pollution hazard: biological
and genetic pollution. In 2000, Purdue University researchers found
that the release of only a few genetically engineered fish into a large
native fish population could make that species extinct in only a few
generations. Meanwhile, scientists at Cornell University discovered
that the pollen from Bt-corn could be fatal to the Monarch butterfly
and other beneficial insects. The Union of Concerned Scientists has
shown that the genetically engineered Bt crops could lead to pests
becoming resistant to Bt. This non-chemical pesticide is essential to
organic and conventional farmers throughout the country. If plant
pests develop a resistance to it, this could fatally undermine organic

farming in the United States. Another significant environmental issue with GE foods is that the crops are notoriously difficult to control. They can migrate, mutate, and cross-pollinate with other plants. If a pest- or herbicide-resistant strain were to spread from crops to weeds, a "superweed" could result and be nearly impossible to stop. Overall, the environmental threat of biotechnology caused 100 top scientists to warn that careless use could lead to irreversible, devastating damage to the environment.

WILL BIOTECHNOLOGY PRODUCE SAFE FOOD?

The biotech industry claims that it is bringing a whole new generation of healthier and safer foods to the market. Yet according to our own government scientists the genetic engineering of foods could make safe foods toxic. GE foods may contain both old and new allergens, which could create serious reactions in millions of consumers. Biotech foods can also have lower nutritional values. In 1999, the British Medical Association recommended banning importing unlabeled genetically modified organisms (GMOs) because of their potential health risks. What makes these risks all the more alarming is that our government requires no mandatory safety testing or labeling of any genetically engineered foods. As a result we have no assurance on the safety of these foods and no way to trace adverse reactions. Far from improving the safety of our food supply, biotechnology is bringing new, unique health risks.

IS BIOTECHNOLOGY CHEAP AND EFFICIENT?

Biotech companies have spent billions of dollars researching the effects of inserting fish genes into tomatoes, firefly genes into tobacco plants, and human genes into farm animals, and creating thousands of other transgenic organisms. It has taken thousands of trials just to come up with herbicide-resistant crops that lead to lower yields and greater chemical use. Biotechnology has yet to bring to market a single product that actually benefits consumers. As companies pass on the enormous costs of their research, why should the public pay more for biotech foods that offer no advantages and only risks?

The biotechnology industry continues to promote itself as the ultimate panacea for all the problems of industrial agriculture. A review of its real impacts reveals that it is not an antidote to modern agriculture but rather simply a continuation and exacerbation of today's food production crisis. Biotechnology increases environmental degradation, causes new food safety risks, and threatens to increase world hunger. It is not the solution, but a major part of the problem.

Part Two

THE AGRARIAN AND INDUSTRIAL WORLDVIEWS

Understanding the
Agrarian Ethic

▼　　▼　　▼

The compelling essays in this section explore the agrarian ethic. Understanding the theory and practice of agrarianism is a critical step in turning away from our current dysfunctional industrial food system. Ultimately, creating a new food future will require us to become "paradigm" warriors against the industrial worldview and for a revived agrarian consciousness.

THE WHOLE HORSE

The Preservation of the Agrarian Mind

WENDELL BERRY

WE CURRENTLY LIVE IN THE ECONOMY AND CULTURE *of the "one-night stand." Industrialism has provided us innumerable commodities, amusements, and distractions, but these offer us little satisfaction. Instead we suffer ever-increasing alienation from our families, our communities, and the natural world. There is another way to live and think: it's called agrarianism. It is not so much a philosophy as a practice, an attitude, a loyalty, and a passion — all based in a close connection with the land. It results in a sound local economy in which producers and consumers are neighbors and in which nature herself becomes the standard for work and production.*

▼

This modern mind sees only half of the horse — that half which may become a dynamo, or an automobile, or any other horsepowered machine. If this mind had much respect for the full-dimensioned, grass-eating horse, it would never have invented the engine which represents only half of him. The religious mind, on the other hand, has this respect; it wants the whole horse, and it will be satisfied with nothing less.

I should say a religious mind that requires more than a half-religion.

—Allen Tate, "Remarks on the Southern Religion,"
in *I'll Take My Stand*

One of the primary results — and one of the primary needs — of industrialism is the separation of people and places and products from their histories. To the extent that we participate in the industrial economy, we do not know the histories of our families or of our habitats or of our meals. This is an economy, and in fact a culture, of the one-night stand. "I had a good time," says the industrial lover, "but don't ask me my last name." Just so, the industrial eater says to the svelte industrial hog, "We'll be together at breakfast. I don't want to see you before then, and I won't care to remember you afterwards."

In this condition, we have many commodities, but little satisfaction, little sense of the sufficiency of anything. The scarcity of satisfaction makes of our many commodities, in fact, an infinite series of commodities, the new commodities invariably promising greater satisfaction than the older ones. And so we can say that the industrial economy's most-marketed commodity is satisfaction, and that this commodity, which is repeatedly promised, bought, and paid for, is never delivered. On the other hand, people who have much satisfaction do not need many commodities.

The persistent want of satisfaction is directly and complexly related to the dissociation of ourselves and all our goods from our and their histories. If things do not last, are not made to last, they can have no histories, and we who use these things can have no memories. We buy new stuff on the promise of satisfaction because we have forgot the promised satisfaction for which we bought our old stuff. One of the procedures of the industrial economy is to reduce the longevity of materials. For example, wood, which well made into buildings and furniture and well cared for can last hundreds of years, is now routinely manufactured into products that last 25 years. We do not cherish the memory of shoddy and transitory objects, and so we do not remember them. That is to say that we do not invest in them the lasting respect and admiration that make for satisfaction.

The problem of our dissatisfaction with all the things that we use is not correctable within the terms of the economy that produces those things. At present, it is virtually impossible for us to know the economic history or the ecological cost of the products we buy; the origins of the products are typically too distant and too scattered and the processes of trade, manufacture, transportation, and marketing too complicated. There are, moreover, too many good reasons for the industrial suppliers of these products not to want their histories to be known.

When there is no reliable accounting and therefore no competent knowledge of the economic and ecological effects of our lives, we cannot live lives that are economically and ecologically responsible. This is the problem that has frustrated, and to a considerable extent undermined, the American conservation effort from the beginning. It is ultimately futile to plead and protest and lobby in favor of public ecological responsibility while, in virtually every act of our private lives, we endorse and support an economic system that is by intention, and perhaps by necessity, ecologically irresponsible.

If the industrial economy is not correctable within or by its own terms, then obviously what is required for correction is a countervailing economic idea. And the most significant weakness of the conservation movement is its failure to produce or espouse an economic idea capable of correcting the economic idea of the industrialists. Somewhere near the heart of the conservation effort as we have known it is the romantic assumption that, if we have become alienated from nature, we can become unalienated by making nature the subject of contemplation or art, ignoring the fact that we live necessarily in and from nature — ignoring, in other words, all the economic issues that are involved. Walt Whitman could say, "I think I could turn and live with animals," as if he did not know that, in fact, we *do* live with animals, and that the terms of our relation to them are inescapably established by our economic use of their and our world. So long as we live, we are going to be living with skylarks, nightingales, daffodils, waterfowl, streams, forests, mountains, and all the other creatures that romantic poets and artists have yearned toward. And by the way we live we will determine whether or not those creatures will live.

That this nature-romanticism of the 19th century ignores economic facts and relationships has not prevented it from setting the agenda for modern conservation groups. This agenda has rarely included the economics of land use, without which the conservation effort becomes almost inevitably long on sentiment and short on practicality. The giveaway is that when conservationists try to be practical, they are likely to defend the "sustainable use of natural resources" with the argument that this will make the industrial economy sustainable. A further giveaway is that the longer the industrial economy lasts in its present form, the further it will demonstrate its ultimate impossibility: every human in the world cannot, now or ever, own the whole catalogue of shoddy, high-energy industrial products, which cannot be sustainably made or used. Moreover, the longer the industrial economy lasts, the more it will eat away the possibility of a better economy.

The conservation effort has at least brought under suspicion the general relativism of our age. Anybody who has studied with care the issues of conservation knows that our acts are being measured by a real and unyielding standard that was invented by no human. Our acts that are not in harmony with nature are inevitably and sometimes irremediably destructive. The standard exists. But having no opposing economic idea, conservationists have had great difficulty in applying the standard.

What, then, is the countervailing idea by which we might correct the industrial idea? We will not have to look hard to find it, for there is only one, and that is agrarianism. Our major difficulty (and danger) will be in attempting to deal with agrarianism as "an idea" — agrarianism is primarily a practice, a set of attitudes, a loyalty, and a passion; it is an idea only secondarily and at a remove. To use merely the handiest example: I was raised by agrarians, my bias and point of view from my earliest childhood were agrarian, and yet I never heard agrarianism defined, or even so much as named, until I was a sophomore in college. I am well aware of the danger in defining things, but if I am going to talk about agrarianism, I am going to have to define it. The definition that follows is derived both from agrarian writers, ancient and modern, and from the unliterary and sometimes illiterate agrarians who have been my teachers. The fundamental difference between industrialism and agrarianism is this: whereas industrialism is a way of thought based on monetary capital and technology, agrarianism is a way of thought based on land.

Agrarianism, furthermore, is a culture at the same time that it is an economy. Industrialism is an economy before it is a culture. Industrial culture is an accidental by-product of the ubiquitous effort to sell unnecessary products for more than they are worth.

An agrarian economy rises up from the fields, woods, and streams — from the complex of soils, slopes, weathers, connections, influences, and exchanges that we mean when we speak, for example, of the local community or the local watershed. The agrarian mind is therefore not regional or national, let alone global, but local. It must know on intimate terms the local plants and animals and local soils; it must know local possibilities and impossibilities, opportunities and hazards. It depends and insists on knowing very particular local histories and biographies.

Because a mind so placed meets again and again the necessity for work to be good, the agrarian mind is less interested in abstract quantities than in particular qualities. It feels threatened and sickened when it hears people and creatures and places spoken of as labor, management, capital, and raw material. It is not at all impressed by the industrial legendry of gross national products, or of the numbers sold and dollars earned by gigantic corporations. It is interested — and forever fascinated — by questions leading toward the accomplishment of good work: What is the best location for a particular building or fence? What is the best way to plow *this* field? What is the best course for a skid road in *this* woodland? Should *this* tree be cut or spared? What are the best breeds and types of livestock for *this* farm? Questions which cannot be answered in the abstract and which yearn not toward quantity but toward elegance. Agrarianism can never become abstract because it has to be practiced in order to exist.

And though this mind is local, almost absolutely placed, little attracted to mobility either upward or lateral, it is not provincial; it is too taken up and fascinated by its work to feel inferior to any other mind in any other place.

An agrarian economy is always a subsistence economy before it is a market economy. The center of an agrarian farm is the household. The function of the household economy is to assure that the farm family lives so far as possible from the farm. It is the subsistence part of the agrarian economy that assures its stability and its survival. A subsistence economy necessarily is highly diversified, and it characteristically has involved hunting and gathering as well as farming and gardening. These activities bind people to their local landscape by close, complex interest and economic ties. The industrial economy alienates people from the native landscape precisely by breaking these direct practical ties and introducing distant dependences.

Agrarian people of the present, knowing that the land must be well cared for if anything is to last, understand the need for a settled connection, not just between farmers and their farms, but between urban people and their surrounding and tributary landscapes. Because the knowledge and know-how of good caretaking must be handed down to children, agrarians recognize the necessity of pre-serving the coherence of families and communities.

The stability, coherence, and longevity of human occupation require that the land should be divided among many owners and users. The central figure of agrarian thought has invariably been the small owner or small holder who maintains a significant measure of economic self-determination on a small acreage. The scale and inde-pendence of such holdings imply two things that agrarians see as desirable: intimate care in the use of the land and political democracy resting upon the indispensable foundation of economic democracy.

A major characteristic of the agrarian mind is a longing for inde-pendence — that is, for an appropriate degree of personal and local self-sufficiency. Agrarians wish to earn and deserve what they have. They do not wish to live by piracy, beggary, charity, or luck.

In the written record of agrarianism, there is a continually recur-ring affirmation of nature as the final judge, lawgiver, and pattern maker of and for the human use of the earth. We can trace the lineage of this thought in the West through the writings of Virgil, Spenser, Shakespeare, Pope, Thomas Jefferson, and on into the work of the 20th-century agriculturists and scientists J. Russell Smith, Liberty Hyde Bailey, Sir Albert Howard, Wes Jackson, John Todd, and others. The idea is variously stated: we should not work until we have looked and seen where we are; we should honor Nature not only as our mother or grandmother, but as our teacher and judge; we should "let the forest judge"; we should "consult the Genius of the Place"; we should make the farming fit the farm; we should carry over into the cultivated field the diversity and coherence of the native forest or prairie. And this way of thinking is surely allied to that of the medieval scholars and architects who saw the building of a cathedral as a symbol or analogue of the creation of the world. The agrarian mind is, at bottom, a religious mind. It subscribes to Allen Tate's doc-trine of "the whole horse." It prefers the Creation itself to the powers and quantities to which it can be reduced. And this is a mind com-pletely different from that which sees creatures as machines, minds as computers, soil fertility as chemistry, or agrarianism as an idea. John Haines has written that "the eternal task of the artist and the poet, the historian and the scholar . . . is to find the means to reconcile what are two separate and yet inseparable histories, Nature and Culture. To the extent that we can do this, the 'world' makes sense to us and can be lived in." I would add only that this applies also to the farmer, the forester, the scientist, and others.

The agrarian mind begins with the love of fields and ramifies in good farming, good cooking, good eating, and gratitude to God. Exactly analogous to the agrarian mind is the sylvan mind that begins with the love of forests and ramifies in good forestry, good woodworking, good carpentry, etc., and gratitude to God. These two kinds of mind readily intersect and communicate; neither ever intersects or communicates with the industrial-economic mind. The industrial-economic mind begins with ingratitude and ramifies in the destruction of farms and forests. The "lowly" and "menial" arts of farm and forest are mostly taken for granted or ignored by the culture of the "fine arts" and by "spiritual" religions; they are taken for granted or ignored or held in contempt by the powers of the industrial economy. But in fact they are inescapably the foundation of human life and culture, and their adepts are capable of as deep satisfactions and as high attainments as anybody else.

Having, so to speak, laid industrialism and agrarianism side by side, implying a preference for the latter, I will be confronted by two questions that I had better go ahead and answer.

The first is whether or not agrarianism is simply a "phase" that we humans had to go through and then leave behind in order to get onto the track of technological progress toward ever greater happiness. The answer is that although industrialism has certainly conquered agrarianism, and has very nearly destroyed it altogether, it is also true that in every one of its uses of the natural world industrialism is in the process of catastrophic failure. Industry is now desperately shifting — by means of genetic engineering, global colonialism, and other contrivances — to prolong its control of our farms and forests, but the failure nonetheless continues. It is not possible to argue sanely in favor of soil erosion, water pollution, genetic impoverishment, and the destruction of rural communities and local economies. Industrialism, unchecked by the affections and concerns of agrarianism, becomes monstrous. And this is because of a weakness identified by the Twelve Southerners of *I'll Take My Stand* in their

"Statement of Principles": under the rule of industrialism "the remedies proposed . . . are always homeopathic." Industrialism always
proposes to correct its errors and excesses by more industrialization.

The second question is whether or not by espousing the revival of
agrarianism we will commit the famous sin of "turning back the clock."
The answer to that, for present-day North Americans, is fairly simple.
The overriding impulse of agrarianism is toward the local adaptation
of economies and cultures. Agrarian people wish to fit the farming to
the farm and the forestry to the forest. At times and in places we latter-
day Americans may have come close to accomplishing this goal, and
we have a few surviving examples, but it is generally true that we are
much farther from local adaptation now than we were 50 years ago.
We never yet have developed stable, sustainable, locally adapted
land-based economies. The good rural enterprises and communities
that we will find in our past have been almost constantly under threat
from the colonialism, first foreign and then domestic and now
"global," which has so far dominated our history and which has been
institutionalized for a long time in the industrial economy. The possibility of an authentically settled country still lies ahead of us.

If we wish to look ahead, we will see not only in the United States
but in the world two economic programs that conform pretty exactly to
the aims of industrialism and agrarianism as I have described them.

The first is the effort to globalize the industrial economy, not merely
by the expansionist programs of supranational corporations within
themselves, but also by means of government-sponsored international
trade agreements, the most prominent of which is the World Trade
Organization Agreement, which institutionalizes the industrial ambi-
tion to use, sell, or destroy every acre and every creature of the world.

The World Trade Organization gives the lie to the industrialist
conservatives' professed abhorrence of big government. The cause of
big government, after all, is big business. The power to do large-scale
damage, which is gladly assumed by every large-scale industrial
enterprise, calls naturally and logically for government regulation,
which of course the corporations object to. But we have a good deal of
evidence also that the leaders of big business actively desire and promote big government. They and their political allies, while ostensibly
working to "downsize" government, continue to promote government

helps and "incentives" to large corporations, and somehow they preserve their notion that a small government, taxing only the working people, can maintain a big highway system, a big military establishment, a big space program, and award big government contracts.

But the most damaging evidence is the World Trade Organization itself, which is in effect a global government with power to enforce the decisions of the collective against national laws that conflict with it. The coming of the World Trade Organization was foretold by the authors of *I'll Take My Stand*, who wrote in 1930 that "the true Sovietists or Communists . . . are the industrialists themselves. They would have the government set up an economic super-organization, which in turn would become the government." The agrarians of *I'll Take My Stand* did not foresee this because they were fortune tellers, but because they had perceived accurately the motive of the industrial economy.

The second program, counter to the first, is comprised of many small efforts to preserve or improve or establish local economies. These efforts on the part of nonindustrial or agrarian conservatives, local patriots, are taking place in countries both affluent and poor all over the world.

Whereas the corporate sponsors of the World Trade Organization, in order to promote their ambitions, have required only the hazy glamour of such phrases as "the global economy," "the global context," and "globalization" — and thus apparently have vacuum-packed the mind of every politician and political underling in the world — the local economists use a much more diverse and particularizing vocabulary that you can actually think with: "community," "ecosystem," "watershed," "place," "homeland," "family," "household."

And whereas the global economists advocate a world-government-by-economic-bureaucracy, which would destroy local adaptation everywhere by ignoring the uniqueness of every place, the local economists found their work upon respect for such uniqueness. Places differ from one another, the local economists say, therefore we must behave with unique consideration in each one; the ability to tender an appropriate practical regard and respect to each place in its difference is a kind of freedom; the inability to do so is a kind of tyranny. The local economists, who have so far attracted the support of no prominent politician, are the true decentralizers and downsizers, for they

seek an appropriate degree of self-determination and independence
for localities. They seem to be moving toward a radical and necessary
revision of our idea of a city. They are learning to see the city, not just
as a built and paved municipality set apart by "city limits" to live by
trade and transportation from the world at large, but rather as a part
of a community which includes also the city's rural neighbors, its surrounding landscape and its watershed, on which it might depend for
at least some of its necessities, and for the health of which it might
exercise a competent concern and responsibility.

At this point, I want to say point-blank what I hope is already
clear: though agrarianism proposes that everybody has agrarian
responsibilities, it does not propose that everybody should be a
farmer or that we do not need cities. Nor does it propose that every
product should be a necessity. Furthermore, any thinkable human
economy would have to grant to manufacturing an appropriate and
honorable place. Agrarians would insist only that any manufacturing
enterprise should be formed and scaled to fit the local landscape, the
local ecosystem, and the local community, and that it should be
locally owned and employ local people. They would insist, in other
words, that the shop or factory owner should not be an outsider, but
rather a sharer in the fate of the place and its community. The
deciders should live with the results of their decisions.

Between these two programs — the industrial and the agrarian,
the global and the local — the most critical difference is that of
knowledge. The global economy institutionalizes a global ignorance,
in which producers and consumers cannot know or care about one
another and in which the histories of all products will be lost. In such
a circumstance, the degradation of products and places, producers
and consumers is inevitable.

But in a sound local economy, in which producers and consumers
are neighbors, nature will become the standard of work and production. Consumers who understand their economy will not tolerate the
destruction of the local soil or ecosystem or watershed as a cost of
production. Only a healthy local economy can keep nature and work
together in the consciousness of the community. Only such a community can restore history to economics.

AGRICULTURAL LANDSCAPES
IN HARMONY WITH NATURE

JOAN IVERSON NASSAUER

THE POPULAR IMAGE OF THE AMERICAN FARM *grows from the out-dated belief that our agriculture is ecologically and socially health-ful. But the reality of industrial agriculture is one of massive soil erosion, monocultured fields, water contamination, and huge cor-porate farms. However, the traditional image of the American farm is not obsolete. It can be our guide in restoring ecological and social values in agriculture. A new vision of healthy agricultural land-scapes marries our traditional expectations of farms with a holistic understanding of ecology.*

▼

The popular image of the countryside is a visual metaphor for human life in harmony with nature. This image is more likely to be found in children's books than in pesticide commercials; it is more likely to be seen in a picture hanging on your wall than on a drive through central Illinois; it is more likely to be part of the view from a home newly constructed on converted farmland than from a home constructed there years ago and sitting in a sea of five-acre lots.

You know this image: A mix of crops weaves a varied field pattern. Livestock graze on the land. Woodlands and streams make sinuous borders along the fields. Tidy farmsteads dot the landscape. There are fish in the pond, birds in the sky, and wildlife in the woods. The air is clean. There is a small town nearby with a school, stores, and churches. You might not live in this landscape, but you would like to visit it, and when you did, you could stop and enjoy a friendly talk with the farmer and buy fresh produce you couldn't find in the city.

The image could be called generic nostalgia, but that is only evi-dence of its broad recognition and enormous appeal. For most Americans this image embodies the same values and expectations they will support in a new vision of the American landscape. These values and expectations include the following:

The countryside is inhabited by friendly people who enjoy farming and are good stewards of the land.

People are safe and welcome here.

The countryside is clean, unpolluted, and uncrowded.

It produces healthful food — better that what you can buy in the supermarket.

The countryside provides habitat for wildlife in a way that is more natural than the city.

The countryside is an attractive place to visit. You can drive through and enjoy the scenery.

In summary, the popular image of the American agricultural landscape grows from beliefs that the countryside is ecologically and socially healthful. It also reflects a belief that even those who do not own farmland or live on farms belong in the countryside as welcome visitors to appealing landscapes. It may not be unreasonable to expect these beliefs to be matched in reality. In fact, the popular image creates a demand for this reality.

A NEW VISION: ECOLOGICAL HEALTH IN BEAUTIFUL NATURE

The new vision of American agriculture should grow from the core of this popular old image. As we learn more about the complex ecologies of all landscapes, harmony with nature becomes more of an imperative than an ideal. The common belief that the countryside is a form of nature coincides with the growing awareness that we must ensure ecological health in the countryside. This makes it possible for popular expectations to propel public policy into achieving ecological health for American agricultural landscapes.

The image of nature in the countryside is at the heart of the beauty people seek and find there. When we construct a new vision of agricultural landscapes, we would be foolish to ignore the cultural power of this image. America has become a suburban nation, and some rural counties have grown wealthy as urban people have ventured from cities in search of beautiful nature in the countryside.

Beauty could be the sole focus of a new vision. Countryside landscapes are integral to the quality of life in metropolitan areas and are
the basis for thriving rural economies. But focusing on beauty alone
tends to leave both beauty and the larger agricultural and ecological
functions of the landscape undefended. In our culture, aesthetics is
mistakenly denigrated as superficial even as advertisers construct
beguiling images to manipulate our behavior. A thoughtful strategy
for American agriculture will use the power of images — not to
manipulate but to communicate the ecological achievements of agricultural policy. The agricultural landscape doesn't need a billboard of
nature to make us feel that the water is clean and the food is good.
The agricultural landscape advertises itself when it conveys the popular image of nature.

Those who track the loss of farmland to exurban development, or
fear the pollution of water by feedlots and fertilizers, or know the sur-
real sterility of monoculture in the grain belt see the jarring contrast
between the image and the reality. But it is just this contrast that sets
up the possibility for a new vision. If we didn't expect the countryside
to be natural, if we saw it as only another form of industry, we might
be complacent about the inevitability of lost habitat. If we did not
personally enjoy the appearance of good stewardship on the land, we
might see the deteriorating health of the countryside as someone else's
problem. But because we expect agriculture to be in harmony with
nature, we hold a collective image of what the countryside is and
should be. A new vision can bring the ecological reality of American
agricultural landscapes closer to the evocative popular image of a
beautiful countryside.

LIMITED KNOWLEDGE AND INTELLIGENT
TINKERING: ECOLOGICAL CONSERVATISM

The popular image of harmony with nature is not enough to tell us
what will actually work to improve the ecological effects of agriculture in the future. The image is a democratic push toward healthy
agricultural landscapes, but it is not an instruction kit.

We know that new agricultural landscapes cannot be simple
replicas of the past and that the agriculture of the future cannot be

based on the limited insights of a single discipline or a narrowly construed scientific method. At its best, scientific understanding gives us a conceptual overview of flows of water, soil, nutrients, chemicals, and plant and animal species through the agricultural landscape and its products. It also partly explains the movements of people in and out of the countryside and their reasons and means for staying there. But science does not give us a definitive understanding of how particular agricultural landscapes work, and it cannot give us the kind of informed permission for wholesale disturbance of functioning ecosystems and communities that some developers and agriculturalists desire. Rather, many scientists have reached a conclusion that parallels that of concerned skeptics, a message of caution: be careful when you change a landscape that works; be cautious about unintended effects of your technology; conserve what works when you experiment with what might work better. Aldo Leopold's 1966 dictum still holds: the first rule of intelligent tinkering is not to throw away any of the parts.

Caution does not prevent change. Rather, it may lead us to reflect on the scale of change that has been introduced into North American landscapes over the past century and to amend that sweeping scale in agricultural landscapes in the next century. Caution may lead us to return some elements that bring variety and ecological balance to the homogeneous patterns of production in agriculture. Clearly, the agricultural landscape must function ecologically. It must positively support large-scale processes of energy conversion, aquifer recharge, soil development, and water and habitat quality. Undoubtedly, we must move to restore some beneficial effects of old agricultural practices that left large-scale ecological processes intact, but this does not mean mindlessly returning to old ways. It means critically selecting what worked in the past and inventing new patterns that will work now and in the future. It suggests we begin tinkering, not by reconstructing the landscape as our grandparents farmed it or as Europeans first encountered it, but by reexamining some old farming practices and indigenous ecosystems. This perspective on agricultural research resembles the assumptions underlying experiments with cultivating perennial grains more than the assumptions underlying pesticide development.

Knowledge of the ecology and culture of a countryside that works may inform us, but that knowledge is incomplete. It cannot tell us what to do. Caution may lead us to a form of conservation that acknowledges our collective hubris. More accurately than the dichotomous stewardship terms of conservation and preservation, ecological conservatism describes a way of farming that is attentive to what we do not know. With ecological conservatism, past landscape patterns that were successful in maintaining large-scale ecological processes would be the primary guide for inventing new landscape patterns. Consistent with the conclusion that we cannot predict all the effects of landscape change, ecological conservatism would suggest that variations on the patterns that work be introduced gradually — at small spatial and temporal scales — and monitored for their effects. Such small-scale monitored experiments suggest an approach like the on-farm research that has become an integral part of sustainable agriculture. Of course, "small" and "gradual" are relative terms. But if we use energy consumption as one measure, we can be certain that industrial agriculture, with its attendant use of fossil fuels, has brought us too far too fast.

Intelligent tinkering gives us a mechanical metaphor for ecological quality. We imagine the tinkerer at the workbench, with all the parts laid out to experiment with how they might fit together to serve a purpose. The machine the tinkerer makes is not necessarily elegant, but it works, and the extra parts have been carefully saved for the next time they might be needed. Someone entering the workshop might not see the order in the parts lying here and there, but the tinkerer knows where everything is.

To use the popular image of the countryside to advance ecological health, intelligent tinkering must be translated into visual terms. The new vision of the agricultural landscape must portray ecological health by drawing on what people already recognize. Our cultural image tells us what nature in the countryside looks like. We can adapt this familiar visual metaphor to portray ecological health.

THE LOOK OF THE LAND: KNOWLEDGE AND IMAGE

Knowledge and image must be intentionally meshed by those who care about public support for the ecological health of the agricultural landscape. As the agricultural landscape recovers characteristics that support ecological health, who will notice, and who will know? Who will advocate, and who will pay? Because image is a reflection of cultural traditions rather than critical analysis, many people will not perceive ecological gains unless the agricultural landscape looks healthy. Because many characteristics that support ecological health are invisible or difficult to see or even contradict the image, knowledge and image will not inevitably converge in the look of the land. They must be designed so that image matches knowledge.

When we don't see ecological health, it isn't because we aren't looking. In Western culture, at least since the 17th century, people have entertained themselves by looking at the land to judge the wealth and character of the landowner and to enjoy the beauty of the scenery. In the 18th century, educated Europeans and Americans began enjoying the look of the landscape for what it told about the natural history of a place. Although that pastime spawned the natural sciences and the conservation and preservation movements, it has remained a rarefied pursuit. Most people say they enjoy nature, but few people can identify plants or animals. Nonetheless, driving for pleasure is the most popular form of recreation among Americans. When we take a drive in the country, we may not know what we see, but we expect to like it.

Among farmers and homeowners the idea that the way your place looks reflects on you is such a commonplace that people seldom talk about it, but we all know it and think about it as we drive through our neighborhoods. Aldo Leopold went so far as to state that "every farmer's land is a portrait of himself." The fact that views of agricultural landscapes are redolent with messages about their caretakers serves to remind us that nature in the countryside is always about people and how they take care of their places. The look of nature so thoroughly infused with human intention should not be confused with nature in the wilderness. Each evokes a different image. Nature in the wilderness may be sublime. In the countryside, the sky and weather bring events of sublime grandeur, but the land is tended.

For knowledgeable viewers, the landscape tells a story that is animated not only by people but by processes and events. Farmers know the drainage and soils and slopes of their land with a subtlety that often surpasses science or engineering. John Fraser Hart coined the term "look of the land" to suggest all that the appearance of the landscape can tell us about its history and use. Mae Watts invited us to "read the landscape" for clues to its ecological character. Kevin Lynch's primer for designers and planners instructed that the environment is an enormous communications device, and he demonstrated how the landscape could be designed to evoke a sense of place. New agricultural landscapes should communicate information so that people can become more knowledgeable about the history and ecological function of the landscape. The landscape should communicate in the most recognizable terms, melding the popular image with cues to ecological function.

CAREFUL CHANGE: MELDING THE POPULAR IMAGE AND ECOLOGICAL KNOWLEDGE

Melding image and knowledge in public perceptions of the agricultural landscape will lead us to ask two questions whenever we introduce change to increase ecological health. The first, most fundamental, question is: What change will increase ecological health? Potential beneficial changes are numerous, from increasing connectivity of uncultivated patches to reducing the use of herbicides. Landscape ecology and conservation biology suggest a rapidly expanding set of principles for change. The second, more strategic, question is: What do people expect that kind of ecological health to look like? This is different from asking what that kind of ecological health actually looks like. It is a question of how we portray nature to fit into a cultural tradition. It is a question of how we take care of our landscapes so that our neighbors will admire and enjoy the nature there. To answer, we begin with how people commonly look at the landscape, not how they might be educated to see it.

For most people the expected image of nature in the countryside more closely matches the appearance of a garden or a park than the wilderness. Nature in the countryside means fields and woodlands, birds and flowers, streams and ponds, hills and valleys, barns and livestock, and very few houses. It is nature at a comprehensible scale, where fences and hedgerows run between fields, trees grow beside streams, and a person could walk from here to there. This is an inhabited nature that invites human involvement, kept neat by those who live there and watch over it. It is nature enhanced by signs of human tending, from freshly painted fences and buildings to straight rows in weed-free fields. All this creates the possibility and desirability of a type of nature that looks quite different from what we expect to find in the wilderness.

Knowing that this is the way people expect nature in the countryside to look should affect our practices and plans for the new agricultural landscape. Those who have worked to restore habitat in agricultural landscapes know that even people who enjoy nature often object to the uneven, weedy appearance of habitat plots, restored wetlands, or reserve parcels. This is not the tended nature they expect. In the past decade, wetlands and prairies have sometimes been obliterated in part because their ecological quality was not apparent to those who saw them. Nature and ecological health will not be unified in popular perceptions unless we plan it that way.

Intelligent tinkering at small scales in agricultural landscapes might monitor many ecological effects, asking, How does this new practice affect water quality, species diversity, or economic productivity? It should also monitor perceptual effects, asking, Does the look of the landscape communicate its ecological quality? Do people enjoy the nature they see here?

Making new agricultural landscapes recognizably beautiful will require working with the familiar landscape language of the popular image. Familiar language does not prevent new statements. It allows parts of the language to be used in new ways. Old, recognizable patterns can be used to signify what new ecological elements mean. Large-scale patterns, edges between types of land cover, and frames around ecosystems that introduce new biodiversity — all are strategies for using what is inherently attractive to convey what actually is healthy in the landscape.

MAKING CHANGE POPULAR:
A NEW AGRICULTURAL LANDSCAPE

In the new agricultural landscape, ecological health and agricultural productivity will be communicated by a landscape that resembles the popular image of beautiful nature in the countryside. At the same time, the beauty of the countryside will be protected and perpetuated by the ecological and economic functions the countryside performs. In this vision, beauty is more than skin deep, and beauty is not a trivial by-product of serious policy. Rather, it is an intentional way to achieve popular support for serious ends: ecological health, agricultural production, and quality of life.

The new agricultural landscape will be beautiful in a way that invites tourism. Scenic roads and byways and places for visitors to stay will become more appealing as parts of the countryside that have lost habitat, streams, or a varied landscape pattern regain a more recognizable image of nature. The countryside will be beautiful in a way that promotes the value of agricultural open space as part of the metropolitan fabric and protects urban agriculture.

The new agricultural landscape also will communicate the ecological benefits of the countryside to the body politic. The pleasure of nature in the countryside will portray the good stewardship of farmers for all to see.

GLOBAL MONOCULTURE

The Worldwide Destruction of Diversity

HELENA NORBERG-HODGE

"IMPORTED EQUALS GOOD, LOCAL EQUALS CRAP." *This is the message being drummed into third world populations. What happens when this message is followed? Rural life collapses, and people who once relied on nearby resources become tied to the global economy. Traditional methods give way to the "modern." Artificial competition and scarcity are created, leading to increased poverty, resentment, starvation, and violence. People become demoralized as they are cut off from their communities and culture. But there is resistance. Third world scholars and activists are reclaiming cultures and are showing that global monoculture need not be our final destination.*

▼

The president of Nabisco once defined the goal of economic globalization as "a world of homogenous consumption," in which people everywhere eat the same food, wear the same clothing, and live in houses built from the same materials. It is a world in which every society employs the same technologies, depends on the same centrally managed economy, offers the same education for its children, speaks the same language, consumes the same media images, holds the same values, and even thinks the same thoughts — monoculture.

Almost everywhere you go in today's "global village," you'll find multilane highways, concrete cities, and a cultural landscape featuring gray business suits, fast-food chains, Hollywood films, and cellular phones. In the remotest corner of the planet, Barbie and Madonna are familiar icons, and the Marlboro Man and Rambo define the male ideal. From Cleveland to Cairo to Caracas, *Baywatch* is entertainment and CNN is news.

Although this sameness suits the needs of transnational corporations, which profit from the efficiencies of standardized production and standardized consumption, in the long term a homogenized planet is disastrous for us all. It is leading to a breakdown of both biological and cultural diversity, erosion of our food security, an increase in conflict and violence, and devastation of the global biosphere.

Human societies have always been embedded in their local ecosystems, modifying and being modified by them. Cultural diversity has come to mirror the biological and geographic diversity of the planet. In arid environments, for example, pastoral or nomadic practices enable people to use more of the sparse resources of their region. In tropical rainforests abundant resources are nearer to hand, and different adaptations — often based on hunting, gathering, and swidden agriculture — have been the solution.

Through such local adaptations, people have met their needs generation after generation, often altering ecosystems without compromising their stability. In many cases human cultures actually enhanced both the security of their food supply and ecosystemic stability by consciously increasing local biodiversity. Farmers in the Peruvian Andes, for example, cultivated more than 40 different varieties of potato in an acre plot, far more than would be found naturally. On Chiloé Island off the coast of Chile there were enough strains of potato to eat a different kind each day of the year. And through centuries of cultivation by traditional farmers in varied ecosystems, more than 17,000 different varieties of wheat have been created. The agricultural biodiversity that exists today is the product of many generations of such farmers selecting seeds for success in a particular place.

Globalization, which attempts to amalgamate every local, regional, and national economy into a single world system, requires homogenizing these locally adapted forms of agriculture, replacing them with an industrial system — centrally managed, pesticide-intensive, one-crop production for export — designed to deliver a narrow range of transportable foods to the world market. In the process, farmers are replaced by energy- and capital-intensive machinery, and diversified food production for local communities is replaced by export monoculture for profit. Thousands of local plant varieties disappear. The same farmers who once grew several hundred varieties of potato on Chiloé now grow just 30, primarily for export. Biotechnology is accelerating this trend, as natural genetic diversity is replaced by clones created and grown in laboratories.

When a new food variety is first introduced, its resistance to pests and disease may be high, but the natural genetic diversity of pests enables them to adapt quickly. As a result, a new cereal variety generally lasts only five or six years before pest problems become so great that it can no longer be grown — even using massive amounts of pesticides. When this stage is reached, farmers must turn to the seed companies for a new variety with an even stronger resistance. But neither Cargill nor W. R. Grace nor any other seed company can constantly create new resistances out of thin air, even with the help of genetic engineering. Ultimately they too must depend on the natural genetic diversity that exists in the wild or in the strains originally cultivated by traditional farmers.

Before long, the credits built up in the gene banks by traditional, location-specific farming will be exhausted. It will no longer be possible to find sources of natural resistance to overcome the genetic adaptation of pests. It could then become impossible to grow major crops like wheat, rice, and maize, and since so many people are now dependent on these staples, starvation on a massive scale would follow.

Much of the cultural diversity that remains in the world today exists in the South, where the majority of people still live in rural villages, partly connected through a diversified local farming economy to diverse local resources. Because of pressures from globalization, those economies are being destroyed, and villagers are rapidly being urbanized and homogenized into the global culture. The urbanization largely results from industrial development, which replaces farmers with agribusiness and large-scale machinery and pushes whole communities off the land. Development also centralizes the few job opportunities and the political power in cities, intensifying the economic pull of urban centers.

Meanwhile, advertising and media images exert powerful psychological pressures to seek a better, more "civilized" life, based on the urban, Western consumerist model. Individual and cultural self-esteem are eroded by the advertising stereotypes of happy, blond, blue-eyed, "clean" Western consumers. If you have been a farmer or are dark-skinned, you are made to feel primitive, backward, inferior. Partly as a consequence, women around the world are now using dangerous chemicals to lighten their skin and hair, and the market is growing for blue contact lenses in such places as Bangkok, Nairobi, and Mexico City.

Once in the cities, people have little choice but to rely on the same scarce resources upon which people thousands of miles away depend. For global corporations, this represents a highly lucrative and efficient market, easy to speak to in their ads. One ad executive in Beijing said the message being drummed into third world populations is "Imported equals good, local equals crap." Corporations and government agencies promoting globalization are conscious of this relationship between urbanization and profit: U.S. grain exporters publicly boast that urbanization of the Asia-Pacific Rim will yield a $14 billion increase in profits in the next five years, as urban populations must use global rather than local resources.

But what happens when rural life collapses and people who once relied on nearby resources become tied to the global economy? Consider traditional architecture in which structures were built from local resources: stone in France, clay in West Africa, bamboo and thatch in the Philippines, and so on. When these building traditions give way to "modern" methods, the plentiful local materials are left unused — while competition skyrockets for the monoculture's narrow range of materials: concrete, steel, and plastic. The same thing happens when people begin eating identical staple foods, wearing the same clothes, and relying on the same finite energy sources. Making everyone dependent on the same resources creates efficiency for global corporations, but it also creates artificial scarcity for consumers, thus heightening competitive pressures.

In this situation, people who are pulled into cities face ruthless competition for jobs and necessities. The gap between rich and poor widens, and resentment, anger, and violence increase sharply. When people are set into such a demoralizing situation while being cut off from their communities and cultural moorings, conflict is all but inevitable.

The prevailing assumption is that the roots of violent conflict lie mainly in the differences among people. By implication, homogenization is civilizing. The basis for such belief often comes from comparing the "civilized" colonies of the third world with the chaos after the colonial powers departed. This analysis doesn't take into account the way colonialism universally destroyed the indigenous systems of governance and the traditional diversified economies that allowed people to produce for their own needs. It may well be that the authoritarian hand of the colonial powers held in check the conflict and violence that would naturally accompany such upheaval, but many of the roots of the violence can be found in the destruction of self-reliant economies and systems of governance.

Most government planners have come to believe that the best way to provide for people's needs is to draw even more of them into urban centers. The Chinese government, for example, is now planning for the expansion of the urban population by 440 million people in the next 20 years. A report by the United Nations promotes urbanization, claiming that urban populations require fewer resources per capita and can be supplied more efficiently with food, water, jobs, and other necessities. But when the real costs of urbanization in the global economy are accounted for, it becomes obvious that urban centers are extremely resource-intensive and that they are actually responsible for a reduction in arable land and therefore in food supplies. Food and water, building materials, and energy for the urban millions must all be brought in from great distances via vast energy-consuming infrastructures; their concentrated wastes must be hauled away or incinerated at great environmental cost. From the most affluent sections of Paris to the slums of Calcutta, urban populations depend on long-distance transport for food, so that every pound of food consumed is accompanied by several pounds of petroleum consumption, pollution, and waste. The urbanized economy is not a product of efficiency but of massive subsidies — tax breaks and direct payments to global corporations and public financing of long-distance transport and communications infrastructures, energy installations, and massive military power to keep recalcitrant communities in line.

How "efficient" is the global economy when it means transporting around the world staple foods that could just as well be produced for local consumption? In Mongolia, a country where there are some 25 million milk-producing animals, the butter in the markets today is primarily German; the water is bottled in Hong Kong. In the marketplaces of France, an apple-producing country, one can find as many New Zealand apples as local ones. How can it be efficient to transport these foods thousands of miles around the planet, using up fossil fuels, polluting the air, and creating food scarcity and global warming? In fact, if efficiency is the yardstick, the goal should be to promote economies that are diversified enough to meet people's needs within the shortest distance possible, depending on long-distance transport only for goods that cannot be produced locally.

There is still time to shift direction, restore diversity, and begin moving toward sustainable, healthy societies and ecosystems. How to begin? In principle, the answer is straightforward: if globalization is the problem, the solution must lie in economic localization. This does not mean an end to all international trade or intercultural communication, as some have unfairly charged. Nor does it mean that industrialized society must always change from a culture of cities to one of villages.

However, the idea of localization runs counter to today's general belief that fast-paced urban areas are the locus of "real" culture, while small, local communities are isolated backwaters, relics of a past when small-mindedness and prejudice were the norm. Most Westerners have a highly distorted notion of what life in small communities can be like. There is only the briefest consideration of cultures and economies that existed before the colonial invaders, nor are there statistics to compare preindustrial and precolonial times with what followed. Recently, however, Southern scholars have begun to unearth this information — finding, for example, evidence about the remarkably high yields in agriculture before the colonial invasions. As for the localized oppression and exploitation experienced in yesterday's smaller-scale societies, people in many parts of the South know very well that being under the boot of today's distant, faceless oppressors can be worse.

Efforts to rein in the runaway global economy need to be international — linking grassroots social and environmental movements from North and South in order to pressure governments to take back the power that has been handed over to corporations. But long-term solutions to today's social and environmental problems will also require a range of small, local initiatives that are as diverse as the cultures and environments in which they take place. Promoting "small-scale on a large scale" would allow specific, on-the-ground initiatives to flourish — community supported agriculture (CSAs), community banks, local currencies and trading systems, rediscovered traditional knowledge, and more. These small-scale steps require a slow pace and a deep and intimate understanding of local contexts and will best be designed and implemented by local people themselves. Over time, such initiatives would inevitably foster a return to cultural and biological diversity and long-term sustainability.

FARMING IN NATURE'S IMAGE

Natural Systems Agriculture

WES JACKSON

FOR 10,000 YEARS TILL AGRICULTURE *has been a disaster for the natural world. Topsoil and biodiversity have been agriculture's most frequent casualties. Current "techno-fixes" like fertilizers and pesticides only make things worse. As a result, nearly one-third of the world's arable land has been lost to erosion, and in the United States we have lost three-quarters of all our agricultural biodiversity over the last 100 years. To reverse our course and find a truly sustainable agriculture, we need to develop a "Natural Systems Agriculture" which features nature's wisdom over human cleverness and brings rewards to the farmer and the land.*

▼

Most people believe that there is a right way to *do* agriculture and that failure to *do* it correctly is simply a failure in character. The very *nature of farming* itself is seldom called into question, and the one who does question agriculture itself may be accused of wanting to return to the bow and arrow way of life.

Agriculture is seen as an essentially wholesome enterprise. The image of a well-scrubbed 4-H kid, clasping the rope on an equally well-scrubbed Holstein heifer at the country fair is *always* fit for the September page of the calendar put up at the local feed store. The kid's bright eyes radiate "new knowledge" and the rosy cheeks "wholesome values."

It isn't just through the kid at the country fair that the notion of the inherent wholesomeness of agriculture gets a boost. The appropriateness of till agriculture is firmly implanted in all civilized peoples. At the United Nations there is a huge statue of a man full of purpose and muscle bent to the task of beating a sword, which does evil of course, into a plowshare, which everyone knows will do good. The developer of a new idea is often described as having "plowed new ground." Saul, the first king of Israel, was anointed in the field where he had been plowing with oxen, suggesting at least a left-handed endorsement of till agriculture from the Almighty himself. The concept of till agriculture is interwoven in our metaphors and symbols. Yet the plowshare may well have destroyed more of the natural world and more options for future generations than the sword.

Till agriculture, almost from the beginning, has to be questioned, not because sustainable till agriculture can't be practiced, but because it isn't and hasn't been, except in small pockets scattered over the globe. So destructive has the agricultural revolution been that, geologically speaking, it surely stands as among the most significant and explosive events to appear on the face of the earth, changing the earth even faster than did the origin of life. Volcanoes erupt in small areas, and mountain ranges require so long in their uplift that adjustments to changing conditions by the life forms are smooth and easy. But agriculture has come on the global scene so rapidly that the life-support system has not had time to adjust to the changing circumstances. In this sense then, till agriculture is a global disease, which in a few places has been well managed, but overall has steadily eroded the land. Unless this disease is checked, the human race will wilt like any other crop.

As I will describe later, I think we have an opportunity to develop a cure for this disease. There is a very real chance that we can arrive at a truly sustainable agriculture. But before arriving at the remedy, it is important to describe the little-noted historical problem of till agriculture. Let us briefly review the epidemiology of the disease.

THE PROBLEM OF AGRICULTURE HISTORICALLY

Greece features a landscape famous for its cultural achievements, from classical times to the present. Here were the landscape and a people that both sponsored and still display the brilliance that has defined much of Western civilization. Here is a land where the impact of agriculture is everywhere, a land where episodes of deforestation and soil erosion have gone on for 8,000 years. History tells us that the ancient Greeks considered themselves careful stewards of the land, people who felt guided by their gods and goddesses in this endeavor. Even so, those early Greeks and their gods, like essentially all agricultural civilizations, failed to hold the topsoil. The recent archaeological evidence of soil erosion in ancient Greece due to agriculture is now well documented. The story begins with the farmers who first settled Greece when the landscape was pristine. But archaeological investigations of ancient ecosystems using soils and fossil pollen along with human relics and artifacts reveal that when hill slopes lose their soil, people move; when usable soils reform thousands of years later, people return to farm. This is no surprise, for here is where both Plato and Aristotle witnessed firsthand land degradation and its consequences. Plato, in one of his dialogues, has Critias proclaim: "What now remains of the formerly rich land is like the skeleton of a sick man, with all the fat and soft earth having wasted away and only the bare framework remaining. . . . The plains that were full of rich soil are now marshes. Hills that were once covered with forests and produced abundant pasture now produce only food for bees. Once the land was enriched by yearly rains, which were not lost, as they are now, by flowing from the bare land into the sea."

As with Greece, Rome relied on the natural fertility and the benign climate of its local geography. The Romans too worshiped nature deities and called the earth "mater terra." Their experience with erosion also mirrored the Greeks' experience: topsoil was lost and fertility declined. The Romans had unbounded faith in human ingenuity, and many believed that intervention on a large scale would pull them through their agriculture woes. Virgil, Ovid, and Seneca were major promoters of such a view. Cicero must also have been a devotee, for he is on record as having said: "By means of our hands we endeavor to create as it were a second world within the world of nature." As would be repeated throughout the centuries in so many cultures, the Romans' interventions were no match for the laws of nature, and their agriculture went into a steep decline.

Egypt fared better. As Herodotus, the Greek historian, said, "Egypt is the gift of the Nile." The Nile received silt from volcanic highlands of Ethiopia, thanks to the predictable monsoon rains arriving from the Indian Ocean each year, bringing minerals into the annual floods of the Nile's tributary, the Blue Nile. Egypt prospered at Ethiopia's mineral expense. The White Nile with its jungle origin and swampy places contributed its organic matter, and the best sources from two parts of the world converged at the confluence. Downstream these fresh nutrients and organic matter so combined to spill over a layer one millimeter thick each year, to be turned into crops for Egyptian farmers and Pharaohs. It seems safe to say that without the steamy jungles and volcanic ash, no pyramids would have been built.

In the New World, the story of till agriculture on sloping ground is much the same as that of the Greeks and Romans. The central Mexican highlands experienced devastating soil erosion 3,500 years before Cortez. Sarah L. O'Hara of the University of Sheffield in Britain and her colleagues took 21 cores of sediment extracted from sites in the central Mexican highlands. Radiocarbon dating of shells and charcoal in the layers determined that there were three periods of severe erosion. The first occurred when Indians began cultivating maize 3,500 years ago, the earliest appearance of maize pollen. A later erosion appeared on steep cultivated hillsides. Most recently, extensive erosion from the hillsides coincided with deforestation. Soil erosion did not increase there after Cortez arrived in 1521. "If anything," she writes, "there was a decrease in the erosion rate after the conquest." We know that not only did the population steeply decline following the conquest, but the forests regenerated.

The industrial agriculture of recent years has accelerated erosion at an almost inconceivable pace. In the last 40 years, nearly one-third of the world's arable land has been lost to erosion and continues to be lost at a rate of more than 10 million hectares per year. Ninety percent of U.S. cropland is losing soil above replacement rates. Loss is 17 times faster than formation on average. At this rate, during the next 20 years, the potential yield of good land without fertilizer or irrigation is estimated to drop 20 percent. Once all soil costs are calculated for the United States, the bottom line is $44 billion in direct damage to agricultural lands and indirect damage to waterways, infrastructure, and health in the United States, and nearly $400 billion in damage worldwide. It has been estimated that to bring soil erosion under control in the United States would require an annual outlay of $8.4 billion.

The ravages of the agricultural disease include not only topsoil loss but also the loss of biodiversity. This age-old problem has become ever more acute. Many crops now altered to conform to industrial farming have been genetically narrowed in the extreme. Nearly a third of the American maize crop comes from four inbred lines. Even in Mexico, farmers abandon the more diverse, locally adapted varieties in favor of genetically narrow, high-yielding strains. In the United States we have lost three-quarters of all our agricultural biodiversity over the past 100 years.

DIGGING THE HOLE DEEPER AS NATURAL FERTILITY DECLINES

Throughout history many have argued that the solution for saving topsoil and biodiversity is more technology. Over the last many decades they have further argued that a new revolution in farming technology will make higher production possible without sacrificing environmental quality. Even a cursory examination of two relatively recent "revolutions" in agriculture demonstrates the folly of this "quick fix" mind-set.

For example, industrial agriculture has offset much of the age-old soil erosion problem with the use of fossil fuels: fossil carbon in the form of fertilizers substituting for soil carbon. This "fossil-carbon" agriculture is startlingly inefficient in terms of materials and energy usage. U.S. agriculture requires ten fossil fuel calories to produce a single food calorie. The trend in countries worldwide is toward even greater consumption of fossil fuels by the agricultural sector. This last-gasp effort to substitute petroleum-based fertilizers for lost topsoil is doomed to failure. Energy scholars now project that global oil production will peak and begin its permanent decline around 2020 and that by the latter half of this century, it will drop to 10 percent of the present annual production. The fossil-carbon answer clearly cannot be a long-term fix for erosion.

Many also see the chemical industry as a panacea for our agricultural woes. But the terrible consequences of this fix become more evident every day. Nitrate from fertilizers, linked to blue baby syndrome and cancer in test animals, is increasingly a problem as it seeps into ground water supplies. Soils that are naturally most productive are alive with everything from earthworms to microorganisms — creatures that build, till, and nourish the soil. Herbicides and insecticides applied to crops kill huge quantities of this life that would contribute to soil health. Nitrogen fertilizers, combined with frequent tillage, "burn up" soil organic matter, thus destroying soil structure. Chemicals may also degrade soil structure, hindering water and gas relationships between the plants and the soil. Data reveal that at best one percent of applied pesticides reach their intended targets; the rest cause unintended damage both on and off site. According to the U.S. Department of Agriculture (USDA), pesticide use on major field crops, fruits, and vegetables nearly tripled from 215 million pounds in 1964 to 588 million pounds in 1997. Numerous studies have also been conducted to verify the suspected link between agricultural pesticides and diseases in humans. Direct links are often impossible to establish because they would require experimentation employing direct dosages. However, a summary of cancer risks among farmers cites "significant excesses for Hodgkin's disease, multiple myeloma, leukemia, skin melanomas, and cancers of the lip, stomach, and prostate" due to pest control chemicals. Another study posits that the herbicide 2,4-D has been associated with two- to eightfold increases in non-Hodgkin's lymphoma in agricultural regions. The study of farm chemicals and their clear role in disrupting the human endocrine system is a fast-growing field. Other reports reveal that numerous pesticides can reduce the immune system's ability to deal with infectious agents.

As the Romans learned a couple of millennia ago, human technical ingenuity is no match for nature's laws. Industrial agriculture's temporary techno-fixes are no panacea for our agricultural woes and never will be. They only exacerbate the problem. But there is a way to escape the current crisis in topsoil and biodiversity loss, a path toward a sustainable agriculture. Once explained the answer may seem obvious, but it is one that humanity has pretty much ignored since the dawn of agriculture.

LOOKING TO NATURE AS THE STANDARD
TO SOLVE THE PROBLEM OF AGRICULTURE

Thinking on the history of agriculture's abuse of the earth, and especially the recent dependency on fossil fuels, chemicals, and the
genetic narrowing of our major crops, it becomes increasingly clear
that the problem of agriculture cannot be solved within our current
conventions of thought and action. These agricultural practices are
based on the idea that nature is to be subdued or ignored. In 1978, I
published an essay entitled "Toward a Sustainable Agriculture," in
which I argued against this paradigm of the subjugation of nature and
for an agriculture based on the way nature works, especially nature's
prairie. I later expanded the argument for a more natural solution to
the "problem of agriculture" in *New Roots for Agriculture*. This seemingly revolutionary idea of "nature as standard" or "nature as measure" goes back at least 2,000 years before Jesus of Nazareth. Wendell
Berry, who has traced this literary and scientific history, begins with
Job, who said, "ask now the beasts, and they shall teach thee; and the
fowls of the air, and they shall tell thee: Or speak to the earth, and it
shall teach thee; and the fishes of the sea shall declare unto thee."
Next he quoted Virgil, who advised that,

> *before we plow an unfamiliar patch*
> *It is well to be informed about the winds,*
> *About the variation in the sky,*
> *The native traits and habits of the place,*
> *What each locale permits, and what denies.*

Edmund Spenser, toward the end of the 1500s, called nature "the
equal mother" of all creatures, who "knittest each to each, as brother
unto brother." Spenser saw nature as the instructor of creatures and
the ultimate earthly judge of their behavior. Shakespeare, in *As You
Like It*, has the forest in the role of teacher and judge. Alexander
Pope, in his Epistle to Burlington, counseled gardeners to "let Nature
never be forgot" and "Consult the Genius of the Place in all."

Berry, himself one of America's great poets, novelists, and essay-
ists, says that this theme departs from English poetry after Pope, with
the later poets regarding nature and humans as radically divided. A
practical harmony between land and people was ignored. The romantic

poets after Pope placed preeminence on the human mind to the point that nature was a mere "reservoir of symbols." The idea that practical lessons could be learned from nature was not advanced.

When poets no longer looked to nature, agricultural writers with a scientific bent reintroduced the theme in the formal culture. The Cornell University professor Liberty Hyde Bailey's *The Outlook to Nature* appeared in 1905; in it he described nature as "the norm": "If nature is the norm, then the necessity for correcting and amending abuses of civilization becomes badly apparent by very contrast." He continued: "The return to nature affords the very means of acquiring the incentive and energy for ambitious and constructive work of a higher order." Later, Bailey's *The Holy Earth* (1915) was published. This time Bailey advanced the notion that "a good part of agriculture is to learn how to adapt one's work to nature. To live in right relation with his natural conditions is one of the first lessons that a wise farmer or any other wise man learns."

Sir Albert Howard published *An Agriculture Testament* in 1940. Howard thought we should farm like the forest, for nature is "the supreme farmer." He wrote: "Mother earth never attempts to farm without livestock; she always raises mixed crops; great pains are taken to preserve the soil and to prevent erosion; the mixed vegetable and animal wastes are converted into humus; there is no waste; the processes of growth and the processes of decay balance one another; ample provision is made to maintain large reserves of fertility; the greatest care is taken to store the rainfall; both plants and animals are left to protect themselves against disease."

At The Land Institute we have carried on this idea of agriculture in nature's image through an effort we call Natural Systems Agriculture (NSA). We began with the goal of relying on the ecological benefits of natural ecosystems with no or minimal sacrifice in food production. We look to the never-plowed native prairie to be our teacher. Nature's prairie features a diversity of species, nearly all of which are perennial. Because their roots do not die as annual roots do, they hold soil through all seasons, even when drenched by rain. Moreover, perennial roots build soil. This ecosystem thus maintains its own health, runs on the sun's energy, and recycles nutrients, and at no expense to the planet or people.

Another consideration: wherever we look, from the Canadian prairies to Texas, from the state of Washington in the west to Ohio in the east, roughly 2,000 miles in both directions, wherever there is prairie, four functional groups are featured: warm-season grasses, cool-season grasses, legumes, and composites. Other species are present, but these groups are featured. Different species fill different roles. Some thrive in dry years, others in wet ones. Some provide fertility by fixing atmospheric nitrogen. Some tolerate shade, others require direct sunlight. Some repel insect predators. Some do better on poor, rocky soils while others need rich, deep soil. Diversity provides the system with built-in resilience to changes and cycles in climate, water, insects and pests, grazers, and other natural disturbances.

The challenge is to feature species diversity and perennialism. We must also try to have all four functional groups represented in our mixture or polyculture, and it must produce harvestable edible grain for direct human consumption. Our primary strategy then is to imitate the structure of the prairie ecosystem in order to be granted the functions described above. Properly designed, the system itself should virtually eliminate the ecological degradation characteristic of conventional agriculture and minimize the need for human intervention.

This sounds idyllic, but is it possible? In order to determine if a "natural systems" agriculture is feasible, we organized our research around four basic questions.

1. Can perennialism and increased seed yield go together at no trade-off cost to the plant?
2. Can a polyculture of species outyield a monoculture?
3. Can perennial species planted in mixtures adequately manage all pests?
4. Can a perennial polyculture sponsor all of its own nitrogen fertility needs?

We have published positive answers in peer-reviewed scientific journals for questions 1, 2, and 3, and have indirect evidence that supports question 4. The functions of a natural system, it is now apparent, can be achieved by replicating its structure. The implications and potential impact of this work are global. By demonstrating underlying principles along with practical applications, we have shown that the "natural systems" approach could be transferable worldwide, as long as adequate research is devoted to developing species and mixtures of species appropriate to specific environments. With additional research, an agriculture that is resilient, productive over the long-term, economical, ecologically responsible, and socially just is within reach.

CONCLUSION: HEALTHIER AGRICULTURE

Natural Systems Agriculture research is predicated on the assumption that to be successful in agriculture we need to know what nature will require of us — a more sophisticated and desirable way of asking, "What can we get away with?"

When we put together several plant species to provide a rough structural analog of the prairie, that prairie we are imitating is a complex polyculture. In our domestic prairies, which will feature grain, we had best not treat these polycultures as wheat or corn fields have been treated. Our plots are more like a whole person that includes a heart. Some medical statisticians are still tempted to take all hearts of a certain age and gender, say, and place them under the likelihood of a heart attack. The problem with regarding hearts as existing in "hearthood," like wheat plants in a field, is that all hearts are not interacting with other hearts in a simplifiable way as an individual wheat plant is with other wheat plants in a monoculture. The heart has to interact with all the other organs of the person's body and respond to the pressures in his or her life, as well as to the history of those pressures, and finally with the hearts of others. The wheat field also has interactions we have chosen to ignore. It is heavily dependent on an economy that is extractive and polluting. On sloping ground it will cause soil erosion. We need ways of thinking about agriculture that are as complex as necessary, meaning an exercise in judgment as to what constitutes "good enough."

We should commit to the journey now to solve the 10,000-year-old problem. It may be an ideal never to be achieved in an absolute sense, just as justice and sustainability are unlikely to ever be ideally achieved. Even so, to commit to this journey would put an end to ratcheting up what Sir Francis Bacon proposed four centuries ago: to torture nature to get truth out of her even as King James had tortured witches to gain truth. Students of Bacon's writings know this was no slip of the tongue on his part, for he also advocated "the enlarging of the bounds of Human Empire, to the effect of all things possible."

And so we are calling for the opposite — emphasizing Nature's wisdom over human cleverness. Agriculture is the best place to begin, for if we don't get sustainability in agriculture first, it is not going to happen. Agriculture has evolutionary biology and ecology as Siamese twins standing behind it. The industrial or materials sector has no such discipline. As progress is made, we can begin to reconfigure human economies, since success in Natural Systems Agriculture will mean that the primary reward will run to the farmer and the landscape, not to the suppliers of inputs. I see no reason why forestry and fisheries thinking and research could not run in concert on this different path for agriculture. Perhaps eventually we can mold all such economies to nature's image, letting her be our ultimate teacher.

Understanding
Industrial Agriculture

▼ ▼ ▼

Industrial agriculture is not only a method of food production. It is also reflects a deeply ingrained way of thinking about nature and ourselves. This section is designed to provide a more holistic understanding of industrial consciousness and its impacts, which will help us grasp the historical and philosophic roots of today's "fatal harvest."

HARD TIMES FOR DIVERSITY

DAVID EHRENFELD

WE LIVE IN A SOCIETY THAT VIEWS *plants, animals, and, yes, even people as mere biological machines. The beauty and uniqueness of each organism has been lost in the reductionism of scientific generalities. Why? Because application of these generalized "laws" allows for manipulation and control over the natural world. And those seeking power over nature find the study of specificity too slow, and the maintenance of diversity too expensive, to be tolerated. Until science and society regain a fascination with diversity and the particular, there will continue to be an accelerating loss of species and devastation of the Earth's living communities.*

▼

B iological riches are the most dependable kind of wealth. Money, if it ever appears, is easily lost. Possessions are equally vulnerable. A good name takes effort to maintain — it can be erased by a momentary carelessness or, in this era of computer files and insatiable news media, by the carelessness of others. Art and architecture are destroyed by war and vandalized by time. Health vanishes; happiness can disappear like silver maple leaves at the approach of winter. Nobody is proof against such changes. But the diversity of living species and communities, even when locally diminished, remains, a cup that fills with every opportunity, although not always with the same wine. One would think that the value of natural and cultural diversity would be obvious to each new generation. Not ours.

The appreciation of diversity has fallen on hard times in Western and Western-influenced societies. The spirit that moved Botticelli to incorporate at least 30 different species of plants in his canvas entitled *Spring*, painted in 1478, the spirit that prompted Shakespeare to mention enough animal and plant species in his plays to provide source materials for entire books, and the spirit that gave Thomas

Jefferson delight in compiling his great collection of comparative vocabularies of 50 different American Indian languages, if it has not vanished, has been effectively sublimated and suppressed in our day. We have in its place the celebration of the sort of pseudodiversity that one finds on the menu of a Chinese-Polynesian-American restaurant, the ersatz variety that is the hallmark of our homogenized world culture.

What has caused the decline of the love of diversity and is causing the decline of diversity itself is, not surprisingly, the ascendancy of its opposite: uniformity. We have abandoned our fascination with the specific, with species, in favor of a preoccupation with the general and the generalizable, with scientific laws. This is the Age of Generality, and every month that passes sees it more firmly entrenched as the official way of seeing and dealing with the world.

GENERALITY AND POWER

Why is generality in the ascendancy? There is one reason, I believe, and it is all but irresistible. Generality confers power. Much of our control (influence is a more accurate word) over the external world is related in one way or another to our discovery of general laws and principles of physics, chemistry, and biology, an explosion of knowledge that is essentially modern. Our ability to manipulate the world, which goes beyond the dreams of the alchemists, is new and addictive. Never mind that the control we claim is almost always flawed, incomplete, and even self-destructive: we humans are poor at giving up power once we get a taste of it. Of course, knowledge of the specific is also useful, but it doesn't very often help us control the world. Penicillin was discovered because of specific observations, but antibiotics as a class belong to the category of applied general theory.

A good example of the power of generality, certainly the one closest to my own experience, is the drastic change that has occurred in biology since 1965. In the modern scientific-technical process, the specific is usually subordinate to the general and is considered the work of lesser scientific intellects and technicians. We expect this mind-set of physicists and mathematicians — not of biologists. Yet the "cutting edge" in biology is now popularly thought to be genetic engineering, a science and a technology that take advantage of the uniformity of the genetic code to toss all organisms into the same grab bag of genes. Most of the genes in this bag are considered trash; a few are withdrawn to be inserted as supposedly useful parts into a small number of recipient organisms such as milk cows or wheat. Here is generality taken to the last degree. Although genetic engineering often does not work as well as its glittering promises, the proof of its power is that the genetic engineers now command higher salaries and more political clout than any previous generation of Western biologists.

It cannot be argued that these biologists have simply shifted the level of specificity from the living organism to the gene. It is the organism that we perceive, that lives in our environments and our history. How can we respect a new view of life that treats plants and animals as mere holders or packages of genes that can be blended at will with genes from other packages? The sanctity of diversity, of separateness, is an ancient belief embraced by people who lived as part of nature and experienced its diversity daily. This belief is no doubt a reason for the biblical prohibitions against sowing several kinds of seeds together in the same field, against weaving wool and linen together in the same cloth, and against interbreeding different species of animals. In the words of the Hellenistic Jewish commentator Flavius Josephus, "Nature does not rejoice in the union of things that are not in their nature alike." How alien this concept seems in today's homogenized, nature-distanced, power-loving society. The sanctity of diversity loses all meaning when designer organisms can be patented and sold to the highest bidder like a new type of cigarette lighter or a new kind of toilet seat.

Generality, as practiced by the genetic engineers, has almost completely taken over the one-time shrine of diversity, the science of biology itself. No longer is diversity celebrated for its own sake. No longer do we see, for example, graduate students who have staked out as their primary life's work a taxonomic group, such as mayflies or topminnows or the birch family; at least we don't see very many of them. Now their work is organized around general questions and themes, such as "foraging strategies" and "habitat fragmentation." Useful as many of these concepts are, they are no substitute for knowledge of the specific. Yet without generality, at least as a cover, few biologists can hope to find employment and support. As I indicated, any academic biologist in any large university can testify to the sheer political power of that most general of all modern biological discoveries, the universal genetic code. So powerful, indeed, is this particular generality that it has all but obliterated the once-prized distinction between pure science and technology, between the academic and the industrial worlds. In the major universities, professorships and even whole departments are now commonly supported by chemical and pharmaceutical companies. But unlike the days prior to the 1980s, when such support had no formal strings attached, it is now contractually contingent on the corporation's first claim to any discoveries and patents that come from the professor's or department's research. No wonder there is a scarcity of top-ranked graduate students who are committed, for instance, to the study of bats per se, and precious few jobs for those who are — except maybe in the field of bat control.

In a world bent on manipulation and control, the study of specificity is too slow and tedious, and the maintenance of diversity is too expensive, to be tolerated by the people who make decisions. Both the study and the appreciation of the particular, of diversity, take time, and time is money. The trouble with differences and particularities, in the economic view that prevails today, is that there is no general rule for coping with them, except, perhaps, to ignore them.

A fundamental problem and paradox of conservation arises from our preoccupation with the general and from the power that an understanding of general laws brings: we are committed to the kind of exploitative approach to nature that places diversity in jeopardy. This is truly a catch-22 situation, or, to use Gregory Bateson's handy phrase, a double bind. Our newfound love affair with generality and general laws, and the resulting power to change the earth, have enabled us to destroy biological diversity at an astonishing rate. They have simultaneously caused us to lose interest in the specific and respect for the people who study it. And that prevents effective conservation.

THE VALUE OF SPECIES

As my philosopher friends would say, nature in its separate elements has lost its intrinsic value to people and now has only instrumental value: we value it for its usefulness. In the long run, this insistence on claiming a general, instrumental need and value for every last species and variety is only going to get us into trouble. It does not occur to us that by assigning only instrumental value to diversity we merely legitimize the process that is wiping it out, the process that says, "The first thing that matters in any important decision is the magnitude of the dollar costs and tangible benefits." People are afraid that if they do not express their fears and concerns in this language they will be laughed at, they will not be listened to. This may be true (although having philosophies that differ from the established ones is not necessarily inconsistent with the power to effect change). But true or not, it is certain that if we persist in this crusade to determine value where value ought to be evident, we will be left with nothing but our greed when the dust finally settles. I should make it clear that I am referring not just to the effort to put an actual price on biological diversity but also to the attempt to rephrase the price in terms of a nebulous survival value.

A concrete example that calls into question this evaluating process comes immediately to mind. I came across it in a paper published in the *Journal of Political Economy* in 1973 by Colin Clark, an applied mathematician at the University of British Columbia. That paper, which everyone who seeks to put a dollar value on biological diversity ought to read, is about the economics of killing blue whales. The question was whether it was economically advisable to halt the Japanese whaling of this species to give blue whales time to recover to the point where they could become a sustained economic resource. Clark demonstrated that in fact it was economically preferable to kill every blue whale left in the oceans as fast as possible and reinvest the profits in growth industries rather than to wait for the species to recover to the point where it could sustain an annual catch. He was not recommending this course — just pointing out a danger of relying heavily on economic justifications for conservation in that case.

In the long run, basing our conservation strategy on the economic value of diversity will only make things worse, because it keeps us from coping with the root cause of the loss of diversity. It makes us accept as givens the technological/socioeconomic premises that make biological impoverishment of the world inevitable. If I were one of the many exploiters and destroyers of biological diversity, I would like nothing better than for my opponents, the conservationists, to be bogged down over the issue of valuing. Economic criteria of value are shifting, fluid, and utterly opportunistic in their practical application. This is the opposite of the value system needed to conserve biological diversity over the course of decades and centuries.

Value is an intrinsic part of diversity; it does not depend on the properties of the species in question, the uses to which particular species may or may not be put, or their alleged role in the balance of global ecosystems. For biological diversity, value *is*. Perhaps nothing more, and certainly nothing less. No cottage industry of expert evaluators is needed to assess this kind of value. Having said this, I could stop, but I won't, because I would like to say it in a different way.

Assigning value to biological diversity involves two practical problems. The first is a problem for economists: it is not possible to figure out the true economic value of any piece of biological diversity, let alone the value of diversity in the aggregate. We do not know enough about any gene, species, or ecosystem to be able to calculate its ecological and economic worth in the larger scheme of things. Even in relatively closed systems (or in systems that they pretend are closed), economists are poor at describing what is happening and terrible at making even short-term predictions based on available data. How then should ecologists and economists, dealing with huge, open systems, decide on the net present or future worth of any part of diversity? There is no way to assign numbers to many of the admittedly most important sources of value in the calculation. For example, we can figure out, more or less, the value of lost revenue in terms of lost fisherman-days when trout streams are destroyed by agricultural runoff, but what sort of value do we assign to the loss to the community when a whole generation of children can never enjoy the streams near home, can never experience home as a place where they would like to stay, even after it becomes possible to leave?

Moreover, how do we deal with values of organisms whose very existence escapes our notice? Before we fully appreciated the vital role that mycorrhizal symbiosis plays in the lives of many plants, what kind of value would we have assigned to the tiny, threadlike fungi in the soil that bring essential minerals to plant roots and are nourished by the roots in turn?

And there is one more corollary of our ignorance, a corollary that takes us to the tropical forest. It is a given of the modern conservation movement that we can earn money to save rain forests by selling renewable products harvested from them by native peoples. Yet when we calculate the value of the chemicals, fruits, and nuts that we extract from the forest to obtain money for conservation, how do we factor in the very real costs of the changes in the forest brought about by our efforts? We know that extraction of forest products can drastically reduce the species being harvested and all the other species that depend upon them, whether or not the extraction is done by natives using low-energy technologies. It is hard to protect endangered species and habitats from legal and illegal demand once the world market is stirred up — even if it is stirred up in the name of conservation. Nor can we predict in advance what will happen once the commercial genie is out of the bottle. It is easier to develop value than it is to calculate the effects of our valuing. Whether it is nuts from the rain forest, ecotourism, or sea turtle farming, I question whether a lasting human relationship with the environment can be based on the premise that conservation should pay for itself so that we don't ever have to limit our desires.

But while building a case against assigning or developing value in wild species and ecosystems in order to save them, I want to leave a very small loophole. Diversity being what it is — diverse — there are no exception-free laws for saving it. Every endangered species or community requires its own unique plan of rescue (which is why conservation is so expensive), and a small number of these plans may legitimately pivot around the market value of species. Separating the few authentic examples from the many spurious ones is a job for ecologists and economists working together.

There is a second practical problem with assigning value to biological diversity. In a chapter called "The Conservation Dilemma" in my book *The Arrogance of Humanism,* I discuss the problem of what I call nonresources. The sad fact that few conservationists care to face is that many species, perhaps most, probably do not have any conventional value at all, even hidden conventional value. True, we cannot be sure which particular species fall into this category, but it is hard to deny that a great many of them do. And unfortunately, the species whose members are the fewest in number, the rarest, the most narrowly distributed — in short, the ones most likely to become extinct — are obviously the ones least likely to be missed by the biosphere. Many of these species were never common or ecologically influential; by no stretch of the imagination can we make them out to be vital cogs in the ecological machine. If the California condor disappears forever from the California hills, it will be a tragedy. But don't expect the chaparral to die, the redwoods to wither, the San Andreas Fault to open up, or even the California tourist industry to suffer — they won't.

So it is with plants. We do not know how many species are needed to keep the planet green and healthy, but it seems very unlikely to be anywhere near the more than quarter of a million we have now. And if we turn to the invertebrates, the source of nearly all biological diversity, what biologist is willing to find a value — conventional or ecological — for all 600,000-plus species of beetles?

I don't deny the real and frightening ecological dangers the world is facing; rather, I am pointing out that the danger of declining diversity is best seen as a separate danger, a danger in its own right. Nor am I trying to undermine conservation; I would like to see it find a sound footing outside the slick terrain of the economists and their philosophical allies.

If conservation is to succeed, people must come to understand the inherent wrongness of the destruction of biological diversity. This notion of wrongness is a powerful argument with great breadth of appeal to all manner of personal philosophies. Those who do not believe in God, for example, can still accept the fact that it is wrong to destroy biological diversity. The very existence of diversity is its own warrant for survival. As in law, long-established existence confers a strong right to a continued existence. If more human-centered values are still deemed necessary, there are plenty available — for example, the value of the wonder, excitement, and challenge of so many species arising from a few dozen elements of the periodic table.

And to countenance the destruction of diversity is equally wrong for those who believe in God, because it was God who, by whatever mechanism, caused this diversity to appear here in the first place. Diversity is God's property, and we who bear the relationship to it of strangers and sojourners have no right to destroy it. There is a much-told story about the great biologist, J. B. S. Haldane, who was well known to be an atheist. Haldane was asked what his years of study-ing biology had taught him about the Creator. His rather snide reply was that God seemed to have "an inordinate fondness for beetles." Well, why not? As God answered Job from the whirlwind in the sec-tion of the Bible that is perhaps the most relevant to biological diver-sity, "Where were you when I laid the foundations of the earth?" Assigning value to that which we do not own and whose purpose we cannot understand except in the most superficial ways is the ultimate in presumptuous folly.

TO PRESERVE DIVERSITY

Conservation is inextricably linked to human values — linked in its methodology and linked in its chances of success. Until science and society regain a fascination with diversity, with differences, with uniqueness, and with exceptions, all in their own right, there will con-tinue to be a shortage of taxonomists, there will continue to be new and faster methods of cutting down tropical forests, there will con-tinue to be an accelerating loss of species and communities, despite all the science, land, and money that conservation can muster.

True, we cannot unlearn exploitative technologies. Nevertheless, the prevailing human value systems can change in response to need and unknown factors, sometimes surprisingly quickly, and perhaps not by any deliberate acts of individuals. The love of diversity is now under a cloud, but it has not gone away — we would have no zoos, botanical gardens, or natural history museums if it had. The world, I believe, is in the process of discovering that the disastrous effects of exploitative generality can be curbed and moderated by a judicious application of diversity of all sorts (maybe including a growing diver-sity of nations). Whether we refer to the failures of global economic and political systems, of endless forest monocultures, or of vast irri-gation and hydroelectric projects, the cure resides in the various cor-relates of diversity: local or here rather than widespread or elsewhere, smaller rather than larger, many ways rather than one way, slow rather than fast, personal rather than impersonal, particular rather than general. And here is a pleasant paradox: diversity does have a general instrumental use after all. It is not that 5 or 10 million species are all ecologically necessary to keep the biosphere intact; but if we relearn how to value this diversity for its own sake, we will discover that we are no longer destroying the world.

In *The Natural History of Selborne*, Gilbert White began his fifth letter to Thomas Pennant with the phrase "Among the singularities of this place . . ." It was the genius of White that immortalized such specificities as the way golden-crowned wrens hang from branches, the number of spines in the dorsal fin of a loach, or even the diameter, in yards, of the pond near his town. However, it required more than White's genius to make the book so popular for 200 years. It required the human ability of his readers to value and prize the singularities of a place. That trait still exists but lies dormant in most people, and can be awakened. One of our prime tasks is to find ways of arousing it again.

In my optimistic moments, I look forward to a world where the genius of a Gilbert White or a Linnaeus can thrive alongside the genius of a Watson and a Crick. This isn't nostalgia; such a world has not existed before. It will demand of us one of the most creative advances of recent human history. Those who will bring about the necessary change are the ones who still love diversity for its own sake.

MACHINE LOGIC

Industrializing Nature and Agriculture

JERRY MANDER

A CENTURY SINCE THE INDUSTRIAL REVOLUTION, *human beings have become immersed within technological forms: cities, factories, high-speed transport, electronic media, as well as industrial practices in forestry, aquaculture, and agriculture. Where humans once coevolved with the natural world, that world is increasingly absent from our experience and awareness. We slowly merge with the machine even in the way we think. In such a confined context, notions of sustainability begin to lose their roots in nature, and themselves become industrial expressions.*

▼

The late French philosopher Jacques Ellul made the case that in technological society all forms of human activity, whether personal behavior or organized social and economic activity, are fundamentally adaptive to the dominant logic and form of the machine. Beyond adaptive, human beings and our political, social, and economic expressions are at one with the machine, part of a seamless symbiotic merger of humans with mechanical and industrial forms, and the human embodiment of industrial consciousness. He argued that the process is now ubiquitous, planetary. It is discoverable not only in the external forms of industrial expression but also in the process of human coevolution with the machines we use. (As we drive our cars, we merge with the machine and the road, becoming ultimately "car-like." As we "watch" TV, we actually ingest its images and store them, and they become our consciousness; we begin to merge with the images we carry. As we use our computers, we are engaged in endless feedback cycles which bring our minds, hands, and bodies in concert with the machine. As we work the assembly line, we are utterly subject to the external repetitive rhythms that the line imposes but that are also internalized and carried by us beyond working hours.) On each side of the human-machine equation, there are adaptations to one another — the machine is adapted for human use, and we adapt to the machine — with the ultimate goal being merger. It is that merged symbiotic form that Ellul labels as "technique," and he applies this as much to human behavior and consciousness and thought as to the metallic expressions of it. In times before the technological age, coevolution was strictly among living creatures with the other expressions of nature. Now, increasingly, our coevolution is with mechanical or electronic forms, while nonhuman nature is dropped from the equation, and from consideration, with already evident disastrous consequences.

If this process of technique can be grasped, merging human thought and behavior into ever more industrial forms, then it is obvious why the organizational forms that we invent and employ are even further expressions of technique. The corporation, for example, itself an example of technique, operates by a system of laws and inherent structural rules that leave it utterly beyond the norms of human "morals," of concerns for community or for the harms that may be caused by industrial activity to a world beyond the technological world — to nature and natural processes. The corporation operates by an internal logic containing certain guidelines: economic growth, profit, absence of ethics and morals, and the endless need to convert the natural world into industrial processes and commercial products, by the fastest, most "efficient" means possible.

All "values" aside from these become secondary; in fact, they do not enter the picture at all in most instances. Questions of community welfare or environmental sustainability are only issues of public relations, under technocorporate consciousness. The intrinsic values of the creatures of the Earth — its plants, its wildlife, its forests — are all reduced to their objective commercial potential, with their ultimate fate determined by what fits technological-industrial processes most neatly.

So, in machine society, it becomes solely the values and forms of the technical instruments — including corporations — that finally determine the organization of human activity and our relationship to nature. This is now clearly evident in every area of economic endeavor, though especially in the areas that corporations have gathered under their control. Whether we speak of the agricultural sector, or manufacturing, or food delivery, or fishing industries, or the care and use of forest communities of living organisms, from trees and humans to insects and microbes, all are subject to the logic of the machine.

All of these economic areas now show the visible symptoms of industrialization, exemplified particularly as monoculture. In agriculture, where many families formerly grew diversified crops to feed themselves and their communities, we now see a global juggernaut of corporate "massification": massive land buyouts, people driven from their farms and cultures to squalid urban situations, and vast farmlands converted to monocultures, using pesticide- and machine-intensive means to care for plants that human beings once nurtured. Where once small farms fed many people and kept the land rich, now most production is in soybeans, or cattle, or coffee for export. This is industrial logic. Meanwhile, the poisons on the lands seep to the rivers and into the food and water. And the people driven to cities, jobless, join the hordes of hungry migrants moving across borders.

Industrial monocultures — single crops where there was once diversity, and single varieties of each crop where there used to be thousands — are also blows against biological and genetic diversity. The Food and Agriculture Organization (FAO) reports that 75 percent of genetic diversity in agriculture was lost this past century. Monocultures are weak, subject to insect blights, diseases, and bad weather. The tremendous volume of pesticides needed to keep monocultures alive kills biological and genetic diversity in the soil. Eventually, little is left but chemical-laden "dead" soil. Then finally, as usable farmland disappears, new pressures are created to encroach upon wilderness areas, yet another threat to biodiversity.

Some corporations say the solution lies with biotechnology. They call it the "ecologically sound solution." But biotechnology operates on the same monocultural principles. Where it has been tried, there have been spectacular failures, costing farmers millions of dollars. And biotechnology introduces a tremendous new danger: biological pollution, a hazard on a scale with nuclear power. Accidental cross-pollination of biotech plants with non-biotech ones could potentially create new, uncontrollable varieties. With the invention of "terminator seeds" — producing plants with sterile seeds — there is the possibility of a crossover gene creating a global "suicide plant" pandemic. Unlike ordinary pollution, genetic pollution might never be stopped. It is madness to take the risk.

Like all of industrial agriculture, biotechnology promotes the idea that the goal of agriculture is to control, simplify, and homogenize, without concern for nature.

The situation with forestry is identical. Where once thriving biotic communities of life permitted a biodiversity rich and stable in its complexities, industrial forestry, following the dictates of the objective rule of technique and the corporate directors of the process, replaces diversity with emptiness: clearcut. Life removed. Sometimes the clearcut areas are replanted into the "tree farms" that corporations will trumpet in their advertising — long rows of single species of pine or eucalyptus or fir — looking just exactly like the assembly lines of other industrial processes, with all diversity of forest life wiped out: a forest community no more.

Similar instances can be cited in the industrialization of fisheries: the giant trawler sweeping quantities of ocean life, thousands of times more than small fisher boats do, killing the oceans and the traditional fishing practices alike. We could enumerate a hundred other areas of economic endeavor. In cities the forms of the industrial-technical process are especially clear: suburbs, freeways, high-rise buildings, concrete on the land, nature nowhere visible, humans moving via machines through industrial canyons at industrial speed.

This homogenizing, massifying process is now being globalized, as the corporate supervisors follow the inevitable growth and expansion dictates of their technological mandates. Technique goes global.

Today, it is only the very rare indigenous society that has managed to stay away from the subjugation of technique. There we can still see the application of non-machine formulas: reciprocal processes as determined by planetary nature-based logic not visible within technological forms. But once those societies succumb to the dictates of the machine, or are pressed to do so, all becomes uniform, at one with the rules of efficiency, objectivity, productivity, economic growth, and profit that are intrinsic to technique.

Only one century into this process, the result is apparent in the looming catastrophes of global warming, ozone depletion, loss of species, pollution of all waters, loss of ecosystem viability, massive loss of biodiversity, and, in the case of small-scale sustainable agriculture, its rapid elimination and replacement with vast wastelands of monoculture, or industrialized farms. The combination of these and other goings-on have brought us directly to the brink of a terrible ecological Armageddon.

Are there beneficiaries? Not judging by what is also simultaneously happening among human populations being similarly industrialized. We now see a level of alienation, suicide, violence, starvation, and a growing gulf between rich and poor that bespeak a society that has been victimized nearly as much as the natural world it worked to destroy. As the industrial processes globalize, the devastation accelerates, and so does the despair of human beings left even more powerless in their decimated communities. Only those few people who are at the driver's wheel of the global industrial machine will benefit, albeit briefly, though one wonders at their joy in drinking champagne toasts on the decks of the *Titanic*.

But if our acceptance of the entire industrial experiment has been a mistake, whether viewed from the social or the ecological perspective, how do we escape from the mess? It is not complicated.

The first step is to gain consciousness and stop engaging in the process that is killing us and killing the planet. Then we need to recover viable practices to reverse it. The immediate need is to abandon the industrial model as quickly as possible and seek to apply such principles and practices as express a reciprocal relationship with nature, beyond the rules of the machine: a human-nature collaboration rather than a human-machine one.

INDUSTRIAL AGRICULTURE'S WAR AGAINST NATURE

RON KROESE

CHEMICAL POISONS, BIOLOGICAL ATTACKS, AIR RAIDS, PILLAGE, AND
DESTRUCTION — *it's agricultural warfare, and nature is the enemy.
For decades agribusiness in its ads and propaganda has used war
as the central metaphor for successful farming. In recent years the
weapons used by industrial agriculture have grown ever more
sophisticated, from genetic engineering to satellite communications.
Meanwhile the casualties among nature, animals, and people continue to mount. It's time to declare a "cease-fire" and transform
modern food production from war against the land to a marriage of
ecology and agriculture.*

▼

*The possibilities of DDT are sufficient to stir the most sluggish
imagination. . . . In my opinion it is the War's greatest contribution to the future health of the world.*
— Brigadier General James Simmons, *Saturday Evening Post*, Jan. 6, 1945

A stealth bomber appears to hover low over an endless corn field, a
mysterious liquid spraying a fine mist from 24 nozzles on a boom
dragging behind . . . Some top-secret photos from the Department of
Defense or a scene from *The X-Files*? No, just one of the scores of agrochemical ads featuring themes of warfare, machismo, or mayhem that
routinely assault farmers from the pages of farm magazines. The barrage
is especially heavy in the late winter, as farmers are planning next year's
crops and the chemical companies unveil their new formulations and
mixtures, each touted as more powerful yet safer than last year's concoc-
tions. Each arrives with a snappy name and is released with a multimedia
marketing blitz as carefully researched and designed and as lavishly
presented as a new car from GM or a new perfume from Calvin Klein.

While some products over the past decade have been marketed with names and ad copy that suggest environmental safety ("Harmony," "Accord," "Finesse," "Unite," "Asana" — this last, a Sanskrit word for yoga positions), most pesticides continue to be sold with logos and messages that convey power, dominance, and often violence. The overarching message they shout again and again at the farmer is that to succeed as a top producer you must do battle with nature and you are dependent on our pesticides to win that fight. The ad with the stealth bomber pulling the sprayer is selling American Cyanamid's herbicide Lightning. The ad's caption reads, "You only have to strike once" — to the corn grower that translates: one spraying with this herbicide is all you need to kill most weeds for the entire growing season, no need for another pass through the field until harvest.

As anyone familiar with popular farm magazines knows, the use of war as a metaphor for successful farming is nothing new. Themes of warfare with the forces of nature as the enemy, along with broader images of dominance and control, have been endemic to farm advertising for farm chemicals and implements for the past 50 years. Understanding the message of these ads is important for what it reveals about the attitudes held and promoted by the major corporate players who make big profits selling "inputs" and machinery to American farmers. An examination of the farming-as-warfare motif is also worthwhile for the insights it provides into the travails of contemporary agriculture and how our food system got into the disturbing social and environmental situation it finds itself in today. For sad as it is to say, during the past 50 years the warfare mind-set the ads convey has increasingly taken hold on the land — the battle imagery of the advertisements manifesting as all too real battles with nature on our nation's farms. As the decades have advanced, the weapons available to farmers have grown more sophisticated, expensive, and, in some cases, more deadly. Equally disheartening is the realization that most consumers are only vaguely aware that this war is raging, separated as most of us are from the sources of our food, inured to the violence that permeates our culture, and constantly reassured by industry and government that we have the safest food supply on earth.

Meanwhile, the casualties to nature, animals, and people continue to mount. Water supplies in most states, even in urban areas, are polluted with nitrates and pesticides. The rain and air carry minute quantities of pesticides — to the extent that even fruits and vegetables grown organically turn up in tests with residues of toxic pesticides, albeit in lesser amounts than conventionally grown produce. An ever larger area of the Gulf of Mexico near the Mississippi Delta becomes a "dead zone" each spring where there is too little oxygen for fish to live — a result of nitrogen loading, much of it from fertilizer runoff into creeks and streams in the Corn Belt. A 1990 World Health Organization report estimated that each year we are poisoning 25 million people worldwide. A 1998 analysis of government data revealed that each day more than a million American children consume unsafe amounts of organophosphates from pesticide residues on fruit and other foods.

Following the big push from President Richard Nixon's secretary of agriculture, Earl "Get Big or Get Out" Butz, soil erosion levels worse than the Dust Bowl days of the "Dirty Thirties" were occurring in much of the Midwest by the late 1970s — two bushels of soil lost to erosion for every bushel of corn produced. (That situation has improved in many areas thanks to the mid-1980s Conservation Reserve Program, which pays farmland owners to take highly erodible land out of production.) Pork and poultry are increasingly raised in factory-like confinements where the animals suffer lives as nothing less than prisoners, requiring routine doses of antibiotics in their feed in order to survive their imprisonment and grow faster. Spills from the growing number of huge, stinking manure lagoons from hog confinements occur almost routinely, fouling streams and killing fish. Family-sized farms continue to go out of business, unable to compete in an increasingly global economy where farm commodity prices are well below the costs of production.

It is impossible to put a date on when the war on the land began. Indeed, it could be argued that it has existed since the dawn of consciousness itself, when humans first saw themselves as separate from the rest of creation. Or perhaps when *Homo sapiens* made the transition from hunter-gatherer to farmer. Some cite the period of the Renaissance and the dawn of mechanistic science. With regard to American agriculture, it is painfully clear that the European explorers and the settlers who followed came for the most part with attitudes of conquest and dominance to the New Land. The process of converting wild

America into what President John F. Kennedy's secretary of agriculture, Orville Freeman, called the "greatest agricultural production plant on earth" can be viewed as one long war on nature and indigenous people. The innovations in technology, as farming became increasingly mechanized and technologically more sophisticated, only served to intensify the battle.

What marked the 20th century, especially the last half of it, was the greatly expanded translation of the discoveries of science into technologies that could be brought into the battle for production. Not surprisingly, war itself, especially World War II, contributed mightily to agriculture's arsenal. The all-out effort required to achieve victory in that war had a profound and lasting effect on American agriculture. It fueled the forces of industrialization and concentration as technologies that were developed or promulgated for the war effort rapidly were brought to bear on American agriculture. The war also established and legitimized the moral tone that continues to dominate agribusiness and government policy today. Indeed, it is scarcely an exaggeration to state that World War II did not so much end as turn its guns and bombs on the land. The result of this battle for production continues to be viewed in many quarters as a triumph. Yields of major crops have doubled and tripled from prewar levels; efficiency in terms of human labor has increased dramatically; and U.S.-controlled transnational corporations dominate global agricultural commerce. It is increasingly obvious, however, that this has been a Pyrrhic victory. We are only now beginning to fathom the real costs of our war on nature as the detrimental effects on the environment become clear and the casualties in terms of social costs continue to mount.

The war-with-nature paradigm that exemplifies industrial agriculture exists in stark contrast to the worldview that defines sustainable agriculture, with its emphasis on ecological health, humaneness, and, at its best, social justice. This clash of values has contributed to the development of two distinct strains in contemporary farming — conventional, industrially oriented production on one hand and ecological/organic ("sustainable") farming on the other. If it is true, as several respected alternative agriculture thinkers claim and ecological studies seem to bear out, that over the long haul the two approaches cannot coexist, it is crucial that this conflict be resolved. Ultimately all of agriculture must be sustainable.

Coming to terms with how and why the war-on-nature mind-set so thoroughly took hold is an important step in setting food production on a path toward peace with nature. At a minimum, such an examination can teach us some things not to do. Reviewing the factors that led to the adoption of certain destructive technologies and practices in the past may help us choose which new technologies to embrace and which to reject. A look at the impact of World War II is key to that understanding.

Why then did American agriculture embrace, or perhaps more accurately become enveloped by, the military-industrial complex during World War II and the decades that followed? The most obvious answer is because the culture as a whole did. That is, as a result of the events involved in the mobilization and victory of the war and the decision by government and industry that our country remain a global military and industrial power after the war, the United States became a national security state — a country constantly poised for war — and militarism became, and remains, an accepted aspect of our national identity. Agriculture merely played its role in that big picture. It should not be surprising then that today the United States is both the planet's number one arms merchant and the world's leading user and exporter of pesticides. Nor is it surprising that some Pentagon contractors are also pesticide manufacturers.

Some of the reasons for this ongoing battle with nature stem from much further back than World War II. Nevertheless, the war on nature was exponentially amplified by the might of U.S. government and industry during and after the war. It is, of course, unfair to argue that the decisions that led to consequences we now see as detrimental were made with ill intent. Indeed, the period of World War II is distinguished in our history as a time of great sacrifice by Americans from all walks of life. Most of the mistakes, which we see today with increasing clarity and the wisdom of hindsight, were a result of ecological ignorance (a flaw from which we still suffer, one hopes to a lesser extent than 50 years ago) coupled with the rationalization that undergirds all wars, namely that the end — winning the war and feeding the world after the war — *justified the means.*

Understanding that it is impossible to segregate agriculture from the culture as a whole and that a range of societal and historical circumstances created the milieu for agriculture's war with nature, why was the battle against nature fully joined after the war? The reasons are many and intertwined. What follows is a brief summary of a few of the major causes.

THE FARMER AS SOLDIER

Demand for food and fiber created by the war pulled the agricultural economy out of a period of depression or stagnancy that had lasted since the boom years of the early 1920s. Farm production increased by one-third during the war years, despite the fact that 5 million people left their farms for military service or to work in cities. Demand for American agricultural goods remained high after the war as the Marshall Plan committed the United States to playing the leading role in feeding and rebuilding war-ravaged Europe. All-out production was promoted by the government as the farmers' contribution to the war effort and to the rebuilding effort after the war.

During the war, the leading farm magazines, such as *Farm Journal*, were filled with ads telling farmers they were "Soldiers of the Soil," that "Food Fights for Freedom" and "wars are fought with food." These ads were paid for by major corporations that during the height of the conflict had few actual goods to sell farmers since most of their production was going to war material. Urged by the federal government, they agreed to join in the campaign to cheer on the war effort. Such boosterism was all the more important in rural communities because of the social unease caused by the exemption of farm boys from conscription. (In 1942, concerned about the growing labor shortage in agriculture, Congress passed a law allowing county selective service boards to exempt farm laborers from military service. In most cases, this meant the oldest son on the farm did not have to go to war.) Those exempted from the draft and their families needed to be assured that the "battle for food production" was every bit as necessary and patriotic as fighting on the front lines.

By 1945, as the eventual outcome of the war was becoming clear, administration plans to encourage reduced production in order to maintain high commodity prices after the war were scuttled as it became obvious that food from the United States — the only major power to survive the conflict with its farm production capacity fully intact — was going to be needed more than ever. By 1946, the message to farmers in farm magazines was: don't let up, "the war isn't over for the farmer," the battle for full production must continue, and thanks to the war, we have some new weapons for you.

CHEMICAL WARFARE

By 1944, articles were appearing in the popular farm press touting the revolutionary inventions developed for the war effort that would soon be coming home to the farm. The most promising (and ultimately the most notorious) of these products was DDT. Although chemists had known about the chemical's insecticidal qualities for decades, it was first widely utilized in the war, to delouse soldiers and to kill malaria-bearing mosquitoes — saving, it should be noted, hundreds of thousands of soldiers from illness and death. Besides being lethal to insects, DDT had the further characteristic of not breaking down when exposed to the weather, thus remaining effective for a long time, and it did not appear to harm people.

By the war's end, DDT and other chlorinated hydrocarbon insecticides were widely available to farmers. These inexpensive new chemicals were widely hailed in farm magazines and the popular press as "miraculous" — the safest and most effective weapons yet developed in the war against insects. An article in the November 1946 *Reader's Digest*, for example, lauded the availability of a new chlorinated soil fumigant with the headline, "Chemical Warfare Invades the Farm." Its subhead proclaimed that "An all-out gas attack on the threadlike worms that ruin crops may greatly increase our food supplies."

Articles and editorials in the farm magazines declared that at last, thanks to modern chemistry, we had the capacity to "totally eradicate" insect pests. Those making that claim, of course, greatly underestimated insects' capacities to adapt. Nor did they foresee the devastating effect the chemical would have on higher life forms. By the end of the decade houseflies were already showing resistance to DDT, and dairy farmers were warned to stop using it in milking parlors because DDT was showing up in milk. By the mid-1950s disturbing declines in raptor populations began to be reported.

Other pesticides that became widely available after the war included organophosphate insecticides, such as the nervous system toxins parathion and malathion, which, along with the nerve gas later used in concentration camps, was developed by German insecticide researchers in the 1930s. Although they have been known for decades to be highly toxic to fish, birds, and humans, organophosphates continue to be the most widely used class of insecticides in U.S. food production. The popular herbicide 2,4-D was developed by the British during the war. Twenty years later, 2,4-D, which is still widely used in agriculture, and on lawns as the chief foe of dandelions, became a weapon of war when it was combined with 2,4,5-T to form the notorious Agent Orange. Millions of pounds of this herbicide combination were used to defoliate forests in Vietnam, exposing our own soldiers and Vietnamese civilians to dangerous levels of toxic chemicals.

Besides the chemicals themselves, more effective technologies for the application of pesticides came out of World War II, most notably mechanical foggers and aerial sprayers. For smaller applications, aerosol cans became available and were promoted as "bug bombs." The foggers could be mounted on jeeps, which also were developed for the war and were marketed as multi-purpose farm vehicles afterwards. While spray planes had been used before the war, primarily for applying arsenic-based insecticides on cotton (Delta Airlines, for example, began as a crop-spraying company), the use of spray planes increased dramatically after the war. This was the combined result of the availability of the new and effective pesticides, thousands of cheap surplus fighter planes, and an abundance of war-trained pilots who liked to fly. Following the war, ads soon appeared in farm magazines urging farmers to "strafe" their fields to win the battle against bugs.

Farms, of course, were not the only targets for these technologies. In 1945, before the discovery of the vaccine for polio, health officials in Rockford, Illinois, enlisted two World War II bombers to spray the city with DDT to kill flies, which they believed carried poliomyelitis. After the war, ads and articles appeared in magazines, such as *Better Homes and Gardens*, celebrating the wonders of the new pesticides and the uses to which they could be put in a modern home in the never-ending battle against bugs and varmints. An article in the June 1948 issue of that magazine included a photo showing a jeep with a fogger parked in front of a house as a thick cloud of DDT billowed out of the doors and windows. The headline proudly proclaimed: "This could happen to your home." The easy availability of the new herbicides and abundant synthetic fertilizer coincided neatly with the birth of the big suburban lawns, as suburbs sprang up around cities, thanks in large measure to GI loans for mortgages.

This push toward industrialization and consumerism, coupled with the growing demand for food to help feed Europe and Asia, contributed to an eightfold growth in the use of natural gas–derived fertilizers in the two decades following the war. The big switch from mined fertilizers and farm-produced manures during and after the war went hand-in-hand with the government's goal of achieving self-sufficiency in fertilizer production as part of an overall effort to achieve national self-sufficiency in vital industrial materials. During the war, supplies of mined nitrate fertilizer and guano from South America, as well as the imported plant-based insecticides rotenone and pyrethrums, had been cut off. Following the war, commercial markets were needed for the excess ammonium nitrate being produced in government-built gunpowder plants around the country. Soon these ordnance factories were sold to private chemical firms and readily switched to the production of inexpensive nitrate fertilizers — although the sales agreements required that the plants had to maintain the capacity to switch back to gunpowder production within a few weeks if ordered to do so by the government.

NUCLEAR AGRICULTURE

While the impact of the development and use of the atomic bomb had a less obvious effect on agriculture than did war-developed technologies that could be directly employed on the farm, its effects were nonetheless real. The dropping of the atomic bombs on Japan was met in the farm press with a mixture of gratitude (that no troop invasion would be needed to force Japan to surrender), awe (at the sheer power of this utterly new source of unleashed power) and fear (that an enemy would have this weapon to use on us sooner or later). In November 1950, after the Russians too had exploded an A-bomb, an article appeared in *Farm Journal* titled, "If an A-Bomb Fell near Your Farm." Clearly aimed at assuaging reader fears that the world was now in danger of a nuclear holocaust, the author, who was introduced as an atomic researcher and lecturer on atomic warfare for the army and navy, wrote that "Even close to ground zero, it is sometimes possible to escape all injury. . . . If worst comes to worst, and we should ever have to fear a bomb burst, it would be wise to wear long trousers and full-sleeved shirts when out-of-doors. The brim of your hat could save your face from heat waves."

Despite the fear it caused, the Bomb contributed to the tremendous faith many Americans came to place in dazzling technologies to solve all human problems. At last, the public was told, Americans had the very power of the sun under our control. Within weeks after release of information about the bombing of Hiroshima and Nagasaki, stories began appearing in the farm press about the great promise nuclear fission held for U.S. agriculture — electricity too cheap to meter from nuclear plants would speed up the process of rural electrification; farmers would be able to light up their fields like baseball diamonds so they could work in the cool of night; tractors would run for a century on a capsule of atomic fuel the size of an aspirin; new super-yielding mutant plants would be created by radiation. As an Iowa State University researcher wrote in a June 1947 article in *Farm Journal*, "thanks to the split atom of World War II, we stand at the threshold of a whole new world of farm research."

In 1946, an article appeared in *Science Digest* that proposed blasting the north polar ice cap to bits with strategically placed atomic bombs in order to warm up the climate enough to expand the grain-growing region of North America into the Yukon. During the 1950s, under the Atomic Energy Commission's "Atoms for Peace" initiative called "Project Plowshares," conferences were held to discuss the prospects of using atom bombs like giant bulldozers to excavate canals and reservoirs for irrigation. Field research continued in various parts of the country through the 1980s on the use of nitrogen-rich, low-level nuclear waste as a fertilizer. Today, of course, food irradiation, using nuclear waste as the radiation source, is on the verge of being widely used as a solution to the bacterial contamination of meat from mechanized packing plants.

POSTWAR MODERNISM

After the war, the notion of "farming as a way of life" was derided as old-fashioned and out of touch with reality. Ads and articles in the farm press told farmers that they had to think and act like business-men who should view their farms as factories. A vivid memory from this writer's youth in rural Iowa is seeing the signs posted by Farm Bureau chapters along highways throughout the rural countryside. The signs boasted that "Today one farmer feeds 50 people." Every year or so the number was painted over with a higher figure: "Today one farmer feeds 57 people," and so on. These signs belied a darker message. They could just as well have stated, "This year another 50 farms went out of business in our county," as millions of family farms were eliminated in the decades after the war.

The farms went out of business because it became more and more difficult for the traditional family farm to make ends meet as farm prices steadily fell further and further below the costs of production. Low commodity prices, on the other hand, served farm-related indus-tries well. Low market prices meant cheap raw materials for the food processing industry as the American diet came to rely increasingly on packaged and processed food. It meant bargain-basement food prices for foreign markets, which translated into big profits for the grain traders and shippers. For our government, surplus farm production became a convenient foreign policy tool and a means for improving growing trade imbalances.

On the farm, however, it meant that farmers were increasingly squeezed between ever-rising costs for machinery and supplies and declining market prices. As a result they felt pressed to expand and to try to get more production out of their acres and their animals by whatever means available. But this tended to increase surpluses and drive prices down farther, exacerbating the situation. This vicious cycle remains in effect today. It is a nasty treadmill that also puts many farmers in an ethical bind, that is, having to farm bigger and use methods they know not to be healthy for the land, their commu-nities, or themselves. This is perhaps the greatest tragedy to emerge from agriculture's battle for production — that many farmers are farming at odds with their own values of stewardship and community in order to make ends meet.

MAKING PEACE WITH NATURE

"The chemical war cannot be won, and all life is caught in its violent crossfire." — Rachel Carson, *Silent Spring*

The increasingly painful irony in all of this, as Rachel Carson and others since have pointed out, is that the war with nature cannot be won, at least not without destroying ourselves in the process. The adaptive capacity of nature is scarcely understood, nor do we have the capacity to begin to foresee all of the unanticipated reactions and consequences that are triggered when we significantly alter natural systems. As Patricia Hynes pointed out in her book *Recurring Silent Spring*, published in 1989, when *Silent Spring* was published in 1962 there were 137 insect species known to be resistant to pesticides; by the late 1980s there were more than 500. In 1945 an estimated 7 percent of crops worldwide were destroyed by insects; 40 years later that figure had nearly doubled.

With what we have learned in the last 50 years about the interdependence of life and the damage we can do even when we are trying to do good, are we anywhere near ready to call for a cease-fire? With regard to mainstream agribusiness, there appears to be little hope that a truce will be coming any time soon. For years the pesticide industry's response to pesticide resistance has been to come up with a new spray. Today the agrochemical companies' answer to growing problems with pesticides is genetic engineering. While biotechnology's proponents promise it will reduce the amount of pesticides unleashed on the environment, it is still based on the notion that nature has to be controlled and fundamentally altered in order for farming to be successful. It seeks to profoundly skirt the forces of evolution that have shaped our ecosystem. In effect, it just moves the battle against nature from under the sun to under the microscope.

The recent resistance to the war against nature from consumers offers some signs for optimism. For example, fear of a reaction from American consumers has kept some big milk suppliers from buying milk from producers who treat their cows with bovine growth hormone. Internationally, the European Union, under pressure from its own consumers and farmers, has thus far stood tough against the importation of herbicide-tolerant soybeans and cattle that have been fed growth hormones. In 1998, some 275,000 Americans complained when the U.S. Department of Agriculture (USDA) proposed organic standards which allowed food that had been genetically engineered, fertilized with sewage sludge, and blasted with radiation to be labeled organic — and the USDA backed down. Sales of organically grown food have increased 20 percent per year throughout the 1990s. Farmers' markets are thriving in cities all over the country. Increasingly stories are appearing in the media of conventional farmers moving to organic production practices, lured by the promise of higher prices.

But it will take more than higher prices for organic production to stop the war on the land and achieve what the sustainable agriculture researcher and author Wes Jackson calls the "marriage of ecology and agriculture." Indeed, the most likely immediate effect of many farmers going organic would be to drive down the prices paid to producers. What is required for real change is a profound shift in all of us, farmers and nonfarmers alike, in how we see ourselves in relation to the natural world.

For the farmer deeply committed to sustainable methods, this means as much as possible working with the impulses and rhythms of nature. It means recycling plant residues and animal wastes to slowly build up the soil so plants are healthier and can better contend with insects and disease. It means using farming methods that stop soil erosion and prevent the runoff of nutrients into creeks and rivers. It means understanding that farm animals are relatives of wild creatures and have the need, some would say the right, to express the characteristics of their species and not be constantly penned up or caged. It means taking a different attitude toward weeds, not loving them or letting them take over the farm, but seeing them as indicators that can reveal what is needed to improve soil conditions. It means looking to biological methods of pest management rather than chemical methods of control. It means switching to the management goal of optimizing production within the constraints of good stewardship rather than maximizing production at all costs.

It also means that organic farming methods are generally going to be more labor intensive, because practices such as mechanical weed control rather than one-shot herbicides and letting animals graze and range naturally rather than locking them in confinements and feeding them growth hormones take more time and management skill. This means that organically grown products are usually going to cost more to produce. And this is where consumers interested in disarming farming can do their part — by "eating with conscience," as the Humane Society of the United States' Michael Fox puts it. If those of us who don't farm want clean water and safe, guilt-free food, we have to learn where our food comes from, stop buying industrially produced food, and be ready to pay more for sustainably produced food. To put it simply: think organically, buy locally, whenever you can.

We consumers also have to be consistent and stop making war with the environment in our own homes and gardens. About a fourth of the more than 2 billion pounds of pesticides that bombard the environment in the United States each year are used off the farm. In our lawns and gardens we need to get off the "weed and feed" battlewagon and accept a little diversity in our backyards. In our homes we need to switch to green cleaning products. There are now an estimated 12,200 farmers in the United States who have put their values on the economic line by going organic. They cannot put farming on the path of peace with nature by themselves. All of us who eat have to become conscientious objectors to the war against nature.

THE IMPOSSIBLE RACE

Population Growth and the Fallacies of Agricultural Hope

HUGH H. ILTIS

THE POPULATION BOMB CONTINUES TO EXPLODE. *Each year, 85 million people are added to the earth's population. That growth means more cars, roads, and dams, more pollution, starvation, and war, and less and less wild nature. It need not be so. As we support the necessary political struggles against oppressive social and economic systems, so we need to fight just as hard for politics that correct the grave and exponentially increasing imbalance between populations and the natural environment.*

▼

Much is being written these days about deforestation and the extermination of biological diversity all over the globe, and, related to these, the genetic erosion of agricultural germ plasm, both of wild crop ancestors and of primitive land races. These alarming problems affect everyone and should be of immediate concern to all the world's people.

TROPICAL DESTRUCTION:
ECOLOGICAL GENOCIDE ON A GRAND SCALE

It is in the wet tropics, particularly in the diverse but vulnerable rain forests and seasonally dry monsoon forests, that this biological genocide is now in full swing. Of the estimated 30 million species of plants and animals on earth, over half live in the tropics, on only 6 percent of the earth's surface. Here, even on a highly localized scale, biodiversity can be overwhelming. Thus, fully 41,000 species of insects, mostly beetles, have been identified in one hectare (2.47 acres) of Panamanian tropical forest! The destruction of tropical habitats, therefore, will inevitably cause the extermination of millions of plant and animal species, for most of which we do not have a name or a description, a life history, or an estimate of their ecological or economic importance. As many as 20 percent of all species on earth may become extinct within 20 years, at least one million species, but very likely many more. The utter devastation that human action wreaks in tropical ecosystems has to be seen to be believed.

In 1962 I stood on a primitive bridge suspended over a clear mountain stream and watched as troops of chattering spider monkeys, on branches a hundred feet off the ground, gracefully jumped from one tree to the next, eating the yellow-orange fruits from a gigantic plank-rooted fig tree. Here, near San Ramon in the eastern foothills of the Peruvian Andes, in a valley overwhelming in its greenness and serenity, giant, brilliantly blue *Morpho* butterflies sailed erratically through a sun-flecked clearing to disappear again into the rain forest canopy. Iridescent hummingbirds hovered over the yellow flower clusters of a trumpet vine liana, while a pair of banana-billed toucans sat motionless on a branch, silently watching. To our small group of biologists, this was a scene straight out of a tropical Eden.

Not one of these living glories has survived. That year, an intelligent but ecologically unaware young man from Lima bought the valley with a development grant provided by the U.S.-sponsored "Alianza para el Progreso" and, even on slopes exceeding 45 degrees, cut down the forest and planted coffee and bananas. Such forest conversion, common throughout the Andes, has resulted not only in the extirpation of species but in massive soil erosion, siltation of rivers, and, locally, climatic change. Lately, the cultivation of coca has had the same effect. The unprecedented fluctuations in Amazonian water levels in recent decades are believed to be the unintended consequence of such land clearing, as is the siltation of the Panama Canal.

With such extensive forest destruction, countless species will disappear. For example, half of the world's primates — the lemurs, monkeys, and apes, our closest evolutionary relatives — are facing extinction. These are all highly endemic, often rare animals, each with its own geography and ecology, that conservation biologists are only now beginning to understand. What must be done to preserve them? The first step, of course, is to *preserve their forest habitat*. But even here, human need for protein — red meat — has hunted out the larger mammals (including primates), birds, and reptiles from vast areas of Amazonia and Central Africa, so that many a forest, though superficially pristine, is in actuality an "empty forest."

The richly diverse forests themselves deserve protection. The lowland forests of the Pacific slope of Ecuador, for example, are the home of many unique plant species. Sharply separated for millions of years from their relatives in the Amazon basin by the snowy Andes, they evolved here in geographic isolation. Near Santo Domingo de los Colorados lies a small remnant of a moist tropical forest, intensively studied by Calloway Dodson and my former student, the late Alwyn Gentry. As described in their *Flora of the Rio Palenque*, this tract of only 167 hectares (420 acres) contains over 1,100 species of plants, almost half of which are trees, shrubs, or lianas. They found nearly 6 percent of the species to be new to science (including several of the giant canopy trees). Fully 4 percent were local endemics, that is, known only from here and nowhere else. The small "sierra" at Centinelas, only six kilometers away, had a strikingly different, but equally endemic, flora, with close to 100 species new to science discovered there. The Rio Palenque preserve is now the only surviving example of "moist tropical forest" in this region, a tiny island of unique natural complexity surrounded by a vast ocean of sterile cultivated uniformity: thousands of square kilometers of pesticide-sprayed sugarcane, African oil palm, banana (mostly for export to the United States and Europe), and cattle pastures for the "Hamburger Society." Even though the Rio Palenque forest is protected, all of its larger forest animals, such as monkeys and tapirs, have long since become extinct, for it is much too small an area to sustain them.

Incredibly, Ecuador — a country no bigger than Minnesota — is estimated to have more than 19,000 different species of plants, over half of them endemic. Compare this to only 17,000 species in all of North America, and only 1,700 native species in all of Minnesota, which boasts only one endemic, an insignificant, semisterile dog-tooth violet lily. In fact, some one-hectare plots of Peruvian rain forest sampled by Gentry contained 300 species of trees! To any temperate-zone botanist, such localized diversity is astounding. But all over the tropics local floras and faunas are saturated with unique taxa: local endemism is the rule, widespread species the exception.

Many tropical plants have turned out to be useful in industry, medicine, agriculture, or horticulture, furnishing drugs, waxes, oils, gums, spices, and fruits. Others, especially some gigantic fruit-producing trees, have been shown to be ecological "keystone species," indispensable to the survival of whole suites of animals, including parrots, Amazonian fish, and monkeys. For these reasons (among others) we need to legally protect extensive areas of tropical forest from agriculture, ranching, plantation forestry, and even from "rubber tapping"; even selective logging of key species will pull the rug out from under many organisms, tightly evolved and totally dependent on them as they are.

About half of the world's tropical forests have already been destroyed. The World Resources Institute estimates that an additional 7.3 million hectares (18 million acres) of closed moist forest are now being destroyed annually, and another 4.4 million hectares selectively logged. Even at these deliberately conservative estimates, most tropical forests may be destroyed within the next 20 years.

The urgency of restraining tropical deforestation is well illustrated in western Ecuador. Only 60 years ago, it was covered with the most inaccessible of tropical forests, uninterrupted for 100 kilometers from Quevedo to Esmeraldas, an area from where almost no biological specimens were then available for scientific study. But today, except for the Rio Palenque Science Center preserve, and an acre here and an *arroyo* there, this entire forest has been recklessly destroyed. Today, only an occasional plank-rooted forest giant, uncut because of its immense circumference, towers alone over a field of bananas, a silent witness to the tropical forest diversity that once was and a pathetic reminder that, from now on, no one in the world shall ever again study these ancient forests or document their unique botanical or zoological treasures. *Extinction is indeed forever!*

THE SIERRA DE MANANTLÁN:
A MEXICAN BIOSPHERE RESERVE PROTECTED

More hopeful are the prospects for the cloud forests of the Sierra de Manantlán, a mountain range of Mexico's Sierra Madre del Sur southeast of Puerto Vallarta. Its preservation started in 1977 with the chance discovery by a young Mexican undergraduate student of a species of wild grass, later named *Zea diploperennis*, a perennial relative of teosinte, the ancestor of maize. This rare weed, which grows nowhere else in the world, may have enormous economic potential: it is immune to just about every known maize virus and readily hybridizes with maize, the world's second most important cereal crop, with a global harvest in 1999 of over 600 million metric tons from 139 million hectares, and worth around $47 billion.

Until 16 years ago, logging steadily decimated the forests of this biological treasure-house. Trucks roared down the mountains every half-hour, hauling gigantic logs of oak, magnolia, and pine, to be made into lumber for building houses, into veneer for furniture, and into broomsticks for export to the United States to gain badly needed foreign exchange to pay off Mexico's staggering $100-billion debt. But because of the discovery of this remarkable grass, and through the efforts of many Mexican educators, scientists, and government officials (and with international moral support), lumbering was stopped in 1984. A year later, 1,200 hectares of the habitat of the diploperennial teosinte, the cloud forests were bought by state funds for the Botany Institute of the Universidad de Guadalajara as a research station. Eventually, with the help of Mexico's National Science Foundation (CONACYT), and under the United Nation's UNESCO Man in the Biosphere (MAB) program, a 140,000-hectare (350,000 acres) Reserva Biosfera de la Sierra de Manantlán was dedicated in 1988 by Mexico's President Miguel de la Madrid. Administered by the Universidad de Guadalajara, the whole mountain chain, with all its diverse ecosystems (home to rare mountain lions, ocelots, crested guans, hummingbirds, as well as to the teosinte and other endemic plants), has now been protected. Most significant has been the creation of the Instituto Manantlán de Ecologia y Biodiversidad (IMECBIO) with a staff of 60, which, attached to the nearby Universidad de Guadalajara's Centro Universitario Costa Sur in Autlán, is devoted to the scientific study and management of its ecology and biota. It is sobering to contemplate what would have happened had agricultural development reached the habitats of *Zea diploperennis*: a few cows in a month's time could have obliterated this species and with it the possibility of mankind's ever utilizing its genetic potential.

THE BIOCLIMATIC PARADOX

Almost without exception, economists, sociologists, scientific advisors, and humanitarians of the developed world have been misled by the overpowering luxuriance of tropical vegetation. How many times have these well-meaning "experts" announced that the problems of world hunger and excessive human population can be solved by increased agricultural production, especially in the tropics? But their deadly ignorance of ecology and geography, their unfailing optimism that the answer to the world's ills lies in growing more food and increased development — leading to a desperately hoped for but illusory "demographic transition" — have been fatal for human life and natural ecosystems, as recent famines in Africa and Asia, floods in Bangladesh, and the horrendous torching of Amazonia since 1988 have so clearly demonstrated.

Botanical reasons for tropical famines are not hard to find. As the geographer J. Chang of the University of Hawaii explained, slender, temperate annual grasses such as wheat, rye, barley, or rice have relatively low agricultural productivity in tropical latitudes compared with their high productivity in cooler temperate climates where they originally evolved. This lower productivity reflects a bioclimatic fact: during the long, warm tropical nights, respiration burns up most of the surplus carbohydrates produced by photosynthesis during the relatively short day. On the other hand, in my own state of Wisconsin (or in the wheat belts of Kansas or Ukraine), the hot 16-hour summer days followed by cool 8-hour nights allow a much greater accumulation of storage photosynthate. Furthermore, in most parts of the lowland tropics, no matter how lush the vegetation, high rainfall interacting with high temperatures tends to leach the already nutrient-poor soils to sterile sands or stone pavements, often useless for agriculture after only three or four years of cultivation. Finally, in the tropics, there are no bitter cold winter temperatures to knock back insect pests.

Humanistic dreams of making breadbaskets out of tropical regions thus quickly evaporate into the fantasies they really are, notwithstanding optimistic editorials in prominent newspapers and lead articles by academic experts (often beholden to industrial financial support) in scientific journals. As the German playwright Bertolt Brecht wryly observed, "He who laughs has not yet heard the bad news." And Canada's Marshall McLuhan was not far behind when he quipped that "An expert is a man who doesn't make the slightest error on the road to the grand delusion," the grand delusion being the unlimited agricultural potential of the tropics.

Tropical forest ecosystems present a climatically determined paradox. Biologically they are super-diverse and valuable beyond belief, but agriculturally usually quite poor. That the biologically depauperate states of Kansas, Iowa, or Manitoba can never become Mexicos, Panamas, or Amazonian Brazils in terms of biodiversity is obvious. At the same time, these tropical countries can never become Kansases, Iowas, or Manitobas in agricultural productivity. But fallacies of hope die hard for nationalistic dreamers of economic glory, biotechnology investors greedy for profit, religious leaders stubbornly determined to ignore demographic realities, and humanitarian do-gooders hungry to rearrange the world. Nevertheless, we must accept these fundamental ecological realities, or the consequences, ecological and political, will be unpleasant indeed.

THE PROBLEM OF NATIONAL PARKS AND BIOSPHERE RESERVES

In the tropics, biopreservationists are thus faced with this low agricultural productivity versus high biodiversity paradox: the less-developed tropical countries blessed with earth's richest biotas, hence with the often unwanted responsibility to maintain in national parks or biosphere reserves their unique biological and ethnological wealth (not just for themselves, but for the whole world), are at the same time often much too poor to afford them. Statistics on park personnel show how critical a problem this is. Compared to the tropical nations, the overdeveloped industrialized countries spend ten times the money, and support ten times the staff, per unit area of park. And parks without biologists, armed guards, and legal protections do not long survive.

Thus, the very countries with the most biodiversity to preserve are able in their poverty to preserve very little and to scientifically study even less. It is a colossal problem in search of a solution. Yet some tropical countries have managed to make nature preservation an important part of their national economy. Tanzania's Serengeti Park, at least, is still well protected, or so we can only hope. Costa Rica and its former directors of national parks, Alvaro Ugalde and M. A. Boza, deserve special praise in this connection. Smaller than West Virginia, but with seven times the number of plant species (over 12,000!), Costa Rica has a national system of 35 well-administered parks, reserves, and *refugios* unrivaled by any other country in the Americas. Fully 13 percent of its total area is under national park protection, and its per capita financial commitment to parks is higher than that of the United States. In fact, including national forests, 20 percent of Costa Rica's lands are under some sort of nature protection. Most promising are the efforts, inspired by an American ecologist, Daniel Janzen, to establish the Guanacaste Area de Conservacíon, which combines fragments of tropical rainforest and seasonally dry tropical forest with adjoining worn-out grazing lands to restore them all to their original forested state.

Other significant reserves have been established in Amazonian Bolivia, Brazil, Colombia, Ecuador, Peru, and Venezuela. During the past few decades, over 12 million hectares of forest have been placed under protection, and, hopefully, many more will be protected soon by the recently conceived instrument of swapping international debt for protection of nature. It is a grim reality, nevertheless, that many of these Amazonian preserves are nothing but "paper parks" now being invaded by squatters, lumbermen, and cattle ranchers.

By the dictates of our own biological evolution, it is our moral duty to be good ancestors to our children by protecting their future environment. We in the overdeveloped nations must learn, as an integral part of any "good neighbor" foreign policy, to approach the problem of tropical biotic extinctions seriously and responsibly. Ecologically enlightened U.S. foreign aid would give priority to the purchase of wild lands, and subsidize the staffing and upkeep of local nature preserves and the building of local museums of natural history throughout the tropics. Such aid would help train local biological (and not just agricultural) expertise by providing fellowships for their teachers of biology to our universities, or ours to theirs, and, by translating scientific monographs, would make the world's biological literature available in the *local* language so that, finally, local scientists themselves could become experts, and defenders, of their own biota. This calls for major international cooperation, which among biologists is already well established, for the enormous complexity of tropical ecology and systematics cannot be mastered by the scientists of any one country alone. Only through the deep appreciation of their own biological patrimony can the less-developed nations protect their biota from opportunistic technocrats bent on development, be they American, European, or Asiatic — or their own.

THE POPULATION BOMB: STILL TICKING, ONLY FASTER!

As of October 2000, the world population registered 6,100 million (6.1 billion) individuals of *Homo sapiens*, double what it was in 1962 when I watched *Morpho* butterflies in that Edenic Peruvian valley, more than triple that of 1925, the year that I was born! In just the last 12 years some 1,000 million people have been added to the Earth's population: 85 million extra to feed each year, 1 million every 100 hours, 250,000 every 24 hours, and 12,000 or so each and every 60 minutes. This cannot, must not, continue. The United States is not exempt from this population explosion. Since the coming of age of the modern environmental movement on Earth Day 1970, we have grown from 200 to 283 million Americans (illegal immigrants not included), a massive increase of 83 million that is doubly catastrophic for the environment if you consider our arrogant affluence, irresponsible resource use, and wanton waste, second to none in this all-too-finite earth. And the predictions that the United States will reach 500 million by 2100 and 1,000 million shortly thereafter, achieving by then crowding and poverty levels of today's Bangladesh or China, is not something any sane person would wish for. That by then the world population would hopefully begin to "level off" at 9, 10, or 11 billion human beings is by no means certain either. If we remember now that these many millions will still need land to grow food on, clean air and water, wood and fiber, housing and energy, *the future of nature is grim indeed.*

Growth of any sort, demographic or economic, means more roads and dams, more cars and concrete, more corn and cows, more erosion and floods, more garbage pits and pollution, more acid rain and green-house effects, more dead elephants and dolphins, more hunger and starvation, more riots and refugees, more poverty, prisons, and torture, more war, mayhem, and disaster — and *less and less wild nature.* It need not be so! We need to stop and reverse human population growth now.

Admitting that the overdeveloped countries must adopt more rea-sonable expectations for their standard of living, that tropical exploitation by their multinational banks and corporations must stop, that their massive commercial development schemes promoted in the third world are among the primary causes of deforestation, and that freedom, justice, and equality are indispensable to a well-ordered world — nevertheless, let all of us (liberals, humanists, socialists, communists, or conservatives) never forget that poverty, lack of edu-cation, and above all overpopulation *in and by itself* are equally responsible for biological extinction: the chop-chop of a billion axes and machetes, the cravings of a billion hungry mouths all wanting to be fed. In fact, it is a poor excuse to blame the "population bomb" solely on capitalism or imperialism or to absolve population growth of its increasingly crucial role in the world's ecological collapse. We must mention here the now increasingly deliberate (but rarely openly expressed) encouragement of large families by leaders of specific reli-gious, ethnic, or racial groups to gain political advantage, to outbreed and so overwhelm their adversaries. In extreme cases this has led, lit-erally, to "Geburten Kriege," wars of birth, so dubbed by the Nazis, even now actively encouraged by one or both parties in Ireland, Israel-Palestine, Kosovo-Serbia, Central Africa, and even in the United States, a policy with terrifying implications for both people and the environment. There is no light at the end of that dark tunnel! As necessary as political struggles against the injustices of oppressive social and economic systems are, they must always go hand in hand with actions to correct the grave and ever-increasing imbalance between human populations and the environment. Encouraging pop-ulation growth, for whatever reason, is the worst way to go.

Thus, although the poverty-stricken people of the world have to have food and firewood, they need birth control even more. By now, any knowledgeable observer of the world's scene must come to the conclusion that, as the first Green Revolution so clearly yet dismally demonstrated, and the siren song of the new biotechnology and the second Green Revolution notwithstanding, *the food versus population race will never be won by growing more food*, but only by decreasing the world's population, preferably through education and persuasion, especially of women, and always with the ready availability of every form of contraception. Let us be clear: to effectively facilitate a modification of our ancient, instinctive breeding behavior, to bring it into line with ecological realities, some forms of birth control must be made available to all men and women. And, here also, the rich developed nations, and modern science, have a vital responsibility. Lastly, let us no more than mention that most contentious issue, abortion, which would largely disappear if contraception were widely available. With its worldwide incidence of over 50 million per year, one can see that this question has enormous demographic implications.

Preventing famine and disease are noble goals. Ending injustice and poverty are noble goals. But none of these will induce an elusive "demographic transition" to lowered birthrates in time to prevent widespread biological collapse, a collapse that would not only intensify human miseries but would further intensify the destruction of nature. We simply cannot allow the natural environment (which, after all, is the only environment humanity is adapted to) to deteriorate any further. In addition, none of these noble goals will be accomplished by furthering the immaculate misconception that raising more food by cutting down more tropical forests, draining more tropical wetlands, or breeding more bountiful crops will solve the demographic dilemma. We are running out of wild nature, space, and water, as we are running out of nonrenewable resources. Meanwhile, the population bomb keeps on ticking, faster and faster. It needs to be defused, now!

The answer to the demographic dilemma is clear enough: we must abandon the fallacies of agricultural hope, for it is not a question of raising more food, but of raising fewer people. If population growth is not curtailed voluntarily, the dictatorial powers of the state (as by sheer necessity in China) or the brutal catastrophes of nature (as in Africa's Sahel and Sudan) will surely do it for us.

Only an ecologically responsible human society, living within limits and sternly self-restrained in both resource use and human reproduction, can give this spaceship world of ours any realistic hope of bequeathing to our children a beautiful, livable, and nature-rich earth.

Part Three

INDUSTRIAL AGRICULTURE'S TOXIC TRAIL

Technological Takeover

▼   ▼   ▼

Agricultural modernization has come at a tremendous environmental and social cost. The first wave of modernization — including the widespread use of pesticides and synthetic fertilizers — has resulted in the pollution of our water, air, and food. Wildlife, fisheries, biodiversity, topsoil, and many other natural resources have been decimated. The second wave of modernization in food production — led by biotechnology — threatens to create even more environmental and human health havoc.

ARTIFICIAL FERTILITY

The Environmental Costs of Industrial Fertilizers

JASON MCKENNEY

IN THE UNITED STATES, THE CONVERSION OF AGRICULTURE *from locally based, natural sources of fertility to sources rooted in fossil fuel consumption has dramatically increased the productive output of our farms, but at the cost of soil health, water and air quality, and the future fertility of our land. Our shortsighted dependence on excessive fertilizer use is a direct consequence of our "industrial" assumptions that we can manage farms as we manage factories, with inputs producing direct outputs. These assumptions have failed and have left us a devastating environmental debt.*

▼

The economic effectiveness of the industrial perspective applied to agricultural ecosystems is rapidly revealing itself to be a myth. The use of fossil fuel–based fertilizers is a graphic example of the failure of the industrial agriculture model. Today, fertilizers, which once primed the soil system's production, are less and less effective in the face of soil loss and degradation, which is largely caused by the fertilizers themselves. Alternatives to this downward spiral do exist — they involve methods that are based in a respect for the biological nature of agriculture. Integrated fertility management and organic methods use little or no fertilizer because they promote healthy soil structure and microbiology to assure long-term fertility on our farms.

THE NATURAL BASIS OF FERTILITY

The natural cycling of nutrients through soils over time is ignored in our industrial model of agriculture. Fertility in functional ecosystems comes from an open exchange and a complex relationship between plants and microbes that is outside of the industrial mind-set. For example, it is convenient for science to understand biology as a well-defined hierarchy in what are called trophic levels. The sun provides energy. Plants absorb and convert it to chemical energy. Animals and fungi live off this energy. Decomposers break down these organisms to their basic components. This general mechanistic model is understood as a basic biological cycle because it involves nutrient movement. The problem with it is its dramatic oversimplification. Plants evolve in radically different soil systems together with microorganisms (not to mention animals, fungi, and other plants) over geologic time scales. The staggering diversity of plants and their interrelationships with these microbes has only recently begun to be explored. What is now commonly recognized is that plant growth and metabolism occur via a complex interrelationship between soil organisms which feed off of plants, help plants grow, feed off of each other, exchange nutrients, nurture one another, eat each other, parasitize each other, form colonies with each other, and on and on. The relationships in soils are exceedingly dynamic and inclusive. In other words, a plant cannot be abstracted from its environment and reduced to a simple machine without adverse effect.

Healthy soil is almost entirely composed of living things and is an inherently biological medium. The historical basis of fertility is contained in the lives of all the organisms that have lived and died in soils over time. This concept was known, if not completely understood, by medieval farmers who left fields fallow for periods of regeneration and by those settlers who plowed the Midwestern prairies. Humus is the basis for this nutrient storage and cycling. It is a matrix of decomposed organic matter in soils upon which microorganisms flourish. Humus is extremely porous, which helps soils absorb and retain water and air, store plant-usable nutrients, and thereby accelerate biological processes. Humus builds up over time in biologically diverse and active soils. As it does, so do accumulated plant-usable nutrients. This is why the fallow strategy works. This is why the Midwestern prairies have been such abundant and resilient agricultural soils. And this is why our indiscriminate use of fertilizers to replace these natural sources of fertility is of such mounting concern.

THE INDUSTRIAL BASIS OF FERTILITY

In contrast to this biological understanding of soil fertility, our current concepts of fertility are based in a chemically oriented industrialist perspective. Some of the earliest botanical experiments over 250 years ago showed how plants require ample supplies of usable nitrogen, phosphorus, and potassium. Later these became known as the "macro-nutrients," elemental compounds which all plants need to metabolize and grow properly. More recently, with a clearer understanding of the photosynthetic process, scientists began categorizing a whole variety of other chemical elements and compounds known as "micronutrients." Iron, calcium, sulfur, zinc, boron, magnesium, molybdenum, and a still growing list of other chemicals were recognized as needed by plants but in lower levels and with less urgency. With this understanding it became easy for scientists to view plants as photosynthetic machines. A checklist had been assembled of all the chemical and energetic inputs needed by plants to adequately produce an output.

Industrial chemistry accelerated its role in agricultural fertility during World War I. At that time the German chemist Fritz Haber and his colleague Carl Bosch derived a method for manufacturing plant-usable nitrogen compounds from atmospheric nitrogen and pure hydrogen. The importance of this discovery has to do with the essential nature of nitrogen. Of all the "macro-nutrients" none is as important as nitrogen because of its role in building proteins and regulating growth and metabolism in plants. It is also one of the most common elements on the planet, comprising over 75 percent of our entire atmosphere. Unfortunately, atmospheric nitrogen (N_2) is useless to plants, because it is locked in a secure and stable bond with itself. Plants can only use nitrogen that has been destabilized by bonding with oxygen or hydrogen. Haber's contribution was a chemical reaction that produces plant-usable nitrogen (ammonia, NH_3). It is important to note that because the bond in atmospheric nitrogen is so strong, the heat and pressure required for the Haber process are immense. (Although his research fundamentally transformed agriculture, Haber is rarely held up as an important scientific figure because his goal in creating volatile nitrogenous compounds was the manufacture of bombs and poisonous gases for Germany's war effort.)

After the war, several nations began to use this chemical process, together with mined phosphate and potash, to synthetically produce "plant nutrition in a bag." With the three major nutrients readily available and relatively easy to apply, we seemed masters of our own agricultural destiny. But this chemical model of fertility ignores fertility's *real* biological basis. If nitrogen compounds are necessary for plant growth, where did they come from before fertilizers? Early civilizations, including the Greeks, Romans, and Chinese, recognized the ability of leguminous plants to restore and improve the quality of soils in which they grew. It was, ironically, another pair of German chemists, Hellriegel and Wilfarth, who in 1888 showed that these plants participate with soil bacteria in a process called nitrogen fixation. In fact, many varieties of plants are capable of establishing a mutually beneficial relationship with soil bacteria. Plants provide a growth medium and energy to bacteria, which in turn convert airborne nitrogen into plant nutrients. It took until relatively recently to classify a whole host of different bacteria living in soils that are capable of this process of nitrogen fixation. It is estimated that 110 million tons of nitrogen are fixed yearly by microorganisms. The rapid proliferation and use of synthetic fertilizers to date is based on the unfounded assumption that we know exactly what plants need and, more pointedly, that we can provide it better than the microorganisms with which plants coevolved.

THE HEYDAY OF FERTILIZER USE

The tremendous increases in food yields through the latter half of the 20th century have been a direct result of the use of fertilizers and other chemicals on hybrid seeds designed to work with these inputs. The methodology of this "Green Revolution" has allowed for fewer farmers to successfully manage larger and larger acreage. Fertilizers, in particular, gave farmers an enormous amount of flexibility and freedom from the difficulties of managing integrated, diverse crop systems. Rather than bearing the burden of fertility management from within the farm, growers now had the ability to purchase and relegate fertility for particular soils as best fit their markets. Any way in which farmers could minimize the uncertainties associated with fertility and the resulting yields was understandably seen as amazing progress for agriculture. Fertility could now be thought of as a direct commodity, and crop plants could be seen as productive machines requiring human-applied nutrients, sunlight, and water to yield predictable outputs. Agriculture became manufacturing.

This kind of chemically based agriculture rapidly became the dominant model in the United States. Within a few short years following World War II, fertilizers were in consistent, heavy use on over 95 percent of soils producing corn, potatoes, and various vegetable crops. Fertilizers were a great way for farmers to hedge their bets. The relatively predictable yield benefits of fertilizer application could be easily weighed against the cost of the product, and initially the disproportional benefit resulted in the overapplication of fertilizers. Perhaps more importantly, fertilizer use was seen as a way of improving marginal soils or as a method for offsetting other deficiencies. What was not evident at the time was the severe environmental debt being incurred for this excessive use of fertilizers.

THE BREAKDOWN OF A SYSTEM

We now know that the massive use of synthetic fertilizers to create artificial fertility has had a cascade of adverse effects on natural soil fertility and the entire soil system. Fertilizer application begins the destruction of soil biodiversity by diminishing the role of nitrogen-fixing bacteria and amplifying the role of everything that feeds on nitrogen. These feeders then speed up the decomposition of organic matter and humus. As organic matter decreases, the physical structure of soils changes. With less pore space and loss of their sponge-like qualities, soils are less efficient at retaining moisture and air. More irrigation is needed. Water leaches through soils, draining away nutrients that no longer have an effective substrate on which to cling. With less available oxygen the growth of soil microbiology slows, and the intricate ecosystem of biological exchanges breaks down. Acidity rises and further breaks down organic matter. As soil microbes decrease in volume and diversity, they are less able to physically hold soils together in groups called aggregates. Water begins to erode these soils away. Less topsoil means less volume and biodiversity to buffer against these changes. More soils wash away. Meanwhile, all of these events have a cumulative effect of reducing the amount of nutrients available to plants. Industrial farmers address these observed deficiencies by adding more fertilizer. Such a scenario is known as a negative feedback loop; a more blunt comparison is substance abuse.

The adverse effects of fertilizer use do not stop at the farm gate. All plant-usable forms of nitrogen are very soluble in water. This is why they are so transient and why they eventually end up in our watersheds.

WATER AND AIR POLLUTION

Every summer, rains carry eroded soils and fertilizer runoff out of Midwestern fields draining 1.2 million square miles of watershed into the Mississippi River, down to the Gulf of Mexico. For several years now, researchers have monitored and studied the by-product of this grand scale pollution. A huge dead zone, at times encompassing the whole water column, forms off the coast of the delta estuary. The only marine life able to survive in this nitrogen-choked, oxygen-depleted expanse are certain forms of algae. It is a twisted irony that the oil pumped from the bottom of the gulf is eventually returning energetically as runoff that pollutes the marine ecosystem. The estuaries of the Chesapeake, Massachusetts, North Carolina, San Francisco Bay, and numerous others all regularly experience the ecological destruction this runoff brings.

Runoff of soils and synthetic chemicals makes agriculture the largest non-point source of water pollution in the country. It is estimated that only 18 percent of all the nitrogen compounds applied to fields in the United States is actually absorbed in plant tissues. This means that we are inadvertently fertilizing our waters on a gigantic scale. When this runoff reaches waterways, it promotes robust growth in algae and other waterborne plants, a process known as eutrophication in fresh waters and algal bloom in oceanic systems. This unbalanced growth depletes the level of oxygen dissolved into waters. Aquatic life of all varieties is literally asphyxiated by the transformation. The additional algae blocks the transmittance of light energy to depth, creating a less biodiverse water column. Over time this addition of nitrogen changes the whole structure and function of water ecosystems. Less aerobically dependent organisms prevail, which compromises the productivity of fisheries. Many of these organisms produce toxic materials as a by-product of their metabolism. Toxic "red tides" and the resulting fish kills and beach closures are brought on by excessive nitrogen levels. Pathogenic organisms such as *Pfiesteria* and *Pseudo-Nitzschia* also proliferate in these polluted waters.

Numerous farming communities in the United States have experienced nitrogen pollution in their aquifers and drinking supplies. When ingested by humans, nitrogen compounds are converted to a nitrite form that combines with hemoglobin in our blood. This changes the structure and reduces the oxygen-holding capacity of blood, which creates a dangerous condition known as methemoglobinemia. Various communities throughout the midwestern United States have suffered from outbreaks of this condition, which is particularly acute in children.

A large quantity of the nitrogen compounds applied to fields volatizes into gaseous nitrous oxides, which escape into the atmosphere. These are greenhouse gases with far greater potency than simple carbon dioxide. Elevated levels of these gases have been directly linked to stratospheric ozone depletion, acid deposition, and ground-level ozone pollution. In this way, our fertilizer use exacerbates the already untenable problems of global air pollution and climate change.

THE DEBT IS DUE

All of these adverse effects of fertilizers result from their application. It is equally important to consider the problems associated with the production of fertilizers. The Haber process first made for the direct link of fertility to energy consumption, but this was in a time when fossil fuels were abundant and their widespread use seemed harmless. The production of nitrogenous fertilizers consumes more energy than any other aspect of the agricultural process. It takes the energy from burning 2,200 pounds of coal to produce 5.5 pounds of usable nitrogen. This means that within the industrial model of agriculture, as inputs are compared to outputs, the cost of energy has become increasingly important. Agriculture's relationship to fertility is now directly related to the price of oil.

This economic model made some sense throughout a farming period in which we were mining the biological reserves of fertility bound in soil humus. Now it is a crisis of diminishing returns. In 1980 in the United States, the application of a ton of fertilizers resulted in an average yield of 15 to 20 tons of corn. By 1997, this same ton of fertilizer yielded only 5 to 10 tons. Between 1910 and 1983, United States corn yields increased 346 percent while our energy consumption for agriculture increased 810 percent. The poor economics of this industrial agriculture began to surface. The biological health of soils has been driven into such an impoverished state at the expense of quick, easy fertility that productivity is now compromised, and fertilizers are less and less effective.

The United Nations Food and Agriculture Organization in 1997 declared that Mexico and the United States had "hit the wall" on wheat yields, with no increases shown in 13 years. Since the late 1980s, worldwide consumption of fertilizers has been in decline. Farmers are using fewer fertilizers because crops are physiologically incapable of absorbing more nutrients. The negative effects of erosion and loss of biological resiliency exceed our ability to offset them with fertilizers. The price of farm commodities is so low that it no longer offsets the cost of fertilizers. We are at full throttle and going nowhere. Economic systems assume unlimited growth capacity. Ecological systems have finite limitations. It would be wise to recognize how the industrial perspective of fertility as a mined resource drives us toward agricultural collapse.

SUSTAINABLE SOLUTIONS

Certainly the adverse effects of fertilizer use come as no sudden surprise to farmers. Even those who manage the most chemically based agricultural systems recognize the important roles of organic matter, microorganisms, and crop diversity in fertility maintenance. Unfortunately, under crushing financial pressure most farmers are limited in the changes they can afford to make.

Some of the greatest reductions in fertilizer use have come from conservation practices and more careful applications. These represent a savings for farmers. Better timing and less indiscriminate application of fertilizers reduce the adverse effect on soil biology and the likelihood of environmental pollution. Equally important are conservation tillage methods in which ground disturbance is minimized and the decomposition of crop residues is promoted. Less tillage disturbance gives a greater opportunity for microorganisms to proliferate, and more crop decomposition helps provide habitat and resources for them. More water, nutrients, and soils are retained on the farm.

Organic farmers approach the management of fertility biologically rather than chemically. Most organic methods work to enhance soil nutrient cycles by relying upon strategies of crop rotation and cover-cropping to provide nutrient enrichment. Nitrogen-fixing and nutrient-building crops are grown explicitly for the purpose of improving soils, increasing organic matter and soil microbes, preventing erosion, and attracting other beneficial organisms. Soil diversity is maintained with crop plant diversity. Multiple varieties of different crops are grown in successions, which maximize nutrient use by different plant types and minimize pests and pathogens. Additional fertility is provided through organic sources. Naturally based organic fertilizers include composted plant materials, composted manures, fishery by-products, blood and bonemeals, and other materials which decay and release nutrients, participating in rather than destabilizing the nutrient cycle. Practiced well, organic methods establish a dynamic yet stable fertility. Costs of outside inputs dwindle, while soil health and overall fertility grows.

As an organic farmer myself, I have seen the overwhelmingly positive effects of these methods. In my experience, soils with an enhanced organic metabolism have a greater productive capacity than that offered by synthetic fertilizers. I am told over and over by all my customers how my vegetables have flavors beyond what they have come to expect. I believe that this is directly related to fertility as a dynamic, interrelated biological process that we have only begun to understand. Plants are far from simple machines with simple needs. To understand them as such is to abuse them and, in turn, to deprive ourselves of the nutrition and taste that we may derive from them.

HIDDEN DIMENSIONS OF DAMAGE

Pesticides and Health

MONICA MOORE

THE IDEA THAT PESTICIDES ARE DANGEROUS IS NOT CONTROVERSIAL. *After all, pesticides are created and released into the environment in order to kill organisms considered pests, be they insects, weeds, bacteria, fish, snails, birds, rodents, or other forms of life. Yet most people do not realize just how dangerous many pesticides are, either individually or in combination with one another, or how far beyond their intended targets the harmful effects of pesticides actually reach. Ultimately, pesticides affect all members of an ecosystem, from the tiniest invertebrates to humans and other large animals living at the top of their food chains.*

▼

Although the true extent of pesticide-related damage has never been (and may never be) fully quantified, enough is known to indicate that these chemicals are very costly to the health of present and future generations. The long list of known and suspected health problems linked to pesticides grows steadily as new scientific discoveries reveal more of the intricate systems in and around us that influence our health and development from the moment of conception until we die. Numerous studies document disturbing levels of pesticide poisonings and other damage in wealthy as well as poor countries, and knowledgeable sources agree that these documented cases represent only a fraction of the actual total. And of course human poisonings are only the beginning of a much larger story of poisonings.

The fact that spreading billions of pounds of toxic pesticides throughout the environment each year results in extensive harm should not be surprising to policy makers, growers, or the general public. Yet somehow it remains not just surprising, but eternally so. This never-ending lack of awareness of the true scale of damage keeps people from challenging assumptions that societies benefit more than they lose from continuing their dependence on pesticides. Meanwhile, the true dimensions of pesticide damage to human health and the environment remain among the best kept, least acted on secrets of agricultural, public health, development, and regulatory authorities around the globe.

This article considers the extent of pesticide-caused damage to human health. Because we humans are an integral part of the environment, environmental health impacts are an important part of this discussion. Assessing pesticide damage requires pulling together information of many different types from many sources, including acute and chronic effects of different kinds of pesticides; fate and transport of pesticides in the environment; pesticide poisonings statistics; and information on pesticide use, sales, and markets. Some of this information is reasonably easy to find, if you know where to look for it. Other pieces of the puzzle exist only as educated guesses or closely guarded commercial secrets that require determined efforts, dumb luck, huge sums of money, or all of the above to bring to light.

Understanding the true dimensions of pesticide health effects also requires the consideration of factors that shield pesticide damage from public scrutiny and outrage. For example, how is it that so many people have no idea either of the scale of pesticide use in conventional agriculture or of the extent of public health problems caused by these chemicals? Why is the public so unaware of the unavoidable exposures to pesticides they endure daily through their food, water, air, workplaces, and living environments? Most disturbingly, why is agricultural reliance on pesticides growing despite often heroic efforts of ecologically minded farmers to meet consumers' preferences for organically produced food and fibers?

Addressing these questions means examining both the biological mechanisms of pesticide poisonings and pest resistance, and the mechanisms of power that operate in corporate boardrooms and national capitols. This means looking directly at the economic, social, and cultural contexts that grant official invisibility to epidemic levels of poisonings and other forms of pesticide damages. Seen from this perspective, pesticides can be important teachers that help us see interconnections among seemingly distant people, places, and ecological communities. But insights into interconnections without actions to reduce pesticide use and promote safer, ecologically based alternatives will not prevent further damage. Unfortunately, the lesson that pesticides should be teaching us — that an ounce of prevention is much better than a pound of cure, especially when the damage is avoidable and no cure exists — has yet to be learned. For this reason, exposing the hidden dimensions of pesticide damage remains an urgent public and environmental health priority and a continuing challenge for the sustainable agriculture movement.

HOW PESTICIDES DAMAGE HUMAN HEALTH

Pesticides can affect human health through acute (short-term) effects, chronic (long-term) effects, or both. Chronic health effects can be delayed effects from an individual exposure or the result of repeated low-level exposures, whose impacts build up over time. Most pesticides have acute toxic effects; many also present serious chronic hazards. Pesticide exposures can also worsen existing illnesses and medical conditions, including asthma and other respiratory illness, liver and kidney disease, and many others.

Acute Pesticide Poisoning. Symptoms of acute pesticide poisonings may be local, causing irritation or damage to the skin or eyes. Some pesticides can cause allergic reactions, another type of acute effect. Acutely toxic pesticides can also affect the body systemically, causing problems as they begin moving through the blood. Many pesticides generate both local and systemic effects. Specific symptoms vary according to the type of pesticide and also within types. The following section describes a range of acute poisoning symptoms for several major types of pesticides, illustrating some of the many ways that pesticides affect human health.

Nerve Poison Pesticides. Two closely related types of nerve poison pesticides, the organophosphates and the methyl carbamates, are responsible for most acute pesticide poisonings and deaths in the United States and worldwide. Both of these compounds kill insect pests by stopping a critical nerve impulse–transmitting enzyme from functioning normally. Unfortunately, they block the same enzymes in the bodies of non-target insects, birds, fish, reptiles, mollusks, amphibians, and mammals, including people. Mild systemic poisoning symptoms produced by these pesticides include blurry vision, headache, dizziness, fatigue, diarrhea, nausea and vomiting, heavy sweating, and muscle or abdominal pain. As the level of poisoning increases, a victim's pupils shrink and he or she experiences difficulty walking, talking, and concentrating. Twitching muscles and generalized weakness are also symptoms. Signs of severe poisoning include pinpoint pupils, convulsions, unconsciousness, difficulty breathing, coma, and death. Organophosphate and carbamate pesticides are widely produced and used throughout the world.

Organochlorine Pesticides. This category includes DDT, the world's most notorious pesticide, along with other less famous compounds. Organochlorines affect the brain and increase the sensitivity of neurons. While better known for their chronic effects, many organochlorines are highly acutely toxic as well. Convulsions are the classic acute poisoning symptom for this category, and may or may not be accompanied by other symptoms, including headache, dizziness, nausea, vomiting, tremors, lack of coordination, and mental confusion. Organochlorines can also cause local irritant effects, including allergic reactions. Although some older organochlorine pesticides have been widely banned, use of others remains common in the United States and throughout the world.

Pyrethrins and Synthetic Pyrethroids. Pyrethrins are naturally occurring compounds derived from chrysanthemum flowers, and pyrethroids are their synthetically manufactured chemical cousins. These compounds also affect the brain and nervous system, although differently than do the two pesticide types mentioned above. Acute poisoning symptoms produced by these pesticides include local skin irritation, multiple allergic reactions, dizziness, tremors, irritability to sound or touch, headache, vomiting, and diarrhea. Because these kinds of insecticides tend to break down sooner in the environment than do many organochlorines, they are often substituted for them, and are used widely in agriculture, as well as in homes and gardens.

Dipyridyl Pesticides. This category includes the herbicides paraquat and diquat, highly toxic compounds responsible for many acute poisonings in the United States and internationally. These pesticides are very strong irritants that can severely damage the skin, eyes, mouth, nose, and throat, including causing blindness and fingernail loss. They destroy lung tissue and cause failure of the kidneys, liver, and other organs. Symptoms of poisoning by these pesticides include pain, vomiting, diarrhea, headache, nosebleeds, loss of appetite, and death. Paraquat in particular is in wide use throughout the world.

Chlorophenoxy Herbicides. This category of herbicides includes the well-known weed killer 2,4-D and also 2,4,5-T, an ingredient of the Vietnam War–era defoliant known as Agent Orange. Products containing 2,4-D are big sellers in both agricultural and over-the-counter home and garden products. While the long-term health effects of phenoxy herbicides are usually considered more serious, acute poisoning symptoms can include skin irritation, headache, nausea, vomiting, low fever, mental confusion, abdominal pain, and temporary changes in heartbeat.

"Inert" Pesticide Ingredients. The already daunting task of evaluating pesticide harm is made much more difficult by the unidentified "inert" ingredients found in all formulated pesticide products. These falsely named ingredients include solvents, emulsifiers, and other substances added to a pesticide product to make it easier to blend or apply or for any other reason not directly related to killing a target pest. So-called "inert" ingredients may have serious negative health effects, and some are even used as pesticides in other products. Although they often make up over 95 percent of the formulated product, the true identity of "inert" ingredients is classified as "confidential business information" and kept secret from both product users and the public. The result is that no one has any idea of what chemical combinations they are being exposed to when they come in contact with pesticides.

CHRONIC HEALTH IMPACTS

Many pesticides are known to cause chronic effects in people, laboratory animals, and/or wildlife. Such effects include many types of cancers, neurological effects, reproductive and developmental illness, and disruption of the endocrine system. Whether subtle or drastic, the pesticide origins of these long-term health impacts are more difficult to prove than are acute poisonings. While not comprehensive, this section presents summary information about several types of chronic pesticide health effects.

Pesticides and Cancer. Many pesticides used in agriculture and in homes, gardens, buildings, and public spaces are linked to different kinds of cancers. According to the Environmental Protection Agency (EPA), 112 currently registered pesticides are known, probable, or suspected carcinogens. Pesticides can increase cancer causation through several mechanisms, including by promoting abnormal cell proliferation, directly altering DNA, or disrupting the immune system. Evidence linking pesticides to cancer comes from three major sources: human epidemiological investigations, studies performed on laboratory animals, and cell-culture studies. The following examples emphasize epidemiological studies:

- The agricultural and home-use weed killer 2,4-D has been associated with malignant melanoma in several studies. One study in the *Journal of the American Medical Association* found that farmers who mixed or applied 2,4-D more than 20 days per year had a six times higher risk of non-Hodgkins lymphoma.
- Overall incidence of childhood leukemia in the United States increased by 27 percent between 1973 and 1990. One National Cancer Institute study found that in homes where pesticides were used even just once a week, children's risk of leukemia increased 400 percent. Other studies show that children whose fathers work in jobs that expose them to pesticides have a threefold increased risk of leukemia.
- Use of the pesticide lindane has been linked with aplastic anemia. One study found that use of lindane shampoos to treat head lice is associated with higher incidence of aplastic anemia in children. Lindane has also been linked with lymphoma and breast cancer in adults.
- Childhood brain cancer has increased by 33 percent in the past 20 years; risks of childhood brain cancer were found to be elevated two- to sixfold in homes where pesticides are used. One study in *Environmental Health Perspectives* found brain cancer rates to be five times higher in homes where

"no-pest" strips were used and six times higher in homes where pets wore flea collars.

Neurological and Behavioral Effects of Pesticides. As mentioned, pesticides that affect the nervous system cause more acute poisoning cases than any other pesticide category. But these pesticides also have serious long-term effects on both the central and the peripheral nervous systems. Many years after the fact, large numbers of people who have suffered serious acute organophospate poisoning have significantly impaired hearing, vision, intelligence, coordination, reaction time, memory, and reasoning. Cognitive symptoms of chronic damage to the nervous system include personality changes, anxiety, irritability, and depression. A growing body of evidence indicates that Parkinson's disease may be linked to exposures to certain pesticides and pesticide classes, among other environmental factors. Specific chemicals implicated in this particular type of damage include the herbicide paraquat, the organophosphates, dieldrin (an organochlorine), and the fungicides maneb and mancozeb. Other herbicides and insecticides also appear to be associated with development of Parkinson's disease. Several fumigants, including methyl bromide, Telone, and sulfuryl floride, are linked with a range of behavioral and cognitive effects. As they are with other health effects, children are particularly vulnerable to chronic neurotoxins, and exposures during key periods of brain growth can result in permanent effects on the structure and function of their brains.

Reproductive and Developmental Effects. Pesticides can damage men's and women's fertility by affecting their reproductive organs directly or indirectly, or by disrupting the normal functioning of their hormones. Fertility can be impaired by occupational exposure to pesticides, as indicated by increased time-to-pregnancy documented in spouses of farmers and agricultural workers and other types of studies in North America and Europe. It may even be destroyed forever, as hundreds of men exposed to the pesticide DBCP in the United States, Central America, and Africa have learned to their deep and lasting sorrow. Widely used pesticides that are known to be reproductive toxins in men, women, or both include the herbicides 2,4-D and chlorosulfuron, the rodenticide 1080, the insecticides oxydemeton-methyl and hydramethylnon, and the fungicides benomyl, myclobutanil, and triadimefon.

Most pesticides can cross the placenta and enter the body of a fetus. Developmental effects of pesticides can include spontaneous abortion, stillbirth, birth defects, low birth weight and smaller infants, and functional impairment. Many studies show that mothers' occupational exposure to pesticides increases risks of congenital birth defects. Others demonstrate that increases in a variety of birth defects are associated with fathers' employment as pesticide applicators. The timing of exposure can be critical: the periods of fetal development and early childhood, in which the body's organ systems are formed, are especially vulnerable times for this type of health effect.

Endocrine Disrupting Pesticides. Many pesticides can disrupt normal functioning of the endocrine system in people and other animals. Such pesticides may strengthen or weaken, imitate or block the effect of naturally occurring hormones, leading in turn to serious problems, including cancer, reproductive illness, or developmental effects. Most pesticides have not yet been studied for their potential to affect hormones or otherwise disrupt the endocrine system, and the tests capable of detecting such effects are still being developed. Pesticides that have been identified as having this type of effect so far include the popular weed killers atrazine, alachlor, cyanazine, and simizine; the insecticides aldicarb, carbaryl, lindane, endosulfan, resmethrin, and other synthetic pyrethroids; the fungicides vinclozalin, metiram, benomyl, mancozeb, and maneb; and the wood preservative pentachlorophenol. Many pesticides that persist for long periods in the environment are known to be endocrine disruptors, including DDT, aldrin, endrin, dieldrin, chlordane, heptachlor, and other organochlorine insecticides.

PESTICIDE POISONING AND CHILDREN

Children are more susceptible to the acute and chronic heath effects of pesticides than adults are for several reasons. Because their bodies and organs are still growing and developing, children's bodies do not process these poisons as well as those of adults. Children are also more exposed to pesticides. Pound for pound, children eat more food, drink more liquids and breathe in more air than adults, so they take in more pesticides per unit of body weight than adults do. Because they are smaller, children's bodies have a relatively greater surface area in contact with the world then adults do, and most pesticide exposures occur through the skin. Children also have more contact with pesticides and other environmental toxins because they crawl around on all kinds of surfaces, often put their hands in their mouths, hug pets more frequently, and generally are in more intimate physical contact with the world than are adults. Children in agricultural settings face particularly high risks. Children ten years and older may work legally on farms, and younger children of farmworkers often join older family members in the fields out of economic necessity. As a result, farm kids often have much higher exposures to pesticides than other children do.

There is some evidence that acute poisoning of children tends to be noticed and treated more readily than occupationally related poisonings, especially when caused by swallowing a pesticide, a spill, or some other specific event in the home. Reports from the national network of Poison Control Centers show that more than 50 percent of pesticide poisoning emergencies reported in the United States each year involve children less than six years old. Poisonings that occur away from home are less likely to make it into the official record.

U.S. AND GLOBAL POISONING ESTIMATES

Although acute pesticide health effects, which occur within moments or days of exposure, are more easily identified than chronic poisonings, most acute agricultural poisonings go unrecognized or unreported. There are many reasons for this. Many symptoms of acute poisonings (e.g., headache, nausea, dizziness, diarrhea, vomiting, and skin rashes) are also associated with other common conditions, making accurate diagnoses difficult even when health care professionals are informed enough to consider pesticide poisoning as a possibility. The fact that most of the world's agricultural workers have no access to health care obviously contributes to a lack of reliable data on agriculture pesticide poisonings. Furthermore, many farmworkers fear being fired or getting labeled as troublemakers if they seek medical help or take time off work to recover when poisoned by pesticides on the job.

Where reliable numbers are unavailable, educated guesses become increasingly important. In the United States, government estimates indicate more than 20,000 farmworkers out of an estimated population of 5 million workers in this country suffer acute pesticide poisonings annually. Yet authorities also acknowledge that their estimates are based on very little knowledge regarding the extent of actual pesticide exposures and resulting health effects. In terms of chronic impacts, no serious effort to develop estimates of annual cases has been attempted.

At the global level, the World Health Organization published an estimate in 1990 that 3 million severe acute pesticide poisonings occur in developing countries each year, including some 220,000 fatalities. This figure is still widely cited today, although another study by the same expert indicates it is a serious underestimation. Based on hospital records in four Asian countries, this expert concluded that between 2 and 7 percent of the agricultural labor force in developing countries is poisoned annually, which would revise his previous estimate upwards to well over 25 million poisoning cases each year in developing countries alone.

Another, more in-depth field study of 228 farmers and pesticide sprayers in Indonesia found that 21 percent of all pesticide applications over the study season resulted in symptoms that strongly indicated organophosphate pesticide poisoning. Asked if they remembered ever having been poisoned by pesticides, 9 percent of the farmers reported at least one incident serious enough that they sought medical attention. The study noted that the farmers "tended to accept this level of illness as part of the work of farming." Most of the farmers also reported pesticide storage, disposal, and other practices that put their family members at risk.

Translating these figures into a fictional nonagricultural setting helps to highlight the social and economic assumptions that allow such astounding rates of occupational hazard to persist without consequences to the suppliers of the injurious product or adoption and enforcement of regulatory measures sufficient to reduce the rate of injury. Consider the following: word processors are basic tools for many firms and industries, and millions of people rely on them for personal uses as well. Now imagine that 21 percent of the time you, or anyone else, used a word processor at work you would receive an electrical shock. That's on average, so it wouldn't be every time, and the shock wouldn't be enough to kill you — at least not most of the time. Then imagine that nearly 10 percent of the people using word processors got shocked severely enough to require medical treatment at some point in their careers and that their families were at risk from the word processors that they kept at home.

Does it seem reasonable for you to be forced to accept being shocked repeatedly as "part of the work of word processing"? Or that the computer company whose products kept shocking you should be allowed to stay in business?

THE BENEFITS OF CHRONIC UNCERTAINTY

In the early stages of learning about pesticide dangers, many people get frightened or overwhelmed and don't want to know more. This is easily understandable. Professionals deeply familiar with pesticide health effects also may numb themselves to the pain and suffering they encounter in laboratory animals, wildlife, and men, women, and children exposed to pesticides in order to stay focused on the task at hand. But overwhelmed individuals and psychic numbing among experts should not prevent public acknowledgement of massive, unnecessary proliferation of dangerous pesticides into the air, water, food, and public spaces we all share.

Chronic pesticide poisonings provide an instructive case in point in considering factors that blunt public awareness of pesticide damages. No one disputes that such poisonings occur, but the extent, frequency, significance, and implications of these poisonings are endlessly controversial. From a public health and welfare perspective, acting to reduce use of hazardous chemicals, getting them off the market, and replacing them with less or non-hazardous alternatives is the obvious and most effective way to address individually the damage — impossible to prove but collectively very real — caused by chronic pesticide poisonings. The same course of action flows easily from an environmental frame of reference.

But somehow, this is not what happens. Instead, industry scientists, regulators, pesticide users, and public interest groups all agree that chronic pesticides are health hazards, but disagree on how hazardous and what to do about it. This is where you start to see the qualifying phrases stack up in both industry and government regulatory positions: yes, they are hazardous . . . *but* they can be applied in a safe and harmless manner when applied according to label instructions. *But* our research indicates that this product presents no significant hazard to the public. *But* by controlling the exposure, we can control the risk, and the exposures are at safe levels. *But* alternatives are not available or cost-effective. *But* we don't know enough about the extent of harm to justify taking "extreme measures" (code for removing a product from the market). *But* the harm done (to many) is outweighed by the economic benefits (to increasingly few) of using the pesticide.

Driven by such assertions, which are rarely if ever subject to open scrutiny, scarce public funds and the greater resources of industry are spent documenting that long latency periods, confounding exposures, and other factors make it difficult to estimate individual and aggregate exposures or quantify risks from chronic pesticides. This is true. Yet such "insights" do little to prevent further damage or develop alternatives to more pesticide use. In this intentionally endless quest for greater knowledge, new studies are designed to better understand a pesticide's mode of action, establish clearer causal relationships, identify so-called "safe" exposure levels, quantify the extent of harm more precisely, etc. Meanwhile, serious measures to reduce and eliminate the source of harm never make it onto the list. As the wheels of investigation grind on, uncertainty is "resolved" in favor of pesticide manufacturers and users, who continue to develop their plans and project future profits based on continuing use of chronic poisons.

PESTICIDES IN THE ENVIRONMENT

Ultimately, most pesticides in the environment degrade upon exposure to air, sunlight, and water, or as they are broken down within plants, animals, and microorganisms. How long this takes and how much damage is done in the meantime varies greatly from case to case, however. Different types of pesticides break down differently, and while the chemical breakdown products of these processes are usually less harmful than the original material, some are even more dangerous than the parent compound, as in the cases of the insecticides aldicarb, malathion, and ethyl parathion, and the herbicide atrazine.

How pesticides break down in the environment is also influenced strongly by temperature, moisture, presence or absence of other chemicals, and many other factors. But predicting the environmental conditions of where a pesticide may end up is no simple matter. Pesticides are highly mobile and can travel vast distances. Once released into the environment, they are like genies let out of their bottles — impossible to put back in. Pesticides applied by aircraft can drift many miles from their supposed targets, evaporating in and out of a solid state within air currents, only to land, revolatilize, and set off again. Tiny pesticide droplets suspended in fog can be deposited onto birds, wildlife, leaves, and any other living or nonliving surface touched by the mist. Rain, storms, and irrigation ditches routinely sweep huge loads of pesticides into streams, lakes, wells, and rivers, with often devastating effects on fish, amphibians, and aquatic invertebrates. Pesticides cross the seas on prevailing currents to contaminate Arctic and Antarctic environments, native peoples, and the animals they depend on for sustenance, thousands of miles from the original application. They also move through aquifers and groundwater, to the horror of those who depend on these sources for their drinking water.

Another way pesticides travel is through food chains. In this mode of transport, pesticides that are taken up within smaller organisms and not broken down or excreted remain stored there until the organisms are eaten by another creature, whose body burden of pesticides increases accordingly. The same thing happens again when that creature becomes a meal for another predator, and so on and so on. These pesticide body burdens travel with their "hosts," and migratory animals such as marine mammals, birds, and fish often carry pesticides over long distances before being eaten by predators.

The continuing process of adding and passing on new loads of pesticides and other toxins through the food chain is called bioaccumulation, and it is the reason that top predators like birds, sharks, some whales, bears, and people carry high concentrations of certain poisons in their bodies. Breast-feeding infants of mammalian predators, including human babies, are at the pinnacle of the food chain, since large amounts of bioaccumulating chemicals collect in breast milk and are passed into the infants' bodies as they feed.

PERSISTENT ORGANIC POLLUTANTS

One particular type of pesticide combines several characteristics that make it a special threat to life. Persistent Organic Pollutant pesticides (POPs) — such as DDT — are linked with serious chronic health effects; they last for long periods without breaking down; they travel far and wide in the environment; and they build up to ever higher and more harmful levels in the food chain. Since their widespread production and use began, less than 60 years ago, POPs pesticides and other POPs chemicals have moved throughout the global environment to threaten human health and ecosystems around the world. All living organisms on earth now carry measurable levels of POPs in their tissues, and evidence that exposure to even tiny amounts of POPs during critical periods of development can cause irreversible damage is strong and increasing. Effects of such exposures can take years to appear, sometimes appearing first in the offspring of exposed parents. In this tragic legacy of damage, children can end up suffering from a parent's exposure to a POPs chemical that occurred decades before they were born.

In an encouraging example of coordinated action to reduce chemical hazards, nations around the world recently recognized and began addressing the extraordinary threat of POPs chemicals with an international treaty. The new POPs treaty mandates global phase-outs of production and use of POPs chemicals. This type of global approach to eliminating chemical damages is both inspiring and much too rare.

WHAT LIES BENEATH

The fact that pesticides continue to be promoted and accepted as the most efficient and desirable form of pest management is a symptom of a different kind of chronic poisoning. Driven by economic policies that put short-term profits and agricultural exports first, and address health and social concerns only later, if at all, extractive, chemical-intensive industrial agricultural is gaining ground despite our greenest intentions and desires.

The approximately $35-billion-a-year pesticide business lies at the center of these expansive lies. Dominated by ten corporate giants based in the United States and Western Europe that control nearly 90 percent of the global pesticide market, this industry is directly (but not solely) responsible for the release of several billion pounds of pesticides into the environment every year. And that's just one piece of the agro-industrial complex. Increasing use of pesticides and other harmful agrochemicals, despite their negative health and environmental impacts and the sustained growth of the organic sector, underscores the power of these industries to thwart attempts toward biologically based pest management and ecological agriculture. Continuing public confusion regarding the true extent of pesticide damages, weak national regulatory and enforcement systems, and a pervasive lack of public investment in already existing and promising new alternative pest management approaches are additional symptoms of these industries' poisonous influence.

Ironically, many people believe that agriculture is gradually giving up its dependence on pesticides. Agrochemical and related industries' investments in marketing, public relations, and political campaigns help explain this misperception. For example, most people mistakenly believe that when pesticide producers proclaim their environmental commitments, this means they are reducing production of environmentally harmful materials. Many people also believe that because organic agriculture is making such rapid gains, levels of pesticide use must be falling as well — and national regulatory authorities neither collect nor publish pesticide-use data showing that exactly the opposite is true. People also assume that pesticides on the market must be safe, or pesticide regulatory agencies would not allow manufacturers to sell them, reflecting a widely held but dangerously inaccurate understanding of these agencies' role. And of course psychic numbing and feelings of being overwhelmed also help shield corporations and governments from scrutiny.

REGAINING GROUND

Acknowledging such barriers and the power of corporate interests to maintain them in no way implies that our societies can never awaken

from the health and environmental nightmares of conventional industrial extractive agriculture. Rather, it points directly to the need for
multiple and reinforcing strategies of public education, analysis, and
actions over time. To be effective, these strategies must facilitate the
development of new leadership and other resources needed to transform agricultural policy and practice. They must also address the
social contexts in which massive unnecessary pesticide damages are
considered "normal" and acceptable and in which companies responsible for these damages are rewarded for inflicting them.

Changing how our societies deal with the uncertainty that surrounds
the hidden dimensions of pesticide damage is an important element
of stemming the rising toxic tide of pesticides. When protecting people
and the environment from pesticide harm, it is not reasonable to require
iron-clad scientific proof or multi-stakeholder consensus that a pesticide
causes a certain number of deaths or percentage of cancers or other
types of health effects before taking action to reduce harm. Even
where our knowledge of the mechanisms and extent of damage is not
complete, awareness of harm should automatically trigger actions to
protect the health of our families, communities, and environment.

Protecting health in highly contaminated and otherwise compromised environments is extremely difficult, and mitigating and healing
damages to health from such contamination is generally prohibitively
expensive and often impossible. That is why preventing the release of
harmful chemicals and other forms of environmental contamination
is the most effective, economical, and morally justifiable approach to
safeguarding people and ecosystems from costly and often irreversible
damages, such as those described here. Acceptance of this straightforward approach is guiding efforts toward cleaner production in several industries and gaining credibility in some nations, most notably
in Scandinavia. Although increasing global pesticide sales and marketing of new genetically engineered pesticides show that the conventional agriculture industry has yet to embrace this precautionary
approach, those of us convinced of the wisdom of moving toward
cleaner production in agriculture have much to work with.

Knowing that we need to move toward an agriculture capable of
supplying the foods and fibers we need without destroying people's
health, environments, and cultures in the process helps us target our

efforts. Since preventing pest problems is essential to healthy and successful agriculture, for example, we know we must figure out much better ways to do this than reflexively using pesticides. Similarly, preventing pesticide-related damage to health implies rapid elimination of pesticides known or suspected to cause such damage. This means we need effective mechanisms for targeting major uses of hazardous pesticides, removing those products from the market, and replacing them with safer alternative approaches.

Fortunately, many proven alternative methods and products are available to reduce our current massive dependence on pesticides, and more are becoming available with time. Where such alternatives already exist, we must move far more quickly to implement them. Wherever they are not available, we need to move urgently to apply the human creativity, financial resources, and other support to ensure they are developed and implemented as rapidly as possible.

Meanwhile, the secrecy and misinformation surrounding the true scale of pesticide use in agriculture remain a huge obstacle to the development of safer pest management alternatives. Think of the billions of pounds of pesticides being released into the environment each year as straws being loaded onto camels' backs. We and our families, communities, and environment are the camels, and the burdens we bear are packed for us by experts who swear they are essential to keeping us fed and are otherwise not a problem — and who make a commission on every straw we carry.

All of us have the right to know what pesticides we are exposed to intentionally or unintentionally, and to be heard in decision-making processes that affect whether or not these exposures continue. In addition to ensuring our right to know, public reporting and disclosure of pesticide use is also crucial to creating effective demands for safer alternatives. The same corporate advertising expertise that helped create chemically dependent agriculture now churns out messages telling us about the greening of agriculture. These messages are all the more easily swallowed because they are partially true — despite industrial agriculture's stalling tactics and thanks to the ceaseless efforts of a small but growing number of farmers leading the way to more ecologically and socially beneficial agricultural systems.

Separating agricultural fact from profitable fantasies requires more information than the public is presently allowed access to. Using new information technologies, it could be easy for any man, woman, or child to find out whether the use of specific pesticides on specific crops in specific places is going up, down, or staying the same in their county, state, and country. Other questions that should be easily answered include whether public and private funds dedicated to research and extension programs designed to reduce pesticide use are increasing, and where to find detailed information about farm ownership and the ecological and labor conditions under which food and fibers are grown and processed. Without constant public tracking of these and other indicators of progress toward ecologically based agricultural production, all we have is assurances from people whose words we know from experience cannot be trusted without independent verification.

UNTESTED, UNLABELED, AND YOU'RE EATING IT

The Health and Environmental Hazards of Genetically Engineered Food

JOSEPH MENDELSON III

THE BIOTECH INDUSTRY CLAIMS *it can insert foreign genetic material, including animal and virus genes, into crops without altering the fundamental nature of our foods. However, a growing body of evidence indicates that these altered products carry potentially serious risks for human health and the environment. Ignoring this evidence, the U.S. government requires no mandatory safety testing or labeling of genetically engineered foods. As a result, millions of consumers have become unknowing guinea pigs, testing the safety of these novel foods.*
▼

Millions of farmers demonstrate in India, burning down the corporate headquarters of a major agribusiness company. Throughout Europe and the United States thousands take to the streets to demand their "right to know." Activists clandestinely rip up crops and burn them. Courts in Europe and South America order halts to crop plantings. The United States threatens an unprecedented trade war with the rest of the world. What's causing this historic food fight? Genetically engineered foods.

Though in existence for barely more than a decade, genetically engineered (GE) or biotech foods have created an international furor that shows no sign of abating. In recent years, the battle over GE foods has been especially heated in the United States. Virtually all the "developed" countries mandate labeling of biotech foods. However, the U.S. government has refused to mandate safety testing or labeling for gene-altered produce. In this regulatory vacuum, up to 60 percent of processed foods in the United States have some GE ingredient and over 70 million acres have been planted with these crops. This has rightfully angered much of the public, who are deeply concerned about the safety of GE foods and furious that they have been denied their right to know which foods have been engineered. Numerous legal actions have been filed against the government and biotechnology food producers, and hundreds of thousands of people, including many scientists, consumer advocates, and religious leaders, have commented to federal agencies, demanding labeling and testing.

Biotechnology companies purport to be amazed by the massive controversy they have engendered. They continuously claim that these foods "are the same as traditional foods." Further, they argue that these "are the most tested and scrutinized foods in history." However, a close look at GE foods belies these corporate claims. Biotech foods are qualitatively different than any foods we have ever eaten, and the failure to regulate the human health and environmental impacts of these foods has resulted in a virtual "black box" of serious and unanswered questions about their consequences.

WHAT ARE GENETICALLY ENGINEERED FOODS?

While the biotech industry is fond of saying that biotech foods have been around since "beer and yeast," in reality the genetic engineering of seeds is the most radical transformation in food production since the dawn of agriculture more than 10,000 years ago. The history of agriculture is largely defined by the use of naturally occurring genetics to produce seeds that result in tastier food, more uniform produce, or greater yields. This process of selective breeding reached its height with the increasingly widespread use of hybridization over the last century.

Genetic engineering is, however, completely different from even the most radical breeding techniques of modern agriculture. It involves artificially manipulating the seed, or food animal, at the cellular level. Because it allows DNA from one type of organism to be placed in that of another, completely unrelated type, it allows for the crossing of natural barriers in ways never before imagined. Biotech researchers have shattered kingdom, phyla, and species boundaries almost at will. They have engineered human growth genes into fish and livestock to make them larger and grow faster, fish genes into tomatoes so that they can grow and be stored at lower temperatures, pesticide genes into corn and other vegetables to resist pests, and firefly genes into tobacco plants, causing the plants to glow 24 hours a day. This process clearly challenges the very integrity of seeds, and much of the earth's other life forms. As noted by the author Michael Pollan, "The introduction into a plant of genes transported not only across species but whole phyla means that the wall of that plant's essential identity — its irreducible wildness you might say — has been breached."

But exactly how do the engineers accomplish this feat? How do they get those flounder genes into tomatoes? The industry claims this process of genetic transfer represents a dramatic increase in "accuracy" over traditional breeding. Such assertions are simply wrong. The current technology being used to genetically engineer seeds is anything but precise. The initial problem facing agricultural biotech was how to "invade" the seed's cell wall and deposit the desired new genetic component in the cell. The current favored solution is to attach the gene to a "vector" that is good at cell invasion. The best candidate vectors to accomplish this cell invasion are, not surprisingly, bacteria and viruses. Most plant biotechnology relies on bacteria to carry the foreign genetic construct into the cell. Viral vectors are more commonly used on animals, including humans. Even when the cell invasion is accomplished, there are still other difficulties in engineering a seed. The host's cells often reject the foreign genetic invader, and often the new genetic material does not produce the desired proteins at the hoped for volume. To resolve these problems, viral promoters are added to "turn on" and promote the activity of the foreign genes.

Once all this has been done, a final problem remains. How do the scientists know that the new genetic construct has become a component of the cell? How do they know they have been successful? To ascertain when their engineering has succeeded, biotech food producers include in the genetic "cassette" being inserted into the cell an antibiotic-resistant marker system. This involves attaching genes resistant to antibiotics such as kanamycin or ampicillin to the genetic construct. Later the plant tissue is flooded with bacteria, and if the antibiotic reacts they know that the genetic construct has been successfully inserted.

There are two critical concerns about this "engineering" at the cellular level that are rarely noted or discussed. Most obviously, it is important that when we speak of GE foods, we refer not only to the insertion of novel genetic material into a cell but to the invasion by the entire "cassette" — the bacterial vector, the new genetic construct, the viral promoters, and the antibiotic marker system. As we shall see, each one of these components being added to our food brings with it potential health threats to consumers.

It is also important to note the imprecision of this process of cell invasion. At this time researchers do not know precisely where this "cassette" will end up in the host organisms, nor do they know enough about the genome (the genetic make-up) of the host organism (be it tomato, corn, or fish) to pinpoint a "safe place" for their genetic additions. Therefore, the very process of genetic engineering creates instability in the seed and resulting foods, and this can lead to health and ecological problems. A reporter visiting a Monsanto lab and witnessing the process described the uncertainty of the engineering process:

> The whole operation . . . is performed thousands of times . . . largely because there is so much uncertainty about the outcome. If the new DNA winds up in the wrong place in the genome, for example, the new gene won't be expressed, or it will be expressed only poorly. . . . I was struck by the uncertainty surrounding the process, how this technology is at the same time both astoundingly sophisticated yet still a shot in the genetic dark.
>
> — Michael Pollan, *The Botany of Desire*

HUMAN HEALTH RISKS

These "shots in the genetic dark" are being taken more and more often. In 2001, there were more than four dozen GE foods and crops being grown or sold in the United States. A majority of processed food items "test positive" for the presence of GE ingredients. In addition, dozens of new GE crops are in the final stages of development and will soon be released into the environment and sold in the marketplace. According to the biotechnology industry, almost 100 percent of U.S.

food and fiber will be genetically engineered within 5 to 10 years. The menu of these unlabeled GE foods and food ingredients includes soybeans, soy oil, corn, potatoes, squash, canola oil, cottonseed oil, papaya, and tomatoes. The large-scale consumption of these genetically engineered crops raises several unprecedented human health risks, discussed below.

Toxicity. As described above, GE foods are inherently unstable. Each insertion of a novel gene, and the accompanying "cassette" of promoters, terminators, enhancers, antibiotic marker systems, and vectors, is random. As a result, each gene insertion into a food amounts to playing food safety "roulette," with the companies hoping that the new genetic material does not destabilize a safe food and make it hazardous. Each genetic insertion creates the added possibility that formerly nontoxic elements in the food could become toxic.

The U.S. Food and Drug Administration (FDA) has been well aware of the "genetic instability" problem for more than a decade. In the early 1990s, FDA scientists warned that this problem could create dangerous toxins in food and was a significant health risk. The scientists specifically warned that the genetic engineering of foods could result in "increased levels of known naturally occurring toxicants, appearance of new, not previously identified toxicants, and increased capability of concentrating toxic substances from the environment (e.g., pesticides or heavy metals)." These same FDA scientists recommended that long-term toxicological tests be required before the marketing of GE foods.

FDA officials also were aware that safety testing on the first GE food, the Calgene FlavrSavr™ tomato, had shown that consumption of this product resulted in stomach lesions in laboratory rats. Even more significantly, the FDA had already concluded that genetic engineering was a possible cause for the 37 deaths and 1,500 disabling illnesses caused by consumption of the dietary supplement L-tryptophan. Showa Denko, a Japanese company, had begun using genetic engineering to produce the dietary supplement in the late 1980s. Apparently, the genetic engineering of this particular lot of the supplement may have created a toxic contaminant by-product that caused these deaths and illnesses.

The FDA's response to the potential toxicity problem with GE foods was, and continues to be, to ignore it. It has disregarded its own scientists, the clear scientific evidence, and the deaths and illnesses that may have resulted from this problem. The agency refused to require pre-market toxicological testing for GE foods or any toxicity monitoring whatsoever. The FDA made these decisions with no scientific basis and without independent scientific review. The agency's actions can only be seen as a shameful acquiescence to industry pressure and a complete abandonment of its responsibility to assure food safety.

Allergic Reactions. Toxicity is not the only health hazard associated with GE foods. In the United States, about a quarter of the population reports some adverse allergic reaction to food. At least 8 percent of children have physically identifiable allergic reactions to food. The genetic engineering of food creates three separate and serious health risks involving allergenicity. First, it may increase the levels of allergy-causing proteins already found in the plant to the point where they prompt strong human allergenic response. Second, genetic engineering can transfer allergens from foods to which people know they are allergic to foods that they think are safe. This risk is not simply hypothetical. A study published in *The New England Journal of Medicine* showed that when a gene from a Brazil nut was engineered into soybeans, people allergic to nuts had serious reactions to the engineered product. At least one food, a Pioneer Hi-Bred International soybean, was abandoned because of this problem. Without labeling, people with known food allergies have no way of avoiding the potentially serious health consequences of eating GE foods containing hidden allergenic material.

There is yet a third allergy risk associated with GE foods. These foods could be creating thousands of different and new allergic responses. Each genetic "cassette" being engineered into foods produces a number of novel proteins that have never been part of the human diet, some of which could create an allergic response in some consumers. The FDA was also well aware of this new and potentially massive allergenicity problem. The agency's scientists repeatedly warned that genetic engineering could "produce a new protein allergen." Once again, the government's own scientists urged long-term testing, but the FDA again ignored its own experts. As these foods are allowed on the market without mandatory allergenicity testing, millions of unsuspecting consumers have been regularly exposed to a potentially serious health risk. The negligence of the government's failure to address this concern is highlighted by the StarLink™ corn fiasco in 2000 — a situation where a strain of potentially allergenic genetically engineered corn not approved for human consumption was found in the human corn supply. As a result, hundreds of food products were recalled and taken off supermarket shelves. The widespread contamination involved in the StarLink™ incident — in addition to the failure on the part of the FDA to act appropriately — portrays the agency's negligence, especially when the potential consequences of food allergies can include sudden death, and the most affected population is children.

Antibiotic Resistance. Another hidden risk of GE foods is that they could make disease-causing bacteria resistant to current antibiotics, resulting in a significant increase in the spread of infections and diseases. As explained, virtually all GE foods contain antibiotic-resistance markers, which help the producers identify whether the new genetic material has actually been tranferred into the host food. Industry's large-scale introduction of these antibiotic marker genes into the food supply could render important antibiotics useless in fighting human diseases. For example, a genetically engineered maize plant from Novartis includes an ampicillin-resistant gene. Ampicillin is a valuable antibiotic used to treat a variety of infections in people and animals. A number of European countries, including Britain, have refused to permit this Novartis corn to be grown, due to health concerns that the ampicillin-resistant gene could move from the corn into bacteria in the food chain, making ampicillin far less effective in fighting a wide range of bacterial infections.

For the past seven years, FDA officials have ignored their own scientists' concerns over the antibiotic resistance problem. During the same time, medical professionals around the world have become increasingly alarmed at how GE foods are leading to a massive infusion of antibiotic genes into the human diet. In 2000, the British Medical Association (BMA) addressed this problem in its study of GE foods. The BMA's conclusion was unequivocal: "There should be a ban on the use of antibiotic resistance marker genes in GE food, as the risk to human health from antibiotic resistance developing in microorganisms is one of the major public health threats that will be faced in the 21st century."

Immunosuppression. In 2000, the well-respected British medical journal *The Lancet* published an important study conducted by Drs. Arpad Pusztai and Stanley W. B. Ewen under a grant from the Scottish government. The study examined the effect on rats of the consumption of potatoes genetically engineered to contain a version of the biopesticide *Bacillus thuringiensis* (Bt). The scientists found that rats consuming genetically altered potatoes showed significant detrimental effects on organ development, body metabolism, and immune function. The biotechnology industry has launched a major attack on Dr. Pusztai and his study. However, they have as yet not produced a single peer-reviewed study of their own to refute his findings. Moreover, 22 leading scientists recently declared that animal test results linking GE foods to immunosuppression are valid.

Loss of Nutrition. Genetic engineering can also alter the nutritional value of food. The genetic instability of these foods can be a major culprit in reducing their nutrients. In 1992, the FDA examined the problem of nutrient loss in GE foods. The scientists involved specifically warned the agency that the genetic engineering of foods could result in "undesirable alteration in the level of nutrients" of such foods. They further noted that these nutritional changes "may escape breeders' attention unless genetically engineered plants are evaluated specifically for these changes." Once again, the FDA ignored findings by their own scientists and never subjected the foods to mandatory government testing of any sort.

PROTECTING THE CONSUMER'S RIGHT TO KNOW

Much of the current controversy over GE food surrounds the important issue of labeling. However, the labeling issue is actually a secondary one. Clearly, given the seriousness of the potential risks, all GE foods should be removed from the market and all seeds quarantined until long-term tests have determined that such foods are safe for human consumption. We do not label unsafe food; we take it off the supermarket shelves. Only after the foods are found safe through proper testing should they be allowed to be sold and labeled.

Not surprisingly, FDA's "no testing, no labeling" policy is opposed by the vast majority of Americans. Each day, tens of millions of American infants, children, and adults eat GE foods without their knowledge. The public clearly believes it has a right to know if food has been genetically engineered. Opinion polls consistently show that more than 90 percent of Americans strongly support the labeling of GE foods. A 1999 *Time* poll revealed that close to 60 percent would avoid such foods if they were labeled. In 1998 more than 275,000 angry consumers protested the Clinton administration's proposal that GE foods could be certified as "organic." More recently, more than a half million people wrote to the FDA to support a legal petition filed by the Center for Food Safety (on behalf of itself and numerous other organizations), which demanded mandatory labeling and testing of biotech foods.

ENVIRONMENTAL RISKS

GE foods require us to reexamine our concept of pollution. When most of us think about pollution, we envision a power plant's smoke-stacks spewing toxic fumes into the air; or automobiles choking us with their exhaust and the resulting smog; or, perhaps, a pipe from a chemical plant pouring out dangerous compounds into a river. Such chemical pollution illustrates a "contamination" model of pollution. Biotechnology creates a very different sort of pollution problem — biological pollution. This is a "disease" model of pollution, in which a living organism invades and causes unexpected havoc to the envi-ronment. Just as bacteria and viruses invade us and create illness, biological organisms can invade an ecosystem and cause massive problems. We have seen this in the past with "exotic" organisms such as the imported fungi which caused chestnut blight and Dutch elm disease. We have also been invaded by thousands of other exotics, from the highly destructive kudzu vine to the killer bees working their way up from South America. Now we are releasing hundreds of thou-sands of genetically altered "exotic" organisms into the environment, and the results could be catastrophic. Because they are alive, gene-altered crops are inherently more unpredictable than chemical pollu-tants — they can migrate and mutate. They will not dilute over time like chemical pollutants; rather they will reproduce, and the problem will only intensify. Once they have been released, it is virtually impossible to recall genetically engineered organisms back to the laboratory or the field. Thus, the rapid adoption of GE crops presents numerous irreversible ecological risks. A research report from Purdue University on fish genetically engineered with growth genes underscores the new biological pollution threat. Scientists found that the GE fish, because of their greater size, had a significant advantage in reproduction. Unfortunately, the new growth genes caused a one-third greater mortality in the offspring as compared to non-GE fish. As a result the researchers predicted that if just 60 of these GE fish were introduced into a population of 60,000 wild fish, the species would become extinct within only 40 generations. Yet, even with independent scientists warning of the dire threat genetic engineering poses to the environment, we do not have a single law in the United States that addresses this new biological pollution risk.

Increased Pesticide Residues. Besides creating bio-pollution, biotech foods also contribute to chemical pollution. "Herbicide-resistant" plants, which accounted for over 70 percent of all GE crops planted in 1998, are genetically engineered to withstand the indiscriminate use herbicides. Normally, if a farmer overuses herbicides, both weeds and the crop are killed by the application. Now, thanks to genetic engineering there can be massive herbicide use without hurting the crop. These GE crops have helped make Monsanto's Roundup the best-selling herbicide ever.

Biological Pollution. With the impending introduction of genetically engineered fish and insects being added to the use of biotech crops, biological pollution is sure to become a major environmental problem in coming years. Bio-pollution from biotech crops has already begun to wreak havoc in farmers' fields and in the larger environment. Vectors such as insect pollinators, wind, and rain are carrying genetically altered pollen into adjoining fields, polluting the crops of organic and conventional farmers. There have been numerous cases where organic and conventional farms in the United States and Canada have been contaminated with genetic drift from GE crops on a nearby farm. As a result many farmers are unintentionally growing GE crops and finding that they cannot sell their product domestically as certified organic or to foreign markets that are looking for GE-free produce. Unless halted, this biological pollution of non-GE crops by the biotech varieties could mean that future generations will have no choice but to buy and consume GE foods. Biological pollution is also affecting the soil and wildlife. In the late 1990s, Cornell University researchers found that pollen from genetically engineered Bt-corn was poisonous to the larvae of Monarch butterflies. This study, published in the journal *Nature*, and several follow-up reports add to a growing body of evidence that GE crops could adversely impact a number of beneficial insects, including ladybugs and lacewings, as well as beneficial soil microorganisms.

"Superweeds" and "Superpests." As noted, we are now growing tens of millions of acres of crops that have been genetically engineered to be herbicide resistant or to produce their own pesticide. Recent research has shown that these crops, because of the way they are genetically altered, could create unprecedented long-term environmental problems. Scientists are finding that pests and weeds are beginning to emerge that are resistant to these new GE crops, which means that stronger, more toxic chemicals will be needed to get rid of the strengthened plant pests. The emergence of the first "superweeds" has been reported as GE herbicide-resistant crops such as rapeseed (canola) spread their herbicide-resistance traits to related weeds such as wild mustard plants. Several laboratory and field tests also reveal that certain common plant pests, including cotton bollworms, living under constant pressure from GE crops, will soon evolve into "superpests" completely immune to Bt sprays and other environmentally sustainable biopesticides. This could pose a significant danger to organic and sustainable farmers whose biological pest management practices may be unable to cope with increasing numbers of superpests and superweeds.

New Plant Diseases. It should not surprise us that when biotechnologists "play God" with the genetic code of food, unanticipated and dangerous outcomes result. This has been especially true of research involving the engineering of viruses and other disease-causing agents into plants. Biotech researchers at Michigan State University have found that when they engineered a weakened virus into a plant to "vaccinate" it, the weakened virus in the plant mutated into new, more virulent forms. Other researchers have discovered that the genetically engineered version of a soil microorganism, *Klebsiella planticola*, completely destroyed essential soil nutrients.

OTHER IMPACTS

Socioeconomic Hazards. The patenting of GE foods and wide-spread biotech food production threaten to eliminate farming as it has been practiced for more than 10,000 years. Patents such as Delta & Pine Land's so-called "terminator" technology, designed to render seeds infertile, could force hundreds of millions of farmers who now save and share their seeds to purchase increasingly expensive GE seeds and chemical inputs from a handful of global biotech/seed monopolies. Already Monsanto controls 60 percent of all utility soybean patents and almost 30 percent of all utility corn patents. If the trend is not stopped, the patenting of transgenic plants and food-producing animals will soon lead to universal "bioserfdom" in which farmers will lease their plants and animals from biotech conglomerates such as Monsanto and pay royalties on seeds and offspring. Family and indigenous farmers will be driven off the land, and consumers' food choices will be dictated by a cartel of transnational corporations. Rural communities will be devastated. Hundreds of millions of farmers and agricultural workers worldwide will lose their livelihoods.

Erosion of Biodiversity. For thousands of years, farmers and plant breeders have attempted to maintain access to a wide range of plant varieties to develop healthier plant strains and meet the changing conditions of agricultural ecosystems. Now much of this diversity is being lost as companies focus plant research on a few selected genetic traits. The rapid adoption of these new, uniform GE crops represents the most radical step in industrial agriculture's trend toward monoculture. As the critics Craig Holdrege and Steve Talbott have elegantly described, first single crops replaced a diversity of crops; then a single variety replaced a diversity of varieties; and now, monocultures are being erected upon a single, genetically engineered trait.

Ethical Hazards. Traditionally, many of our food choices have been governed by principles that allow the consumer to determine whether a particular food or production system comports with his or her ethical or religious beliefs. Every one of us is probably aware of well-established dietary restrictions that flow from either religious practice or personal ethical choice. However, GE foods threaten to rob many people of their ability to abide by their personal religious or ethical beliefs. For example, ethical vegetarians and religious practitioners of certain faiths may be unknowingly consuming crops containing genetic material from animals. And all of us could soon face the disturbing ethical dilemma of genetically engineered farm animals containing human genetic material. Since current government policy does not mandate the labeling of any such GE food, people with ethical or religious concerns are stripped of their capacity to avoid such foods and adhere to their personal beliefs.

CONCLUSION

If only a few years ago some pundit had predicted a world where the pollen of corn plants could poison caterpillars, where taco shells would carry a genetically engineered allergen, where our popcorn was a registered pesticide, where the crops of the world were being genetically programmed to commit "suicide" after one growing season, where farmers by the hundreds were being sued by Monsanto and other corporations because they violated patents on crops, where we purposely created plants that could withstand countless applications of pesticides — we would have thought it bad science fiction. Yet all these scenarios have become science fact.

Clearly, decisions about the path of our food system are at a critical juncture. While GE foods may be an advance for laboratory science, they do not represent "progress" for the farmer or consumer. The GE food future will grant the purveyors of chemical companies greater control over our food supply at the expense of our farm communities, our environment, and even our free exercise of ethical and religious beliefs. Only by initiating a complete moratorium on the production and sale of genetically engineered foods can we hope to forestall the unprecedented risks presented by these foods.

NUCLEAR LUNCH

The Dangers and Unknowns of Food Irradiation

MICHAEL COLBY

SOON MORE THAN 90 PERCENT *of the average American's diet could be eligible for irradiation. But government approval of this technology has been based on heavy industry pressure and bad science. As a result, the consumer has been made a guinea pig, testing these foods and facing potential health risks. Meanwhile leaks from irradiation facilities pose significant risks to public health and to the environment.*

▼

The corporate purveyors and beneficiaries of an increasingly contaminated world food supply are not only destroying indigenous and sustainable forms of agriculture, but are also propagating a destructive myth that agricultural problems largely created by issues of scale and an addiction to toxic technologies can be solved by more of the same. And perhaps nowhere is this phenomenon more obvious than in the new push to promote and implement the nuclear food irradiation technology as a so-called solution to a contaminated industrial food supply. Instead of addressing the known industrial causes of food contamination, irradiation proponents are, in effect, proposing to bathe the food supply in radiation as an alternative to preventing the contamination in the first place.

Beginning in 1986, the U.S. Food and Drug Administration (FDA) gave a series of green lights that have led to the possibility that the vast majority of our food supply will be exposed to nuclear irradiation. The agency has made separate decisions legalizing the use of irradiation for fruit, vegetables, and spices (in 1986); poultry (in 1990); beef, pork, lamb, and horse (in 1997); and fresh shell eggs (in 2000). The FDA is currently considering expanding the use of irradiation to shellfish, unrefrigerated meat, and alfalfa and other sprouting seed. If these are approved it will mean that 90 percent of the average American's diet will be eligible for irradiation.

Staunch citizen opposition is still keeping the technology out of widespread use. However, events such as the *E. coli*–contaminated hamburger recalls and incidences of contamination in imported fruits and vegetables have breathed new life into the struggling industry, as government regulators and corporate food interests aggressively promote food irradiation. As a result, the meat industry in certain locations is using the technology. Today, somewhere in the United States someone is biting into a hamburger that has been irradiated with the equivalent of 150 million chest X rays (perhaps garnished with a spice that has been "treated" with the equivalent of one billion chest X rays). Despite the hype, it is clear that irradiation does not in fact deal with the real and preventable causes of industrial food contaminants such as inhumane factory farming practices, corporate food monopolies with a single-minded fixation on profit, dramatic cutbacks in federal food safety inspectors, dangerous processing and slaughtering facilities, and a citizenry increasingly disconnected from local, sustainable food sources.

Food irradiation was the brainchild of the U.S. Atomic Energy Commission (AEC), now the Department of Energy (DOE), when, in the early 1950s, it became apparent that nuclear waste from military weapons production was (as it still is) a major problem. As a result, President Dwight Eisenhower initiated the AEC's "Atoms for Peace" program designed to create "peaceful uses" for nuclear technologies and nuclear waste products such as cesium-137, one of the most abundant isotopes in the waste from nuclear weapons production. And the DOE has never been shy about articulating its desire to create a commercial need for its cesium-137 waste through the promotion of food irradiation. Consider this 1983 congressional testimony from the DOE's Office of Defense Waste and Byproducts Management:

> The strategy being pursued by DOE's Byproducts Utilization Program is designed to transfer federally developed cesium-137 irradiation technology to the commercial sector as rapidly and successfully as possible. The measure of success will be

the degree to which this technology is implemented industrially and the subsequent demand created for cesium-137.

In addition to cesium-137, other methods of food irradiation include the use of radioactive cobalt-60 and high-energy electron beams, also known as linear accelerators. On average, when food is irradiated commercially, the food receives a radiation dose equivalent to tens of millions of chest X rays, more than enough to break up the molecular structure of the food, destroy essential vitamins and minerals, and create a host of new chemical substances known as radiolytic products. Some of these, such as benzene and formaldehyde, are harmful to human health. Benzene, for example, is a known carcinogen. Other radiolytic products, identified as "unique radiolytic products," are completely new chemicals that have not even been identified, let alone tested for toxicity.

In 1982, the FDA reviewed 441 toxicity studies to determine the safety of irradiated foods. Dr. Marcia van Gemert, the chairperson of the committee in charge of investigating the studies, has testified that all 441 studies were flawed. But in 1986, the FDA, led by political appointees, approved a number of food irradiation applications by declaring that five of the 441 studies were "properly conducted, fully adequate by 1980 toxicology standards, and able to stand alone in the support of safety." Thus, with the shaky assurances of just five studies, the FDA approved irradiation for the public food supply.

To make matters worse, the Department of Preventive Medicine and Community Health of the New Jersey Medical School has found two of those five studies to be methodologically flawed. In a third study, animals eating a diet of irradiated food experienced weight loss and miscarriage, almost certainly due to irradiation-induced vitamin E dietary deficiency. The remaining two studies investigated the effects of diets of foods irradiated at doses below the FDA-approved levels.

Irradiation facilities also pose serious worker-safety, public-health, and ecological threats due to potential radiation leaks, equipment failure, and the production, transportation, storage, installation, and replacement of radiation sources. The U.S. Nuclear Regulatory Commission (NRC) and its state equivalents have recorded dozens of cases of nuclear mishaps, accidents, and administrative negligence at the relatively few irradiation facilities that currently exist in the United States today. To irradiate the food supply on a mass scale, hundreds of irradiation facilities would need to be built, thus dramatically increasing the likelihood of accidents.

In 1988, in what has been called the "Three Mile Island of irradiation," Radiation Sterilizers, Inc. (RSI), in Decatur, Georgia, reported a leak of its cesium-137 capsules into the water storage pool, endangering workers and contaminating the facility. Workers then carried the radioactivity into their homes and cars. Cleanup costs exceeded $45 million and taxpayers footed the bill.

In 1986, the NRC revoked the license of a Radiation Technology, Inc. (RTI) facility in New Jersey for having 32 worker-safety violations, including throwing radioactive garbage out with the regular trash and bypassing a key safety device. As a result of this negligence, RTI's founder and chairman, Martin Welt, was eventually indicted and convicted on felony counts of misleading the NRC and filing false nuclear safety reports.

As a result of the numerous health and ecological threats, coupled with spirited grassroots initiatives, the irradiation industry has faced an uphill battle in its efforts to convince the public to embrace its risky technology. But the once emaciated industry is now being resuscitated by a wave of new government- and corporate-sponsored public relations initiatives that are seeking to "train" the public about the supposed benefits of food irradiation. In addition to the steady stream of dubious claims of safety and simplicity, irradiation proponents are working hard to confuse the public by lobbying Congress and petitioning the FDA to change the labeling of irradiated foods. Current regulations require that irradiated foods bear the label "Treated by Irradiation." Under pressure from the industry and Congress, FDA is considering changing the labeling to a misleading, and therefore less alarming, term for the technology, such as "cold pasteurization."

While such underhanded public relations stunts may make it more difficult for the public to recognize and avoid irradiated foods in the marketplace, one poll after another still indicates that citizens remain extremely distrustful of food irradiation. Putting an end to the irradiation madness will require a continued and tenacious grassroots presence that galvanizes citizen opposition to the technology and seeks to hold wholesale and retail food corporations accountable. But the ultimate nail in the food irradiation coffin will come as a result of a citizenry and culture that turns its back on industrial food and the false and dangerous technological gimmicks, like food irradiation, that continuously prop it up.

Ecological Impacts

▼   ▼   ▼

Even as industrial food technologies are fatal to farmers and farm communities, they also devastate the natural world. Agribusiness practices are among the leading culprits in our current environmental crisis. As the essays in this section describe, industrial agriculture's effects on biodiversity and wildlife are especially profound and tragic.

TILTH AND TECHNOLOGY

The Industrial Redesign of Our Nation's Soils

PETER WARSHALL

SOIL, TO MOST CONTEMPORARY FARMERS, *is simply a utilitarian medium in which to grow profitable crops. Any manipulation of soil that increases its yield at lower costs is good. Petrochemical fertilizers and pesticides, heavy industrial farming equipment for plowing, massive waterworks for irrigation and drainage have become tools for greater profits on larger-sized farms. But they have threatened the sustainability of fertile soils by accelerating erosion, increasing salinization, leaching excess nutrients and toxics into rivers, and reducing the biodiversity of soil microbes, flora, and fauna. Many farmers and soil scientists are rejecting the ag-industrial paradigm and embracing a more holistic understanding of soil as irreplaceable, multigenerational natural capital.*

▼

The ancient Chinese called earth the mother of all things. "She" was a never depleted mammary gland, embedded in the land. Crops suckled her milk and, as they thrived, so did families. Simultaneously, she was a never exhausted womb. Plant a seed, pray for fine weather, and she gave birth to the sustenance of life. To harm the earth was to insult one's ultimate mother.

Agricultural scientists, uncomfortable with these metaphors, have teased "earth" apart. Earths or soils comprise:

- a curious mix of organic matter and mineral granules (clay, silt, and sand)
- a bustling and highly interactive community of organisms, especially microbes
- a unique, complex matrix of pores and channels filled with air, nutrient soup, and aquatic life.

Within the grand variety of earths, amoebas slide over grains of sand, hunting bacteria; bacteria swim through microrivers in search of nutrients; viruses puncture the bodies of bacteria and borrow their DNA; nematodes (a near-visible threadworm) hunt and graze in teeming microforests of algae, devouring like hyenas almost anything that lives.

Just as astronomers boggle the human imagination with cosmic numbers, soil ecologists have amazed us with down-in-the-earth population surveys. One teaspoon of rich grassland soil can contain 5 billion bacteria, 20 million fungi, and 1 million protists. More microbes live in a teaspoon of earth than people on the planet.

In one square meter, the top few centimeters of topsoil might contain galactic numbers of the above microbes, but also 1,000 each of ants, spiders, wood lice, beetles and their larvae, and fly larvae; 2,000 each of earthworms and large myriapods (millipedes and centipedes); 8,000 slugs and snails; 20,000 pot worms; 40,000 springtails, 120,000 mites, and 12 million nematodes.

Soil is literally alive with a networked complexity greater than that of human brain tissue. Besides growing food, soil's powers include influencing greenhouse gases in the atmosphere, the creation of more soil from bedrock, and the purification of all the freshwater on and in the planet's surface. If anything, the mother of all things has achieved an enhanced status. "Her" planetary tissue is the heart of the biosphere, lithosphere, atmosphere, and hydrosphere of the planet.

Over the millennia farmers and consumers have lost, forgotten, suppressed, or changed their feelings for earth. They have definitely abandoned ancient rituals such as the Asian and European festivals in which making love on early spring fields encouraged the generation of crops. Questions like "What soil grew the food on your dinner plate?" or "How friable is the earth that yielded these sliced tomatoes or crescents of cantaloupe?" have become almost absurd. We thank the Lord for our daily meal, whose ingredients arrive from mysterious places, as if the veggies were babies transported home in diapers in the beaks of storks.

Before reaching the table, most American food moves over 1,300 miles from the farm soils it grew in. And most American farm soils now contain seeds, and mineral and petrochemical additives harvested hundreds to thousands of miles from the farm.

Soil, to most contemporary farmers, is simply a utilitarian medium in which to grow profitable crops — a substrate that can be improved upon and reengineered. Soil is a financially calculated asset in the larger economic strategy of collateral, loans, subsidies, price supports, investments for maximum returns, and government payments. Any manipulation of soil that increases its yield at lower costs is good. And soil is political. Dangling the dollar, Congress decides which soils should be rested or tilled, abandoned or restored.

THE REDESIGN OF VIRGIN SOILS

After hundreds to thousands of years of sorting silt, clay, and sand granules; of balancing chemistry, water, and life forms, a soil gains a local personality. The soil profile evolves into a layer cake with special textures and structures adapted to the local climate, hillslope, or river terrace. These naturally created soils, called virgin soils, remained essentially intact until the plow. Today, of the 20,000 soil types in the United States, fewer than 1,000 examples remain virginal.

In 1837, John Deere began to sell his all steel, nonsticking, unstoppable moldboard plows. They required oxen or horses to move them across the fields. By the mid-1800s, numerous British inventors applied steam engine technology to harvesters and then plowing. Early steam engines, the size of locomotives and powered by wood, coal, and straw, sat immobile on the edge of a field; they pulled a plow across the farm by pulleys attached to poles set on the opposite fenceline. In the United States, in the Dakotas and California, some farmers tried mobile locomotive/tractors that pulled plows. The tractors weighed up to 14 tons and spurted flying sparks that set the field aflame. They were quickly abandoned.

As internal combustion engines shrank in size and engine weight decreased with distillate, gasoline, diesel, and liquid gas fuels, specialized, steam-engine-traction machines (today's "tractors") could pull plows on a truck-like chassis. By the 1930s, over a million tractors crossed American farm fields. With Henry Ford's invention of a better rear hitch, tractors, with very few exceptions, replaced horses and oxen. Farmers could pull a variety of earth-moving equipment — plows, disks, drag levelers, scrapers, seed planters, and harrows.

All this new machinery accelerated the demise of American virgin soils. From 1870 to 1900, a period of plummeting farm prices and dreams of increased exports, farmers tilled more and more land just to stay in the same financial place. During this 30-year period, farmers sod-busted an area of virgin soils equal to the total tilled since the 1600s.

Even virgin soils that had been off limits because of their cantan-kerous personalities felt the impact of the new machinery and capital. Dredges, draglines, hydraulic revolving hoes, ditch diggers, and pump excavators "reclaimed" wetland soils at ever-increasing rates. Caterpillar dozers filled swamps and bogs, and blocked river terraces from flooding by building dikes, levees, and walls. Backhoes dug trenches to control water tables and to remove saline water. Rippers cut into hardpans that stopped root penetration. Dozers, scrapers, and levelers helped terrace formerly unplantable hillslopes, leveled hump-and-hollow prairie landscapes, and, in arid watersheds, increased the capture of runoff with contoured berms. As agricultural machinery grew in complexity and cost, farmers became deeply involved in credit and needed to till still more contiguous land to pay off debts.

Some futuristic industrial agriculturalists see a planet that grows its food without any soil. They dream of a soilless agriculture in which dirt has been replaced by rock wool, fiberglass, and styrofoam "soils." Other techno-farmers have begun to design greenhouses which simply spray crop roots with appropriate petrochemically derived fertilizers. Specialty crops like hydroponic tomatoes have become cost-effective for some off-season markets. But the ability to supply basics — rice, soy, wheat, and corn — through soilless agriculture remains a fantasy.

THE REDESIGN OF SOIL WATER

Soils can be too wet or too dry for too long to maximize yields. In humid watersheds, soils can become hyperwet and flooded. In arid watersheds, dry soils demand irrigation, but the irrigated fields may not drain well and the soils become waterlogged; eventually salts build up. Thus, agricultural engineers have long sought to control the amount and timing of soil water and to prevent salinization.

Like the soil profile, the soil's capacity to hold water fell to mechanization's powers. Pumps and aqueducts altered the life and biochemistry of millions of acres of farmland. At first, the steel wind-mill drew down shallow water tables for supplemental and crisis irri-gation. By the 1930s, with rural electrification and improved diesel engines, windmills lost favor. More powerful pumps and new drilling equipment opened access to formerly unreachable aquifers. After World War II, farmers irrigated huge dryland ecosystems that had not experienced long and extensive soil wetness (e.g., the Great Plains Ogallala region). In parts of the west, so much water was pumped out that the soils compacted and then cracked. Some of these cracks are big enough to swallow pickups and can be seen from satellites.

Along with pumps, the invention of special cements, rebar, large construction equipment, and other techniques encouraged massive waterworks. Surface water from dammed rivers now travels for hun-dreds of miles by aqueducts to irrigate hundreds of thousands of acres of arid and desert soils west of the Rocky Mountains. From Denver to Tijuana and from the Oregon border to Tucson, the world's largest hydraulic civilization pumps and shunts the Colorado and the rivers of California for the sake of increased soil moisture and monocrops.

Irrigation has accelerated the threat of salting up soils. It took over 2,500 years for the Tigris-Euphrates societies to ruin their soils with salt. Modern U.S. agriculture — irrigating with salty waters, adding salty fertilizers, cultivating salty soils, forcing the water table into the root zone by irrigation, and letting canals leak — has degraded arid land soils in 50 years or less. Some 55–60 million acres (about 10 percent of all U.S. cropped land) have been degraded by salinization. Thousands of acres have been removed from cultivation, and tens of thousands need to be overirrigated to leach the salts to drains below the root zone. In the San Luis districts of California, some of these drains are seven feet below the surface. The leached water must then be carried to a river or internal basin. Where to "dispose" of the brine has not been resolved in either California or Arizona. Pollution of wells and rivers and the poisoning of wildlife are common.

Too much water, rather than too little, has plagued farmers in the eastern United States and Mississippi Delta region. One hundred and ten million acres of wetlands have been drained for agricultural crops. Many of these drainage works devastated wetland wildlife, and only recently have attempts been made to slow down the conversion of wetlands to farmed lands and restore some previously farmed soils.

The U.S. industrialization of drainage began in the 1800s with hand-dug ditches and clay-tile drains. After World War II, large equipment excavated muck and buried plastic pipes with 24-hour drainage. This process also included yield monitors, wet-patch rehabilitation schemes, and precision farming.

These drainage works had harmful side effects. Applied fertilizers can seep into the drainage networks used to manage soil water. The tail waters (waters released by the drainage network into a river) can harm downstream peoples. Forty percent of Minnesota River basin farm soils, for instance, are overwet for desired crops. Drainage fast-tracks unused fertilizer into the river. The fertilizer eventually settles out in the Mississippi Delta where it hyperstimulates the growth of plant and microbial life. The fast-growing plants consume the delta's oxygen and asphyxiate local fish and shellfish. In short, upstream drainage creates a downstream dead zone about the size of Connecticut at the Mississippi's mouth. Despite protests from downstream fisherpeople, various techno-fixes (e.g., "conservation tilling," constructed wetlands, wider tile spacing) have been largely ineffective.

THE LOSS OF SOIL

At the heart of farming is a complex quandary: you must cut into the earth to increase its productivity but, at the same time, prevent the cut soil from washing or blowing away. For millennia farmers have plowed to loosen the soil for seeding, to increase rain infiltration, to solarize disease pathogens, to stir up nutrients from below the root zone, and to reduce competing weeds. They have also allowed the soil to erode. Plowing has been the necessary wound.

Our plow-begotten farmlands repeat this story — the human inability to balance the cutting and the conserving of soil. The humid Midwestern grainbelt is the major region of runoff erosion from bare earth ("fallow"). In the arid Great Plains and western states, cropping and livestock produce high rates of soil loss from wind erosion. The sodbusters of North America allowed one-third of our topsoil to wash downstream or downhill. Great Plains soil productivity fell 71 percent during the first 28 years of sodbusting. And since 1950, about one-third of American cropped land has had to be abandoned because of erosion problems.

Every farmer knows that soil erosion is self-destructive. Lose topsoil, and the soil loses its capacity to retain moisture; in turn, the soil becomes more sensitive to droughts. Lose organic matter and natural or synthetic soil nutrients, and production costs go up as yields go down. Lose the topsoil, and the subsoil becomes the surface soil. Most subsoils have less organic material, too much clay, and reduced phosphorus, and limit root extension as the depth to bedrock decreases. Erode uphill soil, and it may wash to the lowest part of fields, burying seedlings and seedbeds. As if this were not enough, the eroded fields — part rilled, part gullied, part buried in sediment — are harder to cultivate and fertilize.

David Pimentel and his collaborators estimate the harmful impacts of eroded soil (called sediment once it is displaced) will cost downhill and downstream users $7.4 billion to correct. For instance, dredging sediment from waterways costs about $520 million, and repairing damage to recreational facilities might cost $2 billion. Even if this is an overestimate, the costs to taxpayers are far from trivial.

It took the Dust Bowl in the 1930s to force the U.S. government to recognize that intact soils are a long-term public benefit. Congress now taxes all citizens to subsidize soil conservation measures such as strip-cropping, contour plowing, set-asides of more fragile soils, and grassed waterways. The Food Security Act of 1985 launched a strategy to prevent erosion by cutting government subsidies that promoted cultivation of fragile lands. Erosion of cropland has fallen 40 percent since then. Nevertheless, even today, after many conservation efforts, American farmland still loses topsoil faster (averaging about 17 times faster) than it is formed. Of the 375 million acres in crops, 112 (about 30 percent) have excessive soil loss. Since the measurement of erosion does not include gully losses, total soil losses could be twice that of topsoil alone.

Soil erosion varies perversely with the price of corn/soy, wheat, and cotton. Higher prices stimulate the hope of greater incomes, and farmers cultivate more marginal land. Higher prices have meant more erosion, not less. In addition, financial capital works as much to destroy the natural capital values of soil as to conserve them. Farmers, for instance, still receive greater government payments for growing high-erosion monocrops. They have been penalized financially for good soil-retaining practices such as rotating diverse crops and shortening the time that bare soils remain exposed to weather.

Ironically, some farmers now replace the wounding plow by herbiciding weeds. In "no till" systems, the weeds are poisoned — with claims of no erosion. All farmers face a difficult trade-off: herbicides or sediment.

Land programs to essentially pay farmers to remove their most vulnerable lands from plowing and allow fallow cycles have been sporadic (1956–72 and again from 1986, but winding down). In 1937, the government spent $460 million on erosion management. In today's dollars that equals about $5.3 billion. Total programs concerned with soil conservation now equal less than half the adjusted 1937 allocation ($2.1 billion). Conversion to no-till and minimum tillage cultivation has also plateaued at about 40 percent of the nation's farmland. Erosion control practices have diminished.

THE PETROCHEMICAL ECOSYSTEM: FERTILIZERS AND PESTICIDES

Fertilizers. Natural fertilizer (especially nitrogen) comes from the excreta of soil fauna such as nematodes and protozoa, fixation by free-living and plant nodule bacteria, the biochemical weathering of bedrock, rainfall, and the decaying bodies of all the soil's flora and fauna. Agriculture removes these nutrients by harvesting, accelerated erosion, leaching, and accelerated microbial metabolism from plowing.

To keep a soil productive, farmers have added what they could, given transport costs and knowledge. Native Americans, with no livestock, added fish. Euro-American farmers added livestock manure and bonemeal into their soils, and rotated green manure crops like alfalfa and clover with market crops. About 150 years ago, farmers began to replace some of these organic inputs with inorganic mineral salts. In 1847, Justus von Liebig discovered that nutrients removed from the earth by crops could be replaced by minerals in specific rock formations. With increasingly sophisticated machinery and exploration, potassium, phosphorus, and other mineral supplements have been extracted, processed, and shipped by railroad to the farm, especially from Canadian and Floridian mines. The imported minerals altered the metabolic personalities of local soils. Soils, especially in the Midwest, began to converge toward a homogeneous commodity medium.

After World War II, synthetic fertilizers became a necessity for crop production, and many soils can be considered addicted to them: they must receive high inputs or they cannot sustain crops. In 1946–47, for example, the United States manufactured about 800,000 tons of synthetic fertilizers. In 1947–48, the amount leaped to 17 million tons and kept on rising in subsequent years. These chemical fertilizers boosted yields beyond any farmer's expectations.

But all was not gold with synthetic fertilizers. As quick stimulants, synthetic fertilizers encourage the loss of organic matter and hurt a soil's buffering powers, including resistance to soilborne disease. Some fertilizers increase soil acidity and most leach quickly, stimulating downstream pollution. Synthetic fertilizers, in fact, are not very efficient. Only about 50 percent of any chemical fertilizer actually contributes to crop growth. Microbes and weeds absorb the other half; or the fertilizer washes and volatizes off the field. In 1997, 72 percent of our waterways were affected by agricultural pollution, mostly fertilizers.

Pesticides and Fungicides. In the last half of the 19th century, arsenic and other soil fumigants began to receive serious attention. By the 1950s, many farmers started their yearly work with heavy soil fumigation. (High-value crops received more expensive granular biocides.) The 1960s sported a vibrant agrochemical optimism. Farmers directly injected or fumigated pesticides into the soil to reduce root fungus, larval, and nematode diseases. There was mirex for fire ants and pineapples; DBCP for soil nematodes; the organophosphate Diazinon™ for sod farms and golf course soil pathogens such as cutworms, wireworms, and maggots; and carbamate pesticides to fight nematodes in sandy soils with high water tables in Wisconsin, Long Island, and Florida. At the height of agrochemical pesticide enthusiasm, organochlorines were especially popular. Aldrin and dieldrin specialized as preemergence soil insecticides for corn and the control of ants and termites. The menu also included chlordane, the halocarbon fumigant EDB, and strychnine.

Pesticides held such power that American farmers reduced or eliminated crop rotations, which, in turn, encouraged the expansion of soil pathogens. As the industry sang pesticide praise, the soil microbes exchanged genes, and each generation showed increased resistance to the applied pesticide. The more monocropping with soil fumigants, for instance, the stronger the nematode resistance to chemical attack.

By the 1980s, pesticide paeans had quieted. The Environmental Protection Agency (EPA) began canceling or severely restricting the use of many soil-injected pesticides because of their cancer-causing, resistance-enhancing, and wildlife-damaging properties. Integrated pest management (IPM) promoted crop rotations, organic composts and compost teas, and natural biological control agents. IPM — with its aim of building a soil with microbial inhabitants that outcompeted or effectively attacked soil pathogens — proclaimed itself the alternative to soil fumigation.

But soil-root ecology has proved a great mystery, and early detection of soil pathogens has not yet been perfected. IPM is still learning how to combine economics and soil health to prevent nematode and fungus attacks. And in the 1990s, biotechnology and soil solarization with plastic sheets entered the farm field and tried to co-opt IPM; biotechnology attempts to replace natural biological control organisms with engineered organisms.

Though herbicides and foliar insecticides seldom reach the soil in harmful concentrations, they can work through the plant itself to the root where they inhibit the release of protective root exudates and nitrogen-forming nodules; or they can kill helpful microbes. On the other hand, pesticides directly injected into the soil or fumigated clearly diminish the diversity and complexity of soil communities. One microbe, for instance, may ingest a pesticide but may be unable to transform it. It excretes the pesticide, and another microbe tries. When successful, microbes transform contaminants by breaking off carbon dioxide groups. The new molecule is usually more soluble in water, which increases the opportunities for other microbes. One hopes this all occurs fast, for some "breakdown" or transient molecules are more toxic than the original.

At present, methyl bromide is probably the most dangerous soil pesticide to human health. It is scheduled to be banned in 2002. An international agreement on persistent organic pollutants, including pesticides for fungal and nematode root diseases, has been signed. It awaits U.S. Senate approval and the president's signature. While foliar pesticide and herbicide application increases, toxic soil biocides may have seen their day.

PETROLEUM REMAINS AG-INDUSTRIAL KING

In summary, since World War II, petroleum has been seated firmly on the throne of modern agriculture. It powers earth-moving machinery and groundwater pumps. It is a stock for fertilizer, pesticides, plastics, and seed varnishes. It is the major energy source for fertilizer factories and ag-industrial transport. Petrochemical herbicides and pesticides move by barge, train, and trucks to be sprayed, fertigated (mixed with irrigation water), and fumigated onto and into the soil.

Petrochemical-derived products, especially plastic pipes and seed varnishes, have thoroughly entangled industrial processes with every aspect of soil management. Clay-tile pipes have lost out to giant reels of plastic drainage and irrigation pipe and drip system lines. In 1976, U.S. farmers, for the first time, spread transparent polyethylene sheets across fields to raise soil temperatures, reduce soil evaporation, and kill off soil pathogens. Polyvinyl and now black ethylene sheeting are currently in vogue. Companies have developed a sprayable biodegradable plastic soil covering which they hope to market. In addition, some seeds are now coated with special bacteria, as well as limestone and phosphate powders, to improve sprouting. The seed coatings can be a water-soluble adhesive such as polyvinyl acetate, polyurethane, or polyurea. Similarly, some fertilizer granules have been varnished with plastics to slow the release of nutrient.

As the 21st century begins, infotech agriculture vies to share the throne with petrochemical-based farming. Infotech equipment hopes to increase ag-industrial efficiencies, and biotechnology hopes to add or subtract genetic information to optimize crop yields. Though not fully proven, "precision agriculture" is a budding example. Mounted on the cab of the tractor, a differential navigation receiver can determine field location from satellites and feed farm field coordinates to an onboard computer that has stored information on the farm's soils and slopes. The computer directs equipment to appropriately dose agrochemicals at each field coordinate. "Precision agriculture" is but one of many infotech inventions. Others include laser-leveling of soils to improve irrigation and tillage efficiency, time domain reflectometry (TDR) to determine soil moisture, infrared spectral leaf reading to reveal soil deficiencies, and DNA probes to identify soil pests.

Soil biotechnology — the manipulation of soil organisms and their metabolic processes to optimize crop productivity — engenders extravagant hopes as well as fears of ecological catastrophe. Biotech agronomists dream of corn plants with root nodules that produce nitrogen and eliminate the need for added fertilizers; of inoculating soils with bioengineered microbes that will target root pathogens; and of bioengineered soil bacteria that will transform harmful pesticides into innocuous molecules or inhibit nitrates from leaching into streams. The impact of bioengineered crops on soil ecology is hardly known. Studies of what happens to biotech pollen that falls onto soil or root exudates from bioengineered plants have just begun. Given the complexity of soils and the ability of microbes to disperse explosively, the need to go slow cannot be overemphasized.

SOILED HISTORY AND ORGANIC IDEALS

The struggle between a highly mechanized, high-input, and highly networked agricultural marketing system and a highly diverse, high-humus, and bioregionally adapted agriculture intensified after the industrial revolution. From the 1920s to the early 1950s, jeremiads and political tracts called industrial agriculture's attitude toward soil arrogant, exploitive, ruinous, greedy, short-sighted, and speculative. Critics pointed the finger at misguided scientists, corporate profiteers, farm organizations, and congressmen. They warned of the end of civilization. Hugh Bennett, a father of U.S. soil conservation, told the public that with erosion, it was "not just the land which goes. The people, the cities and towns, and the civilizations decay with the land. That's history."

The tone has calmed since U.S. farming and society did not collapse in the following decades. But the "permanent agriculture" movement of the 1930s has resurged again and again, as biodynamic agriculture, permaculture, organic agriculture, sustainable agriculture, and alternative agriculture. These movements have made sure the public learns that high-input agriculture remains a mixed blessing, and they have carried the morality of earth as expressed in early Chinese thought. To permanent farming, agrochemical soil inputs and highly mechanized earth-works keep channeling farming toward practices that wound both land and people — increasing erosion, soil deformation, toxic chemical pollution, human health problems, poor quality food, and soil salinity.

In the 21st century, the ag-tech and permanent agriculture views of soil will continue their contentious debate. "Permanent" agriculture will find ways for the soil of one generation to be as rich as the soil of the previous. Those involved in industrial agriculture will continue to see soil as simply a medium for engineering maximum yields and profit and pursue techno-fixes toward these ends.

For both permanent farming and more conventional farming, global warming is the wildcard. Soil microbes produce 85 percent of the atmosphere's greenhouse gases. Soil conservation could reduce the production of U.S. greenhouse gases by 16 to 42 percent, depending on the estimate. There may be new emphasis on government technical assistance and payments to further reduce plowing and soil out-gassing. Organic farming has not yet resolved how much and what kind of plowing is appropriate.

Both permanent and high-tech agriculture must also deal with the globalization of basic crops (soy, corn, cotton seed, rice, and wheat) and more specialized ones like sugarcane, grapes, and oranges. Tens of thousands of local farm soil types and global economic and trade agreements have merged. Those concerned with soil health must think and act both locally and globally simultaneously.

In my view, the ideal farm produces excellent foods, keeps its soils in place, eliminates health harms to field hands and downstream citizens and wildlife, and encourages future fertility. The ideal government and market give earth great value as multigenerational natural capital; and give durable, sustaining soils priority over financial gain. Over the past 150 years, the more maternal interest in soil's long-term fertility has been transmogrified into an attitude dominated by concerns for short-term cash turnover and maximum tilled acreage. But, as long as one can picture the ideal farm, ideal market, and ideal government in practical detail, a future with permanent farms and rich soils is much more than a quixotic dream.

WATER

The Overtapped Resource

MARK BRISCOE

FRESHWATER IS ARGUABLY OUR MOST PRECIOUS *and our most squandered natural resource. Nearly 40 percent of the world's food supply is produced using highly wasteful irrigation systems that are depleting nonrenewable groundwater, sterilizing the soil, and carrying carcinogens and other toxins into our drinking water. A quick glance at history reveals that civilizations dependent upon unsustainable irrigation practices, as is ours today, are ultimately doomed. If we are to save ourselves, it is vital that we choose sustainable means of food production and alternative water management strategies.*

▼

Water, a simple compound of one oxygen atom and two hydrogen atoms, is fundamental to all life. Indeed, water and life are so intricately associated that we can scarcely conceive of a situation where the latter might arise without the former. The human body is 60 percent water, and water is essential to all of the body's physical processes, from the conduction of electrical nerve impulses to the maintenance of a steady body temperature. People can survive extended periods, up to several weeks, without eating food. But a person who fails to replenish water used by the body and lost to evaporation will die within a matter of days. Water, of course, plays similarly crucial roles in the life of plants and is therefore also integral to food production.

It is not surprising that water has been a determining factor in the development and history of human civilization and agriculture. The earliest agricultural societies were clustered in regions where rainfall was sufficient to produce adequate crops to feed their populations. Around the year 4000 B.C.E. all this changed, when members of an established farming society migrated into the Mesopotamian plain between the Tigris and Euphrates Rivers. There long, dry summers often ruined their crops before harvest time. Rather than move on to an area with a more hospitable climate, these farmers, known to us as the Sumerians, devised a means of diverting water from the Euphrates River to their fields — thereby developing the world's first irrigation system.

Irrigation greatly increased crop yields, and before long the Sumerians were producing food surpluses. This allowed some members of the society to devote themselves to pursuits other than subsistence agriculture. Archeological evidence indicates that the Sumerians became the first people to develop the wheel, the sailboat, and yokes that allowed them to plow their fields with the assistance of domesticated livestock. On top of these achievements, the Sumerians were the first civilization to employ writing.

A number of other irrigation-based societies arose in the centuries after the Sumerians — in Pakistan's Indus River valley, in China's Yellow River basin, and eventually in several different parts of North and South America, to name but a few. Almost all of these civilizations have two things in common. First, they rose to great heights of cultural and agricultural achievement. Second, with a single exception, they ultimately failed. History demonstrates that irrigation places great strain on the environment by depleting natural water sources and reducing the quality of the land. And, says director of the Global Water Policy Project Sandra Postel, "The inherent environmental instability of irrigated agriculture can weaken seemingly advanced cultures, rendering them less able to cope with political and social disturbances."

Today, approximately 40 percent of the world's food production comes from irrigated land. In the United States, some 21.4 million hectares of farmland — about 11 percent of all the land in production — is irrigated. In parts of the American West, the percentage is much higher.

Given the dismal success rate of earlier irrigation-dependent societies, the sustainability of the developed world's current irrigation dependency is uncertain. "Westerners call what they have established out here a civilization, but it would be more accurate to call it a beachhead," writes Marc Reisner in his classic work, *Cadillac Desert: The American West and Its Disappearing Water.* "And if history is any guide, the odds that we can sustain it would have to be regarded as low. Only one desert civilization, one out of dozens that grew up in antiquity, has survived uninterrupted into modern times. And Egypt's approach to irrigation was fundamentally different from all the rest."

Indeed, from antiquity until recent decades, irrigation in the Nile River valley centered on the river's natural flood cycle, which allowed farmers to irrigate without depleting water resources. Of equal significance, the Nile floods replenished the soil by washing fertile silt from the Ethiopian highlands down onto the valley's croplands. Only recently has the sustainability of Egypt's irrigation practices come into question. "For thousands of years Egyptian farmers irrigated by simple diversions from the Nile and nothing went badly wrong," explains Reisner; "then Egypt built the Aswan High Dam and got waterlogged land, salinity, schistosomiasis, nutrient-starved fields, a dying Mediterranean fishery, and a bill for all of the above that will easily eclipse the value of the irrigation 'miracle' wrought by the dam."

WATER SCARCITY

The most immediate and obvious problem associated with unnatural irrigation-based farming is that it requires a steady source of water but does nothing to replenish this source. In many places, depletion of underground aquifers, primarily from irrigation, far exceeds the natural rate of renewal. Thus, underground water reserves are shrinking. In the United States, this problem has become particularly acute in California and other agricultural sections of the West. "California is overdrafting groundwater at a rate of 1.6 billion cubic meters (bcm) a year, equal to 15 percent of the state's annual groundwater use," says Postel. Well over half of the state's use is in the highly productive agricultural region of the Central Valley, which is the origin of about half of the fruits and vegetables grown in the United States.

Even greater depletion is occurring in the massive Ogallala aquifer, which stretches from the Great Plains to the Southwest and underlies portions of eight states. This single groundwater formation, says Postel, contains more water than would flow through the

Colorado River in two centuries, and provides more than 20 percent of all the water used by U.S. irrigation projects. The depletion rate for the Ogallala is about 12 bcm per year. In the decades since massive irrigation projects drawing on the Ogallala began in Nebraska, Kansas, Colorado, Oklahoma, Texas, and New Mexico, the United States' largest groundwater reserve has lost over 325 bcm of water that has not been replenished by nature. This staggering total equals the amount of water that would flow through the Colorado River over the course of 18 years.

Groundwater depletion is not merely an American problem. In addition to the United States, countries and regions accumulating severe groundwater deficits include India, China, North Africa, and Saudi Arabia. Worldwide, the annual depletion of aquifers, due primarily to agricultural irrigation, amounts to at least 163.6 bcm.

The overuse of nonrenewable underground aquifers carries with it a number of consequences. Even before wells run completely dry, depletion increases the cost of pumping the water above ground, and irrigation in agricultural communities can become prohibitively expensive. In time, small farmers with tight operating budgets are squeezed out. Only large, wealthy operations that can afford the technology to pump water from deep beneath the surface remain in business, thus exemplifying the maxim in the West that "water flows uphill toward money." However, even those farms able to afford higher irrigation costs are likely to recoup their expenses by switching from staple crops to high-priced luxury crops.

Depending on local characteristics and the extent of the depletion, declining groundwater sources can bring the utter collapse of communities and farms that owe their existence to irrigation. In *Cadillac Desert*, Reisner says that thanks to irrigation and federally funded water projects, "states such as California, Arizona, and Idaho became populous and wealthy; millions settled in regions where nature, left alone, would have countenanced thousands at best." When the water dries up or becomes too expensive to extract from the ground, farms reliant upon irrigation fail, and communities built around them disappear. When the pumps shut down, farmers either struggle to make a living with lower yielding dry-land farming or take their acres out of cultivation.

Moreover, population growth and a growing trend towards urbanization often pit city dwellers against farmers in competition for what remains of overtaxed water supplies. An influx of people into regions like the American West places even greater stress on water resources that are already strained. In yet another example of water flowing uphill toward money, wealthy urban areas are obtaining the water rights held by rural irrigation districts in exchange for cash payments. A number of these deals have proven very controversial, with some rural advocates arguing that the cities' water demands will force farms to take acres out of production. As the population of the West continues to climb, disputes over water are likely to follow a similar track.

Even more may be at stake than the future of the West's urban and rural communities. A likely ultimate loser in these disputes over water is nature itself. "I think when the crunch comes and you have four or five or six endangered species demanding more water, and agriculture demanding more water, and urban areas demanding more water, the situation becomes politically intolerable," says Reisner. "And I think that given the political forces arrayed against each other, you're more likely to lose the Endangered Species Act or at least modify it, than you are to cut L.A. back by 60 to 70 percent or to cut some of the farmers off entirely."

Of course, even if we somehow overcome the problem of dwindling water resources, unnatural irrigation carries with it other inherent and potentially devastating consequences.

SALINIZATION OF THE LAND

Carthage, the greatest rival to the Roman Republic during the first and second centuries B.C.E., finally succumbed to a lengthy siege which ended the Third Punic War in 146 B.C.E. Roman soldiers, motivated by rage, vengeance, and a desire to prevent a fourth Punic War, demolished the city and its harbor, slaughtered most of the citizens, and sold those who were spared into slavery. As a final touch, the Romans sowed the farmland surrounding the city with salt to render the countryside sterile and ensure the absolute extermination of Carthaginian civilization.

Today, much of the American West faces a fate similar to that of the Carthaginian landscape. The threat comes not from Roman legions, but from self-inflicted irrigation projects that over time leave substantial salt sediments in the soil. "Nowhere is the salinity problem more serious than in the San Joaquin Valley of California, the most productive farming region in the entire world," Reisner tells us in *Cadillac Desert*.

Mineral salts, including sulfate, carbonate, and chloride salts of sodium, calcium, magnesium, and potassium, are naturally dissolved in all potential sources of irrigation water, from rivers and lakes to underground aquifers. When farmers apply this water-salt mixture to their crops, the plants absorb the water but leave the salts behind. As if that were not enough, irrigation can also promote another type of salinization. Water applied to frequently irrigated croplands can cause water tables, which also contain dissolved salts, to rise beneath the fields. As the water tables approach the surface, a portion of the water evaporates, leaving its salt in the soil. In many irrigated fields, both types of salinization occur simultaneously.

A typical irrigation scheme that applied 10,000 tons of water per hectare annually would simultaneously deposit between two and five tons of salt in the soil. In the United States, salt buildup affects about 23 percent of irrigated land — though in some areas a much higher portion of the land is affected. In fact, significant salinization is damaging about 35 percent of the irrigated land in California and nearly 70 percent of that in the lower Colorado River basin.

Eventually, unremoved salt buildup lowers crop yields, or, in extreme cases, renders the land completely sterile. Such is the case in parts of the San Joaquin Valley. "There are already thousands of acres near the southern end of the valley that look as if they had been dusted with snow; not even weeds can grow there," says Reisner. "An identical fate will ultimately befall more than a million acres in the valley unless something is done."

Managing the salt buildup in the soils can be tricky and expensive. In the San Joaquin Valley, federal and state governments proposed a massive canal project designed to drain salty agricultural runoff from the fields. The project proved an utter failure. First, a lack of funds necessitated scaling back the grand scope of the endeavor. Then problems arose when natural and man-made poisons in the runoff water contaminated waterfowl nesting lands at the terminus of the drainage canal. Even if we manage to solve the problems of finance and disposal of contaminated runoff, it is likely we will be fighting a losing battle so long as inefficient and unsustainable irrigation practices remain in place.

AGRICULTURAL RUNOFF

Of course, irrigation is not the lone culprit behind agriculture's water-related problems. Each year, U.S. farmers apply approximately 800 million pounds of pesticides to their fields. When these pesticide applications are followed by rains or irrigation, the poisons can seep into the groundwater or contaminate waste water running off of the fields and into nearby streams and rivers. The federal government's 1998 National Water Quality Assessment (NWQA) Program found pesticide contamination in all of its river and stream samples and in more than half of its samples taken from shallow groundwater wells. Altogether, the program detected 83 different pesticides or pesticide breakdown products, and almost invariably the contaminated samples contained residues of multiple pesticides. Some 66 percent of the stream samples contained five or more pesticides. Most of these pollutants were originally sprayed or spread on cropland and then either washed into nearby streams or absorbed by underground aquifers.

The NWQA found the highest concentrations for commonly used herbicides, including the suspected human carcinogens alachlor, atrazine, and cyanazine. These chemicals are found in dangerously high concentrations in the drinking water of many people who live in rural agricultural areas, and they are not removed by water treatment systems. The problem of pesticide contamination is not one that can be cleared up overnight. Even poisons that have not been used for decades persist in groundwater and streambed soil sediments. The NWQA found numerous stream samples contaminated with DDT, the highly toxic insecticide which the Environmental Protection Agency (EPA) banned in 1972.

Even more highly concentrated in farm runoff than pesticide residues are plant nutrients, such as nitrogen and phosphorus. Each year in the United States, farmers apply about 12 million tons of man-made nitrogen and 2 million tons of man-made phosphorus fertilizers to their fields. Applications of manure add an additional 7 million tons of nitrogen and 2 million tons of phosphorus to the soil. Not surprisingly, a significant portion of these nutrients eventually winds up in aquifers and streams. Approximately 20 percent of the shallow wells located on farmland tested in the NWQA had nitrate concentrations exceeding the EPA's drinking water standards. The problem is most serious in the Central Valley of California and in parts of the Great Plains and the Mid-Atlantic. Nitrate in the human body reduces the ability of the blood to transport oxygen. The most serious health threat posed by excessive nitrate levels is methemoglobinemia, a type of nitrate poisoning that can be fatal to infants.

In the NWQA, phosphorus levels exceeded suggested EPA standards in 80 percent of stream samples. High phosphorus levels promote the growth of nuisance plants and algae, which can kill fish and other aquatic life by reducing levels of dissolved oxygen in streams. These algal blooms can also damage municipal water systems.

FIXING WATER PROBLEMS

Water covers two-thirds of the earth, yet a mere 3 percent of this total is in the form of freshwater, suitable for drinking and agricultural use. Much of this 3 percent is inaccessible, locked up in permanently frozen glaciers and ice caps or located too deep within the earth to be reached from the surface. Freshwater is both rare and precious.

Nonetheless, the greatest portion of the water used by people goes into woefully inefficient irrigation for agricultural production. The vast majority of irrigation around the world relies on simple systems in which either fields are flooded or water is channeled down furrows. Experts estimate that as a result of spillage, seepage, and evaporation, nearly half of the water diverted for irrigation never makes it to the fields.

Other types of irrigation have proven much more efficient. A new type of sprinkler irrigation in which nozzles are placed low to the ground has resulted in up to 95 percent efficiency. This compares very favorably with traditional sprinkler systems in which the water is shot high into the air and a significant portion of it is likely to evaporate or be blown away from target crops.

Farmers have achieved the best efficiency with drip irrigation systems, which slowly provide the crop roots with water a single drop at a time. Drip irrigation uses from 30 to 70 percent less water than flooding and has been shown to increase crop yields by 20 to 90 percent over that typical for fields irrigated in other ways. Making efficient irrigation systems economically viable for small-scale and poor farmers around the globe could reduce agricultural water usage by around 37 percent. These efficient systems, by reducing the amount of water applied to the fields, also decrease problems associated with salinization, erosion, and agricultural runoff.

Perhaps even more important than improving irrigation efficiency, farmers and consumers can change their habits and practices to make better use of the water resources available to us. For instance, farmers can elect to grow crops better suited to the soil types and water availability of their lands. Planting of drought-resistant crops in semi-arid climates can reduce irrigation without taking land out of production.

Another option involves intercropping, the planting of a variety of crops together in a single field, rather than the conventional monoculture method of growing a single crop in regularly spaced rows. The consistent and complete groundcover of an intercropped field not only maximizes the use of soil moisture, but also cuts down on evaporation and reduces the need for irrigation.

Governments can encourage farmers to make decisions that support these sustainable practices by doing away with water subsidies that promote inefficient irrigation farming. Such subsidies have made large-scale irrigation projects relatively inexpensive in regions where free-market economics would have otherwise placed a premium price on scarce water resources. "In an arid or semi-arid region, you can irrigate low-value, thirsty crops such as alfalfa and pasture grass only if you have cheap water," explains Reisner. "If you need forty or fifty thousand pounds of water in places like California and Colorado to irrigate enough fodder to raise two dollars worth of cow, you can't even consider it if forty thousand pounds of water costs seven or eight dollars (as it would if you bought it from the California Water Project). But it makes perfectly good sense if the government sells you the same quantity for thirty or forty cents — as it does if the Central Valley Project is your source." By actually placing a price on water commensurate with its value, governments could go a long way toward reducing wasteful and unsustainable practices.

As consumers, the choices we make can also affect the amount of water used by agriculture. Producing a pound of corn requires somewhere in the neighborhood of 100 to 250 gallons of water. However, as Reisner suggests, growing enough grain for livestock consumption to produce a pound of beef can require 20 to 80 times more water, up to 8,500 gallons. Food production for the diet of an average North American requires twice as much water as for the diet of an average Asian, who eats significantly less meat. "By moving down the food chain, Americans could get twice as much nutritional benefit out of each liter of water consumed in food production," writes Sandra Postel. "Stated otherwise, the same volume of water could feed two people instead of one, leaving additional water in rivers and streams to help restore fisheries, wetlands, recreational opportunities, and ecological functions overall."

OUR FORGOTTEN POLLINATORS

Protecting the Birds and the Bees

MRILL INGRAM, STEPHEN BUCHMANN, AND GARY NABHAN

POLLINATORS, INCLUDING BIRDS, BEES, AND ANIMALS, *are critical to fruit and seed production. Without them, the ability to regenerate the biotic community would be lost. Yet worldwide, we are currently facing a pollination crisis, in which pollinators are disappearing at alarming rates as a result of habitat loss, pesticide poisoning, diseases, and pests. As a society, we must work together to confront this impending crisis and devise workable plans for protecting these pollinators that are essential to healthy functioning of wild and agricultural communities.*

▼

Pollination — the transfer of pollen from one flower to another — is critical to fruit and seed production and is often provided by insects and other animals on the hunt for nectar, pollen, or other floral rewards. Insect pollination is a necessary step in the production of most fruits and vegetables that we eat and in the regeneration of many forage crops used by livestock. In fact, animals provide pollination services for over three-quarters of the staple crop plants that feed humankind and for 90 percent of all flowering plants in the world.

Recent surveys document that more than 30 genera of animals — consisting of hundreds of species of floral visitors — are required to pollinate the 100 or so crops that feed the world. Only 15 percent of these crops are serviced by domestic honeybees; at least 80 percent are pollinated by wild bees and other wildlife. Who are the pollinators? Our recent analyses of global inventories of biodiversity indicate that more than 100,000 different animal species — perhaps as many as 200,000 — play roles in pollinating the 250,000 kinds of wild flowering plants on this planet. In addition to countless bees (the world contains an estimated 40,000 species of bees), wasps, moths, butterflies, flies, beetles, and other invertebrates, perhaps 1,500 species of vertebrates such as birds and mammals serve as pollinators. Hummingbirds are the best-known wildlife pollinators in the Americas, but perching birds, flying foxes, fruit bats, opossums, lemurs, and even geckos function as effective pollinators elsewhere in the world.

We must recognize that pollinators are not providing a free service. Economic assessments of agricultural productivity should account for the "cost" of sustaining wild and managed pollinator populations. Investment and stewardship are required to protect and sustain them, and we are failing in this crucial task. According to the U.S. Department of Agriculture (USDA), there is an "impending pollination crisis," in which both wild and managed pollinators are disappearing at alarming rates owing to habitat loss, pesticide poisoning, diseases, and pests. For the first time ever, local bee shortages in 1994 forced many California almond growers to import the bulk of the honeybees they needed from other states to ensure that their $800-million-a-year crop would be pollinated. Recent monitoring of pumpkins in New York State determined that their blossoms were still laden with pollen five hours after they opened in the morning, long after they are typically stripped of all pollen by bees.

THE PLIGHT OF THE HONEYBEE

The decline in pollinators is vividly demonstrated in the current plight of the honeybee. The number of commercial U.S. bee colonies plummeted from 5.9 million in the late 1940s to 4.3 million in 1985 and 2.7 million in 1995. The loss of one-quarter of all managed honeybee colonies since 1990 signals one of the most severe declines U.S. agriculture has ever experienced in such a short period. There are fewer bee hives in the United States today than at any time in the last 50 years.

This decline has been brought on by the spread of diseases and parasitic mites, the invasion of Africanized honeybees, exposure to pesticides, climatic fluctuations, and the elimination of government subsidies for beekeepers. And an increasing number of places around the United States are reporting pollinator scarcity. Studies of cucurbit pollination in Arizona, Alabama, and Maine revealed that honeybees are in fact frequently absent from fields and that bumblebees and ground nesting squash bees are doing the majority of the pollination. In recent years, some wildland habitats have lost 70 percent of their feral honeybees, which make hives in rocky outcroppings and other cavities.

The arrival of Africanized bees in 99 U.S. counties since 1990 has forced some beekeepers to abandon apiaries in highly populated areas for fear of liability suits from neighbors. In addition, Africanized bees are among the carriers of parasitic mites infecting thousands of U.S. apiaries, killing off additional colonies.

To minimize further losses, honeybee colonies need better monitoring and management. Yet the USDA is currently considering closing bee research laboratories. Bee research must be strengthened and expanded to include research on management of pollinators other than honeybees. Increasingly, other pollinators will have to be deployed to take up the slack created by the decline of honeybee colonies. Orchard growers and farmers need to ensure that neighboring wild habitats remain suitable for wild pollinators if they are to secure pollination services for their crops.

U.S. policy makers responsible for the recent cut in long-standing subsidies to beekeepers for honey production have further jeopardized the pollination services provided by honeybees, estimated to be 60 to 100 times more valuable than the market price of honey. Policy makers must begin devising programs that reward farmers for implementing practices to protect habitats of wild pollinators and provide incentives for those who wish to manage a wider variety of pollinators to assist farmers and orchard growers.

For such reasons, government agencies such as the USDA, SARH/ Mexico, and Agriculture Canada should invest more resources in programs to manage a diversity of pollinators, to stabilize remaining apiaries, and to reward farmers for setting aside cropland and retaining hedgerows or windbreaks where wild pollinators nest and forage.

PESTICIDES AND POLLINATORS

As noted, a major contributor to the decline in honeybees and other pollinators is exposure to toxins. Whether managed or wild, pollinators need protection from pesticides and other chemicals that can poison them or impair their reproduction. These chemicals can also eliminate nectar sources for pollinators, destroy larval host plants for moths and butterflies, and deplete nesting materials for bees.

Few people realize the United States now applies twice the amount of pesticides as when Rachel Carson published *Silent Spring* in 1962. In Canada during the mid-1970s, aerial spraying of coniferous forest pests so reduced native bee populations that blueberry yields fell below the norm for four years.

A large number of insecticides used in agriculture are toxic to pollinating insects, but only honeybee colonies can be moved away from fields prior to spraying. Even so, it has been estimated that 20 percent of all losses of honeybee colonies involve some degree of pesticide exposure. According to a study on economic costs of pesticide use, honeybee poisonings result in an annual loss of $13.3 million in the United States. Wild insect pollinators such as small solitary bees are even more vulnerable than honeybees to organophosphate pesticides that have largely replaced organochlorines like DDT. Field studies in U.S. deserts have found that pollinators remaining in small fragments of natural habitat are particularly susceptible to insecticide spraying on adjacent croplands.

Moreover, many crops that would benefit in quality and quantity from more thorough pollination are not sufficiently pollinated because of heavy pesticide applications. Cotton harvests, for example, could increase by as much as 20 percent if the flowers were fully pollinated by bees, and farm income could potentially increase by $400 million per year. However, using bees to enhance cotton has proven impossible on a large scale where there has been continued intensive use of insecticides.

Although applying toxic chemicals always runs the risk of harming the biotic community, at a minimum pesticide applicators need training in monitoring pollinators as well as pests. Pollination ecologists familiar with particular species can work with pesticide applicators who know about timing and the drift distances of chemicals under various weather conditions. When pesticides are applied by aircraft, as much as 50 to 75 percent of the chemicals sprayed can miss their target, leading to inadvertent exposure of nontarget organisms such as pollinators.

Alternative agricultural techniques can provide nontoxic methods of weed and insect control that incorporate use of habitat set-asides for beneficial insect populations and require the use of fewer toxins. Alternative strategies may help farmers reduce costs involved in crop management, and at the same time allow them to market organic produce at premium prices.

Both gardeners and farmers can rely on alternative nontoxic methods to control pests and weeds. More widespread practice of such methods has the potential to reduce wildlife exposure to insecticides, herbicides, and fungicides. Urban dwellers can also reduce the amounts of toxins used around their homes, and by purchasing organic produce, they can provide economic incentives for growers to switch to more pollinator-friendly organic methods.

HABITAT LOSS: A MAJOR THREAT

Small isolated patches of wild habitat may look natural and healthy, but they often lack essential pollinators and seed dispersers that ensure regeneration of the biotic community. These animals typically require more habitat area than that covered by populations of the rarest plants. When large habitats are fragmented into small isolated patches, it is not long before some of the animal residents decline in numbers to the point that they no longer provide effective ecological services beneficial to plants. Globally, more than 100 species of birds and mammals in 60 genera of vertebrate pollinators are already listed as threatened, and untold numbers of invertebrates are also at risk.

Because some wild pollinators need undisturbed habitat for nesting, roosting, and foraging, they are very susceptible to habitat degradation and fragmentation. Some pollinators require plants that flower sequentially, so that they have food sources throughout the season. Elimination of these sources by herbicide spraying or clearing of native vegetation can literally starve pollinators. In Costa Rica, wild bee diversity in degraded forestland dropped from 70 to 37 species in just 14 years. Population declines have also been confirmed for butterflies, moths, flying foxes, and a host of other pollinators of food crops. We must find ways to reward farmers for setting aside land to support wild pollinators. Unplowed farmland set aside for several years can produce vegetation that supports considerable insect diversity and aids nearby crops by providing pollinators and other beneficial insects. Land use planners should work to create seminatural buffers around small wildlife reserves to connect protected areas with undeveloped corridors and to designate pesticide-free zones within this matrix. Greenbelts and habitat set-asides need not always consist of pristine vegetation, but they must be large enough to provide safe nesting sites and a range of floral resources.

ENDANGERED POLLINATORS, ENDANGERED WILD PLANTS

In the larger picture, native pollinators are as important for wild plants as they are for crops. Yet the ultimate reproductive consequences of pollinator scarcity on wild plants is not appreciated and remains understudied.

In Iowa, where only 200 acres of unplowed "virgin" prairie remain intact, prairie wildflowers now suffer low seed yields for lack of adequate visitation rates by pollinators. Rare cacti in national parks and adjacent to heavily sprayed cotton fields also suffer high levels of floral abortion due to a paucity of moths. There are small nature reserves nested within urban areas that contain rare plants, but their flowers wither without producing fruit. In one small reserve within urban Tokyo, for example, a primrose almost completely fails to set seed, owing to local disappearance of its bumblebee pollinator.

The last remaining natural populations of a rare evening primrose live in California's Antioch Dunes National Wildlife Refuge. Though the primrose is protected, its hawkmoth pollinator has not reappeared after years of pesticide spraying in nearby vineyards, and reproduction of the plant has remained low. The primrose remains in jeopardy as it produces few fruits and low percentages of viable seeds, while its weedy neighbors produce many. This is just one of many examples where pesticide use, decrease of nectar sources or larval host plants, and other threats have triggered the decline of pollinators of endangered plants.

Unfortunately, not even federally listed endangered plants are regularly monitored for pollinator availability. A survey of federal recovery plans for 16 endangered plants growing near the U.S./Mexico border revealed that the range of available pollinators had been determined for only two of them, and threats to pollinators themselves had not been taken into account at all. Because of such "reciprocities," conservation policy and practice should move toward sustaining or restoring ecological relationships, rather than treating species as isolated organisms. "Critical habitat" needs to be redefined to include the needs of both rare plants and their animal associates. When critical habitat has been designated for endangered plants, it has almost always been done without determining foraging and nesting areas required to ensure sufficient pollinators and seed dispersers for long-term recovery of the plant in danger. To begin to resolve some of these discrepancies, the Forgotten Pollinators Campaign is currently working with entomologists and conservation biologists to create pollinator monitoring protocols that can be used by land managers around the country.

PROTECTING MIGRATORY POLLINATORS

Bats, hummingbirds, moths, and butterflies are among the pollinators that seasonally migrate long and short distances between mountain ranges, regions, and countries. Their migratory routes are often well-defined "nectar corridors" where the sequence of flowering over a season offers pollinators sufficient energy to sustain their journey. Many of these nectar corridors are no longer fully intact, however; land conversion has eliminated some floral resources over 20 to 60 mile segments, in some cases longer than the distance energy-depleted pollinators can fly in one day.

Scientists and policy makers need to collaborate across political boundaries and regions to assess the continuity and health of migratory corridors used by pollinators. Because some migrants travel 2,000 to 4,000 miles a year, habitat loss in one area of their range may limit their populations overall. Certain migratory pollinator species aggregate in large numbers in temporary roosts that are vulnerable to human disturbance. Such roost sites should be protected throughout a species' entire range, since a refuge in just one portion will be insufficient to support a viable population. International policy agreements and environmental education efforts are needed to champion migratory pollinators.

RECOGNIZING THE FORGOTTEN POLLINATORS

Interactions between plants and their pollinators are essential to healthy functioning of wild and agricultural communities. Habitat loss, disease, and pesticides take their toll in different ways, but all imperil these vital ecological relationships, many of which developed through thousands of years of natural and cultural selection.

The vast majority of the 100 or so crop species that feed the world depend on animals as go-betweens to ensure that crops are pollinated. Crises like those now faced by the honeybee industry demonstrate the lack of safety nets to protect agricultural yields. We can no longer justify devoting all research and management dollars to a single or even a few pollinators, but instead must support a diversification of the entire pollination industry.

As a society, we need to recognize our debt to the "forgotten pollinators." To successfully confront the impending pollinator crisis, we must work together. Foresters, entomologists, and conservationists must devise workable plans for endangered plant species that include pollinators. Farmers, orchard growers, and other land managers need to consider pollinators as they make decisions about pesticides and land use. Educators must emphasize the importance of pollinators in wild and agricultural lands and the interconnectedness of life in general.

Urban dwellers can purchase organic produce, include nectar and host plants for pollinators in their gardens, and rely on organic methods of pest and weed control. Pollinator gardening provides hummingbirds, butterflies, and other wildlife with important sources of nectar and increases our awareness of the diversity of ecological relationships in our own backyards. In an era when human activities place increasing pressure on both natural and rural landscapes, we cannot ignore the vital role of pollination services and the frequently negative impacts that we are having on plant/pollinator relationships.

CAN AGRICULTURE AND BIODIVERSITY COEXIST?

CATHERINE BADGLEY

MODERN INTENSIVE AGRICULTURE *is a major contributor to the alarming loss of species and ecosystems and increasing rates of extinction. By reducing total land area devoted to agriculture and implementing alternative farming practices, modern agriculture could become compatible with biodiversity and habitat conservation. Such changes would require incentives and regulations for farmers, as well as changes in consumer buying habits.*

▼

For the first time in 65 million years, the world is in the early phases of a mass extinction, this one resulting from human impacts on the biosphere. Agriculture, more than any other human activity, has the greatest collective negative effect on Earth's biodiversity. Modern industrial agriculture transforms habitats, displaces populations of native species, spreads non-native species, and pollutes terrestrial and aquatic ecosystems with agricultural inputs and by-products. One of the many reasons to implement more sustainable forms of agriculture is to reduce the effects of current agricultural practices on native biodiversity.

MODERN AGRICULTURAL PRACTICES: TRANSFORMING NATURAL HABITATS

Farming began about 10,000 years ago, and the diversity of agricultural practices today reflects some of the stages of this lengthy history. In less industrialized parts of the world, farming methods have varied little over the last several thousand years — the same lands are cultivated, the same crops planted, the same tools and style of labor employed. By contrast, industrialized regions have moved to the intensive, large-scale production of monocultures, which involves crops, machinery, and soil additives that are introductions of the second half of the 20th century.

Farming practices can be placed on a spectrum of agricultural intensification. At one end of the spectrum are the agroecosystems that bear a strong resemblance to the native, pre-agricultural ecosystems of a region. Practices that give rise to these agroecosystems are often called "traditional" or "indigenous." They include the family subsistence farms of many cultures and often support many kinds of plants and animals. In some regions of the world, traditional farmers cultivate native species as well as introduced crop species.

AGRICULTURAL INTENSIFICATION

LOW				HIGH
Javanese garden	small-scale	horse-powered	midsized	industrial
Mayan garden	organic farm	Amish farm	farming in U.S.	agriculture

At the other end of the spectrum are the highly regulated monocultures of modern industrial agriculture, dependent on synthetic fertilizers, pesticides, and heavy machinery. These agroecosystems do not resemble any natural ecosystems and represent the most substantial transformations of the original native ecosystems, in terms of both displacing native biodiversity and altering soil-forming processes. Modern industrial agriculture is prevalent in industrialized nations and is expanding in many developing nations.

Many practices are intermediate in terms of agricultural intensification. For example, Amish horse-powered farming in the United States and Canada usually involves conversion of original forest to fields of grain or pasture, but the use of horses rather than tractors and of manure rather than synthetic fertilizer usually sustains the original soil structure and texture.

The levels of intensification along this spectrum closely reflect the amount of biodiversity which remains present in farm ecosystems. Three aspects of biodiversity apply. The first is the original "native biodiversity" — the array of plants, animals, and other organisms that inhabit a particular area before farming. This collection of species is dynamic but fluctuates around a characteristic level for each ecosystem. In contrast to "native biodiversity" systems, farms have "planned biodiversity" and "associated biodiversity." Planned diversity is what the farmer intentionally raises, which typically consists of introduced species or domesticated varieties of local wild species. Associated biodiversity includes species that interact with the planned biodiversity, through pollination, predation, and competition. As agricultural production intensifies, both native and associated biodiversity declines, reaching the lowest levels in chemical-intensive, monoculture systems. Planned diversity can remain steady for decades or longer, under a range of production methods. However, irreversible degradation of farmland — through erosion, desertification, salinization, or loss of soil fertility — has also occurred under a wide range of methods.

LOSSES OF BIODIVERSITY DUE TO AGRICULTURE

Estimates of current extinction rates range from three to four orders of magnitude greater than "background" extinction rates. A global assessment of the status of modern species indicates that 11 percent of birds, 18 percent of mammals, 5 percent of fish, and 8 percent of plant species are facing extinction. In the United States, freshwater animal groups are the most vulnerable, including freshwater mussels (69 percent of species at risk), freshwater fishes (37 percent at risk), stoneflies (43 percent at risk), and crayfishes (51 percent at risk). Since these aquatic groups have unusually high species numbers in the United States, the high percentages also reflect large numbers of species. Over 5,000 species of U.S. flowering plants are at risk. E. O. Wilson estimates that 27,000 species are lost each year due to tropical deforestation alone. The major processes that endanger species or cause extinction are the loss and fragmentation of habitat, displacement by introduced species, pollution of habitat, and overharvesting. Global climate change is expected to add to this disruption of species habitats.

Habitat Loss or Fragmentation. Habitat destruction — which includes clearing of vegetation, replacing one kind of vegetation with another, and urbanizing and polluting natural areas — has contributed to the extinction or endangerment of about 90 percent of threatened species. Agriculture is the leading cause of habitat destruction in terrestrial ecosystems. As much as 40 percent of global net primary productivity — the base of all food chains — has been appropriated by humans and their commensal species. On land, the lion's share of this appropriation involves agriculture. Of the 8.9 billion hectares of the Earth's land area that are capable of supporting substantial vegetation, 1.5 billion hectares are currently used for production of agricultural crops and 3.3 billion hectares are used to pasture livestock.

Thus, many natural ecosystems have significantly shrunk, primarily because people have converted the original vegetation to farmland or pasture. Examples include the North American prairie and many lowland tropical rainforests. Shrinking ecosystems reduce the habitat size of native plants and animals. This, accompanied by the fragmentation of the native vegetation, results in smaller, scattered populations of native species in patches of the original ecosystem. Populations in each individual patch are much more vulnerable to disappearance than is a larger population spread over a greater area. Species with very small geographic ranges or small population sizes are especially vulnerable to extinction as their original habitats become smaller and more fragmented. In Australia, several species of native marsupials and rodents are extinct or endangered as a result of overgrazing by introduced livestock and the conversion of natural habitats for agriculture.

Disruption of Natural Processes. Soil degradation and erosion, contamination of local aquatic systems with silt or pesticides, and loss of micro- and macrobiota often result from agricultural practices. In Michigan, three species of fishes have become extinct and another three have been reduced to relict populations as a result of siltation or pesticide contamination of streams by adjacent agricultural lands. In monocultural agroecosystems, insect pest species are fewer in number but greater in abundance than in untransformed ecosystems. Fertilizer applications may contribute to outbreaks of pathogens or insect pests.

Extirpation of Large Mammals. In North America, most native ungulates and large carnivores have suffered substantial range reductions as a result of habitat conversion, hunting, or government-sponsored predator-control programs that benefit livestock producers.

Affected animals include bison, bighorn sheep, elk, grizzly bears, and wolves. In the United States not including Alaska, wolves were nearly exterminated, not because they posed a direct threat to people, but because they occasionally preyed on livestock. As a result, populations of these predators' prey species, such as deer and rodents, have increased to the extent that they may become subject to additional control programs. Thus, the loss of predators also represents a loss of important ecological interactions among species.

Exotics. Competition between native and introduced species may result from the highly managed support of non-native agricultural crops as well as from the less managed or unintended spread of exotic species. For example, arid grazing lands in the western United States were seeded with non-native grasses that have choked out native grasses in many areas. Bees introduced both to produce honey and to pollinate crops readily compete with native bees and bumblebees for nectar and pollen.

Soil Degradation and Pesticides. All agriculture involves some disturbance of the soil. Plowing, tilling, removing weeds, harvesting crops, and grazing livestock are all disruptive processes, particularly if they are performed too often or with very heavy equipment, as they are in mechanized farming. As soil structure and texture are degraded, the soil holds less water, recycles nutrients more slowly, and is more prone to erosion by wind or water. Eventually, the soil biota diminish — leading to a further decline in soil structure and function. Severely degraded soil may take decades, centuries, or even millennia to recover. Soil erosion is a substantial problem: 80 percent of agricultural lands show moderate to severe soil erosion. In the United States, the average rate of soil erosion is the equivalent of one inch in 20 years; the natural formation of an inch of soil is a 300- to 1,000-year process.

Synthetic insecticides and herbicides contribute to the loss of biodiversity by reducing or eliminating both targeted and nontargeted species. Worldwide, 5 million tons of pesticides are applied to crops every year. Few pesticides are species-specific, so their application generally affects many local populations other than the intended ones. Soil organisms are often among the unintended victims. Making matters worse, some pesticides remain in the exposed organisms and then accumulate in the tissues of their predators and the predators' predators and so on. This process can spread pesticides extensively through the food webs of a local ecosystem. Modern technology has promoted ever greater use of pesticides and herbicides. Genetic engineering of crops is now at the cutting edge of agricultural technology. While publicized as safe and ecologically benign, many manipulated crops contain genetically engineered resistance to a particular herbicide so that more of that herbicide can be applied to weeds in the same field.

Some of these negative effects of farming practices have accompanied agriculture through its history, whereas others are more recent. Certainly, modern industrial agriculture, with its synthetic inputs and heavy equipment, is more intense and destructive than traditional methods. The average farm size has increased under industrial agriculture, with fewer families engaged in farming. As farm size has increased, woodlots, hedgerows, and shelter belts have disappeared, resulting in reduced protection against soil erosion and reduced habitat for wildlife.

ALTERNATIVE FARMING PRACTICES

The seemingly inherent conflict between agriculture and biodiversity is by no means absolute. Implementing viable alternatives to modes of farming that destroy biodiversity involves changing agricultural practices and reducing the land area devoted to agriculture. Such changes will require different incentives and regulations for farmers and will be effective only if consumer buying habits support them.

Changes in Farming Practices.

1. Preserve areas of native habitat on farms. Preserving existing habitats is the most effective way to protect local biodiversity. Many small farms do this by maintaining woodlots for firewood, fenceposts, and recreation and by keeping remnants of native vegetation as hedgerows and riparian growth along streams.

Often, small areas of native habitat could more effectively preserve local biodiversity if they remained connected to each other by habitat corridors. These would facilitate dispersal of individuals from one area of habitat to another and reduce the likelihood that populations of rare species would disappear completely. In areas with little remaining native habitat, ecological restoration of native vegetation would be a slow but effective way to promote native biodiversity. For many ecosystems, a more concerted effort to preserve linked areas of native habitat, including wildlands, interspersed with sustainably managed farmland would go a long way toward maintaining or restoring local biodiversity, especially for species with large geographic ranges.

2. *Incorporate native species into agroecosystems.* Much of the world's agriculture consists of a dozen usually non-native species grown in massive quantities. Exotic species generally do not support as much of the associated biodiversity of a farm as would native species, which engage in a set of ecological interactions that have arisen over many hundreds of generations in the context of a particular climate and environment. Exotic species must interact with collaborators and competitors that differ from those of their original ecological and evolutionary contexts. Native species tend to be more resistant than exotics to climatic stresses, diseases, and other disturbances. In addition, native populations often have greater genetic diversity than do agricultural exotics, because the natives can breed with members of local wild populations, whereas the exotics usually have no such ability. Promoting diversified mixtures of native and non-native species would be an intermediate stage in the movement toward agroecosystems that feature native species and varieties derived from them by artificial selection.

In the United States, native species that could play a more prominent role in agriculture are trees that bear fruits, nuts, or sap; perennial grasses; and herbs that produce edible seeds, fruits, or leaves. Many important crops already in cultivation are derived from native species; these plants should receive greater emphasis in the agroecosystem.

3. *Use mixtures of perennials.* Appropriately designed mixtures of plants can complement each other — in terms of nutrient cycling and water use, for example. The cultivation of perennials rather than annuals would result in soil being plowed less than once per year. Perennial mixtures would sponsor greater soil health and greater biodiversity, particularly of microbiota and insects, than do

annual monocultures. This approach becomes even more effective if the agroecosystem mimics the structure and function of the native vegetation. Bill Mollison's "permaculture" and Wes Jackson's Natural Systems Agriculture are examples of this approach.

4. *Eliminate practices most destructive to associated biodiversity*. The practices recommended above would have little positive effect on biodiversity if they entailed substantial use of synthetic fertilizers and pesticides. Rather, non-synthetic fertilizers and pest-control methods would better promote the soil biota, keep persistent toxins out of groundwater, and reduce the impact of pesticides on non-targeted species. Using crop residues, animal manure, and compost to promote nutrient cycling on the farm mimics nature's regime of soil fertility. Diverse species in the agroecosystem should reduce the vulnerability of crops to pests and diseases. Control of pests should rely on native predators and parasites to the greatest extent possible. The guiding principle is to manipulate ecosystem processes to support the farmer's goals, rather than replace ecosystem processes with synthetic inputs.

These are not radical suggestions. Established agricultural methods, such as organic farming, intercropping, and use of cover crops, already incorporate the principles cited above and accommodate greater biodiversity than mechanized, chemical agriculture. However, to diminish the rate of species extinction and prevent further loss of biodiversity, these sustainable farming practices must supplant industrial agriculture on an increasingly wider scale.

Changes in Consumer Habits. Changes in society, not only on farms, will determine whether the reform of agricultural practices can succeed. Reduced per capita consumption of animal products, for example, would reduce the amount of land needed for growing grains. Grains make up about 80 percent of the world's food supply. Worldwide, 37 percent of the annual grain harvest is fed to livestock. In the United States, 60 percent of the total grain supply (about 70 percent of the grain produced) is fed to livestock. Additionally, a greater bioregional approach to food consumption and less reliance on imported luxuries would focus more attention on the health of local farms and farmers, reduce the costs of transporting food, and reacquaint consumers with the sources of their food. Farm policies should provide incentives for farmers to preserve biodiversity and to design more ecologically sound agroecosystems. Popular support is also needed for farm policies that favor small, diversified, family farms over large, corporate-owned monocultures. Such an emphasis on localized farming would prove more socially and economically sustainable, as well as more supportive of biodiversity.

WILDLIFE HEALTH

KELLEY R. TUCKER

THE IMPACT OF AGRICULTURE ON WILDLIFE HAS BEEN PROFOUND. *Activities such as tilling, mowing, drainage, rotation, and the application of pesticides and fertilizers have significant implications for wildlife health, habitat, and diversity. The potential for agricultural lands to provide quality habitat for some wildlife species is substantial. By keeping common species flourishing, agriculture can add diversity at the local level and beyond — and that goal should be in the interests of farming and biodiversity alike.*

▼

The intensification and specialization of agriculture in recent decades has led to dramatic changes in habitat availability and type. Cropland diversity has been reduced, small farms have been integrated into larger management units, and adjacent woodlots, hedgerows, and native plant borders have declined in number and size. The isolation of natural and semi-natural habitats, and of the wildlife species supported by them, has increased as a consequence. If it is unrealistic to undertake restoring the full complement of wildlife species once associated with an agricultural area, it has also become increasingly evident that the diversity of wildlife species cannot be expected to thrive solely in unconnected oases set aside for conservation. Instead, a level of habitat quality useful to a variety of wildlife species can be maintained by cropland managers in partnership with others invested in wildlife health. An inclusive agricultural model can be developed that integrates some wildlife species groups into the agricultural landscape instead of isolating them.

AGRICULTURE AND WILDLIFE

The simplest of agricultural activities — clearing land, tilling soil, and replacing a diversity of growth with specific crops — leads to changes in wildlife foraging and land use. In North America, it is difficult to separate the effects of developing agricultural practices on wildlife patterns or species diversity from those of the myriad other activities associated with European settlement. Nevertheless, the clearing of eastern forests and the cultivation of grass crops farther west are seen by many scientists as key elements in species shifts such as that from a predominance of forest-specialist bird species to those more capable of utilizing clearings and grasses. These shifts likely parallel those involving other wildlife species groups, such as small mammals, that draw less attention in scientific and historical literature.

Today about 52 percent of the mainland United States and 11 percent of Canada — an astonishing figure, given that only 1 percent of Canadian land is considered agriculturally prime — is in agriculture. The transformation of native landscapes, together with increasing urbanization and the intensification of agriculture in recent decades, has led to some notable species changes. Conversion of native habitats into agricultural lands has led to local extirpations of some wildlife species, shifts in abundance, and alterations in range. Some of the best-documented cases concern birds. For example, in the past, agricultural practices left edge and field habitats that resulted in Neotropical migratory bird use; the recent decline of dense edge habitats and related larger field sizes has affected significant declines in these species. Avian conservationists are increasingly aware that grassland birds in eastern and western North America are declining rapidly, according to recent analyses of Breeding Bird Survey data. And David A. Kirk points to significant declines in farmland bird species in Canada between 1966 and 1994 (the most recently analyzed period).

Such warning signs go beyond a valid focused concern for the conservation of bird species. Birds have often been considered excellent sentinel species for environmental health. In the agricultural setting they are once again useful in this manner. A decline in bird species diversity suggests not only decreases in gross avian habitat but also decreases in diversity of plants and subsequently of insect and pollinator species in agricultural environments. What are the implications for wildlife when the vast tracts of land now occupied by agriculture in the industrial world seem to be suffering serious declines in generic species diversity?

This is not a purely North American phenomenon. Similar population concerns for birds have been raised in Britain, where a member of the United Kingdom's Game Conservancy recently stated, "We are facing a second silent spring." Declines in farmland bird species have occurred across Europe as well. Furthermore, increasing agricultural development in the nonindustrial ("third") world may well result in many of the same shifts and associations among wildlife species. The landscape changes that have occurred over roughly two centuries of settlement and expansion of agricultural practice in North America parallel changes that took close to a millennium to achieve in Europe. Given the demands of technology and local economies in a global market, it is not unreasonable to assume that countries beginning to expand their agricultural bases today will arrive at this impasse between nature and culture at an ever-increasing pace.

From a more agricultural perspective, this decline in bird species should be of great concern to those involved in integrated pest management, as birds are important natural predators of pests in the farm landscape. Birds are control agents for a variety of pest species. A 1996 study by Kirk and colleagues identified four groups of crop "pests" reduced by bird species: mammals, other birds, invertebrates, and plant species. While not the whole solution, a diverse bird population can depress insect populations that are at moderate to low densities. Anecdotal information suggests they may also help reduce local outbreaks of pest species. However, birds cannot be expected to exert such control without habitat nearby to fulfill their basic needs.

Although sustainable agriculture initiatives focus on biological controls, they do so for insect and not avian predators. One reason for this may be that many bird species are considered to be cropland pests themselves. Yet a 1993 study by Nicholas L. Rodenhouse and colleagues estimated that only 10 of the 215 migratory landbird species caused significant damage to agricultural crops over widespread areas in the United States. Of these, the Red-winged Blackbird caused by far the most damage. Another study suggests that by providing certain species with vast areas of uninterrupted feeding opportunities and by reducing competition from other species because of insufficient habitat and intrusive farming techniques, we ourselves have elevated certain bird (and insect) species to the rank of major pest.

Given our historic fascination with birds, their potential benefits to agricultural environments, and their role as environmental sentinels, their population declines augur poorly for other wildlife species that have failed to capture the popular imagination to the same degree. While crop losses to vertebrate wildlife do occur and should not be trivialized, they must be balanced against the largely unmeasured benefits of natural controls — in terms of pest control, the direct ecological benefit derived from species diversity, and the maximizing of the gene pool for future improvements to crop species.

THE IMPACT OF AGRICULTURAL PRACTICES ON WILDLIFE

Today's agricultural activities are highly manipulative, fields are vast, and natural habitats are increasingly scarce. The ecological roles of many species have been displaced in favor of more "efficient" agents such as pesticides. In terms of wildlife habitat, agriculture has interrupted the diversity of natural species assemblages. Soil loss, reduction in soil and water quality, alteration and contamination of watersheds in combination with frequent disturbance of remaining habitat, use of biocides, and the proliferation of non-native species have all contributed to the "unsustainable" nature of modern agricultural ecosystems. Recent trends such as no-till farming, which seems to alleviate soil erosion, have unwittingly contributed to other problems such as compromising the value of field edge habitat and increasing the availability of pesticides to wildlife. The cumulative loss of habitat to agriculture, especially to intensive agriculture, is one of the primary challenges to biodiversity and to wildlife species health today.

Farmland Structure. Before the 1950s, farmland included a variety of natural plant communities that in turn provided useful wildlife habitat. Field margins, ponds, shelterbelts, woodlots, and other uncultivated adjacent areas were typical elements of farms. No one argues that such agricultural "edges" are prime habitat for wildlife species, but given generic declines in quality and quantity of habitat and the increasing isolation of wildlife, the role of edge areas should not be underestimated. Neotropical migratory birds, for example, use edge areas for foraging, nesting, singing/territory marking, preening, and more. Indeed, edges support many migratory bird species that do not use fields. Groundcover provides habitats for reptiles and small mammals. These native plant edges are critical to a host of invertebrate species which provide food for wildlife and play important pollinating roles as well. While certain "pest" insect species are bound to thrive in edge environments and potentially spread into crops, so do their natural predators, vertebrate and invertebrate. According to Pierre Mineau and Alison McLaughlin, "most evidence indicates that field margins have the best potential to enhance [plant and invertebrate] species richness and may even help to restore predator-prey relationships."

The average field size in the United States doubled between 1940 and 1967. Larger farm machinery and increased specialization in one or two crop commodities by many farmers contributed to this trend. Edge habitat declined as farm size increased — from 30 to 80 percent has been removed in the central United States since the 1930s. Birds have been the subjects of the majority of studies on the wildlife impacts of these changes. The increasing homogeneity of the U.S. farm landscape has led to notable declines in the abundance and diversity of Neotropical migratory birds, in the number of native bird species that nest in edge habitat, and in grassland and farmland bird species. A 1979 study of land use in Illinois tracked changes on a 1,117 hectare (2,793 acre) plot from 1939 to 1974 and concluded that loss of permanent grassland, wood cover, and edge habitat to intensifying agriculture resulted in extirpation of Greater Prairie-Chickens, a 78 percent decline in Bobwhite, and a 95 percent decline in cottontail rabbits. In Britain, where the relationships between bird populations and edge habitats have been studied most extensively, losses of some songbird species populations of up to 75 percent have been reported among fairly common species such as the Linnet, Song Thrush, and Corn Bunting. The loss of traditional hedgerows to the same pressures described above is seen as the primary culprit. Smaller plot sizes, an increase in continuous woody edges, a more significant depth to wood-

lots, the maintenance of naturally occurring wetlands, and thoughtful management of roadside areas and nearby public lands can all
contribute to the integration of wildlife in agriculture.

Mechanical Operations. Tilling, mowing, and harvesting affect
wildlife species directly and indirectly. Mammals, reptiles, and ground-
nesting birds may be accidentally killed by farm machinery, and birds'
nests disturbed or destroyed. Many birds are theoretically able to
reestablish nests after early season disturbances such as tilling, though the
cycle of planting and mechanical ground application of some pesticides
may limit such recovery. The extent to which the persistence of local
avian populations is affected by tilling activities is not well studied.

The earlier and increased frequency of cutting and mowing forage
crops has raised significant concern about the number of direct kills of
grassland species' nesting young and possible local population-level
effects. First cuttings are occurring weeks earlier than ever before and
forage crops are being cut up to four times per season. Several studies
have concluded that mowing probably contributes to declines in
grassland-nesting species populations. Evidence also suggests that
mowing and harvesting during breeding and nesting season result in
abandonment of territories. Mowing at night can cause increased
mortality of adult birds attending nests or roosting. Summer harvesting
of small grains or soybeans has some of the same impacts as mowing.

Indirect effects of mechanical operations include alteration of soil
and water quality in the agroenvironment and the reduction of shelter vegetation, plant diversity, and — in the case of tillage — in the
abundance of food. Tilling the soil does result in a temporary abundance of foods for birds and some small mammals, but it also buries
75 percent or more of crop residues, including grains and seeds that
serve as forage for birds and that provide habitat or food for the
arthropods some birds consume.

Reduced till and no-till practices have, at first glance, largely positive associations with wildlife and especially birds. Crop residues
provide cover and increased forage opportunities. The timing and frequency of planting and harvesting operations can, however, lead to
accidental mortality and nest destruction. Increased field herbicide
use, a tendency to manage field margins aggressively with chemicals,
and midsummer mowing or burning may result in the same level of

environmental contamination, habitat and nesting loss, and general disturbance of wildlife as conventional tilling. Faced with these dilemmas, most ecologists still lean toward no-till methods if chemical applications are minimized and controlled. The effects on wildlife of conventional tilling versus no-till remain to be studied.

While direct kills of some animals may be inevitable with farmland machinery, changes can be made that better accommodate wildlife. Subsurface tilling blades and seed drills with narrow disc openers and packing wheels are examples of possible equipment improvements, but do require farmers to be aware of nest locations in order to save significant proportions of birds. In some areas, farmers concerned about ground-nesting birds have erected fencing around field nests to lessen wildlife mortality during mowing. The rescheduling of mechanical operations to allow for the completion of breeding cycles, however, would result in the greatest gains for wildlife species using farmland. ***Intercropping and Crop Rotation.*** These practices break up monocultures, add a level of diversity, and foster development of predator-prey relationships in ways that could decrease the need for chemical applications. Intercropping may even include certain weed species that serve as a "trap" for pest insects and add to soil quality.

Drainage. Recently heightened awareness of the need to conserve remaining wetland areas throughout North America has not prevented their loss at an estimated rate of 450,000 acres a year. In Canada, where a federal standard has been established for "no net loss of wetlands," a survey of 6,142 farmers determined that 17 percent of those with wetlands remaining on their land had drained one or more of these between 1990 and 1992. Wetlands are essential to a wide variety of aquatic plants and animals; 190 species of North American amphibians are dependent on wetlands for breeding. Drainage of wetlands leads to fundamental changes in vegetation and wildlife species use. Government support and independent partnerships to protect wetlands — large tracts and smaller areas within farms — are critical to conserving wildlife and species diversity.

Pesticides. The use of pesticides in agriculture has increased dramatically since the 1940s. Relatively soon after their introduction, organochlorine compounds like DDT, toxaphene, and heptachlor were found to have a variety of adverse effects on wildlife populations. In 1972, DDT was banned for all uses in the United States. Since then, most other chlorinated insecticides have been banned. Organophosphate and carbamate class pesticides became increasingly popular in their stead. While less persistent in the environment, these two classes of chemicals are generally more acutely toxic to many wildlife species. In 1985 organophosphates and carbamates accounted for 85 percent of insecticide use on major agricultural crops in the United States. Today, farmers can use a wide array of pesticides, including insecticides, miticides, fungicides, and — at ever increasing rates — herbicides, which account for 60 percent of all pesticides used on field and forage crops in the United States and 70 percent in Canada.

Wildlife comes into contact with pesticides dermally, via direct spray or contact with residues on treated vegetation or by ingesting treated forage, granular pesticides mistaken for food, or poisoned prey. Animals may also bathe in or drink contaminated water or ingest residues through preening or grooming. Laboratory testing and incident reporting suggest that certain species are particularly sensitive to specific pesticides or pesticide classes, but the toxicity of a given pesticide can vary greatly from species to species (even within the same genus) making it difficult to define "indicator" species for pesticide risk assessments. Variations in sensitivity or toxicity may also be affected by pesticide formulation or application method, the sex or age of the animal, the route of exposure, or the level of body fat reserves.

Pesticide effects on wildlife can occur after an acute exposure (brief exposure to single or multiple doses of a chemical) or after chronic exposure (long periods of uptake or repeated pulse doses of a small amount of chemical). Direct effects include changes induced in an animal after exposure. For ease of discussion, they can be broken down into the categories of lethal, sublethal, and reproductive. Lethal effects may be immediate or delayed and are generally more frequent for neonates than adults. But mass die-offs of adult birds in agricultural fields have been documented in several countries. It takes only one or two small granules of some of the more toxic carbamate and organophosphorus compounds to kill a small bird. And while organophosphates and carbamates generally have lower environmental persistence, they can remain in and accumulate in food chains and lead to secondary poisoning.

Sublethal effects include but are not limited to weight loss and lower fat reserves; lethargy that may lead to increased predation, inability to mark or defend territory, or failure to attract a mate; loss of migratory orientation; and decreased care of eggs or young. In addition, animals experiencing difficulty in coordination or movement may be the victims of other lethal encounters such as a being struck by cars — in which case poisoning may not be considered as a cause of death. In young birds, decreased begging behavior has been noted as a sublethal response, leading to losses in body weight.

Endocrine and/or reproductive effects have gained increased attention in recent years and include decreased reproductive capacity, effects on embryo development, eggshell thinning, and decreased viability of young. Research suggests that hormonally active pesticides have negative effects at extremely low doses and do not follow the classic linear dose model that informs traditional toxicology. Seventy individual chemicals or chemical families have been identified as endocrine disruptors. In addition, over 60 percent of the total amount of herbicides used in the United States are capable of endocrine and/or reproductive effects in animals.

Indirectly, pesticide application alters food resources available to wildlife; it also alters habitat structure and availability, and predator populations. Pesticides contribute to farm monoculture by narrowing species composition of crop fields, especially of edge areas purposefully or inadvertently sprayed. Insecticides are generally more toxic than herbicides to soil fauna and wildlife species. Populations of beneficial arthropods and nontarget prey species are often reduced after broadcast applications of nonselective insecticides. Yet, increasing agricultural herbicide use in recent years has raised concerns. Nonselective herbicides tend to simplify the vegetation structure and reduce general forage and ground cover that provide habitat and support wildlife prey items. Herbicides are also used to control weeds on roadsides, rights-of-way, and other areas adjacent to cropland. Reductions in diversity and cover in these locations may have negative impacts on wildlife species.

Wildlife is regularly exposed to pesticides, regardless of the environments frequented. David Pimentel estimates that 672 million birds are exposed to pesticides on farms alone each year, and that 10 percent of these, or 67 million, die. Regardless of the precautions taken — calculating droplet size, spray angles, height of spraying equipment — limiting applications to target areas is difficult. Drift can occur, particles can bind to soil and become airborne, and spraying onto margin areas is not unusual. Many of the most commonly used pesticides are themselves nonselective. Indeed, U.S. Fish and Wildlife Service biologists list approximately 50 pesticide active ingredients used in the United States — many in agricultural settings — that have caused documented mortality incidents in migratory birds. But our knowledge of the extent of pesticide effects on wildlife populations is hampered by the paucity of independent scientific research and difficulties in collecting and verifying wildlife mortality data.

Pesticide-induced deaths of wildlife are rarely observed. Carcasses are difficult to locate — easily camouflaged by underbrush or hidden in burrows — and up to 92 percent are scavenged within 24 hours of death. Centralized databases and standardized protocols for storing and analyzing such information are lacking. And, while biomarkers exist for the popular organophosphate and carbamate classes of pesticides — making it possible to test for and measure their presence in the blood or brain of an animal — many new products are being developed that have different modes of action and do not have reliable biomarkers.

Preliminary comparisons from Europe seem to indicate that bird prevalence on conventional farms may be 37 to 51 percent of that on organic farms. But pesticide use worldwide is entrenched. The use of persistent organochlorine compounds and acutely toxic organophosphates continues in many countries. Neotropical migratory birds, for example, that are protected from some of the more deadly and most reproductively toxic chemicals in the United States and Canada, nevertheless migrate through and to areas where these chemicals are still in use. The removal of those pesticides most hazardous to wildlife from markets worldwide and a shift to more highly selective pesticides would be enormously beneficial. In North America, ongoing scientific discovery regarding risks to wildlife and reassessment of farmland structure and agricultural practices by farmers and land managers to lessen pesticide use is necessary to protect wildlife health.

Fertilizers. Chemical fertilizers may pose a greater direct threat to water and soil quality and biodiversity than to wildlife. But indirect effects to wildlife are evident. Use of inorganic fertilizers tends to reduce overall plant species diversity and may lead to farm edges dominated by one or two plant species. This can affect wildlife use of and dependence on such edge areas. Also, inorganic fertilizers directly and indirectly affect arthropod and soil organism diversity and abundance, leaving some bird species, for example, with a decreased food supply. Manures, on the other hand, have beneficial effects on soil pH, soil structure, erosion, organic matter content, and more. Studies have suggested that increased use of organic manures on farms, even in combination with chemical fertilizers, may be cost-effective and beneficial to crop production in the long run.

Genetic Engineering. In 1999, only three years after the first large-scale harvest of genetically engineered (GE) crops, the amount of U.S. land in GE crop is sobering: 35 percent of all corn, 55 percent of all soybeans, half of all cotton — a total of one-fourth of U.S. cropland. Corresponding U.S. Department of Agriculture figures for 1998 — approximately 33 percent GE corn, 44 percent GE soybeans, and 40 percent GE cotton — emphasize the rapid adoption rate by growers. Genetically engineered crops are created for one of several purposes: to provide certain crops the ability to produce their own insecticide (e.g., Bt-corn, potatoes, and cotton); to provide resistance against a particular herbicide so that spraying allows complete knockdown of other plants (e.g., soybeans, canola, and corn); to protect a plant or crop from disease using genes from a virus (e.g., squash and papaya); or "enhancing" certain crops so that they deliver certain benefits (e.g., increased vitamin content — no currently marketed crops).

Scientists concerned with wildlife health and toxicology concede that the speed and degree to which U.S. farmers have invested in GE crops has left independent science on the issue lagging behind. Two recent entomological studies, however, have raised questions about detrimental effects to wildlife. In the first, pollen from genetically modified corn was found to harm Monarch butterflies — important pollinators and a sensitive environmental indicator species. Monarch caterpillars eating Bt-corn pollen in the lab had higher death rates and signs of stunted growth compared with the control group. In a subsequent field study conducted in Iowa, 20 percent of monarch cater-pillars fed milkweed leaves from Bt-corn fields and adjacent areas died, compared to no deaths of the control group. Some European studies reported in the British popular press detail adverse effects on ladybugs and green lacewings — both beneficial insects.

GE crops are touted as requiring fewer pesticide applications. Industry has released limited data covering only one year, 1997, and the results are mixed. Significant reductions in herbicide use do occur in some fields, but in others herbicide use remains the same or slightly higher. Further data will be required before any consistent reductions become evident. In the meantime, the indirect effects of herbicide-tolerant crops on wildlife using fields and field edges raise many of the same problems as traditional herbicide use: decreased ground cover, less diversity of plants to support prey variety, decreased weed seed forage base, and a general decline in habitat.

LIMITING THE AGRICULTURAL LANDBASE: AN INDUSTRY PROPOSAL

In response to many of the concerns detailed above — especially those tied to habitat destruction — one suggestion of the chemical industry is to conduct even more intensive, higher-input agriculture on a lim-ited landbase, thereby freeing up more land for conservation. Such an approach would not achieve its stated goals.

1. As Mineau and McLaughlin argue, "The expansion of intensive agriculture has taken place without the benefit of land use plan-ning to ensure that a suitable quantity of representative natural habitat was set aside for conservation." In western Canada, for example, the remnant prairie has been reduced by 80 percent; one half of Canada's endangered and threatened mammals and birds compete for this habitat. Given this history, there is reason to be skeptical about the selection of sites to be allocated for such high-input agriculture.

2. What incentives could possibly convince a large proportion of pri-vate farm owners to give up managing their own land in perpetu-ity? Furthermore, in a capitalist system where agricultural land is largely privately held, there is no way to insure that land set aside

as wildlife habitat would remain as such.

3. Wildlife is inherently mobile. Birds and other animals cannot be restricted to set geographical boundaries. Any wildlife management plan must avoid the idea that populations can be isolated from supplemental habitat for the purposes of conservation.

4. Pesticides and fertilizers — integral to intensive agriculture — are not easily restricted to targeted areas. Numerous examples exist in the toxicological literature of chemicals that have spread in wind-carried soil and rain to contaminate distant areas.

It is not simply a matter of growing more food on less land. Nor is it enough to restrict the conservation of wildlife species to a system of largely unconnected, protected areas or to threatened and endangered species alone. Instead, it is the integration of wildlife species into agricultural environments that should be the long-term goal, in the interests of farming and biodiversity alike.

CONCLUSION

"As a general rule," remarks Louis B. Best, "almost any practice that reduces soil erosion, diversifies farming practices, and/or reduces pesticide use will probably benefit wildlife." Furthermore, John T. Ratti and J. Michael Scott point out, "most wildlife-habitat development within agricultural lands also has beneficial effects on soil erosion, stream siltation, chemical runoff, and other factors associated with increased wildlife populations (e.g., recreation)," in addition to having little impact on operating costs. Taken together, these provocative remarks suggest that the same processes and techniques that will foster a healthy farm environment will also integrate limited wildlife habitat. Further research on the part of agricultural scientists and wildlife biologists would help farmers accomplish these goals in their own specific circumstances: climate, soil type, crop, and wildlife population. But changes in farmland structure; dedication of unproductive patches, roadsides, and edges to permanent cover without chemical use, burning, or mowing; protection of wetlands on and off farms; reassessment of mowing schedules; increased crop diversity; reductions in pesticide use; and increased selectivity of pesticides used are useful starting points.

Agricultural lands are primary habitats for a minority of wildlife populations. But, as noted, they take up a significant proportion of the total land surface. Privately owned agricultural cropland alone accounts for 29 percent of all lands — the largest land category in the United States. Industrial agricultural practices, like many technologies, have their limits. Loss of soil, reduced soil and water quality, declines in native species and biodiversity, and significant impacts on wildlife health and habitat can all be attributed to this dominant mode of farming. But the potential for agricultural lands to provide quality food as well as quality wildlife habitat for some species, and a secondary or overflow habitat for many, is substantial. They can help keep common species common by providing critical way stations for migrants, habitat for housing significant local breeding populations, and corridors for species expanding or shifting their territories — thus adding to diversity at the local level and beyond. It seems a goal worth attaining.

Part Four

ORGANIC & BEYOND

REVISIONING AGRICULTURE
FOR THE 21ST CENTURY

Name the Enemy

▼　　▼　　▼

After reviewing the impacts of industrial agriculture, it is imperative to identify the real sources of so many of these problems — corporate control and globalization. By identifying, understanding, and ultimately confronting the power structures behind the industrial agriculture system, we can begin to institute successful alternatives.

THE END OF AGRIBUSINESS

Dismantling the Mechanisms of Corporate Rule

DAVE HENSON

ACTIVISTS TODAY ARE FIGHTING *numerous environmental and sustainable-agriculture battles. As in the past, we may win many of these struggles, but they will be only temporary victories unless we confront the real source of so many of these problems — corporate control. In all of our issues the underlying problem that we face is protecting public, democratic decision making from being usurped by private, corporate decision making. Without aggressively confronting the tremendous power wielded by multinational corporations, we will never halt industrial agriculture or succeed in instituting successful alternatives.*

▼

For decades, the U.S. mainstream environmental movement has used a strategy of regulatory and administrative law remedies to address the litany of environmental harms caused by industrial agriculture. Environmental organizations have focused campaign attention on arguments with corporations over how many parts per billion of a particular pesticide can be put in our rivers, how much of our public lands can be exploited, or how many individuals of a particular species it is acceptable to kill. The arenas of these struggles have been the courts and regulatory agencies, with occasional passage of legislation that restricts corporate harms.

What have we won? Indeed, the environmental movement has won some major legislative victories: the National Environmental Protection Act, an Endangered Species Act, a Clean Water Act, a Clean Air Act, and dozens of other laws that limit the damage that corporate agriculture and industrial society in general can do to nature and to people. In addition, the movement has created hundreds of national and state regulations and administrative rules that limit pesticide use, restrict farming near riparian corridors, require soil conservation efforts by farmers, and so on.

However, an honest assessment of the overall effectiveness of this strategy of *regulating* corporate harms must conclude that it is a limited strategy and that it has ultimately *licensed* an unsustainable and unacceptable level of ecological destruction and marginalized our most fundamental concerns. We have been fighting corporate assaults against nature timber harvest plan by timber harvest plan; factory farm by factory farm; dying stream by dying stream. We are constantly being called to fight against new and more virulent crises. If we win one, there is little time to celebrate because there are many more crises created by corporate agribusiness every day. Corporations have grown and become far more powerful in this regulatory environment. In short, corporations have successfully framed both the arena of struggle and the terms of the debate, and have limited us to incremental compromises.

Consider the national struggle around the new federal organic standards at the end of the 1990s. Congress appointed a blue-ribbon panel — a diverse committee of organic farmers, nutritionists, scientists, product manufacturers, and retailers — to propose a new law. After several years of research and hearings, the panel presented a carefully considered, comprehensive set of recommendations to the U.S. Department of Agriculture (USDA). In 1997, however, the USDA, on Democratic President Bill Clinton's watch, rejected those recommendations and instead issued to the nation draft organic standards obviously heavily influenced by corporate agribusiness and "life science" corporations. This proposal potentially allowed into the "organic" definition products with genetically engineered ingredients, food grown with toxic sewage sludge used as fertilizer, and products that had been irradiated. It was a slap in the face to the organic movement's hard work and to the trust it had placed in the regulatory system.

It then took almost two years of mass mobilization, including organizing the writing of a record 275,000 letters to the USDA, to fight industrial agriculture's attempted takeover of organic. We finally exposed the hypocrisy and shamed the USDA into retreating from the worst aspects of their industrial agriculture agenda for organics. Did we "win"? What might we have done during those two years of struggle if we had not had to fight that corporate takeover? What could we have done with 275,000 people mobilized proactively to *further* the sustainable agriculture agenda instead of having to drop everything and *react* to the attack on organics?

CORPORATE VS. DEMOCRATIC DECISION MAKING

The real struggle around the national organic standards was not over the federal definition of organic, important as that is. The real struggle was about public, democratic decision making versus private, corporate decision making on issues of food and agriculture.

This is one major case — and there are hundreds like it — where private capital, amassed as the wealth of multinational corporations, exerted much more decision-making authority than the people of this country.

Another example of corporate decision making usurping the public democratic process can be seen in the current struggle over genetically engineered foods. In the United States, the life sciences corporations have succeeded in setting the terms of the debate. The corporate media have framed the struggle as one of "right to know" and of bad science versus good science. We are told that we are in a grand battle over whether or not to *label* genetically engineered foods. In fact, if we "win" labeling — just another regulatory "fix" — we are actually giving license to the ongoing harm.

The *real* issue we should be fighting around genetic engineering is the patenting of life and the consolidation of the ownership of all the major food and medicinal crop genomes into the hands of a few multinational corporations. The *real* issue with genetic engineering is: Who is making this fundamental decision? Who is going to decide what we ought to do with the most consequential and potentially dangerous technology since the splitting of the atom: corporations and "the free market" or people and democratic process?

These are not just cases of putting profit over people and ecosystems, but of governments and courts legally defending corporate decisions over democratic decision making, and of corporate private-property rights being ruled as supreme over individual or communal property, human and environmental rights.

The big questions here are (1) what the appropriate role of institutions of economic enterprise in a democratic society is; and (2) what economic and cultural decision making should be public and what should be private.

CORPORATE PERSONHOOD AND CORPORATE "RIGHTS"

What happens when we try to reassert democratic, public control over major economic decisions? What happens when we seek to halt corporate abuses or insist upon the "precautionary principle," the "polluter pays principle," or even the "right to know"? Corporate attorneys (and they are plentiful) respond with legal defenses based on the fiction that a corporation is a legal "person" in terms of constitutional protections. They use the interstate commerce clause of the U.S. Constitution to assert that states, counties, and cities have no authority to restrict interstate and transnational commerce. They assert for the corporation the property rights, due process, and equal protection guarantees meant in the Constitution for real, human persons.

They have used Fourth Amendment constitutional protections (intended to safeguard natural persons against unreasonable search and seizure by the state) to limit environmental, health, and safety inspectors from investigating conditions in industrial farms and factories.

They have claimed, and legally achieved, First Amendment free speech protection as a way to overturn public initiatives and legislation aimed at limiting billboards, banning advertising in schools, and controlling the information agenda of *our* public airwaves. They have won major U.S. Supreme Court rulings equating financial contributions to political campaigns and political ads with political free speech, disabling "we the people" from keeping corporate money out of *our* elections. Once the corporations strategically acquired personhood status, Philip Morris (Corporation) and your grandmother, for example, are both treated as *people*, with the same constitutionally protected rights.

While real people die, their wealth is subject to estate and inheritance taxes; "corporate persons" live forever. Corporations also receive extensive limited liability, making it nearly impossible to imprison individual corporate managers, board members, or shareholders for far worse crimes than those that often result in incarceration of real human persons. If a real person steals a motorcycle for his/her third felony ("third strike"), California mandates a sentence of 25 years to life in prison. But if, for example, the UNOCAL Corporation, based in California, is convicted for the 15th time for breaking the law (as it has been), it suffers a very small fine and goes on with business as usual.

Under World Trade Organization (WTO) rules, this logic of corporate personhood is extended to its grandest illogical conclusion. Multinational corporations can sue nations for "lost future profits" if a country limits that corporation's "right" to extract, exploit, and pollute more than the lowest common denominator "harmonization" of international WTO deregulation.

It is very important to remember that nearly all of the rights of natural persons, which corporations now enjoy, were handed to them by courts, not legislatures. Most of these rights were neither granted in the U.S. Constitution nor ever voted on by the people.

HOW DID CORPORATIONS ACQUIRE SO MUCH AUTHORITY?

The first giant U.S. corporations were the banks and railroads that emerged after the Civil War. They set out for a decades-long court shopping spree, biding their time to find the right court, packed with the right elite judges, to give them the rulings that they needed to continue the march toward full legal personhood. They followed with a strategy of rewriting state constitutions and state corporate codes to further set themselves apart from the direct control of the people.

In the 135 years since the Civil War, the corporate class has succeeded in constructing a corporate form, empowered with the rights of natural persons, that is essentially outside the control of the sovereign people. While they have been strategically molding law and culture to favor their control of economic and governmental decision making, "we the people" have been struggling to ensure that all *real* people are legal persons, fully protected by the U.S. Constitution. In a nation that was founded with only white, land-owning males defined as "persons," people of conscience have struggled mightily to bring African Americans, women, Native Americans, Asians, debtors, men without property, and all other classes of human beings to full personhood at the roundtable of democratic sovereignty. We are still struggling to insure that gays and lesbians, and new immigrants, have full rights. And we are working for the day when the flora and fauna, ecosystems, and the very natural processes that insure life for all will be fully represented at the decision-making table as we steward our common wealth.

Corporations, on the other hand, have no business being present at that decision-making table. Or rather, they *only* have business. A corporation has concern for only growth and profit. That is what it is set up to do. When "we the people" sit down to discuss how we can develop a sustainable agriculture that strengthens local, diverse culture and restores, not degrades, our Mother Earth, the corporations should be out of the room. It is our duty to set the parameters for economic activity. If a corporation does not like our terms, it can disappear — there will be plenty of others willing to do good business on the terms we have defined.

Does this seem too idealistic? It was not so long ago, in nearly every state in the Union, that corporations were all given *limited* charters of incorporation (as opposed to today's *general* charters that grant corporations perpetual life). Typically, a manufacturing charter would be limited to 40 years, a mining charter to 50 years, and other corporate charters to 30 years. After that, the corporation was dissolved, or the corporate officers could reapply for a new charter but would then receive public scrutiny of their past actions. The question would be: "Have they served the interests of the people of our state?" If not, why would we give them a new charter to continue to harm the land or the people?

Under the Wisconsin State constitution until 1954, for example, a corporation could not own excess property outside the direct use for the purpose of their charter. The corporation could not own another corporation. The corporation existed for a limited life span, written into the charter. And it was a felony for a corporation to give money to a political campaign.

Corporations are chartered, given the basic license to do business, by the states. A typical early attitude toward charter incorporation was stated in 1834 by the Pennsylvania legislature: "A corporation in law is just what the incorporating act makes it. It is the creature of the law and may be molded to any shape or for any purpose that the Legislature may deem most conducive for the general good."

Private banking corporations were banned in many states until the Civil War era. That makes great sense. Think about it: Why would we allow a few private individuals through private banks to amass unprecedented wealth from the interest on the collective capital of all of us? Why would we turn over the decision-making authority on where to invest our collective wealth to the self-interests of the industrial elites? Further, banks in those days were forbidden to engage in trade and could not merge.

IS "CORPORATE RESPONSIBILITY" AN OXYMORON?

When we speak of corporations, we must make a distinction between private corporations and public corporations; between small, community-based corporations and multinational corporations; and between for-profit corporations and not-for-profit corporations. Small, family, or community-scale corporations are most often privately held and have much more flexibility in how they do business (for example, not being forced to yield high quarterly profits — no matter the environmental or social cost — for shareholders). The corporate owners and managers most often live locally, where the company does its work, and the surrounding community can more easily hold them accountable to local democratic decision making.

These corporations are more likely to be of a human scale at which each worker can have a personal stake in the business and a relationship with the owner and with the community. Conversely, the largest of the multinational corporations have gross net incomes greater than many nation states and are at such an inhuman scale that "enlightened" managers can rarely temper the giant organization's insatiable urge toward growth and short-term economic returns.

For decades, many environmentalists, ecological farming advocates, and other social movement activists have focused on campaigns for "corporate responsibility" — trying to convince the leaders of huge, polluting companies to be "better corporate citizens." But trying to change the hearts of CEOs very rarely works. Courts often rule that "shareholder rights" to maximum profits limit management's prerogative to do the "right thing," like stopping the factory farm from polluting the river, or pulling the business out of Burma, or building a child-care center for employees.

When a multinational corporation signs some "voluntary code of conduct" it usually results in the movement's stopping a boycott campaign and celebrating the corporation as a "model good citizen." Yet there often comes the day come when the corporation's managers decide they can no longer afford to abide by the codes. They were only voluntary codes, after all. We then have to start the campaign all over again.

Corporate public relations departments long ago learned that it pays well to use a small fraction of the surplus wealth earned from overcharging us on whatever product or service they sell to blast us with propaganda. They tell us that Chevron "cares," that Weyerhauser is "the tree planting company," and that Archer Daniels Midland will "feed a hungry world." Further, some of the worst criminal corporations and corporate officers win local or national "good citizen" awards for donating small fragments of *our* surplus wealth (that they hoard) to the symphony or the Girl Scouts, or by donating their corporate logo–laden goods to our public schools. Corporate foundations also fund many of the largest environmental, civil rights, arts, and other groups in the nation.

The result of this "corporate philanthropy" is that it gives control of much of our national culture and social movement agenda to these corporations through their decisions on which groups receive grants (and thus have their campaigns reach the public) and which groups die on the vine for lack of funding.

CORPORATE CONTROL OF FOOD AND AGRICULTURE

With regard to food and agriculture, the multinational corporations' strategy has been to establish the unchallengeable right to their control over the food system. They have done this through monopo-lization by strategic underpricing of smaller-scale competition and by developing a revolving door of corruption between corporate man-agement and the very government agencies charged with enforcing regulations. Through vertical integration — from financing to seed patents to value-added products to distribution — they have cultivated farmer dependency on credit, seed, chemical input, and farmgate pricing worldwide.

They have successfully appropriated much of our public educa-tional and research resources, crafting "private-public partnerships" with universities, governments, and even the United Nations. Through TRIPS (the Agreement on Trade-Related Aspects of Intellectual Property Rights) and the WTO, multinational corpora-tions have successfully gained control of intellectual property rights, international trade regulation, and dispute resolution.

To fully control the global food system, the global corporations must continue to colonize and homogenize the remaining independ-ent and resistant cultures around the world. Over many decades of trial and error, they have developed enough institutional memory to utilize — even create — regulatory structures that insure that the eco-nomic bottom will not drop so low on any potentially resisting people that they will, as Marx put it, "have nothing to lose but their chains" and rise up in revolt.

DEVELOPING AN EFFECTIVE COUNTERSTRATEGY

The fight against corporate chemical-industrial agriculture, against corporate control of the global food system, against corporate owner-ship of life, and against corporate control of economic decision mak-ing is the fight on this planet. All the cultures of the world, and all ecosystems, have a common interest in replacing corporate rule with democratic rule in service of diversity, cooperation, sustainability, and the common wealth.

To win this fight — much of it needing to be fought in the United States, which is the source of so much of the corporate problem — our movements must rapidly evolve new strategies. Specifically, we must do three kinds of activism at once.

1. Fight Fires

For the past 30 years, our conservation and environmental movements have been focused on "fighting fires." We have built ten thousand local or national groups to fight ten thousand corporate assaults on nature and people. David Brower often said that "there are few real environmental victories, only holding actions." He meant that, for example, after a five-year campaign using much of our local movement time and resources, we *may* stop a clear-cut or new dam, but the corporation will be back to take the trees or the river as soon as it can maneuver a change of judge or politician, or a lull in our vigilance. We have to fight them off forever. They just have to win once.

Of course, we have to fight fires. When the "Hogs 'R' Us Corporation" comes to put a 2,500-hog farm on the banks of our "Salmon River," we *must* mobilize and put our all into the campaign. We have no choice. But this form of struggle alone will rarely have an effect on corporate destruction everywhere else in the world and may just chase the corporation (and the problem) to another community.

2. Create Alternatives

The ecological farming movement has grown steadily for the past 30 years, but we are being far outpaced by the multinational corporations' destruction of small-scale and traditional farming in the United States and around the world. We must, however, provide an articulated, accessible platform of specific vision and practices that reflect the values of ecological, economic, and cultural sustainability. We have many examples of how to do agriculture right; they are just dwarfed by the number and scale of the corporate wrongs.

Our alternatives must be based on farmland and watershed protection and restoration. Our vision includes restoring polycultural diversity in farming systems and appropriate scale in agriculture. We seek local, national, and international economic policies that reward and subsidize sustainable farming and business practices, and punish, tax, and disallow unsustainable farming and business practices. We must integrate and reward economically and socially just farm-labor practices. Our vision for agriculture must highlight the enhancement of wildlife habitat and wildlife corridors, and we must work quickly toward the elimination of synthetic insecticides, fungicides, and herbicides.

But as we work to build alternatives and as we become effective at modeling "how it might be," we must be clear that the corporations can be and *always are* ruthless in buying out, making illegal, marginalizing, or destroying people's most successful efforts at getting off their treadmill.

3. Dismantle the Mechanisms of Corporate Rule

A group of people was bathing by a river. One saw a baby floating by and yelled for the others to help pull it out. As they were giving resuscitation to the baby on the riverside, they spotted another floating downstream, then another, then another . . . They were all working feverishly to rescue each new baby that floated by. This went on for some time, until someone thought to go upstream and stop the people who were throwing babies into the river.

While we must fight the fires (save the babies) that get forced upon us, *we cannot confuse reaction to a problem with proactive strategy*. And while we must build sustainable alternatives, we will create a safe and open space for sustainable practices to become the norm *only* if we dismantle the mechanisms of corporate rule that stand in our way. We need to focus on *defining* the authority — and the legal limits to that authority — that corporations are allowed. We need to stop yielding to them the rights of personhood while we try to *regulate* their harms from the edges.

Our movement is full of activists who know all about the legal maximum for chemical pesticide applications, the details of timber harvest plans, and how to file injunctions to stop a polluting factory farm. But how many of us have read our state constitution or corporations code, or know the last time the corporations rewrote key clauses of either of those documents? While we have become experts at the game of fighting to regulate corporate destruction, the corporations have been writing and rewriting the rules of the game.

We must focus on new strategies that change the ground rules on who is in charge, to reclaim our constitutional right to sovereignty over economic activity. *We must choose appropriate arenas of struggle*. The really meaningful fights that will win a reality of sustainable agriculture everywhere are over what we put in our state constitutions, corporate codes, and corporate charters.

Part of developing new strategies is to pay closer attention to the language we use. The language of our struggle is important because it is how we cultivate literacy among the population: ecological literacy, watershed literacy, economic literacy, global literacy, and democratic literacy.

It took us a decade in the antinuclear movement to move from talking about "safer nukes" to calling clearly for "no nukes." The civil rights movement evolved its language from calling for "desegregation" to demanding "equal rights." Importantly, our current movement language has been changing from talking about "corporate responsibility" to "anti-corporate" and "anti-globalization." Further, we now hear in the streets the call for "dismantling corporate rule." Our new language juxtaposes corporate grabs for "intellectual property patent rights" for seeds and plant genomes with our clarity about "collective heritage," "traditional, communal property rights," and "the rights of nature."

BY WHAT AUTHORITY?
DIRECTLY CHALLENGING CORPORATE RULE

We can get considerable mileage by asking the refrain, "By what authority?" By what authority do large corporations wield so much power over nature, our lives, cultures, and economies? "By what authority?" or "Quo warranto?" is also a legal writ. In state constitutional law, when a corporation is acting outside of its charter, we can file a motion in court that demands to know by what authority this corporation poisons our rivers or steals our seeds. We demand a ruling of Ultra vires — or "beyond its authority" — and the revocation of that corporation's charter.

In 1998, such a charter revocation was initiated in New York State, under Republican Attorney General Dennis Vacco. The state sought to revoke the charters of two nonprofit public relations and lobbying groups for the tobacco industry — the Tobacco Institute and the Council for Tobacco Research. Before the court could rule, and as a part of the Master Settlement Agreement against tobacco companies, the lobby groups voluntarily forfeited their charters. Their assets were distributed to the state's antismoking education fund, and their documents and files to the School of Public Health at the State University of New York.

In the 1870s to 1890s, American farmers built an anti-corporate movement that was clear about what it wanted. The Populists, Knights of Labor, Greenbacks, Alliance, and even the Grange worked to oppose the monopolizing consolidation of the banks and railroads. They understood that what was at stake was the control of their independence, their culture, and their decision-making power around prices and distribution. While not an overtly conservation-minded movement, these groups struggled to maintain control of their direct relationship to and stewardship of the land. They also understood the importance of who controls currency policy and access to credit. They fought to keep farming as the foundation of rural culture and local democracy — much like the agrarian democracy that Thomas Jefferson had envisioned.

We need to revive the passion and clear anti-corporate, pro-democratic focus of that populist movement. Times have certainly changed, but the fundamental struggle against rule by large corporations is much the same. Any successful national and international movement will have to be based in strong local movements that have a clear sense of strategy and the courage to stay strong and focused as the corporations fight back.

In the United States it can often seem that we have no chance to turn back corporate rule. To get perspective and develop strategies, we must have the wisdom to learn from the still-intact cultures and movements of resistance in many other parts of the world, where communities have not yet succumbed to monoculture and corporatization. Huge, radical anti-corporate movements in Mexico, India, France, and many other countries can give us inspiration and ideas. The fact is, however, that we in the United States have the responsibility to take the lead in new campaigns to dismantle the mechanisms of corporate rule, for it is in our nation that so many of the world's most criminal and destructive corporations are incorporated and headquartered.

Our best strategy is to act at the local and state levels, at the scale where we can possibly win initial campaigns. We need to pass local and state laws that declare our sovereignty over economic decision making in our communities and in our states. To do this, we will need to choose the fights that can organize a voting majority to democratically declare our decision. There is no shortcut to get this done. This is about community organizing, about motivating people to take history into their own hands and create their own destiny.

However, when we pass a local or state law that bans or restricts corporate control of our land and culture, we will certainly face intense opposition from the corporations we seek to contain. The corporate lawyers will argue in courts that we are violating their "corporate free speech," their "private property rights," their "intellectual property rights," their "right to do business," and their "right to future profits." They will say our new laws in favor of local culture and sustainable agriculture violate the commerce, the equal protection, and the due process clauses of the U.S. Constitution, and they will seek a federal court injunction against our democratic decision. They will say our local laws restricting corporate exploitation of soil, water, air, people, and culture are "unfair trade barriers," and they will seek a ruling from the secret WTO panel so they can threaten to crush us with trade sanctions.

Well, let's bring on those fights! We need to create *crises of jurisdiction*: direct clashes between laws that people of a local or state jurisdiction have just democratically debated and passed and the ruling of some international tribunal of corporate attorneys who tell us, "You don't have authority to decide on matters of the market — that's for the corporations to decide." It will be these crises of jurisdiction that will mobilize people to resist such tyranny.

There are dozens of ways we can begin dismantling the mechanisms of corporate rule from the local level on up. Some of these strategies have been tried and are holding up against corporate counterattack; others are ideas waiting to be tried for the first time. Among them: (1) Amend state constitutions by inserting *defining* language that will declare, for example, that a corporation does not have the constitutional rights of a person, that patents on life are not allowed, and that the polluter pays. (2) Amend state constitutions and state corporation codes to revive restrictions on corporate charters, declaring (among other things) that it is a felony for corporate officers of a corporation to finance political campaigns or try to influence elections; that corporate charters are for a limited number of years; that corporations cannot own property outside the specific needs of the business they are chartered to do; and that corporations cannot own other corporations. (3) Ban corporate ownership of farmland, as has been done at the state level through constitutional amendment or legislation in Nebraska, South Dakota, and seven other U.S. states. (4) Attack so-called "corporate free speech" head-on at the local level — at school boards, ban the use of corporate logos on campus; at city or county council, ban billboards and ban corporations from running political ads. (5) Disallow criminal corporations from doing business with a jurisdiction: prohibit "repeat offender" corporations, those with multiple criminal convictions, from conducting business within a city or county jurisdiction (i.e., corporate "three strikes" laws); and initiate *Quo warranto* charter revocation proceedings against the worst criminal corporations.

All of these practical strategies require substantial campaigns and a lot of strategic forethought. When we move to disable the global corporate system, we had better have a well thought-out strategy! In this corporatized culture that steers all radical thought toward short-term compromises, we need to revive a sense of long-term struggle. We are not going to "win" in a few years. As every branch of our environmental and social justice movements must continue to "fight fires" *and* create sustainable alternatives, we each must also dedicate a substantial part of our day-to-day and long-term work to these new strategies that aim to dismantle the mechanisms of corporate rule. We do this for our ancestors and our descendants, and we do this for our Mother Earth.

INTELLECTUAL PROPERTY

Enhancing Corporate Monopoly and Bioserfdom

HOPE J. SHAND

INCREASINGLY, THE LAWS OF INTELLECTUAL PROPERTY — *including patents, plant breeders' rights, trademarks, and trade secrets — are being used by corporations to seize monopoly control of genes, plants, animals, and microorganisms. Patents are even being granted to corporations for exclusive "ownership" of biological processes — the building blocks of life. Intellectual property policies are turning farmers into bioserfs, deprived of the right to save, sell, or exchange seeds. Fortunately, some governments and organizations are fighting against intellectual property regimes that threaten food security, jeopardize basic human rights, and marginalize public sector research.*

▼

Intellectual property is the oil of the 21st century. Look at the richest men a hundred years ago; they all made their money extracting natural resources or moving them around. All today's richest men have made their money out of intellectual property.
— Mark Getty, grandson of the oil magnate J. Paul Getty

Twenty years ago, the concept of "intellectual property" was little known or discussed outside of corporate boardrooms, government patent offices, or an exclusive circle of trade negotiators. Today, intellectual property has become a powerful tool to enhance corporate monopoly and consolidate market power. Exclusive monopoly patents are giving a steadily shrinking number of corporate "Gene Giants" unprecedented control over the biological basis for commercial agriculture.

Intellectual property is being used to eliminate the right of farmers to save and exchange seed, and to breed their own crops. Instead of promoting innovation in agriculture, patents are stifling research and hindering competition. Monopoly control over plants, animals, and other life forms jeopardizes world food security, undermines conservation and use of biological diversity, and threatens to increase the economic insecurity of farming communities. What is intellectual property? How have intellectual property laws evolved over the past 30 years, and what role do they play in industrial agriculture?

WHAT IS INTELLECTUAL PROPERTY?

The term "intellectual property" (IP) refers to a group of laws — such as patents, plant breeders' rights, copyright, trademarks, and trade secrets — that are intended to protect inventors and artists from losing control over their intellectual creations — their ideas. Intellectual property rights are granted by a state authority for a specified time period. The inventor has the right to exclude others from making, using, or selling his/her creation, and to determine under what circumstances others may use the protected idea or innovation. The types of intellectual property most relevant to plants and other life forms are patents and plant breeders' rights. Proponents of intellectual property argue that these laws promote innovation by rewarding inventors of new technologies and that IP laws are essential because a temporary monopoly enables companies to recoup their research investment.

THE EVOLUTION OF INTELLECTUAL PROPERTY IN U.S. AGRICULTURE

Historically, farmers have been the primary innovators in agriculture. They have played, and continue to play, a major role in contributing to the introduction and development of crops and livestock. One hundred years ago, virtually all of the crops grown in the United States were farmer-bred varieties. In his book *Unnatural Selection*, Cary Fowler describes a free seed distribution program established by the U.S. government to encourage farm-based plant breeding. In 1897, when this program was at its peak, the U.S. government freely distributed 22 million packets of seeds to U.S. farmers. The goal was to utilize the ingenuity and skills of the nation's farmers in geographically diverse regions to select, breed, and multiply thousands of novel plant varieties. It was the innovation of farmers that helped to build the agricultural base of the United States.

In the 20th century the rights of farmers to freely exchange and control their genetic materials were severely eroded as plant and animal genetic resources became subject to monopoly control under evolving intellectual property laws. As outlined below, the history of intellectual property laws in the United States demonstrates the seed industry's quest to sever the age-old relationship between the farmer and the seed.

The Plant Patent Act of 1930, the first plant intellectual property law in the United States, was designed to reward the developers of asexually propagated plants (mostly flowers, fruits, and ornamentals). Food crops were intentionally excluded from coverage under the 1930 law on moral grounds, because food was considered too important to human well-being to permit monopolization. But times have changed. The past 35 years have witnessed the privatization of plant breeding and seed sales. The seed industry, increasingly dominated by agrochemical and drug companies, began lobbying vigorously for stronger intellectual property protection for plants as a way to stimulate innovation and to create incentives for corporate breeders. In reality, plant patenting was exactly what the industry needed to privatize, through legal means, what it could not control by physical means.

In 1970, after years of seed industry lobbying, the U.S. Congress passed the Plant Variety Protection Act (PVPA), a type of intellectual property designed to reward developers of new sexually reproduced plant varieties such as soybeans, wheat, cotton, and many vegetables. This breeders' rights law contained two important traditional features. It allowed plant breeders to freely use each other's protected varieties for further breeding experiments; and it also permitted farmers to reuse seed from their harvests, and to sell small quantities to their farm neighbors, without having to pay royalties or ask permission. This was known as the Farmer's Right — or farmer's exemption.

The fundamental right of the farmer to save his or her seed for replanting was considered so important that the seed industry made assurances to Congress that no further attempts would be made to expand proprietary rights over seeds or endanger the farmer's exemption. But those promises were quickly forgotten. In 1994 the U.S. Congress delivered a crushing blow to farmers' rights when it amended the PVPA and eliminated the farmers' right to resell proprietary seed from their harvest to farm neighbors. The pattern is a familiar one. Every time plant intellectual property laws have been amended, the scope of protection and the rights of corporate breeders have been expanded at the expense of farmers, diversity, and society. It is clearly in the interest of those with money and power to amend any intellectual property system to strengthen their legal monopoly.

CONTROL OF BIOTECHNOLOGY

Intellectual property has been a major factor in the growth and consolidation of the U.S. biotechnology industry. In the 1980s, U.S. patent laws were redefined to allow for exclusive monopoly control of all biological products and processes. Over the course of a single decade, the U.S. government took giant steps to accommodate the corporate desire to patent life:

- In 1980, the U.S. Supreme Court ruled in the landmark case of *Diamond v. Chakrabarty* that genetically engineered microorganisms are patentable.
- In 1985, the U.S. Patent and Trademark Office ruled that plants (previously protected by Plant Variety Protection laws and the Plant Patent Act) could qualify under the stronger utility patent laws.
- In 1987, the U.S. Patent and Trademark Office ruled that animals are also patentable.

As a result of these decisions, virtually all living organisms in the United States, including human genetic material, became patentable subject matter, just like any other industrial invention. As one industry analyst explains:

Since 1980 it can no longer be said that something is not patentable just because it is living. . . . Biotechnology has advanced so rapidly in recent years that there is now virtually no life form which does not have the potential as the subject of patent application.

The patenting of life forms represents a radical departure from the scope of traditional intellectual property law. In addition to the basic criteria for patenting (novelty, usefulness, and nonobviousness) there is a well-established doctrine in patent law that "products of nature" are not patentable. But with the advent of genetic engineering, it did not take long to redefine what is considered human "invention" and legally patentable.

THE GENE GIANTS

Seeds are software. And we have the seeds.
    — Alfonso Romo Garza, CEO of Grupo Pulsar, a Mexico-based
conglomerate that controls 25 percent of the global vegetable seed market

Recent years have seen a breathtaking consolidation of power over plant genetic resources worldwide. Seed is the first link in the food chain. Whoever controls the seed controls the food supply. For companies that have combined interests in seeds and agrochemicals, the patented seed is the ideal delivery system for a package of proprietary technologies — genes and related inputs. As a result, many of the world's largest agrochemical and pharmaceutical corporations have spent billions of dollars acquiring seed and biotech companies. For example, Monsanto has spent over $8 billion acquiring seed and biotech companies; DuPont acquired Pioneer Hi-Bred, the world's largest seed company, for $9.4 billion; Dow bought Cargill Seeds North America last year.

Today, the top ten seed companies control almost one-third of the $24.7 billion commercial seed market. But corporate market share is much higher in specific seed sectors and for certain crops. For example:

- Forty percent of U.S. vegetable seeds come from a single source. The top 5 vegetable seed companies control 75 percent of the global vegetable seed market.
- DuPont and Monsanto together control 73 percent of the U.S. seed corn market.
- Just four companies (Monsanto, DuPont, Syngenta, Dow) control at least 47 percent of the commercial soybean seed market. An estimated 10 percent of the market is in public

varieties. An estimated 25 percent of North American soybean seed is farmer-saved, not newly purchased.

- At the end of 1998, a single company, Mississippi-based Delta & Pine Land, controlled over 70 percent of the U.S. cotton-seed market. Delta & Pine Land is perhaps best known for its notorious patent on genetic seed sterilization (a.k.a. terminator).

With the advent of genetic engineering the Gene Giants are staking far-reaching claims of ownership over a vast array of living organisms and biological processes. As a result, fewer and fewer companies are making critical decisions about the agricultural research agenda and the future of agriculture worldwide. The power of exclusive monopoly patents is giving these companies the legal right to determine who gets access to proprietary science and at what price.

BIOSERFDOM

With the evolution of intellectual property laws farmers are losing the right to use and develop plant diversity. Today, under U.S. patent law, it is illegal for farmers to save patented seed and reuse it. Why does this matter? Farmers have been selecting seeds and adapting their plants for local use for over 200 generations. Up to 1.4 billion people in the developing world depend on farm-saved seeds as their primary seed source. Crop genetic diversity enables farmers to adapt crops suited to their own ecological needs and cultural traditions. Communities that lose traditional varieties, adapted over centuries to their needs, risk losing control of their farming systems and becoming dependent on outside sources of seeds and the inputs needed to grow and protect them. Without an agricultural system adapted to a community and its environment, self-reliance in agriculture is impossible.

When genetic engineers at Monsanto or DuPont develop a new variety of soybean, corn, or cotton they are building on the accumulated success of generations of farmers who have selected and improved seeds for thousands of years. The companies insist that they "invented" their genetically engineered plants and that they should be rewarded with exclusive monopoly patents. In reality, corporate plant breeders are fine-tuning and modifying plants that were developed by anonymous farmers and the more recent contributions of institutional breeders.

Monsanto, the world's second largest seed company (now itself owned by Pharmacia), requires farmers — its customers — to sign a gene-licensing agreement before they buy the company's patented, genetically engineered seeds. The licensing agreement prohibits the farmer from reusing the seed for any reproductive purpose, even on his/her own land. If farmers are caught infringing the patent, Monsanto is "vigorously prosecuting" them in court. In some areas, Monsanto is literally policing rural communities with Pinkerton investigators — hired detectives — to root out seed-saving farmers. The company has filed more than 475 lawsuits against farmers for patent infringement and violation of technology user agreements.

In other words, farmers are being turned into criminals, and rural communities are becoming corporate police states. The fundamental issue is control. With the advent of genetic engineering, the farmer is becoming a renter of proprietary seeds and livestock — and he or she is losing the right to make farm-level decisions. Companies like Monsanto are attempting to dictate how farmers will farm and under what conditions. This is popularly known as "bioserfdom." The result is that food production is being taken out of the hands of independent farmers.

The economist Michael Boehlje calls it the "Wal-Marting" of American agriculture. Farmers will raise animals or grow crops according to a formula dictated by the end processors. Farmers will sign contracts that stipulate precise levels of inputs, dictating what seed, fertilizer, chemicals, row spacing, irrigation, harvesting technique, and other details will be used. As the Gene Giants gain control over every phase of production, processing, and marketing — from "farm to fork" — the role of the farmer is reduced to that of a contract worker. The American farmer becomes a "renter of germplasm," rather than an independent owner-operator.

RIGHTS FOR WHOM?

There is no doubt that patents are a powerful tool to protect corporate monopoly, but they do not necessarily promote innovation. The monopolistic nature of the patent process can restrict innovation, limit competition, and thwart new discoveries. Over time, intellectual property regimes have grown into mechanisms that allow corporations (not individual inventors) to protect markets rather than ideas. In today's knowledge-based economy, intellectual property assets have surpassed physical assets such as land, machinery, or labor as the basis of corporate value. At the end of 1995, for example, the Hoechst group held 86,000 patents and patent applications. According to Dr. Richard Helmut Rupp, head of Hoechst R & D, "The most important publications for our researchers are not chemistry journals, but patent office journals around the world." The cover of Novartis's 1997 annual report boasts that the company holds more than 40,000 patents. IBM is now getting ten new patents every working day.

Increasingly, access to new agricultural technologies is legally restricted by a complex pedigree of patented gene traits. For example, one of Pioneer Hi-Bred's genetically engineered insect-resistant corn hybrids requires access to 38 different patents controlled by 16 separate patent holders. The control of patented genes and traits has created legal barriers that make it difficult or impossible for small companies or public sector researchers to compete or to gain access to new agricultural technologies.

The uncertainty and confusion over the application of patent law to living materials has resulted in immense legal battles between corporations competing for ownership of strategic genes, traits, and biological processes. Not surprisingly, the number of intellectual property lawyers in the United States is growing faster than the amount of research. In order for patents to have economic value, corporations must defend their patent claims and enforce licensing requirements. The transaction costs are enormous. The legal costs alone of obtaining a patent approach $10,000, and it typically costs $1.5 million per party to litigate a patent. Billions of dollars are being spent on legal fees, diverting resources away from agricultural research and societal needs.

Today, the battleground over intellectual property has moved to the international arena. The World Trade Organization's (WTO) rules on intellectual property obligate all member countries to implement minimum standards of IP for plant varieties and microorganisms. In the developing world, where the majority of farmers depend on farm-saved seed as their primary seed source, the notion of legal restrictions on seed saving is perceived by many as both alien and life-threatening.

CONCLUSION

IP laws require urgent societal review. Patents and plant breeders' rights are stifling the free flow of information and genetic resources that are so vital to human survival and sustainable agriculture worldwide.

Civil society organizations and some governments are campaigning actively against the patenting of life. Farmers and indigenous peoples' organizations are vocally denouncing patents which they believe threaten food security and human dignity and are predatory on their resources and knowledge. In August 2000, the United Nations Sub-Commission for the Protection of Human Rights warned that the WTO's intellectual property rules could infringe on the rights of poor people and their access to both seeds and pharmaceuticals. The 1999 United Nations' Human Development Report concludes that "the relentless march of intellectual property rights needs to be stopped and questioned." The future of agriculture depends on the promotion and protection of the farmer's inalienable right to save and exchange seed. If we are to reclaim agriculture, we must resist monopoly control of life. If we are to make agriculture truly sustainable, it must be built on biological and cultural diversity, not uniformity, and on democratic institutions that are people-centered, not profit-centered.

GLOBALIZATION AND INDUSTRIAL AGRICULTURE

DEBI BARKER

FOR MILLENNIA COUNTRIES AROUND THE WORLD *have practiced self-sustaining, localized agriculture. A new industrialized agriculture model is now being forced on these countries — a global system dependent on massive chemical inputs, invasive technologies, and corporate control. This globalized agriculture has devastated the environment, farm communities, and farmers. Yet corporations and international trade agreements continue to foist this dysfunctional agriculture on third world countries. Fortunately, we are witnessing a worldwide movement against globalization, while farmers and consumers are actively developing cooperative strategies to promote successful alternatives.*

▼

Over the last several centuries, farmers around the world have developed diverse crops and foods that have been adapted to specific geographies, ecosystems, climates, available natural resources, cultures, and tastes. Farmers developed seeds and saved them from harvest to harvest, invented a variety of cultivation methods and crops that were unique to an ecosystem and a culture; nurtured natural resources; and kept a careful balance between regional fish, fowl, and other wild creatures. Food was grown locally for local communities, creating an accountability and responsibility to maintain a balance of all of these elements.

This self-sustaining ecological approach to growing food and fiber has endured for thousands of years, but during the last century a radical new approach to agriculture emerged. A rapid global conversion to an industrial agriculture system has resulted in a world in which environmental destruction has accelerated, millions of farmers and livelihoods have disappeared almost overnight, hunger has increased, and the nutrition and safety of our food has been compromised.

A global industrial agriculture model is inherently devastating to the environment and citizens for many reasons:

1. Local, self-reliant food systems that provide food and livelihoods for millions and a secure food supply are replaced by corporate, often foreign, control over farm inputs, energy, crop commodity prices, food production, and food marketing.

2. Biodiversity — of microorganisms, plants, insects, and animals — is replaced by monoculture.

3. Pollution caused by industrial agriculture's use of pesticides and chemicals increases on a planetary scale, destroying soil, water, and air and causing harm to wildlife and humans.

4. The import/export-driven model of globalization requires a huge increase in transport infrastructures, often constructed at the expense of nature.

5. The massive movement of agricultural commodities requires additional fuel usage, packaging, etc., and fosters exotic species invasion, and the spread of viruses, bacteria, and disease.

6. Control over and access to essential elements of life — the commons — are being stripped away from local communities and given over to corporations.

7. Genetically modified organisms and plants further destroy biodiversity and bring unknown, potentially catastrophic danger in the form of biopollution.

This industrial agriculture regime is promoted and enforced by international institutions and agreements such as the World Bank, the International Monetary Fund (IMF), the World Trade Organization (WTO), the North American Free Trade Agreement (NAFTA), and the proposed Free Trade Area of the Americas (FTAA). The rules and policies of these agreements and institutions are negotiated between governments, but they are mainly crafted by the large corporations that benefit from a globalized industrial agriculture model.

The global bodies governing this system have powerful tools to ensure, among other things, that an industrial agriculture system is enforced. For example, rulings by WTO dispute resolution panels, which are binding for all WTO members, have forced the European Union (EU) to accept U.S. beef that is injected with artificial hormones or face stiff trade sanctions on EU agricultural commodities. The WTO also rejected the EU's right to favor small-scale, often organic, banana farmers in the Caribbean, requiring it to buy bananas from huge plantations in Latin America (owned mainly by Chiquita, a large U.S. company) notorious for using environmentally damaging techniques as well as exploiting cheap farm labor. Almost every WTO ruling on environmental matters has favored corporations over the environment.

THE GLOBAL TAKEOVER OF INDUSTRIAL AGRICULTURE: THE "GREEN REVOLUTION"

Many areas of the planet began to shift to forms of industrial agriculture during the time of European colonization, when colonizers used labor and land to produce and extract raw materials — from cotton to minerals — that would supply the industrial and consumptive needs of colonizing nations. Simultaneously, industrial nations created systems of agriculture that required importing a cheap labor resource — and met that need through the slave trade.

Almost a half a century ago, another dramatic, rapid shift took place in agriculture in the United States and parts of Europe — farm inputs such as labor, fertilizers, seeds, water, and others that were previously produced on the farm were replaced by inputs that had to be purchased off of the farm. Fossil-fuel-driven machines were manufactured, which replaced human labor and enabled larger tracts of land to be farmed. Commercial "high yield" hybrid seeds were developed, along with the chemicals and pesticides that were a prerequisite in order for these seeds to produce any bud of food. Such seeds also required huge amounts of water, and, just in time, great feats of engineering enabled large dams to be built and rivers to be totally rerouted/diverted, allowing water to be delivered to formerly arid lands.

These mechanized, modern tools of farming — the seeds, the fertilizers, the chemicals, the farm equipment — quickly became commercial farming inputs that took control away from local farms and communities and gave more control to large corporate structures which supplied the inputs. Along with creating dependence on farm inputs, industrial farming also dictated a much higher use of energy. In Canada, for example, on-farm energy use alone grew by 9.3 percent between 1990 and 1996. In developing countries, energy used for agricultural production as a percentage of total commercial energy rose approximately 30 percent from 1972 to 1982 — this increase was directly driven by Green Revolution agricultural production. Such energy use, with emissions of carbon dioxide, methane, and nitrous oxide, has severe consequences for global climate.

A whole new attitude toward nature was also part of the move toward industrial agriculture systems. Working with and within ecological systems was replaced by subjugation and conquest. Diversity was replaced by uniformity. Self-reliance was replaced by dependence. These new attitudes also significantly disrupted local social arrangements and cultures. Many of the violent conflicts and wars of the last several years have been attributed to tribal and ethnic hostilities and religious differences; however, often these societal and political upheavals can be traced to disruptions in local ecosystems brought about by changes in agricultural systems. The Indian state of Punjab is a prime example. A region in which Hindus and Muslims had lived together relatively peacefully for many years turned into an area of tremendous violence, partially due to the stress put on local resources — especially water — when Punjab was turned into India's center of the Green Revolution. Likewise, tribal conflicts in regions in Africa can often be traced to food and natural resource scarcity caused by the denuding of forests for export crops, the rerouting of water for irrigation, and other such requirements of the industrial agriculture system.

Beginning in the 1970s this industrial model of agriculture was marketed to other parts of the globe as the "Green Revolution." In addition to transforming farm systems from providing their own inputs to a system that depended on seeds, fertilizers, and pesticides, high energy use, mechanized equipment, and fossil fuels from mainly foreign sources, the Green Revolution food system was based on an import/export model. Whereas developing nations primarily grew diverse, local crops for local consumption, the new agricultural model dictated that they grow crops for export — coffee, flowers, wheat — to be shipped to already well-fed, richer industrial nations.

Another characteristic of industrial agriculture is that it is based on a monoculture system, or monocropping, where one crop is planted over large swaths of land. Monocultures replaced more sustainable models, which planted many different crops together or near one another (intercropping), a centuries-old method that, among other benefits, provided natural pest controls through the beneficial insects and other creatures that thrive in such systems. Many of these species have now disappeared. Soil quality also suffered from loss of diversity. And, within only the last few decades, monocultures have eliminated plant diversity, crops, and foods. Thousands of varieties of rice were once grown in the Philippines; today two varieties account for 98 percent of production. Mexico has lost more than 80 percent of its maize varieties since 1930. In China 10,000 wheat varieties were cultivated in 1949, but in just 20 years the number dropped to 1,000. In an era when efficiency is the buzzword associated with success, it is ironic that these diverse, sustainable systems gave way to the hugely inefficient industrial system. Numerous studies confirm that when all internalities and externalities are used to calculate crop yields — amount and cost of inputs, farm animal and human labor, and other factors — a monoculture system is highly inefficient compared to smaller, diverse models.

The Green Revolution dramatically transformed not only farmers and peasants in many third world countries, who had developed highly sophisticated horticulture systems over thousands of years, but also entire societies and communities. Agriculture was and still is the basis of most community activities and livelihoods around the world. In India, millions of farmers grow approximately 6,000 million tons of wheat every year. A chain of traders (artis) bring the wheat from the farm to local shops. Most wheat is bought by consumers from the local corner store (kirana) and taken to the local mill operator (chakki wallas) for processing — there are more than 2 million flour processing shops in India. In addition, flour is also produced in the household by millions of women.

Similar small-scale local economies exist throughout Asia, Latin America, and Africa. These self-sustaining models began to be disrupted under the Green Revolution as local food crops were replaced by crops for export, leaving local artisans and livelihoods displaced, and people hungry. Soon, ecological crises followed — soils became depleted, water resources became overused, the web of insect and animal life was disturbed, and air quality turned foul as fossil-fuel farm machinery and vehicles transporting crops overtook the landscape. Ensuing political and social conflicts often followed. Globalization policies as enforced by trade agreements of the last decade have increased stress on local economies on a massive scale.

The industrial agriculture model was first promoted and enforced by the World Bank, the IMF, and major American foundations. The World Bank teamed up governments and financial institutions and provided loans to huge agricorporations to distribute (initially free or discounted) hybrid "high yielding" seeds and accompanying chemicals to farmers in many developing countries. The Bank also financed large water projects, which would be needed to maintain the industrial system. At first, the Bank worked with some national governments to help establish national seed banks that provided low cost seeds to farmers. However, a few years later, the Bank and the IMF set criteria for countries seeking loans for development projects that effectively dismantled such programs. Among the requirements of these structural adjustment programs (SAPs) were reducing or eliminating national seed banks that provided seed for farmers, thus giving more control to private seed corporations, and reducing or eliminating government low-interest loan programs for farmers.

INTERNATIONAL INSTITUTIONS AND AGREEMENTS: GLOBAL COERCION FOR INDUSTRIAL AGRICULTURE

Although the Green Revolution occurred on a rather grand scale, huge agri-corporations saw vast untapped market potential remaining, as most of the world still maintained food systems of local production for local consumption. The commercial seed market alone represents billions of dollars. Worldwide it is estimated to be worth about $23 billion, but the total market, which includes farmer-saved seed and state-run seed programs, is about twice that — around $45 billion. In India, the average farm size is less than two hectares — that's a lot of farmers and a lot of seed — a huge market to be gained.

The agenda of the 1994 Uruguay Round of the General Agreement on Tariffs and Trade (GATT) was to force a trade "über alles" economic model on the world. The basic GATT premise was that market principles reigned supreme over every other social or cultural consideration and were to be applied uniformly around the globe. Agriculture became increasingly prominent in the negotiations. Previously, agriculture had been a minor part of the GATT, limited to setting quotas and tariffs; agriculture policies largely remained as domestic matters. The Uruguay Round changed all of that and produced agreements that greatly expanded its rule over agriculture while limiting the power of national governments to protect their own farmers, consumers, and natural resources.

One of the biggest reasons that the United States pushed to include agriculture as part of the Uruguay Round was because U.S. agriculture subsidy costs were spiraling in the effort to remain competitive with other developed nations, all eager to secure export markets. As farm inputs became more expensive, governments had to spend more and more to help farmers meet their cost of production. Recently about 65 percent of the EU's budget went toward agricultural programs.

By the end of the negotiations, which resulted in the creation of the WTO, every aspect of food and agriculture was covered in the new trade rules and policies. The Agreement on Agriculture (AOA) is committed to achieving specific binding commitments in each of the following areas:

1. market access
2. domestic support
3. export competition

(It also includes a section on sanitary and phytosanitary standards.) While the AOA is very complex and full of annexes and "boxes" that assign specific targets to countries based on their place on the development ladder, the overall goal of the agreement is for countries to reduce or eliminate tariffs (i.e., import taxes), import quotas on commodities, or any other type of "barrier" that would prevent goods from entering a country. Another major aim is to reduce or eliminate subsidies, or direct payments, to farmers.

For decades, subsidies and farm price supports were a way of sheltering traditional livelihoods, small communities, and local culture.

In the United States, the government issued direct payments to farmers to ensure that they would receive adequate compensation for their crops, and it set loan rates that would maintain a stable price for certain commodities. Most southern countries could never afford to make payments to farmers. The few farm subsidy programs in the South that exist do not come close to matching the amount of funds available in the North.

Although the WTO claims to mandate the elimination of farm subsidies, the reality is that northern countries are still issuing subsidies, some of which have increased over previous years. This can happen because northern countries are allowed a subsidy-reduction schedule based on very high, some claim artificial, baselines. In addition, many of the northern subsidies are exempted or remain untouched in the agreement. In the meantime, import quotas were the only means that southern countries could use to protect themselves against northern subsidized commodities. With the elimination of these import controls, cheaper commodities from the subsidized North have come flooding into southern markets, decimating domestic farmers who are unable to compete. In the Philippines, it is estimated that over 350,000 rural livelihoods will be destroyed as this country shifts from growing corn, rice, and sugarcane to cut flowers and vegetables for export. While the AOA reduces or eliminates any supports or controls that would help farmers, it maintains and even increases a variety of corporate export subsidies and marketing promotion programs. Many of these export subsidies are paid for with taxpayer dollars. For example, the U.S. Overseas Private Investment Corporation, supported by U.S. taxpayers, provides vital insurance to U.S. companies investing overseas. This kind of subsidy significantly reduces risk for these companies and lowers the costs of doing business overseas. So, while corporations are subsidized to roam the world and take advantage of the scramble among countries to outbid one another in providing the cheapest labor, production costs, commodity prices, etc., farmers and livelihoods in both the North and the South are destroyed.

In addition to reducing farmer supports and eliminating import controls, the AOA requires that governments eliminate supply management programs and emergency food stocks, thus destabilizing food supply. Agreements such as the AOA, NAFTA, and the proposed

FTAA further ensconce the import/export-driven model. Under NAFTA, the Mexican border was opened up to food imports from the United States and Canada, which has created food insecurity in Mexico. In 1992 — pre-NAFTA — Mexico imported 20 percent of its food; by 1996 — two years after NAFTA — it imported 43 percent. Further absurdity of the import/export model is illustrated by the simultaneous swapping of commodities as ships pass in the night — one carrying grain from the United States to India, one with grain from India heading to the United States. In 1998, Britain imported 240,000 tons of pork and 125,000 tons of lamb at the same time that it exported 195,000 tons of pork and 102,000 tons of lamb.

Combined with the policies of the World Bank and the IMF, the AOA agreement also further ensures that governments cannot supply their domestic farmers with low-cost seeds and other farm inputs. This results in increased instability of food supplies, hunger for millions of people, and devastating consequences for farmers, communities, and nature. In India, thousands of farmers have committed suicide by swallowing the very pesticides that promised prosperity but instead left them in debt and not even able to grow enough food to feed their families. Farmers in Chiapas, Mexico, unable to compete with cheap corn imports that flood the Mexican market from the United States, are destitute — their protests against NAFTA agricultural policies are met with military force. In many Southeast Asian countries, thousands of farmers have been driven from their lands into already overcrowded cities to seek jobs in factories.

THE HIDDEN HAZARDS OF GLOBAL FOOD TRANSPORT

In addition to globalizing the pollution of soil, water, air, and the destruction of forests, wildlands, and species habitat that occurred in industrial countries, the import/export-driven model inherently causes catastrophic damage to ecosystems because it requires a massive global transportation infrastructure. More and larger airports, waterways and bays, superhighways, railroad tracks, fuel pipelines, and other huge projects are constructed to service the global economy — a large portion of which is agricultural commodities. Often these projects are constructed at the expense of remaining wilderness, forests, and rural or pristine lands.

The increase in transporting of goods globally is astounding in terms of pure inefficiency and the further amount of damage caused to the planet. For example, the average components of a 150-gram strawberry yogurt travel about 2,000 kilometers in the process of being made into yogurt and then shipped to consumers, according to the Wuppertal Institute of Germany. The strawberries come from Poland, corn and wheat flour and syrups from Holland, jam and sugar beets from Germany, as does the yogurt itself, and plastic and paper containers and wrappings come from various other places. The average plate of food on American dinner tables has traveled approximately 1,300 miles from source to plate.

Such increased transport has tremendous costs for the environment. Ocean shipping currently carries nearly 80 percent of the world's trade in goods. The fuel commonly used in shipping is a mixture of diesel and low-quality oil known as "Bunker C," which is particularly polluting as it is very high in carbon and sulfur. Bunker C would be considered a waste product if not consumed by ships. Given the current volume in global trade, the shipping industry is anticipating major growth over the next few years — the port of Los Angeles, for example, is planning and building for a 250 percent cargo increase by the year 2020. Increased air transport is even more environmentally damaging. Each ton of freight moved by plane uses 49 times as much energy per kilometer as when it is moved by ship. A two-minute takeoff is equal to 2.4 million lawnmowers running for 20 minutes! Due to economic globalization, freight transport in the EU is expected to increase by 70 percent in ten years. It is also predicted that truck transportation will have increased sevenfold in the ten years since NAFTA was passed.

Other environmental problems are associated with increased movement of goods. More transport means producing and disposing of more packaging materials — manufacturing plastics, paper, wood pallets, and other wares causes additional air and water pollution and destruction to forests, and further strains the earth's sink capacity when items are disposed of. Increased transport is also bringing increased devastation from bioinvasion. Wave after wave of invasive species — bacteria, parasites, viruses, insects, and animals — hitch rides on planes, trains, trucks, and ships heading for new locales. Finally, shipping perishable items requires refrigeration, which further contributes to ozone depletion and climate change.

Public health is also threatened as transport of agriculture goods increases the spread of viruses and food-borne illnesses and disease. In most industrialized countries, the number of food-related illnesses has risen sharply in the last decade. The origin of foot and mouth disease in parts of Europe, where, in spring 2001, over a million farm animals were killed in order to rid the region of the disease, has been traced to animals that were imported in from Asia. The slaughter of these animals may seem a curious way to deal with the problem. Why did a disease that does no harm to humans and from which most animals recover in a matter of weeks lead to the slaughter of healthy animals? The answer is to ensure that there would be no threat to ever greater exports of meat products — as Dr. Vandana Shiva wrote, the killings were a "ritual sacrifice to the gods of the global market."

NATURE AS A CORPORATE FREE-FOR-ALL: BAD TRIPS

The Agreement on Trade-Related Aspects of Intellectual Property Rights (TRIPs) is another measure in the WTO that affects agriculture and the environment. It enshrines the rights of corporations and expands their control over basic elements of life — seeds, plants, and other biological elements — and takes away the rights of millions of farmers and citizens who have developed and cared for elements of life without commercial intent for centuries. Much of the raw materials and knowledge of seeds and plants that has been developed and exchanged freely in the South for centuries can now be owned by northern corporations.

The TRIPs agreement is also one of the tools that gives the biotechnology and seed industries monopoly control over seed throughout the world. Genetically engineered (GE) seeds would not be a profitable venture unless corporations had a guarantee to the exclusive right of genetic plant and animal material needed to manufacture GE products. *TRIPs allows corporations to patent and own plant life and other life forms on a global scale.* In simple terms, the TRIPs agreement requires all WTO members to adopt, as their own domestic law, a system of intellectual property rights protection based on the U.S. model. TRIPs covers rules on copyright, trademark, and patent protection. Patents can be claimed for microorganisms, plants, seeds, and other elements of life.

Many southern countries have historically opposed patenting crucial elements of the "commons" — seeds, plants, and other living resources necessary for food and health — believing that they should be freely available. For millennia, the commons have been clearly understood to be part of the cultural, spiritual, and biological inheritance of all people.

Such a global patent system sanctions biopiracy. For example, foreign corporations now have the right to take traditional indigenous seed varieties that have been developed by small farmers over centuries, "improve" them by minor genetic alteration, and then patent them. These corporations then have the exclusive right to sell the patented seeds to the communities that once owned them in common and used them freely.

Under the WTO, virtually all life forms and resources can be turned into commodities available for corporate ownership. TRIPs was an agreement written by corporations, for corporations. The Monsanto official James Enyart explained the process of putting TRIPS into the GATT discussions:

> Industry has identified a major problem for international trade. It crafted a solution, reduced it to a concrete proposal, and sold it to our own and other governments. . . . The industries and traders of world commerce have played simultaneously the role of patients, the diagnosticians, and the prescribing physicians.

There are other agreements in the WTO that hand over immense powers to corporations while stripping away power from nations, communities, and citizens. The Agreement on the Application of Sanitary and Phytosanitary Measures (SPS) sets rules for food safety standards — from pesticides and biological contaminants to inspection, product labeling, and genetically engineered foods. Its intent is to establish rules to "guide the development, adoption and enforcement of sanitary and phytosanitary measures in order to minimize their negative effects on trade." Downward harmonization of food safety standards is the practical effect of the agreement. For example, the body of standards used by the SPS to set standards, called the Codex Alimentarius, allows certain levels of DDT pesticide residues on fruits and vegetables.

The Agreement on Trade-Related Investment Measures (TRIMs), which requires member countries to further liberalize and open their borders to foreign finance and investment, is another WTO agreement that gives more powers to corporations and constrains governments from protecting its citizens and local businesses. Agribusinesses now have easier access to markets around the globe because of TRIMs.

BIOTECH FOODS: EXTENDING GLOBAL CONTROL OVER FARMERS AND SEEDS

The advent of biotechnology in agriculture can be viewed as being yet another way of capturing and controlling the market and, ultimately, controlling the food supply for the entire planet. The penetration of seed and chemical companies into the agriculture market peaked around the 1970s. Development of inbred/hybrid seeds that inhibited a second-generation plant from reproducing had been marketed for several crops but was not cost-effective to develop for large, important crops such as wheat and soybeans. In order for agribusiness to grow, it had to find a way (1) to control the biology of agronomic species and (2) to ensure that this control was maintained by corporations (as discussed above, TRIPs largely filled this requirement).

Biotechnology is sold as the panacea to cure hunger in the world. However, the products developed by the industry reflect that its concern is not about human health and hunger but about control and profit. The advent of biotechnology has brought terminator seeds, which render seeds sterile, and genetic trait–controlled seeds, such as Roundup Ready, that will only respond to specific herbicides/pesticides sold by the same company that sells GE seeds. Other developments are GE plants that emit their own toxins, as is the case with Bt-corn and Bt-cotton.

The products created by these seeds include the FlavrSavr™ tomato, which was designed to withstand long-distance transport. Golden rice is the poster product that the biotech industry trots out over and over as evidence that the industry is altruistic in its intentions. It claims that golden rice, a GE rice in which a petunia gene is spliced into rice, giving it a slightly orange color, will help cure vitamin A deficiency in children from developing countries. A recent ad in *The New York Times* read: "Because rice is a crop eaten by almost half the world, golden rice could help relieve a global vitamin A deficiency that now causes blindness and infection in millions of the world's children. Discoveries in biotechnology, from medicine to agriculture, are helping doctors treat our sick, farmers protect our crops, and could help mothers nourish our children, and keep them healthier."

How could anyone be against that? The problem is that the claims made by the industry don't really pan out. In this case, they have not yet established how much vitamin A the GE rice can produce. The goal is 33.3 micrograms of vitamin A per 100 grams of rice. Even if this target is achieved, the consumption of a single serving of golden rice will only provide 1.32 percent of the recommended daily allowance of vitamin A.

Biotech does nothing to address the political, social, and financial instability of the global food system. The fact remains that the GE seeds and the requisite herbicides would not be given away for free. How will the hungry afford the seeds and the herbicides? Who will pay for and distribute the food after it is harvested? GE products are designed to create a further and more lasting dependence on the corporations that manufacture them and will also create a more unstable food supply as use of GE crops results in the elimination of locally adapted varieties.

Additionally, the environmental effects of GE seeds are largely unknown and untested. However, growing evidence suggests that there could be grave unintended harm caused by this technology, including harm to beneficial insects and the environment. Other indirect problems are associated specifically with GE Bt plants. Recently, scientists and farmers have found that major plant pest insects develop a tolerance to Bt when it is constantly expressed by a plant, as is the case with Bt-corn and -cotton plants. Resistance happens within a relatively short period of time — from two to ten years — resulting in "superpests" which can only be eliminated by a massive increase in synthetic pesticide use. Concurrently, one of organic farming's principal pest-management tools could soon be rendered ineffective. Biopollution is another by-product of biotechnology that has not been fully tested. While other forms of pollution can potentially be stabilized or cleaned up, genetic pollution cannot be recalled or controlled. Already, "superweeds" are emerging as biotech crops cross-pollinate with neighboring crops of the same or a closely related species or with wild plants.

BREAKING THE GLOBAL SYSTEM: ALTERNATIVE MODELS TO INDUSTRIAL AGRICULTURE

A global industrialized agriculture system is not the only future. It is not an inevitable system of progress — rules were created that favor and enforce this system. As the grave consequences of industrial agriculture are being played out around the globe, many citizens and communities are beginning to develop international cooperative strategies to counter this dangerous trend and to clearly articulate successful alternative models. Many of these "alternatives" are simply systems that have been proven and have endured for centuries. Globalization policies have, in fact, taken away the space for these and other models to flourish.

The tremendous citizen movements that are becoming more and more visible on the streets, beginning in Seattle, Washington, at the WTO Ministerial Summit, are demanding that communities and citizens have a voice and a choice about the quality and quantity of food they eat, the system of production they use to grow and process food, the quality of the environment and life-support systems in their regions, and other issues relating to justice, equality, and sustainability. How we grow our food and maintain food systems determines the dignity, fundamental rights, and survival of the planet and all of us who inhabit it.

Going Organic & Beyond

▼ ▼ ▼

The ultimate goal of The Fatal Harvest Reader *is to outline a specific vision for the future of agriculture: an agriculture that incorporates farming practices that are "organic and beyond." Organic agriculture is the beginning of the evolution of a food system that respects farmers, communities, the land, biodiversity, animals, and the wild. The essays in this section provide a blueprint for our collective efforts to fundamentally reshape our food future.*

UNCLE BEN

Goin' Organic Just Like We Used To

JIM HIGHTOWER

BY THE STANDARDS OF MODERN AGRICULTURE, *Hightower's Uncle Ben would be considered a fool of a farmer, failing to make use of all the chemical products and technology available, and farming on a mere 30 acres. Over the last generations traditional farming has been replaced by the chemical sprayer, synthetic pesticides, and genetic engineering. As a result, soil, water, and food itself have been contaminated, and fewer farmers are working the land. But with consumers increasingly demanding fresh, safe, and healthy organic foods, Uncle Ben's ways look more and more like the future, not the past.*

▼

Apparently my Uncle Ben Fletcher was a fool. Actually, he was my great-uncle, already an old man by about 1950, when I first recall my brother and me visiting him and Aunt Emma on their little truck farm outside Weatherford, Texas. At the time we had no idea Uncle Ben was a fool, and we probably would have jumped anyone who said he was. In our boyish innocence, Jerry and I thought Uncle Ben was clever as could be — he was brimming with pranksterish fun, always had a story to tell, could pitch washers like nobody's fool, never dressed in anything tighter than bib overalls, raised everything from chickens to watermelons (and a family, too) on that 30-acre hardscrabble plot, was blessed with a quick and exuberant laugh, and plainly enjoyed life.

By the standards of modern agriculture, though, he was a fool of a farmer, failing to make use of the full arsenal of petroleum-based inputs and chemical products today's agribusiness employs to maximize profits. Still, this failure and fool did manage to make a crop, as did his neighbors, supplying the whole area with a terrific variety of succulent fruits, flavorful meats, fresh vegetables practically bursting with nutrition and taste, rich milk and cheeses, hearty grains, and . . . well, a cornucopia. God, the food was good!

And no one who bought it had to wonder or worry if any of it contained such contaminants as pesticide residues and genetically engineered hormones, because Uncle Ben and the others raised this abundance without a trace of chemicals. Imagine. The fools simply did not know any better.

Farmers have been taught a lot since then, of course. In only a generation, Uncle Ben's plow was replaced by the chemical sprayer as the apt symbol of agriculture. Thanks to the introduction of synthetic fertilizers, insecticides, herbicides, and fungicides, instead of a hundred Uncle Bens nurturing crops on 30 acres each, we now have one farm operator managing 3,000 acres . . . and trying to manage the big bank debt incurred to underwrite such high-tech production. This is a result that agricultural economists (who have the collective vision of dung beetles) cite in their learned journals, lectures, and chemical company consultancy reports as the very model of agricultural "efficiency."

Theirs is an efficiency that conveniently factors out what is known in the jargon of economists as "externalities." (Literal Translation: big, ugly numbers that would cause our equations and conclusions not to add up; therefore we shut our eyes tight as can be and pretend they are not there.) But in your and my real-life environment, unlike in their EconomicsWorld, externalities are hard to ignore. For example, the sheer volume of chemicals being used in their "model of efficiency" crops up in the most unpleasant ways, costing far more than our good earth, farmers, and progeny can stand to pay. Since the mid-1960s, pesticide use on farms has doubled, with nearly a billion pounds of active ingredients now being applied each year. Another 4 billion pounds of "inert" chemicals are added to the pesticide mix, too, including known cancer causers and other toxics. This total pesticide dosage of almost 5 billion pounds a year is *20 pounds* for every man, woman, and child in America. Good grief, we consume only about 5 pounds of butter per capita, and 8 pounds of coffee (and the health patrol gives us a hell of a tongue-lashing for this excess), yet there goes agribusiness merrily peppering out dinner with 20 pounds of poisons apiece.

We pay for this — in taxes, in illness, in health-care costs, and in suffering. For example, farm pesticides run off into our drinking water — nearly a hundred different pesticides are now found in the groundwater of 40 states, contaminating the essential liquid of life for 100 million of us. Our taxes have to be increased to try to filter out some of these toxics before they reach our taps, then we have to pay even more dearly for the crushing health costs — monetary and otherwise — of the poisons that are not filtered out.

Frontier communities had a quick and certain remedy for anyone who poisoned the town's well: they hanged the son-of-a-bitch. Today, though, when the ag economists draw up their efficiency equations, well poisoning is not even marked down as a cost charged to the poisoners — instead, it's dismissed as an "externality." Did people get breast cancer? Did the pesticides run off into the bay and shut down the fishing industry? Was a farmworker's baby born with birth defects? Hey, pal, stuff happens, life ain't fair, not our fault, get out of the way of progress . . . and if you're so prissy about poisons, maybe you oughta start boiling your water.

Of course, boiling water to eliminate poisons would be as ineffective as the poisons are proving to be against the pests. It turns out that bugs, weeds, and other agricultural pests are amazingly adaptable — some 500 species of insects have already developed genetic resistance to pesticides, as have 150 plant diseases, 133 kinds of weeds, and 70 species of fungus.

Yet the industry urges farmers to charge dead-ahead, to apply ever more poisons and ever more poisonous poisons. Ever more expensive ones, too, now costing farmers $8 billion a year, not counting the cost of spreading them. While the pests are adapting and surviving this chemical onslaught, farmers are not — ironically, thousands are killed off financially each year by the escalating cost of the very pesticides that were supposed to make them so efficient. Worse, thousands of farmers, farmworkers, and rural residents die prematurely each year, victims of their prolonged exposure to agriculture's "chemical revolution."

Old Texas Saying Number One: "If you find you've dug yourself into a hole, the very first thing to do is to quit digging." The good news is that farmers everywhere are eager to quit digging, but like people hooked on drugs, they find themselves caught up in a culture of chemical use, with everyone from the government to the banker pushing more chemicals on them.

Old Texas Saying Number Two: "Where there's a will, there are at least a thousand won'ts." Try to change and you are up against the whole ag system. Start with the extensive rural network of traveling agents for corporate agribusiness, pushing poisons from county to county and from farm to farm. Go to the public agencies — the county extension office, the federal farm research station, or the state ag college — for advice or help, and you'll find them singing hosannas for whatever is industry's pesticide du jour. Ask about organic production and they treat you like you walked in wearing a pink tutu. Politicians are no help, because practically all of them take money from the pesticide peddlers, so they are always quick to defend even the industry's worst excesses and insist that chemicals are nothing less than manna from heaven. Then there's the Farm Bureau, a blowhard agribusiness bureaucracy that falsely fronts as the "national representative of farmers." The bureau not only preaches pesticide use relentlessly but is in the pesticide business itself. Or go to the real power in a rural community — the bank — and you'll get a hard and quick lesson about the industry's grip on agriculture. When farmers seek crop loans from banks and federal lenders, they are handed applications that include a promise that they will follow a detailed schedule of applying chemicals to their land. No poisons, no loan. No loan, no farm. Gotcha.

Still, despite the pervasive power of the chemical industry, despite a nay-saying, foot-dragging, brain-dead agricultural establishment, change is coming — inexorably and with accelerating speed. Agriculture is and will continue shifting to low-chemical use and eventually to organic production because of two irresistible forces: you and farmers.

First, the collective "you" — consumers, the public, the market. All together now: *"We don't want your damn poisons in our food, in our water, in our babies!"* It is not merely a few sprout-eating ex-hippies who feel this way, but the mainstream, the center, the majority — even Republicans, for God's sake. Pollsters confirm that nine out of ten of us are demanding what the trend-trackers have dubbed the

Clean-Food Diet, which is described in *The New York Times* as "foods free of artificial preservatives, coloring, irradiation, synthetic pesticides, fungicides, ripening agents, fumigants, drug residues, and growth hormones," as well as foods that are "processed, packaged, transported, and stored to retain maximum nutritional value."

By far the biggest surge in food marketing is toward clean food and natural products: organic product sales doubled from 1989 to 1994 and now are rising by more than 20 percent a year; overall, the sales of natural foods were nearly $6 billion in 1999; the number of natural-products retail storefronts increased almost 7 percent between 1998 and 1999, when the number of stores was 17,613, and most conventional supermarket chains are now compelled by consumer demand to carry lines of organic foods; organic cotton clothing and linens are becoming all the rage, mass-marketed not only through upscale, enviro-trendy catalogues, but also at Kmart and JCPenney; and if you think the market has nowhere else to go, let me be the first to inform you that a Texas company wants to pamper you with Organic Cotton Toilet Paper. Who says we do not live in exciting times?

"Hrumph," grump the hidebound heads of ag-biz, "organic farming is nothing but a bunch of frou-frous on farmettes, refugees from Haight-Ashbury trying to get you gullible consumers to buy a basket of spotted, bug-infested tomatoes they brought to town in their graffiti-flecked '65 VW bus. Turn farming over to organic producers and half the world will starve, because these dips cannot — repeat *not* — produce the massive yields that our Miracle of Modern Agriculture turns out every day, God bless America and the Chemical Manufacturers Association, end of discussion."

Of course, their adamancy is rooted in the sterility of their argument. It is an argument they are doomed to lose because of the second irresistible force propelling us toward an organic future: farmers. As happens to power establishments everywhere, agriculture's long ago began sniffing its own BS and believing it to be perfume, so it has lost touch with terra firma and those who farm it. To get back in touch, and to see where agriculture is headed, they could do no better than to visit Jim Crawford — one of America's *real* organic farmers. He doesn't hail from Berkeley, as would befit the establishment's stereotypical profile of an organic producer. Crawford comes from just outside Muleshoe, Texas. As the name suggests, this Panhandle town (population 4,842) is in unabashed, unrelenting farm country. It is a no-nonsense place where folks are not much given to trendy frou-frou, and I can attest that Jim Crawford is a true son of the place, with more John Wayne in him than John Lennon. A fourth-generation Panhandle farmer, he graduated from Muleshoe High, got an ag degree at Texas Tech, then returned to Muleshoe to apply what he was taught in college, which was to apply layer after layer after layer of synthetic fertilizers and pesticides to his 900 acres of corn and cotton. He did this for 17 years, until he concluded in the late 1980s that he had had all the conventional wisdom about "how to farm" that he could stand: Jim was on the brink of broke.

With his spreadsheets on the kitchen table and his red pencil in hand, he saw that his costs were only going to keep going up and the price of his crops was not, so something had to give, or he had to give it up. Right then and there is when Crawford became an organic farmer — not through some Earth Day epiphany, but through a hard-eyed examination of the bottom line. It dawned on him that generations of folks before him had farmed successfully without all those chemicals he was using, so maybe they knew something worth knowing. He began to talk to old-timers, check out books, make calls to what the experts dismiss as "oddball" groups, and generally to study the possibilities — all of which led him to discover that the solution had been right under his nose all the time: manure.

With more cattle than people, the Muleshoe area has beaucoup manure, and Jim's self-education project was teaching him that plowing composted manure or other organic matter into his fields literally would restore life to soil that had been killed with repeated poisoning. The manure begins putting back microbes, minerals, and other natural elements, while also improving the soil's "tilth" so it retains moisture and holds plants more firmly.

Organic farming is not simply a matter of doing away with chemicals; indeed, farming organically is more complex and difficult than farming chemically, because it requires an understanding of how soil, plants, and pests interact, and it puts a priority on strengthening the soil and nurturing it. Far easier just to nuke the pests, plants, and soil with some 2,4-D, and let the devil take the hindmost. At its core, organic farming recognizes that agriculture is the art and science of *cooperating* with nature, rather than always trying to overwhelm it.

Crawford started his shift from synthetics to organic on his corn crop. The first year, just as the snickering nay-sayers of ag-biz had predicted, he got only half the yield he used to get. But the next year, as his manure applications began to work their natural wonders, his yield was nearly back to what it had been, plus he was not spending money to buy chemicals and spread them. Less snickering. By the third year his soil was getting plenty stout, and his corn yield was one-and-a-half times better than what his neighbors were getting the chemical way. End of snickering. Plus his corn crop used only half the water others required, and his premium-quality corn earned him a premium price. The snickering was replaced by area farmers stopping by, digging their boot heels into his plowed field, and saying: "Manure, huh?"

Uncle Ben was no fool ... just ahead of his time.

ORGANICS AT THE CROSSROADS

The Past and the Future of the Organic Movement

MICHAEL SLIGH

FED UP WITH INDUSTRIALIZED AGRICULTURE, *many farmers and individuals, starting in the 1960s, looked to an alternative food system that was safer, cleaner, and fairer. From the start, organic farming was ecologically sound, locally rooted, and a way to sustain family-sized operations. But today, what was once a niche market has exploded into the fastest-growing sector in U.S. agriculture. This growth has not come without consequences. With the development of national standards, we still must fight to ensure that the integrity of these standards is maintained and that they remain a "floor," allowing more stringent standards — and ultimately a just food movement — to be built on their foundation.*

▼

GETTING THERE

The fatal flaw of today's food production is that it is modeled on the industrial system. It does not attempt to remain within the bounds of nature but rather is designed to "beat" nature — beat it with technology, cheap labor, and cost externalization. For much of the last century this industrial agricultural system has reigned supreme. Indigenous and older forms of agriculture were viewed as hopelessly primitive and unworkable. Progress in food production meant ever more and larger machines, larger corporate farms, and ever more chemical inputs.

The alternative to the industrial model is a food system in which food trade raises incomes, and increases food security and food safety at both ends; one in which the environment is preserved; one in which farmers have fair access to the means of food production and consumers have fair access to food at fair prices. These principles are best associated with organic agriculture — which set out to be the fair, safe, and sane food alternative. However, as it has become ever more successful, organic agriculture is at a crossroads. It can continue to embody the key organic principles, or it can be co-opted by agribusiness and become just another adjunct of industrial agriculture. The direction the organic movement takes will determine much of our food future in the 21st century.

THE ROOTS OF ORGANIC

To better understand the current value of organics, it is important to take a quick look at organics in historical perspective. We must always remember that the organic approach is very ancient as well as modern and scientific. It is not a U.S./European creation but rather an ongoing adaptation of indigenous knowledge. As such, we need to stop and honestly embrace and pay tribute to the enormous continuing contributions of indigenous peoples to agriculture, especially the organic approach. This genius is the foundation of modern organics, and the basis for the continued survival of indigenous peoples. The preservation of their knowledge of techniques, practices, and biodiversity is the hope for the future of all of us.

The roots of the U.S. organic movement can be traced directly back to this indigenous influence. In the early 1900s, F. H. King, the former head of the U.S. Department of Agriculture's (USDA) Bureau of Soils, Division of Soils Management, came back from China and wrote about the permanent agriculture of the Far East in his book *Farmers of Forty Centuries* (1911). King had clearly seen the wisdom of another agricultural model, but he died before completing his recommendations. In the 1940s Paul Keene and J. I. Rodale came back inspired by studying organic agriculture in India and began to farm and promote this kind of agriculture. They were branded "kooks" at the time, but today they are widely seen as U.S. agricultural visionaries. However, organic remained very fringe for a long time. The "back to the land" movements of the 1960s and early 1970s embraced these indigenous ideas and influences, and organics continued to be perceived as both fringe and "hippie" farming, if not downright countercultural.

But many family farmers and farmworkers also saw organics as a very common-sense alternative to the increasing environmental and social problems they were facing with industrial agriculture. Slowly, organic agriculture became a more widely accepted alternative to agribusiness as usual: ecologically sound, locally rooted, a way for farmers to farm with dignity, a way for family-sized operations to be fairly compensated. It was agriculture "with an attitude" — the marriage of values and standards.

Perhaps the first great blow to industrial agriculture came in 1962 with the publication of *Silent Spring* by Rachel Carson. Carson was a noted marine biologist who worked with the Department of the Interior for 17 years. She then wrote several best-sellers on sea life. Finally, profoundly disturbed by the growing evidence of the environmental havoc being caused by pesticides, she wrote her historic tome on the chemical danger. The book caused a firestorm of controversy. Carson — fighting terminal cancer — took on her corporate opponents and did not back down. Her work launched an entire movement against the misuse of pesticides, the very cornerstone of industrial agriculture. It created a new public awareness of the tremendous danger of the use of pesticides and began a consumer movement against the use of harmful chemicals in food.

The late 1960s also saw the rise of Cesar Chavez's United Farm Workers union, which organized tens of thousands of mostly Chicano migrant farm laborers into a union of solidarity and mutual support. The union's struggles garnered national attention and became the focal point for mobilizing literally millions of consumers, both in the United States and abroad, to support their boycotts of agribusiness giants. A major demand of the union was the end to hazardous pesticide application practices that imperiled the lives of thousands of farmworkers. Chavez's work also created a bridge between the interests of consumers and those producing and harvesting foods — a relationship that was to become key in the building of the organic food movement.

Another significant challenge to corporate agribusiness was the organizing among America's farmers and ranchers by groups such as the National Farmer's Organization, the American Agriculture Movement, and the National Family Farm Coalition. These groups led crop-holding actions, dumped milk, and blocked highways to protest the control by a few corporations over the food chain and the resulting low prices for farmers — so low they were forcing family farmers out of business.

The U.S. organic movement evolved more fully in the early 1970s with the formation of many local and state-level organic farmer organizations. This happened in a very bicoastal way. In 1971, a handful of organic farmers calling themselves the Maine Organic Farmers and Gardeners Association, (MOFGA) kicked off activism on the East Coast. Today MOFGA has grown to over 3,000 members. In 1973 a group of about 50 such farmers in California kicked off West Coast activism by forming the California Certified Organic Farmers (CCOF). The success of MOFGA and CCOF was mirrored in numerous other organic farmer–led organizations across the country. All of these groups were founded to define uniform standards for organic food and to establish a certification program to verify farmers' practices. By 1979, CCOF had helped push through state legislation defining organic standards — the first in the country.

Soon the research community began to take an interest in the changes farmers were making. The University of Washington economic report on organic agriculture in 1976 was the first to document that U.S. organic agriculture was economically feasible. At the end of the Carter administration, a young USDA scientist, Dr. Garth Youngberg, published the now-famous USDA report and recommendations on organic farming. It was a clear scientific validation of the benefits of organic agriculture and laid out an ambitious research agenda to guarantee organic agriculture would be taken seriously. It also alerted consumers that this was a worldwide phenomenon and outlined the choice between family farm agriculture or the industrial model. This seemed like the dawning of a new age, but within a year the Reagan administration took over. The Reagan USDA, under the leadership of Secretary J. R. Block, was very different from the Carter USDA, which had been led by Secretary Bob Bergland, a strong proponent of sustainable agriculture. As might be expected, Youngberg was forced out of the Reagan USDA, and the printing of the organic report was halted.

In the 1980s, despite the hostile political climate, farmers, a very few brave researchers, and the nonprofit community increased organizing around organic/sustainable agriculture. There were several Congressional attempts at funding organic research, but these attempts failed. However, the Sustainable Agriculture Research and Education (SARE) program was passed in the mid-1980s, and Congress authorized the program at $40 million per year — a figure that no administration's USDA has yet to actually request in full. A small amount of research did begin to trickle toward organic farming through this program. Even after a decade of private sector growth, the creation of over 40 different certifiers, and the boom and crash effects on organic sales from the Alar pesticide alert in the late 1980s, there was still very little public sector support for organics.

Soon, however, there was concern among organic proponents that a state-level system might not be consistent enough to ensure the integrity of organic standards as trade expanded to other states and countries — an integrity that was critical for consumer confidence and the continued success of the organic movement. Consumer and farmer organizations coalesced around urging the then chair of the Senate Agriculture Committee, Senator Patrick Leahy of Vermont, to introduce The Organic Foods Production Act of 1990 (OFPA). The goals were to put research, enforcement, and harmonized standards in place to ensure continued growth and continued consumer confidence. This was particularly important because organic was no longer just "fresh and local," it was entering interstate and global trade channels — standardization and harmonization of those standards were needed.

Two key deals were made that ensured the bill's passage. First, the House struck out all mention of the research agenda — making the bill one concerned solely with marketing organics, not furthering research on it. For its part, the organic community agreed to agree to the USDA's primary role in setting organic standards only if the authority of the USDA was balanced by that of the National Organic Standards Board (NOSB). The NOSB was set up to have the primary ongoing responsibility for establishing the national list of approved and prohibited substances for organic agriculture and to guide the USDA toward sound regulations. The NOSB membership, as mandated by the OFPA, consists of organic farm owners and operators, organic handlers and retailers, numerous members who represent consumers and environmental protection, and a science expert. The congressional record clearly stated at the law's passage that the USDA was not to "reinvent the wheel" but to form a partnership with the organic community, in part through the NOSB process. (Keep in mind that the USDA testified against the passage of this permanent law.) With the passing of the OFPA, the organic movement had come of age, but its greatest challenges lay ahead.

THE ORGANIC MOVEMENT TODAY

By the 1990s organic food had arrived. Millions of Americans were rejecting industrial food and purchasing the organic alternative. What was once a niche market has exploded into the fastest growing sector in U.S. agriculture. Organic products are now purchased by food buyers in every corner of the United States, and that market is increasing by more than 20 percent a year.

Most importantly, organic agriculture has currently established itself as a real competitor to industrial food. The organic movement has understood that the current food system's concept and design has caused the near catastrophic environmental and health impacts described in earlier sections of this book. In contrast, organic agriculture has evolved into an ecological production management system that promotes and enhances biodiversity, biological cycles, and soil biological activity. It is based on minimal use of off-farm inputs and on management practices that restore, maintain, and enhance ecological harmony. More specifically, organic farming systems do not use toxic chemical pesticides, fertilizers, genetic engineering (GE), or sewage sludge. Organic foods are minimally processed to maintain the integrity of the food without artificial ingredients, preservatives, the use of genetic engineering, or irradiation.

When a consumer today buys a product certified organic, she knows that food has been grown and processed according to strict uniform standards, verified annually by independent state or private organizations. Certification includes inspection of farm fields and processing facilities. Farm practices being inspected include long-term soil management, buffering between organic farms and any neighboring conventional farms, product labeling, and record keeping. Processing inspections include review of the facility's cleaning and pest control methods, ingredient transportation and storage, and record keeping and audit control.

As required by the OFPA, from 1992 to 1996 the NOSB held 15 public sessions around the country that resulted in numerous recommendations on what could, and could not, be considered acceptable organic practices or products. In December 1997, however, the USDA issued a proposed organic rule which failed to comport with these NOSB recommendations and which proposed allowing genetic engineering, irradiation, and sewage sludge as acceptable organic practice. In the strongest public outpouring on a food issue in U.S. history, over 275,000 consumers commented to the USDA on the proposed rule. They strongly and often angrily called on the agency to obey the NOSB and to ensure that biotech, irradiated, and sewage sludge–produced food would not be sold as organic. The USDA, clearly shocked by the huge public rebuff of its proposed rule, quickly announced that it would abandon this proposal and prepare a completely new organic standard. These new national standards were finalized in early 2001. They cover the production, handling, and processing of foods produced using organic methods.

The new national rule remains controversial, and how it is implemented will determine its impact on organic integrity. Some very basic questions still remain: Will the rule help the early farmer-innovators of organic agriculture or hurt them? Will the costs, red tape, and paperwork drive the small-scale farmer out of organic? Will the rule allow the entry of industrial-style confinement livestock operations? Will its regulations enhance or hurt consumer confidence? We must fight for answers to these questions that will ensure fairness and integrity, that will ensure the marriage of values and standards. This is an ongoing struggle for food with a place, a face, and a taste.

ORGANIC AT THE CROSSROADS

The problems with the new national standards and the federal implementation of OFPA mean that constant vigilance is required if the integrity of organic standards is to be maintained. Additionally, the looming threat of corporate takeover of organic as it becomes more profitable is of grave concern. Corporate control of organic could mean the end of small-scale organic farming and a serious eroding of the standards themselves. Decisions now, at this critical moment, will determine how the great organics experiment will be judged. Will we retain our collective organic integrity by building on our core values, or will the advent of governmental oversight and the expansion of participants result in a loss of support for these core values and thus set up the climate for co-optation?

Working to maintain organic integrity during its national "institutionalization" is one of the most difficult phases, because it is the interface between something informal that has been, up until now, mainly developed and promoted by the private and grassroots sectors and a new, formal national, and even international, regulatory oversight. Governments and large multinational corporations in both hemispheres are getting involved. Bilateral and multilateral trade arrangements, national and state laws, FAO/WHO Codex Alimentarius organic food labeling standards, and corporate concentration, mergers, and buyouts are daily influences and pressures on the organics value system. All public and private stakeholders, including farmers, laborers, processors, handlers, retailers, suppliers, and consumers, must actively participate in this process. It is essential for all of us to recognize that governments cannot and will not be able to solve all of the problems that come with growth, success, and new players entering into organics. If we want a light hand of governmental oversight, then we must manage ourselves to a greater extent. We cannot have it both ways. We must develop our own mechanisms to proactively preserve and enhance organic integrity. We must create ways to continually renew our organic vision.

Clearly, organic food — a crucial alternative to industrial agriculture — is at a historic crossroads. It will take a continued strong public response to ensure that the integrity of the national organic standards is maintained and that the current standards remain a "floor" allowing more stringent standards to be built on their foundation. As we engage in the critical battle to protect organic during this institutionalization phase, it is vital that we define some key elements that are at the very core of the organic alternative and that must be aggressively protected and vigorously maintained.

KEY ELEMENTS OF ORGANIC INTEGRITY

We associate organics with sound environmental stewardship and improvements of the quality of life and social justice for those participating. We associate organics with fairness, openness, and doing the right thing. We associate organics with values that include improved health and food and worker safety. Finally, we associate organics with reforming agriculture from its present system to one in which people live within the bounds of nature. These associations help reveal the following key elements of organic integrity.

Environmental Stewardship. This stewardship includes production and processing systems that promote and enhance biodiversity and ecological balance. Organic integrity will not survive if it supports expedient practices that in the long run damage the environment. Proper stewardship requires that we develop standards for animals to have real access to pasture and the out-of-doors. We must also have sustainable energy use in organics, including in production, shipping, and processing. Additionally, we must clearly confront the pollution of genetic engineering and the patenting of biological processes and their impacts on organic agriculture and our ecosystem. We must rapidly develop and preserve germplasm for the non-GE agricultural alternative.

Accountability. The lifeblood of organics is grassroots, consumer-based confidence in and demand for safe foods that are produced and processed using environmentally sound, humane, and socially just practices. These are based on public openness, honesty, and direct consumer access. Organic integrity also requires accountability to local communities for the impacts of our organic production and processing on local, regional, and international economies. Organic integrity embraces the promotion of fair trade practices, which support local food systems, family farms, food security, and nongovernmental participation. Organic integrity cannot survive through allowing organic colonialism or any other practices perpetuating historically unjust relationships between nations of the North and those of the South. Processors and retailers must find their enlightened self-interest in supporting these principles and must take a greater share of the risks and costs associated with the organic approach.

Fair Pricing Systems. Fair pricing is essential for the survival of organic integrity. It must be fair for all stakeholders in this system: farmers, laborers, processors, retailers, and consumers. A fair relationship between the costs of production, the price the consumer pays, and the profit taken along the way must be maintained. This is fundamental to the future of organic. If the organic approach becomes solely a predatory pricing system emulating historical agribusiness practices, then we will have lost a major part of our organic integrity. Fair trade and farmer and farmworker rights are essential ingredients for this approach.

A Model for an Alternative System. We must develop an alternative approach to agribusiness as usual. Organics set out to combine environmental stewardship, accountability, and fairness into an alternative model, as well as enlightened labor standards that set the mark for other food systems to strive for. This movement did not start out to establish expensive niche-market foods for rich people, but to model an alternative system for all of agriculture. We must make this accessible for all peoples.

OUR CHALLENGE

Our challenge is to develop strategies to preserve and promote organic integrity in these key areas. We must do so swiftly and in an equitable manner. We are collectively responsible for shaping this and the next phase of organics. This phase will be one which creates a new movement not simply to preserve organic integrity but to foster a large and generous vision for organics: the emergence of environmental stewardship and improved quality of life as norms. The challenge is about organic and beyond — nurturing, protecting, and preserving the parts of this vision that have taken root, but also going beyond. We must graft "just" food on this sapling: it's not about "just" having lunch but about having a "just" lunch. A crucial part of the post-institutional phase of organic must be the call for the just food movement.

Again, our challenge is to develop practical strategies for promoting and preserving organic integrity. We will be evaluated and judged on what organics becomes as well as what we choose to leave out. It is up to all of us. We must not become what we set out to be the sane alternative to.

It is always important to remember that the human spirit is stronger than corporate greed or governmental incompetence — we can have the food system that we want if we vote with our feet and our food dollars.

THE ETHICS OF EATING

Why Environmentalism Starts at the Breakfast Table

ALICE WATERS

JUST AS THERE IS AN ETHIC TO GROWING FOOD, *there is also an ethic to eating. As we continue to be more aware of what we are eating, we must also think about how we eat. The ritual of coming together to break bread was once the basis of community; yet with the onset of instant dinners and television, fewer and fewer meals are eaten together; more often than not we now consume our food alone and "on the run." This disrespects food and ourselves. Let us reclaim the family and community meal where values are taught and senses are heightened.*

▼

The choices we make when we buy food are *serious* choices. More and more people understand this. They no longer see themselves as passive food "consumers." Rather, they embrace their roles as "creators," knowing that the foods they decide to grow or purchase will create a different future for themselves, their families, generations to come, and the natural world. As an obvious example, we all know that when people choose organic foods and avoid mass-produced and fast foods, they are voting for a sustainable future and against a network of supply and demand that destroys human health, local communities, traditional ways of life, and the environment.

But there is another ethical choice we make about food which is equally important. It's not just what food we are purchasing, but also how we decide to eat our food. Just as there is an ethic to growing or obtaining food, there is also an ethic to eating.

Perhaps the first step in eating ethically is to eat together, with each other and our children. When you eat together, and eat a meal you cooked yourselves, you are involved with the process in a different way. You shelled the peas, you peeled the potatoes, and you want everyone to enjoy every last bite. These are the kind of meals we should be eating with our children. To paraphrase Wendell Berry, such meals honor the materials from which they are made; they honor the art by which they are done; they honor the people who make them and those who share them.

I think we can all agree on the importance of this, no matter where we fall on the political spectrum. Certainly it is the least we can do for our children. Far too many children today are living in not just inhumane, but inhuman conditions. And this is true not just of the kids who are being pressed into military service in vicious wars, and not just of the kids around the world who are at the edge of starvation, but of the kids in our own country who have never sat down and shared a meal with their own families outside of the glare of the TV screen. We have raised a generation of kids, far too many of whom have never participated in the growing of food or the preparation of meals and have never sat down together at a table with other generations and learned the meaning of mutual responsibility, and the caring and love that families can only express, I believe, by sharing nourishment. Is it any wonder that many kids are greedy, violent, and nihilistic?

Once, not so long ago, food preparation and food service were both the solemn duty and the reward of family living. Once, families were food-producing and food-processing units. And humanistic values were instilled, more than *anyplace* else, at the dinner table. Families eating together passed on values such as courtesy, kindness, generosity, thrift, respect, and reverence for the goodness of nature — pretty much the whole Boy Scout package of virtues. But notice that William Bennett and his ilk don't talk much about food; and that is because of a paradox at the heart of political conservatism: on one hand it values old-fashioned family virtues, but on the other it supports a rapacious economic system that, more than any other factor, is responsible for the disappearance of these values.

The ritual of coming to the dinner table was once the *basis* of community. Recently, Francine du Plessix Gray wrote an essay in *The New Yorker* aptly titled "Starving Children," which said, among other things, "The family meal is not only the core curriculum in the school of civilized discourse, it is also a set of protocols that curb our natural savagery and our animal greed, and cultivate a capacity for sharing and thoughtfulness. . . . The ritual of nutrition helps to imbue families, and societies at large, with greater empathy and fellowship."

Polls tell us that in the United States today, something like 57 percent of the nation's children never regularly share meals with their families. Why do families not eat together? One insidious factor has been television. Of the families who do eat together, a high percentage do so with the TV on. T. S. Eliot said television makes it possible for many people to laugh at the same joke, at the same time, and still be lonely. In a similar fashion television makes it possible for us to eat in one room but not eat together. And television is addictive. The average household watches seven hours of TV a day. A recent and very convincing study links the post–World War II decline in membership in associations of all kinds — political parties, fraternal organizations, churches — with the rise of television. I think TV wears away the ties that bind us together in the family, as well as in the society at large, because TV obviates the necessity for a family unit to amuse itself with its own resources and for its members to communicate with each other.

Another compelling reason for the decline of the family meal has been the onward march of commercial "convenience" foods at the very same time the new economic order was devaluing the role of women in the home. Modern technology makes it easy for food to be consumed on the run, in small units. Fast foods, microwaves, dehydrated foods put a premium on speed. Speed is the enemy of the ethical preparation and eating of food. It dishonors food and ourselves. We have to *make* time for our food. People who have adopted the fast food pattern of eating have forgotten what well-prepared, delicious food is.

One group fighting against the onslaught of fast food is Slow Food, an international food and wine movement, active in 45 countries worldwide, with 65,000 members and about 560 local branches. The aim of the Slow Food movement is to rediscover the richness and aromas of local cuisines and to fight the standardization of fast food. Slow Food is a response to the fast pace of modern culture, which has changed our lives and threatens the environment and the landscape in the name of productivity. In our ongoing efforts to change how people relate to food, the Slow Food movement represents principles well worth fighting for.

But perhaps our greatest challenge is working to get our kids to join us at the dinner table. So we have to teach them why they should. And one of the biggest reasons is that you learn at the table. Above all, you learn to use your senses. And you either use your senses, or you lose 'em — they get dulled, you settle for the routine and the mediocre, in food and everything else. There is so much information that comes from sensual stimulation — information that comes to you immediately, even faster than over the Internet. I am convinced that teaching children to eat food together is the best way to teach them to open up their senses and use them — after all, eating is something everybody does every day. If children learn to use their senses, it will improve their ability to communicate — not just about food, but about everything else. And they will grow up to be wiser, happier people.

This is going to have to be done in the schools, too. But if all of us were to encourage our local schools to start programs in gardening and eating, we could have an impact. Kids have to be taught that fresh, nourishing food is their birthright — that wholesome, honest food should be an entitlement for all Americans, not just for the rich.

To try to get this message across, I have joined some neighbors, parents, and teachers at the Martin Luther King, Jr. Middle School in Berkeley, California, to plan a food curriculum. For years, whenever I drove by the school, I was struck by how run-down the schoolyard looked, and I thought, what a great garden this would make. And what a great thing it would be if the students not only got to plan, plant, and cultivate a garden, but if they got to actually use that food to cook school lunches for themselves. To my delight, the principal at the school thought this was a good idea, too, and now we are well under way to making a food curriculum a reality.

This project is called the Edible Schoolyard, and these are some of the events we have created: We have initiated a ritual seeding with 150 adults and children who broadcast seeds for the cover crop with drums timing the march across the field. We have made sherbets for 500 kids who had to decide which flavor they like best: lemon, tangerine, blood orange, or lime. There was a raffle and the winner won dessert of the fruit he liked best. We have built an adobe oven near the garden site for bread and pizza baking. And every October, we gather the community together on the full moon to celebrate harvest.

The kids are extremely receptive. Now at King School, they are getting boxes of produce from a community supported agriculture farm — each class receives a box every week. One of the teachers was telling us at a garden design meeting for the schoolyard about how the kids in her class washed and trimmed and cut up the ingredients and made a big salad. "Now wait," she said. "Before we start eating, let's stop and think about the person who tilled the ground, and planted the seeds, and harvested the vegetables. And then we chopped up the vegetables and put them in this bowl and made this big salad . . ." — and the kids stood up at their desks and gave the salad a huge standing ovation!

FULLY INTEGRATED FOOD SYSTEMS

Regaining Connections between Farmers and Consumers

REBECCA SPECTOR

WITH OUR FOOD TRAVELING ON AVERAGE 1,300 MILES *from farm to table, and the consolidation of distribution systems, consumers continue to get farther away from their food source, and farmers continue to receive lower prices for their products. A fully integrated food system connects the farm to its local community, allowing consumers to regain a lost connection with the farmers growing their food. By connecting consumers directly with farmers — through farmers' markets and community supported agriculture — fully integrated food systems provide consumers with the freshest produce available and farmers with a higher price for their products.*
▼

The mechanization and industrialization of agriculture has played a significant role in the changing of the agricultural "culture" in America. Industrialization turned "agri-culture" into "agri-business," as farmers were encouraged to grow crops in large-scale monocultures, primarily for export. The growth of such agribusinesses has had many consequences, among them the decline of small-scale diversified farming, an increase in the use of chemical inputs, a decrease in the need for human labor on the farm, and the separation between food consumers and food producers.

THE CREATION OF CULTURAL DISTANCE

With the growth of large-scale, monocultured farming and a continuing focus on mass production, marketing, and processing, America's agricultural distribution system became a corporatized giant by the mid-20th century. This centralized distribution system resulted in a decrease in farm income, with a greater percentage of the food dollar going to middlemen for processing, packaging, storage, and distribution. And the loss in farm income has only grown worse through the century. Since 1950 the average farmer's income has decreased by 32 percent — for every dollar a consumer spends on food, farmers today now receive 10 cents or less, compared to anywhere up to 70 cents just a few decades ago.

But decreased farm income is not the only negative result of our centralized distribution and export system. It has also created a huge separation between food consumers and food producers. On average our food is shipped 1,300 miles from production to processing to our plates. Although this system appears to offer us more choices in the supermarket, the increased distance between producer and consumer has resulted in a breakdown of environmental accountability and responsibility, and a lost connection between farmers and the public at large.

For one thing, this distance serves to block feedback between producer and consumer, so consumers have little knowledge about the production practices used in creating their food or the impact of these practices on their health or the environment. Costs associated with agricultural production are hidden. When purchasing strawberries in the winter, for example, few consumers are aware of the highly toxic pesticides needed to grow that crop in a tropical climate or the impact of those pesticides on wildlife, the environment, or farmworker health. Distance between consumer and producer enables the shopper to make such a purchase without any knowledge of the impacts of his or her decision.

This distance between producer and consumer is also reflective of the separation between life and work. Before industrialization, farming in the United States was much more widespread and it was possible for almost anyone to farm. The early American farmer had the opportunity to work and live on (and off of) his own land. But along with mechanization and industrialization in the United States came the new goals of quantity and efficiency. Human values were removed from the process of mechanization, and from farming, and work became something people did in order to support their "true life-styles" on the weekends. On this subject Wendell Berry posits, "If human values are removed from production, how can they be preserved in consumption?" Aldo Leopold has said that by working on, with, or near the land (or perhaps having a connection to that land through the farmer), conservation becomes a way to understand and preserve the environment from which we gain our sustenance. In "The Land Ethic," Leopold writes that under the nation's economic system, individuals are separated from the land their food comes from, which creates further separation between individuals and their food growers, and hence individuals and their natural environment.

But these are not the only impacts created from distance between producer and consumer. With this distance we have lost our connection to food seasonality — few folks these days know what areas foods come from at different times of the year. And as the famed chef Alice Waters will tell you, this lack of knowledge about eating in season most surely leads to compromised freshness and flavor. The best tasting foods are always the ripest, and therefore the foods that are grown nearby, in their appropriate season. By contrast, strawberries flown in from Mexico in the winter must be picked well before they are ripe and treated with chemicals to survive their long trip to U.S. supermarket shelves. Yet most people would agree that few things taste better than a ripe, juicy strawberry bought at the farmers' market in the height of the season.

Through all of this, we have created a profound cultural divide between farmers and the rest of society. No longer do we see small, diversified farms scattered across the American landscape. No longer do the majority of farmers maintain farming as their only occupation. As we have lost farmers to this "efficiency" in agriculture, we have also lost farmland — nearly a million acres a year just in this past decade. And we have lost our connection to our food source and to the land.

BIOREGIONALISM: REGAINING CONNECTIONS

The good news is that we are finally seeing a shift in attitudes about agriculture and food. Consumers now more than ever have an interest in purchasing foods directly from farmers and are demanding that these foods be grown in an environmentally responsible manner. At the same time, farmers are also changing their attitudes, and their production practices, as they recognize the importance of connecting with their buyers. This shift in attitudes and production practices is also having a more significant effect — it is closing the gap between farmers and consumers and encouraging more bioregionalism. In the words of Kirkpatrick Sale:

> We must try to understand ourselves as participants in and not masters over (the) biotic community . . . but to become dwellers in the land, the crucial and perhaps only and all-encompassing task is to understand place, the immediate specific place where we live . . . the limits of its resources; the carrying capacities of its lands and waters; the places where it must not be stressed . . . and the cultures of the people, of the populations native to the land and of those who have grown up with it, the human social and economic arrangements shaped by and adapted to the geomorphic ones, in both urban and rural settings — these are the things that must be appreciated. That, in essence, is bioregionalism.

The concept of bioregionalism works to "correct" a number of ethical implications that are indicative of a deterioration of agriculture and the environment in the United States. For one, bioregional economies seek to maintain rather than use up natural resources and to adapt to the environment rather than exploit or manipulate it. Bioregional economies also seek to establish a stable means of production rather than one fixed on continual growth. Additionally, bioregionalism suggests that people tend to not pollute or damage the natural system on which they depend for their livelihood if they *participate in* and see directly what is happening to that natural system. By connecting directly with the farms and farmers growing our food, we can gradually make a shift from being a passive consumer to becoming a more active one — one who takes the time to know the farmer growing our food and to learn about the ways in which that food is grown.

Bioregionalism is gradually becoming an essential part of today's agricultural economy. Many farmers seek more stable means of production, and of sales, and recognize the importance of diversification in both their production and marketing practices. At the same time, consumers are seeking a more direct connection to their food. As a result, we are beginning to see an increase in direct relationships between farmers and consumers. These relationships are created through various outlets

— farmers selling their produce directly through community supported agriculture programs, farmers' markets, and roadside stands; farms holding more public events, including farm tours, volunteer days, and "u-pick" opportunities; and even farmers selling directly to small stores and restaurants that feature the farm in marketing materials or on menus to further the connection between farmer and consumer.

This change in the agricultural economy begins to reflect a "fully integrated food system" — one that connects the farm to the local community and allows the public to regain a long-lost connection with the people who are growing food. By connecting consumers directly with farmers, fully integrated food systems provide the public with the freshest produce available locally and farmers with a higher percentage of the food dollar than they would receive selling their produce through a distributor.

The following are just a few examples of how farmers and consumers are working together to develop more fully integrated food systems.

ALTERNATIVE MARKETING STRATEGIES: CONNECTING FARMERS AND CONSUMERS

Community supported agriculture farms (CSAs) are a form of mutual cooperation between farmers and consumers who come together to produce healthy food in a sustainable way. In a typical CSA, community members purchase a share in a local farm's operation at the start of each growing season and in return receive a fresh, nutritious box of produce directly from their grower on a weekly basis. In this arrangement, members agree to pay the costs of production regardless of the actual harvest, so many of the financial burdens typically borne by the farmers are shared by farmer and consumer. Other CSAs act more as a subscription service, allowing members to pay month to month, or even week to week. In most cases, members receive whatever produce is available at the farm each week, although some farms do "exchanges" with other farms, so they can provide their customers with products — such as certain fruits or flowers — that they are unable to grow. CSAs range from small gardens with 5 to 20 members to large farms serving nearly 1,000 families. The number of CSAs in the United States was estimated at 50 in 1990 and has since grown to over 1,000.

Because CSA involves a direct and personal relationship with the farmer — and often the land on which the food is grown — it sets itself apart from the conventional agriculture system in which the farmer-consumer relationship is indirect and anonymous. CSA seeks to bring consumers closer to their food source, with many farms encouraging visits through harvest days, meals, and tours of the farm. Such inter-action connects consumers with the land where their food is grown by viewing, participating in, and learning about farming practices. The CSA farm model offers a positive alternative to the conventional food system, where consumers purchase days- or weeks-old produce from the supermarket shelf. It also provides farmers with a viable eco-nomic alternative — allowing them a greater percentage of the food dollar (close to or at 100 percent) and a stable revenue stream.

Farmers' markets are designated public places where a group of farmers sell their produce one or twice a week. Like CSAs, the num-ber of farmers' markets has soared in the past few years, up from 1,755 in 1994 to more than 2,800 in 2000, according to the USDA's Agricultural Marketing Service. Farmers' markets allow buyers to pick and choose exactly what seasonal produce they would like to purchase and whom they would like to purchase it from. At many farmers' markets, farmers provide samplings of their best fruits, nuts, and even olive oils, and proudly display photos of their farms and dis-tribute educational materials or recipes. The market environment encourages shoppers to walk around, meet and talk with the farmers, and learn more about specific production practices, such as organic or integrated pest management techniques. It is also a place for peo-ple to meet others in their community, and it is a wonderful place for children to explore. Also like CSAs, farmers' markets provide farmers with close to 100 percent of the food dollar (minus a fee or small per-centage paid to the market for maintenance) and a direct connection between farmer and consumer. In the words of the peach grower and writer David Mas Masumoto, farmers' markets "are one of the saviors of the family farm. All those barriers created by the conventional mar-keting system are torn down. The consumer sees it isn't just a com-modity — it's a peach, or a carrot, or a cabbage."

Farmers' markets and CSAs provide an opportunity for all mem-bers of the community to reconnect with their food source and to have access to the freshest and most nutritious produce available. Many farmers' markets are located in the heart of cities and are easily accessible by public transit. Additionally, produce at the farmers' market is often cheaper than at the supermarket, especially if purchasing organic. The government-sponsored Women, Infant and Children program (WIC) offers special food coupons that can be used at the farmers' market, and most markets also accept food stamps.

Other direct marketing alternatives provide even more ways of connecting farmers with consumers. Many farmers today sell their produce directly to local restaurants and local food stores, instead of going through a distributor. Many of these restaurants and stores are so pleased with the quality and freshness of the produce that they acknowledge the farms on their menus or use point-of-purchase materials as an opportunity to share the farmer's story with the consumer. Rainbow Grocery in San Francisco, for example, distinguishes products that are "farmer direct" using a stylish hangtag attached to the price display. Restaurant Nora in Washington, D.C., often lists the name of the farm where each local food item was grown. These and other examples can be seen across the country, from large cities to rural towns. And they are all encouraging regional economies and giving control over the sale of the product back to the farmer.

CHANGING LIFE-STYLES

Fully integrated food systems are a way of putting the culture back in agriculture and giving consumers and farmers a new attitude toward food and toward life. In the words of E. F. Schumacher, to attain sustainability "we must thoroughly understand the problem of production and begin to see the possibility of evolving a new life-style, with new methods of production and new patterns of consumption: a life-style designed for permanence." By changing how we think about food and farming, we are changing our life-style from one of alienation to one of relationship. Through the new connections of fully integrated food systems, we are healing our farm communities, the earth, and ourselves.

COMMUNITY FOOD SECURITY

A Promising Alternative to the Global Food System

ANDREW FISHER

LOCALIZED GRASSROOTS MOVEMENTS NATIONWIDE *have been promoting community food security to address deficiencies in a food system that is unresponsive to the food needs of lower-income communities. Programs that promote farmers' markets, establish school salad bars, and support urban agricultural enterprises help forge ties between farms and inner cities, provide education on sustainable agriculture and nutrition, and ensure that everyone has access to healthy, affordable foods. This concept of community food security has linked these efforts and many others into an increasingly promising and powerful movement for food system reform, while providing communities with a needed measure of food independence.*

▼

At first glance, America's food system may seem exemplary, at least for those of us with access to stores and who can afford grocery prices. We can visit a local supermarket almost anywhere in the country and purchase Mexican mangoes in May, Chilean grapes in March, or even organic cherry tomatoes in January.

Yet, upon closer scrutiny we discover that serious problems abound in a food system that is highly concentrated in ownership and unresponsive to community needs. Small and medium farmers are regularly squeezed out of business by high input costs, low prices for their products, and poor access to markets. The family-farm-based agricultural system is fast becoming a thing of the past. The average age of the American farmer is over 55, and few of their children are choosing to continue family agricultural traditions. The number of farmers is in such decline that farming is no longer listed as an occupation on census forms. An increasingly globalized food system not only provides unfair competition for the nation's growers, but is energy inefficient, threatens regional self-sufficiency, and discourages consumer acceptance of regional and seasonal foods. Suburban sprawl threatens prime farmland nationwide. After decades of struggle, farmworkers continue to earn poverty-level wages while suffering from high rates of tuberculosis and pesticide poisoning.

The ills of the food system hit hardest at the nation's most vulnerable. Supermarkets have redlined inner cities, choosing to target the more lucrative suburban middle class. Access to healthy and affordable food has become difficult for those without cars. In Los Angeles County almost one million people live in areas where food access is deficient. A nationwide study of nineteen metropolitan areas found that zip codes with high levels of poverty had 30 percent fewer supermarkets than higher income neighborhoods. This isn't because these neighborhoods can't support new markets. In fact, some of the most profitable supermarkets in the Pathmark chain are located in inner city Newark and Harlem. Back in Los Angeles, low-income communities hit by the 1992 riots were found capable of supporting an additional 750,000 square feet of supermarket floor space, or the equivalent of 15 to 20 average sized stores.

The lack of transportation options compounds the dearth of adequate food outlets for low-income shoppers. Transit planners rarely design bus routes around community food shopping needs, leaving residents little choice but to carry their groceries long distances, make multiple bus transfers, or spend limited funds on taxi rides. All too frequently, car-less residents rely on corner mom and pop stores, which rarely carry the ingredients for nutritious diets, such as fresh produce or low-fat milk. Their prices also can be exorbitant, up to 70 percent higher than in supermarkets. Even those supermarkets that remain are second-class institutions, charging prices far above those of their suburban counterparts for foods of lesser quality in dirtier stores with poorer service. By way of example, the South Central Los Angeles-based Community Coalition recently led a campaign protesting a local supermarket chain for selling rotten green meat at a neighborhood store.

All of these factors reduce access to and household income available for nutritious foods, leading to an above average incidence of diet-related diseases, such as diabetes, hypertension, obesity, and cancer among minorities. From 1976 to 1980, National Center for Health Statistics (NCHS) figures show that 6.5 percent of children aged 6 to 11 were considered overweight. By 1990 to 1994, that figure had doubled to 11.4 percent. Latinos and African-Americans and their children suffer from higher than average rates of obesity. For example, 17.7 percent of Mexican-American children are overweight, according to the 1990-94 NCHS study. Obesity puts children at risk for other diseases, including hypertension, adult obesity, cancer, heart disease, and strokes.

Television has a negative effect on children's health beyond the fact that it discourages physical activity. The average child views 10,000 food ads per year, most of which are for candy, fast food, sugary cereals, soft drinks, and other junk. These marketing campaigns, combined with "supersizing" trends in the fast food and convenience market industries, encourage the consumption of excess calories and fat.

AN ALTERNATIVE

To address these issues, grassroots activists across the country have been busy developing an alternative food system, based on the principles of social justice, economic viability, and ecology. This new food system is small yet flourishing. This growth is perhaps best exemplified by the boom in farmers' markets, the number of which increased by 63 percent from 1994 to 2000. Now, over 2,800 markets operate nationwide. Sales at farmers' markets total approximately $1 billion annually. Other ways of bringing food closer to home, such as community-supported agriculture (CSA), community gardens, and buying clubs, have also been on the rise, as people look for better quality and desire a closer connection with their food sources. The concept of community food security has linked these efforts and many others of a similar nature into an increasingly promising and powerful movement for food system reform.

Guided by the Los Angeles-based Community Food Security Coalition, the community food security movement hosts a diverse array of organizations committed to a more equitable food system. The movement includes organic and family farm groups, food banks, community gardeners, nutritionists, environmentalists, and community development organizations. Promising new alliances between farmers and low-income communities are being forged around the mutually beneficial strategies of community food self-reliance and direct farm-to-consumer connections. Squarely within the anti-globalization community, these groups are developing concrete alternatives that promote locally grown foods instead of globally sourced ones and encourage community self-reliance rather than dependence.

Community food security as a concept is as diverse as its constituencies. Building on the concept of national and household food security used in the Global South, the program integrates elements from various disciplines into a holistic framework for action and understanding of the food system. Like public health, it tends to be prevention-oriented, preferring to head off hunger rather than treat it with charitable handouts. Like ecology, it encourages a systems approach and encourages a participating community to conduct an analysis of its food system as a planning tool. The community food security concept borrows from the community development field as it uses food as a vehicle for building relationships and developing indigenous resources.

In addition to the development of model programs that can better meet the needs of their constituents, community food security groups have been reframing the way food is recognized in the public sphere. No coherent food policy exists at either the federal level or municipal levels. Historically, national nutrition efforts have developed in the context of our policies to support farmers. Commodities were purchased to raise farm prices and in turn were donated to schools, food banks, and other institutions. At the local level, food has been seen as a private sector concern, quite different from other basic needs such as water, housing, and transportation, which are all regulated by municipal agencies.

The community food security movement has begun to put food on the map as a concern. It was successful in convincing the Clinton Administration to create within the U.S. Department of Agriculture a Community Food Security Initiative, which undertook the lengthy and contentious process of developing collaboration among multiple internal agencies for the purpose of promoting food security. At local levels, the movement has successfully advocated for the creation of city, county, and state food policy councils in such places as Hartford, Connecticut, Knoxville, Tennessee, Pasadena, California, and Austin, Texas. These councils recommend food-related policy changes to the executive and legislative branches of government, and generally increase the prominence of food as a matter of public concern. In other communities, such as Berkeley, California, community food security advocates have created school district policies that encourage the purchase of organically grown foods and focused more attention to food within the curriculum. Numerous other communities are coming together to develop successful food security programs.

PROMOTING GOOD FOOD AND EDUCATION TO FACE HEALTH ISSUES

"The salad bar is the greatest thing that could happen to the 59th Street School's cafeteria," begins a letter from student Diana Garcia to the Los Angeles Unified School District (LAUSD). "It helps me stay healthy and have a better life. Going on the field trip to Farmer Phil's, I learned to tell the difference between seeds, flowers, stems, leaves, and roots." Diana is referring to the Farmers' Market Fruit and Salad Bar, started by Occidental College's Center for Food and Justice in conjunction with LAUSD. Its success prompted the development of dozens of fruit and salad bars in the second-largest school district in the nation, which serves 722,000 students.

The Fruit and Salad Bar program's primary goals have been to augment local farmers' incomes while making fruits and vegetables available to school-age children, and to provide education on food production and healthy food choices. School gardening activities and field trips to farmers' markets and local farms have provided rich opportunities for hands-on nutrition education.

The Fruit and Salad Bar has the potential to be an important tool to help schools address growing health problems among children. A 1998 UCLA study found that 40 percent of children in 14 low-income elementary schools in LAUSD were obese. Studies show 40 percent of overweight 7-year olds and 80 percent of overweight teens remain so into adulthood.

Pilot programs, with food sourced from local farmers' markets, were launched at the Castelar Elementary School, which serves predominantly low-income Asian students in the Chinatown neighborhood, and at the 59th Street School, whose students are mainly low-income African-American and Latino children. The schools marketed the program with an all-school assembly on salad bar food choices and etiquette, presented by 5th-grade students. Classroom curriculum was also developed to promote healthy food choices.

While the farmers' market salad bars were discontinued at LAUSD for a variety of reasons (but continue in every school in Santa Monica and are starting up in multiple school districts across California), conventional salad bars are now offered at more than 55 schools. While the district discontinued purchasing directly from local farmers, nutrition education and outreach activities continue. Students, teachers, and parents have all shown strong interest in school gardening projects and trips to local farms and farmers' markets.

URBAN AGRICULTURE AS A COMMUNITY RESOURCE

The San Francisco League of Urban Gardeners (SLUG) is a shining example of an organization making use of community resources to meet its community's needs. SLUG seeks to develop job training and resources to address community challenges. In one of its primary projects, SLUG helps develop city gardens that produce fresh fruits and vegetables and also contribute to economic development, personal growth, and community pride. SLUG's urban agriculture projects include the development and maintenance of four youth gardens around San Francisco, the Youth Garden Internship at St. Mary's Urban Youth Farm, and sales and marketing for its local enterprise, Urban Herbals.

SLUG's Urban Agriculture and Marketing Department oversees four gardens located in low-income communities and run by at-risk teenagers. Over 10,000 pounds of produce were harvested at these four urban agriculture sites in 2000. The largest site, St. Mary's Urban Youth Farm, is a 4.5-acre plot in a neighborhood with an unemployment rate of 84 percent. After clearing the site of garbage and construction debris, SLUG started the garden in 1995 with a few raised beds of vegetables for use by the housing project and surrounding community. Since then, the project has expanded to include an orchard with over one hundred apple, peach, pear, avocado, olive, and loquat trees surrounding a large plot of organic vegetables, a flower production garden, beehives, a greenhouse, and garden plots for the nearby residents. In addition, St. Mary's Youth Farm has a recycling/compost education area with an amphitheater, a wetland restoration project, a windmill, and a green waste-chipping program that benefits San Francisco residents.

SLUG's Youth Garden Internship (YGI) trains and employs over one hundred teens every year to work after school and during the summer in the orchards and organic vegetable gardens. The youths plant, harvest, and deliver the produce to the local community, especially to senior citizens and disabled residents. SLUG not only uses the farm as an educational site for community workshops, school field trips, and internships in gardening, but also provides mentoring services to the youths and the community. The YGI program teaches teens about landscaping, horticulture, and restoration of wetlands and native plants, and conducts workshops in leadership, violence prevention, and health promotion.

Those who have graduated from the YGI program may choose to continue working for SLUG, in their organic food business, called Urban Herbals. These 18- to 22-year-olds learn skills in production, marketing, and business management. The program uses fruits, vegetables, flowers, and beehives from St. Mary's as well as from family-run, organic Bay Area farms to make "Jammin' Jam," "Bee Real Honey," herbal vinegars, "Slammin' Salsa," unfiltered virgin olive oil, flower arrangements, and gift baskets. SLUG provides employees with a 12-week business-training course, a kitchen health and safety course, and opportunities to travel and participate in gift shows and conferences.

According to Paula Jones, Urban Agriculture program manager, the main ingredient that ties the project together is "pride." SLUG is immensely proud of having trained hundreds of people in organic gardening and community service. The community members are proud of the skills they have learned, the produce they have grown, the areas they have beautified, and the sense of community spirit the project has brought them.

SLUG's projects are an excellent example of how a community food security project can be used to build capacity and expand opportunities for low-income communities, contributing to urban renewal, food security, and grassroots economic development.

CONCLUSION

Community food security programs like SLUG and the Fruit and Salad Bar project are beginning to address some of the ills of industrial food production that lurk just beyond the perception of many Americans. While mainstream food producers and supermarket chains may view low-income areas as secondary markets, whose specific desires and needs they can ignore, community-based programs allow people to act in their own self-interest and reclaim a degree of food independence. And with time, successful community food security ventures can spread their reach, and their benefits, well beyond the inner city.

Over the past decade, numerous community programs have proven that equitable food systems can build alliances between farmers, young people, and low-income communities. The time is ripe for a more integrated approach to addressing the nation's food system deficiencies based on self-reliance, local food systems, and collaboration. Community food security provides an excellent framework from which we may build toward absolute food independence.

ECO-LABELS

Promoting Alternatives in the Marketplace

BETSY LYDON

AS THE ECONOMIC VIABILITY OF FARMING *continues to spiral down-*
ward, farmers are seeking to differentiate their products by commu-
nicating to consumers positive messages about sustainable and
socially responsible production practices. One of the fastest growing
ways of differentiation is through "eco-labels" — a seal of approval
identifying a product as having particular attributes, such as
"reduced pesticide use" or "grown locally." As consumers better
understand the profound impacts of industrial food production on
the environment, eco-labeling initiatives will continue to proliferate
at the local and national level.

▼

For the past two decades, the sustainable agriculture movement
has been gaining momentum and greater acceptance. Individual
farms across the United States and throughout the world have woven
together principles and practices of agricultural sustainability.
Research and educational support have gradually improved,
transforming individual pockets of knowledge into whole and
replicable systems.

Production practices, the environment, and to a lesser extent,
quality of life issues have received much-needed attention during this
early era of development. Recently, however, there has been growing
recognition that the marketplace may be one of the most important
factors pushing sustainable agriculture into the mainstream. In fact,
farmers, retailers, and consumers increasingly comprehend the connections between healthy food, viable rural communities, environmentally and socially responsible farming methods, and choices at
the supermarket.

As a consequence, farmers and retailers alike seek to differentiate their products in the marketplace by communicating positive messages about production practices and social issues to consumers. As consumer interest in sound production practices grows, labeling initiatives, especially "eco-labeling" initiatives, are proliferating at the local, national, and international level. With conventional farmers experiencing some of the lowest prices for raw commodities ever, the future of agriculture is at stake. Many farmers now realize that they have to add value to their produce and use credible eco-labeling in order to survive.

ECO-LABELING SCHEMES: THE BASICS

American consumers are now accustomed to reading nutrition labels and ingredient lists when shopping for food. Like other food labels, eco-labels help shoppers distinguish among products on the supermarket shelf and allow them to make their choices based on product information. But eco-labels differ from nutrition and ingredient lists in that they inform consumers about production practices and social issues in addition to product attributes. And, much like the Good Housekeeping seal, eco-labels act as a seal of approval, clearly identifying products that have been produced according to specific guidelines.

Eco-labels typically perform one or more of three key functions: ***Standard Setting.*** To determine eligibility requirements for participation in their program, eco-labeling organizations set standards. Some eco-labeling organizations develop a list of prohibited practices to determine eligibility, while others use positive point-based systems, assigning various points to specific practices and determining minimum point requirements for participation. Standards commonly involve environmental considerations, such as pesticide use, soil and water conservation practices, and attention to wildlife habitat. More recently, eco-labeling organizations have begun to incorporate standards for socio-economic considerations as well, such as fair trade, locality, and fair treatment of workers.

Verification of Compliance. Regardless of the specific standards set, eco-labeling organizations should be able to verify compliance, that is, ensure that the standards are actually being met. Methods typically used for verification include, but are not limited to, written applications, signed affidavits, lab testing, and on-farm inspections.

Consumer Education and Marketing. Eco-labeling, in and of itself, is cause-related marketing and an educational tool. Eco-labels provide a vehicle for environmental, technical, or farmer-related information and stories, which inform both consumers and wholesale buyers alike. An eco-labeling organization's role in consumer education and marketing can vary widely, from letter-writing campaigns and consumer advocacy to simple product identification.

Eco-labels are entering the marketplace in increasing numbers, both in the United States and throughout the world. While some older labels have been in existence since the 1940s and 1950s, a new wave of labels has sprung up in the past decade. By some estimates, there are now over 150 independent eco-labeling programs, including organic, operating in the United States alone.

The organic label is perhaps the most recognized and widespread eco-label in the marketplace today. It communicates valuable information to consumers about the production practices of organic agriculture and differentiates organic products from other natural and conventional products in the marketplace.

In an attempt to build markets for sustainably produced agricultural products, numerous other eco-labeling initiatives have been developed in recent years. Some are relatively small efforts focused on distinct geographic regions, while others concentrate exclusively on one specific environmental issue, such as preservation of bird habitat. Some labels do not focus on traditional environmental issues at all; rather they encourage consumers to "buy local" or "pay fair prices." Still other labeling initiatives, such as the certified organic label, are quite ambitious in scope, with national and international accounts and multiple products endorsed.

PROMISING EXAMPLES: NATIONAL TO REGIONAL PROGRAMS

Nationally, The Food Alliance (TFA), a nonprofit organization based in Portland, Oregon, uses market-based incentives to promote foods grown in a manner that reduces or eliminates pesticide use, conserves soil and water resources, and provides safe and fair working conditions. Farmers who meet TFA's strict eligibility requirements earn the right to market their products with the TFA seal of approval. From artichokes to zucchini, over 80 different varieties of fruits and vegetables are now marketed with the Food-Alliance Approved label in grocery stores nationwide.

In the northeastern United States, CORE Values Northeast (CVN) is a program whose mission is to create a supportive market environment for farm products that are locally grown and ecologically responsible. Founded by Mothers & Others for a Livable Planet in 1994, the program identifies orchards and farms in the Northeast that have adopted biointensive integrated pest management practices. Selected farms go through a rigorous certification process, which involves the submission of a comprehensive farm plan, adherence to a detailed set of production guidelines, maintenance of detailed records, an annual knowledge-based evaluation by a third-party inspector, and regular attendance at CVN meetings. Farmers who pass the certification process may take advantage of a recognizable CVN label and other point-of-purchase information. About 42 growers from 7 different states in the Northeast participate in this program. CVN apples are sold in major supermarket chains, numerous food co-ops, specialty stores, farmers' markets, and school and corporate cafeterias.

Also on the East Coast, a program called Local Hero — run by Community Involved in Sustaining Agriculture (CISA) — distinguishes products that are grown in western Massachusetts in an effort to promote the local farming community. The program uses an easily identifiable Local Hero label and point-of-purchase information in supermarkets and restaurants, so shoppers can easily tell products grown locally from other products in the marketplace. The program also uses advertising and local media to "tell the stories" of the local farmers and to further connect these farmers with their local community. Although the program does not have specific standards for environmental stewardship, it highlights small, family farms that represent a century-old tradition of farming in New England.

THE CHALLENGE AHEAD

Through diverse strategies, the more than 150 eco-labels in the United States promote many of the goals of sustainable agriculture. At their best, eco-labels act as conduits for societal change: first, by offering consumers greater choices of environmental and social values with their purchases; then by channeling marketplace rewards to producers who farm sustainably.

The potential for wielding eco-labels as tools for change is tantalizingly great. Yet, at present, eco-label programs are still relatively inexperienced, with the exception of the organic label. Many have little marketplace savvy or technical on-farm knowledge, are isolated from one another, and have limited resources. The increased interest at all levels of the sustainable food and farming community in creating a more comprehensive and coherent approach to eco-labeling — one that will strengthen eco-labeling programs themselves, reach more consumers, and provide a web of support for the farmers, retailers, and others involved — is critical at this stage in agriculture. Industry standards or common principles that could be used as guidelines do not yet exist. Common language for communicating information about the sustainable marketplace is also lacking. Perhaps as a sign of maturation, the labeling community has recently begun to recognize the need for more formalized networking, collaborative research, and cross-evaluation among efforts to maximize the limited resources in this arena.

FARMING WITH THE WILD

A Conservation Approach to Agriculture

DANIEL IMHOFF

FARMING AND RANCHING ACTIVITIES *now affect over two-thirds of the U.S. land base in the Lower 48 and are respectively responsible for 42 and 26 percent of the species listed under the Endangered Species Act. Action must be taken so that agriculture can coexist with, and even encourage, the proliferation of wildlife. "Farming with the wild" offers an expanded vision for the future of sustainable agriculture — one that promotes smaller farms that fit into the natural landscape and allow for wildlife corridors. Fortunately, a growing number of farmers and activists are working to encourage more wild farming, and restoring healthy ecosystems across the country.*

▼

First, a confession. Last summer, while driving home late at night through the flat belly of the intensively farmed Anderson Valley, I fatally struck a bobcat. It had appeared in my peripheral vision in mid-chase, eyes wide, legs tensed, a rare glimpse of feline intensity. Though I stood down on the brake and clutch, the collision was inevitable, punctuated by a bone-chilling thud. I carried my victim, a male weighing about the same 40-plus pounds as my five-and-a-half-year-old son, to the roadside. In the light of my car beams I sat with the cat for what seemed to be an endless existential hour, absorbing the burden of my deed, composing the most fitting plea for forgiveness I could muster. In the morning I revisited the corpse, still numb and nauseous, finding no graceful closure on my side of the encounter.

The episode points to what is increasingly evident in farming regions across the country. Agriculture and development — particularly of the "clean" variety characterized by an absence of wild edges, woodlands, and wetlands — dominate an ever-increasing portion of the landscape. Few people can deny that we face the prospect of a zoo-like world, in which truly wild areas are reduced to islands floating in vast seas populated by just a handful of plant and animal species specially selected for industrial manipulation. By the mid-1990s, of the 631 species of plants and animals listed as threatened or endangered in the contiguous states, farming was cited as a contributing factor to 42 percent of listed species and grazing and ranching to 26 percent. Our farming and ranching practices, then, hold a precious key to the prevention of such a minimalistic future. Like the great swaths of forests which function as the "Earth's lungs," revitalized or "re-wilded" rural areas could potentially restore the flow of native biodiversity and natural processes to the heartland.

THE SHORTCOMINGS OF ORGANIC STANDARDS

Not too many years ago, a piece of undersized, pockmarked fruit often symbolized the organic alternative to a farm system dependent on chemicals known to damage wildlife. "When we started farming in the early 1970s," remembers the California organic farmer Warren Weber, who began his career market gardening with a horse and plow, "just charting a pesticide-free course was a substantial challenge." Three decades later, organic producers are now growing multi-thousand-acre monocrops of just about any conventional commodity, including grains, grapes, dairy, meats, vegetables, cotton, and rice. And the organic industry has lurched into an era of consolidation and globalization.

The organic movement's David versus Goliath success story against industrial agriculture is a deserved cause for celebration. The mainstream success of the movement, however, has caused a growing number of people to question whether organic farming, through commercialization, has strayed too far from its roots. If organic production ends up mimicking conventional agribusiness (huge, faraway operations minus the chemicals, with centralized distribution and processing) what becomes of the independent, regionally- and quality-oriented, stewardship-minded farmer?

Weber, who served on the committee which drafted California's first organic rules in 1979, and whose Star Route Farms has become the largest working vegetable farm in Marin County, California, believes it is time to consider farming to a higher standard. "One thing we failed to include when we devised California's organic standards was the ecological perspective of how a farm fits into a watershed," he told me some years ago. In northern California, where he farms half of the year, Weber listed siltation, erosion, irrigation, waste water, and runoff as key farm management issues that must be addressed as producers and organizations look toward organic certification in this new century. "Conserving habitat for endangered species and using water responsibly are real concerns in this area," Weber continued. "People are just starting to think about what standards and principles we want in place, how they should be implemented, and whether or not they are verifiable."

Other key concerns include non-lethal controls for native predators, the creation of on-farm habitat for migratory species (including pollinators, birds, and mammals), the need for connectivity between farming regions and larger wilderness areas, and the prevention of genetically modified organisms from interacting with native species.

MOVING BEYOND ORGANIC

In their essay, "Tame and Wild: Organic Agriculture and Wildness," the North Dakota wheat farmer Fred Kirschenmann and the organic certifier David Gould have eloquently phrased the need for higher standards for sustainable agriculture:

> We cannot have healthy "organic" farms within degraded landscapes. Quite apart from the problem of "drift" — whether chemical or genetic — there is the fact that the biodiversity necessary to produce the ecosystem services on which our organic farms depend can only be restored and maintained at the ecosystem level. It is the coevolution of a diverse array of species interacting with each other that gives nature its dynamic resilience — something Stuart Kauffman calls "interacting dancing fitness landscapes." (1993)

Just as the community supported agriculture (CSA) movement has opened the door to new models and opportunities for local, small farming–based production and distribution systems, the concept of "farming with the wild" offers an expanded vision for the future of sustainable agriculture. Such a vision would begin with far more and far smaller farms that gracefully meld into landscapes pulsing with a wide range of native species. Every farm, while still being an ecosystem unto itself, would in some way function as a corridor connecting it to a larger, ultimately wilder landscape — through clear and free-flowing watersheds, through woodlots, grasslands, or wetlands, on into roadless areas beyond human intervention. Society would also do its part to actively encourage and support community-oriented farmers who grow a different mix of crops in every region and who are rewarded for not farming at the expense of bobcats, bears, bobolinks, or any other members of wild nature that they are living amidst. Ultimately, entire regions would be recognized or certified by their "wild" aspects. It is a legacy worth striving for.

EMERGING MODELS AND WILD FARM PIONEERS

The good news is that, for some time, in farm areas across the country (and in other countries), people have already been leading by example, attempting to take Sir Albert Howard's edict of "farming in nature's image" to a higher level than previously accomplished: ranchers who have given over wetlands to be regulated by beavers rather than irrigation districts; vineyardists interplanting rows with wildflower habitat to serve as corridors for wild pollinators and beneficial insects; farmers who are proactively scaling back the size of their farms, returning certain woodlots or grasslands or riparian zones to the wild through permanent conservation easements; wildlands philanthropists and land trusts who are purchasing former ranches and farmlands for large-scale restoration efforts; and many others.

By way of example, in the early 1990s, the Sacramento Valley farmer John Anderson, a former University of California veterinarian, began his journey to becoming one of the country's pioneer restoration farmers. Over the past decade, Anderson has been learning, one step at a time, how to recreate California's lost prairie savannas. More than half of Anderson's 500-acre farm has been dedicated to the nearly full-time task of farming for wildlife. He has incorporated over

50 locally adapted species of native perennial grasses, forbes, sedges, rushes, shrubs, and trees along the meandering riparian zones and unused strips of Hedgerow Farms. And on some 60 acres of cultivated fields, Anderson raises a variety of native grass seed for sale to other restoration projects around the state. Surrounded by farms with denuded ditch banks and roadsides nearly devoid of trees, Hedgerow Farms stands out like some 19th-century landscape painting, with woodland corridors of native oak, cottonwood, and willow rising high above the irrigation canal. For that reason, beavers, carnivores, and dozens of bird species (up to ten protected species in the Sacramento Valley) now find haven there. Instead of farming via the conventional commodity subsidy system, Anderson has become savvy about the grants available through such programs as the Conservation Reserve Program (CRP) and other local Resource Conservation District incentives to help support his work.

To have truly "rewilded" farming areas, however, we cannot have exemplary farmers like Anderson working in relative ecological isolation. One can only imagine the result if every Central Valley farm, or even one out of every ten for that matter, were encouraged to farm for wildlife. An amazing turnaround could take place in a state where rivers have literally been run dry for row- and tree-crop irrigation and up to 95 percent of all riparian systems have been impacted. (In his later years, Marc Reisner, the author of *Cadillac Desert* and an activist on California water issues, played an inspirational and diplomatic role in convincing Sacramento Valley rice farmers of the value in converting their fields into seasonal wildlife habitat by eliminating straw burning and allowing winter flooding.)

Anderson's passion, scientific bent, and abundant energy have helped make Yolo County a model for conservation agriculture efforts. As a board member of the National Audubon Society, Anderson inspired a collaborative program between Audubon California and the Yolo County Resource Conservation District to win a $636,000 grant from CalFed, a state and federal effort to resolve water conflicts. This brought the restoration ecologist Jeanne Wirka and the watershed coordinator Judy Boshoven into the effort, to provide technical and financial assistance to regional farmers. According to an article in *Audubon* magazine by Jane Braxton Little, "Wirka and

Boshoven have spent much of the past two years bouncing over rutted roads to meet with landowners on stream banks, in pastures knee-deep in invasive yellow star thistle, in farmhouse kitchens, and in community centers." In 18 months the resulting partnerships have built exclusionary fences to keep cattle out of streams, created ponds to trap sediment and filter runoff from fields, and planted sloughs and creek banks with native shrubs and trees. It is a slow and painstaking process, just gathering momentum. Yet one project begets another, and Yolo County is emerging as a model, not just for the largest agricultural state, but for the country as well.

"The idea that organic farms are enclaves of purity — that everything within their boundaries is God-like and everything that lies outside is evil — is a patch ecology perspective that must be reconsidered," says Kirschenmann, a long-time organic farmer and director of the Leopold Center at Iowa State University. Farming with the wild, then, must be a unified effort, employed region by region, gaining the participation of the entire farming community and agencies as well. As Kirschenmann and Gould have written:

> The kind of future for organic agriculture that we need to envision, therefore, is one in which we begin to identify ecological neighborhoods, learn as much as we can about how the ecologies of those neighborhoods function, and how we can fit agriculture into those neighborhoods by effectively using the ecosystem services they provide. Such services include everything from microorganisms that restore soil quality, to predators that keep pests in check, to plants that invite predators to specific pest problems, to habitats that invite native pollinators — and much more.

The Nature Conservancy (TNC) began such a landscape-based project in 1984 when it started the The Cosumnes River Preserve, now a 42,000-acre watershed on one of the last undammed rivers flowing out of the Sierra Nevada mountains. Located 30 miles south of Sacramento in one of the world's most rapidly urbanizing areas, TNC's flagship project incorporates organic rice farming, livestock grazing, and other agricultural activities in select buffer areas surrounding the recovering river system. Annual flooding has been restored to the preserve, resulting in the creation of winter habitat for waterfowl and wading birds as well as the full recovery of native fish populations. New stands of valley oak forest native to the lower Cosumnes are growing and spreading, complementing the remnant old growth patches saved by the preserve. Shallow summer flooding provides habitat and also helps to control weed species in the rice fields.

Similar cooperative landscape-level planning projects are underway throughout the country, such as the effort being spearheaded by a diverse group of activists in New York State's Adirondack region. There, through coordinated land trust purchases and other individual initiatives, a wildlands corridor known as the Coon Mountain to Split Rock Wildway is being established to link Lake Champlain with Adirondack State Park. This includes Black Kettle Farm, which has been inspired by the principles of maximizing biodiversity on a working farm. And the 800,000-acre Parque Pumalin Project in Chile's X District offers yet another wild farm model. All visitor entrances also serve as working demonstration organic farms, part of a larger attempt to address the challenge of creating viable rural economies for settlers living adjacent to protected wilderness (and supplying healthy food to visitors as well).

CERTIFICATION AND ECO-LABELS

Inevitably, the practicality and success of farming with the wild will boil down to economics. Balancing economically viable forms of land use with biodiversity protection will also inevitably serve as an incubator for controversy. Government programs which support conservation rather than subsidizing overproduction must be stepped up. Increasing the budgets for underfunded and increasingly desired cost-share programs like the Conservation Reserve Program (CRP), Wetlands Reserve Program (WRP), and Environmental Quality Incentive Program (EQIP), were the subject of intense debate in the 2002 Farm Bill. A number of certification programs and eco-labels are already attempting to create market-based incentives that address species-specific and regional issues: shade-grown coffee and cacao; fish- and predator-friendly cultivation programs. Perhaps the most evolved certification schemes are the various shade-grown coffee labels, which have attempted to quantify and qualify the actual ecological values embodied by those efforts.

"Salmon Safe" certification began in 1997 as a project of the Pacific Rivers Council (PRC), an Oregon-based think tank with a history of forest activism. "Eighty percent of the non–point source pollution on the Willamette River comes from agriculture — nurseries, grass seed farms, orchards, dairies, and vineyards," says Dan Kent, director of PRC's "Salmon Safe" program. "We knew that changing farming practices could drastically reduce that." By 2000, after nearly five years of science-based research and farmer outreach, Salmon Safe farms ranged from Washington State to the Feather River in northern California.

Winter cover cropping is probably the most important step that certified Salmon Safe growers are taking to curtail runoff from fields and vineyards, a baseline practice that is recommended but not required by organic certifying programs. Other important practices include minimizing chemical use and managing buffer strips along riparian areas. In addition to holding the soil in place during rainy seasons, leguminous cover crops can be planted to fix nitrogen, alleviating yet another emerging issue for northwest farmlands: ground water contamination due to decades of over-fertilization with synthetic nitrogen. Throughout the growing season, flowering cover crops can also attract a diversity of insects to fields, serving as natural pest control.

"We really struggled with whether a farmer had to be perfect or not," says Kent. "But we knew that no matter what we did, there was still going to be agriculture in salmon watersheds. So we tried to include a wide variety of farms in the program." In addition, the labeling program has continually tried to raise the bar on its ecological standards. Through the difficult process of creating a self-funding agro-ecologically based label, Kent has learned that price premiums may not be the most important incentive that can change farmer behavior. Market access, through an enhanced value of the producer's efforts, says Kent, can perhaps be the most significant benefit.

THE WILD FARM ALLIANCE

In January of 2000 the Foundation for Deep Ecology hosted a three-day conference in an effort to jump-start an organization focused solely on the emerging wild farms concept. A year later, the Wild Farm Alliance (WFA) was officially established as a project of the San Francisco–based Tides Foundation. Spearheaded by an engaged and interdisciplinary advisory board of conservationists and sustainable agriculture activists from around the United States, among the WFA's primary strategies is to identify and promote on-the-ground models that can help to inspire credible and valuable results. Another important thrust of the WFA will be to build alliances with leaders and organizations to create a dynamic, regionally based movement.

At present, the challenge of making farming more harmonious with biodiversity conjures more questions than ready answers, but one thing is certain. If the past three centuries of North American agriculture have been about demonstrating how much of the land can be appropriated to feed and clothe the world, this century must be about carefully assessing how much we can give back in the pursuit of living not industrially, but organically and bioregionally. Fortunately, after decades of working in relative isolation, conservationists, farmers, and sustainable farming activists are beginning to view agricultural areas as critical terrain in the effort to restore large and healthfully functioning ecosystems throughout the continent. We can only hope that time is on the wild's side.

Afterword

▼

HOPE

WENDELL BERRY

I will not be altogether surprised to be told that I have set forth a line of thought that is attractive but hopeless. A number of critics have advised me of this, out of their charity, as if I might have written of my hopes for 40 years without giving a thought to hopelessness. Hope, of course, is always accompanied by the fear of hopelessness, which is a legitimate fear.

And so I would like to confront directly the issue of hope. My hope is most seriously challenged by the fact of decline, of loss. The things that I have tried to defend are less numerous and worse off now than when I started, but in this I am only like all other conservationists. All of us have been fighting a battle that on average we are losing, and I doubt that there is any use in reviewing the statistical proofs. The point — the only interesting point — is that we have not quit. Ours is not a fight that you can stay in very long if you look on victory as a sign of triumph or on loss as a sign of defeat. We have not quit because we are not hopeless.

My own aim is not hopelessness. I am not looking for reasons to give up. I am looking for reasons to keep on. In outlining the concerns of agrarianism, I have intended to show how the effort of conservation could be enlarged and strengthened.

What agrarian principles implicitly propose — and what I explicitly propose in advocating those principles at this time — is a revolt of local small producers and local consumers against the global industrialism of the corporations. Do I think that there is a hope that such a revolt can survive and succeed and that it can have a significant influence upon our lives and our world?

Yes, I do. And to be as plain as possible, let me just say what I know. I know from friends and neighbors and from my own family that it is now possible for farmers to sell at a premium to local customers such products as organic vegetables, organic beef and lamb, and pasture-raised chickens. This market is being made by the exceptional goodness and freshness of the food, by the wish of urban consumers to support their farming neighbors, and by the excesses and abuses of the corporate food industry.

This, I think, gives the pattern of an economic revolt that is not only possible but is happening. It is happening for two reasons. First, as the scale of industrial agriculture increases, so does the scale of its abuses, and it is hard to hide large-scale abuses from consumers. It is virtually impossible now for intelligent consumers to be ignorant of the heartlessness and nastiness of animal confinement operations and their excessive use of antibiotics, of the use of hormones in meat and milk production, of the stenches and pollutants of pig and poultry factories, of the use of toxic chemicals and the waste of soil and soil health in industrial row-cropping, of the mysterious or disturbing or threatening practices associated with industrial food storage, preservation, and processing. Second, as the food industries focus more and more on gigantic global opportunities, they cannot help but overlook small local opportunities, as is made plain by the increase of community supported agriculture, farmers' markets, health food stores, and so on. In fact, there are some markets that the great corporations by definition cannot supply. The market for so-called organic food, for example, is really a market for good, fresh, trustworthy food, food from producers known and trusted by consumers, and such food cannot be produced by a global corporation.

But the food economy is only one example. It is also possible to think of good local forest economies. And in the face of much neglect, it is possible to think of local small business economies — some of them related to the local economies of farm and forest — supported by locally owned, community-oriented banks.

What do these struggling, sometimes failing, sometimes hardly realized efforts of local economy have to do with conservation as we know it? The answer, probably, is *everything*. The conservation movement, as I have said, has a conservation program; it has a preservation program; it has a rather sporadic health-protection program; but it has no economic program, and because it has no economic program it has the status of something exterior to daily life, surviving by emergency, like an ambulance service. In saying this, I do not mean to belittle the importance of protest, litigation, lobbying, legislation, large-scale organization — all of which I believe in and support. I am saying simply that we must do more. We must confront, on the ground, and each of us at home, the economic assumptions in which the problems of conservation originate.

We have got to remember that the great destructiveness of the industrial age comes from a division, a sort of divorce, in our economy, and therefore in our consciousness, between production and consumption. Of this radical division of functions we can say, without much fear of oversimplifying, that the aim of producers is to sell as much as possible and that the aim of consumers is to buy as much as possible. We need only to add that the aim of both producer and consumer is to be so far as possible carefree. Because of various pressures, governments have learned to coerce from producers some grudging concern for the health and solvency of consumers. No way has been found to coerce from consumers any consideration for the methods and sources of production.

What alerts consumers to the outrages of producers is typically some kind of loss or threat of loss. We see that in dividing consumption from production we have lost the function of conserving. Conserving is no longer an integral part of the economy of the producer or the consumer. Neither the producer nor the consumer any longer says, "I must be careful of this so that it will last." The working assumption of both is that where there is some, there must be more. If they can't get what they need in one place, they will find it in another. That is why conservation is now a separate concern, a separate effort.

But experience seems increasingly to be driving us out of the categories of producer and consumer and into the categories of citizen, family member, and community member, in all of which we have an inescapable interest in making things last. And here is where I think the conservation movement (I mean that movement that has defined itself as the defender of wilderness and the natural world) can involve itself in the fundamental issues of economy and land use, and in the process gain strength for its original causes.

I would like my fellow conservationists to notice how many people and organizations are now working to save something of value — not just wilderness places, wild rivers, wildlife habitat, species diversity, water quality, and air quality, but also agricultural land, family farms and ranches, communities, children and childhood, local schools, local economies, local food markets, livestock breeds and domestic plant varieties, fine old buildings, scenic roads, and so on. I would like my fellow conservationists to understand also that there is hardly a small farm or ranch or locally owned restaurant or store or shop or business anywhere that is not struggling to save itself.

All of these people, who are fighting sometimes lonely battles to preserve things of value that they cannot bear to lose, are the conservation movement's natural allies. Most of them have the same enemies as the conservation movement. There is no necessary conflict among them. Thinking of them, in their great variety, in the essential likeness of their motives and concerns, one thinks of the possibility of a defined community of interest among them all, a shared stewardship of all the diversity of good things that are needed for the health and abundance of the world.

I don't suppose that this will be easy, given especially the history of conflict between conservationists and land users. I only suppose that it is necessary. Conservationists can't conserve everything that needs conserving without joining the effort to use well the agricultural lands, the forests, and the waters that we must use. To enlarge the areas protected from use without at the same time enlarging the areas of *good* use is a mistake. To have no large areas of protected old-growth forest would be folly, as most of us would agree. But it is also folly to have come this far in our history without a single working model of a thoroughly diversified and integrated, ecologically sound, local forest economy. That such an economy is possible is indicated by many imperfect or incomplete examples, but we need desperately to put the pieces together in one place — and then in every place.

The most tragic conflict in the history of conservation is that between the conservationists and the farmers and ranchers. It is tragic because it is unnecessary. There is no irresolvable conflict here, but the conflict that exists can be resolved only on the basis of a common understanding of good practice. Here again we need to foster and study working models: farms and ranches that are knowledgeably striving to bring economic practice into line with ecological reality, and local food economies in which consumers conscientiously support the best land stewardship.

We know better than to expect a working model of a conserving global corporation. But we must begin to expect — and we must, as conservationists, begin working for, and in — working models of conserving local economies. These are possible now. Good and able people are working hard to develop them now. They need the full support of the conservation movement now. Conservationists need to go to these people, ask what they can do to help, and then help. A little later, having helped, they can in turn ask for help.

CONTRIBUTORS

CATHERINE BADGLEY is a research scientist and lecturer at the University of Michigan. Her research concerns the fossil history and paleoecology of terrestrial ecosystems, especially their mammals. She teaches courses on environmental issues, ecology, the history of life, and sustainable agriculture in the Environmental Studies Program. She holds a B.A. in geology (Radcliffe College), an M.S. in wildlife ecology (Yale School of Forestry and Environmental Studies), and a Ph.D. in biology (Yale University). She lives in southeastern Michigan on an organic farm, where the landscape, garden, and farm animals are continuing her education.

DEBI BARKER is the deputy director at the International Forum on Globalization (IFG) based in San Francisco, California. She coauthored *Invisible Government—The World Trade Organization: Global Government for the New Millennium* with Jerry Mander and has edited several IFG publications, including *Blue Gold: The Global Water Crisis and the Commodification of the World's Water Supply* and *Views from the South*. She began working on globalization issues as an assistant for *The Case against the Global Economy* by Jerry Mander and Edward Goldsmith. She currently serves on the board of the International Center for Technology Assessment.

WENDELL BERRY is considered one of America's greatest living men of letters, having achieved national recognition as a poet, novelist, and writer of nonfiction. He lives on a farm in Port Royal, Kentucky, where he and his wife raise sheep and grow home produce. His has written several books on agriculture and related topics including, among others, *The Unsettling of America: Culture and Agriculture*, *Home Economics*, *The Gift of Good Land*, and *Another Turn of the Crank*.

MARK BRISCOE has worked as a professional writer and editor for over 12 years. Since 1999, he has been director of publications at the International Center for Technology Assessment and the Center for Food Safety in Washington, D.C. His published articles and essays have covered topics ranging from environmentally friendly tourism to zero-emissions automobile technologies and from global warming to sustainable agriculture.

STEPHEN BUCHMANN, PH.D., runs The Bee Works, LLC, out of Tucson, Arizona. He is coauthor of *The Forgotten Pollinators* (Island Press), and has written 3 books and 150 scholarly articles. Dr. Buchmann is active in global pollinator conservation efforts, and currently serves as a steering committee and founding member of the North American Pollinator Protection Campaign of the Coevolution Institute in San Francisco.

MICHAEL COLBY is the executive director of Food & Water, Inc., a national political advocacy organization that focuses on issues concerning culture, agriculture, and ecology. He is also the editor of its quarterly magazine, *Food & Water Journal*, a leading forum for creative and strategic advocacy, provocative and inspiring essays, and commingling of the arts and activism. Mr. Colby and the work of Food & Water have been featured in hundreds of media venues, including *The New York Times, Newsweek, ABC's 20/20, The CBS Evening News,* and *The Wall Street Journal.*

DAVID EHRENFELD is a professor of biology at Rutgers University, where he teaches courses in ecology and conservation biology. He is the author of numerous books and articles, including *The Arrogance of Humanism* and *Beginning Again: People and Nature in the New Millennium,* from which his essay in this book was excerpted. His latest book is *Swimming Lessons: Keeping Afloat in the Age of Technology.* He is the founding editor of Conservation Biology and is considered an important thinker in the fields of environmental ethics and conservation biology.

ANDREW FISHER is cofounder and executive director of the Community Food Security Coalition, a national alliance of 265 organizations working to create a just and sustainable food system, based in Los Angeles. He is a nationally recognized expert in the field of food security and has co-authored numerous articles and studies on the topic. He is active in the sustainable agriculture movement in California, and played a lead role in the adoption of a hunger policy by the city of Los Angeles. He holds graduate degrees from UCLA in Environmental Policy and Latin American Studies, and is a dedicated community gardener.

DAVE HENSON is the director of the Occidental Arts and Ecology Center (OAEC), an 80-acre farm, ecology education center, and intentional community in Northern California. An environmental and social justice activist for over 20 years, Mr. Henson has held staff positions with the Highlander Research and Education Center, the National Toxics Campaign, Greenpeace, and the Earth Island Institute. He is also a principal with the Program on Corporations, Law, and Democracy, which instigates democratic conversation and actions that contest the authority of corporations to govern. Mr. Henson also serves as an organizational development and strategic planning consultant to community-based environmental, social justice, and farm groups.

JIM HIGHTOWER is a national radio commentator, author, and renowned public speaker, and former Texas Agriculture Commissioner. Known as "America's most popular progressive populist," Mr. Hightower publishes a monthly newsletter called *The Hightower Lowdown*, which was recently named Best National Newsletter at the annual Alternative Press Awards. He also broadcasts daily radio commentaries in 60 markets across the country, writes a weekly newspaper column, and has a monthly column in *The Nation*. His best-selling books include *There's Nothing in the Middle of the Road but Yellow Stripes and Dead Armadillos* and *If the Gods Had Meant Us to Vote, They Would Have Given Us Candidates*.

HUGH H. ILTIS is professor emeritus of botany and director emeritus of the Herbarium at the University of Wisconsin in Madison. He has won numerous awards, including the Society for Economic Botany's Distinguished Economic Botanist in 1998 and the Asa Gray Award of the American Society of Plant Taxonomy in 1994. His ongoing research has made important contributions to our understanding of the evolution of maize, and of the flora and plant geography of Wisconsin, North America, and the Sierra de Manantlán Biosphere Reserve in Mexico. He has conducted numerous field studies on the botany of North, Central, and South America and has trained numerous scholars of plant taxonomy, conservation, and economic botany.

DANIEL IMHOFF is the cofounder of SimpleLife Books and the executive director of Watershed Media, a nonprofit communications agency located in Northern California. He is currently completing The Wood Reduction Trilogy, a series of resource guides designed to help targeted audiences find or maximize alternatives to wood in paper, building materials, and packaging. The author of a number of articles on agriculture and the wild farm concept, Mr. Imhoff is also researching *Farming with the Wild: Strategies for Enhancing Biodiversity on Farms and Ranches*, a book identifying models and resources to help farmers incorporate conservation practices onto their farms and watersheds. He is also a founding member of the Wild Farm Alliance.

MRILL INGRAM is currently working at the University of Wisconsin, Madison on a project exploring the potential of environmental management systems to improve environmental performance on farms. She is also a Ph.D. candidate in geography at the University of Arizona, and is focusing on alternative knowledge in U.S. agriculture. Her larger interests include community-based research and food security.

WES JACKSON is president of The Land Institute, founded in 1976. After attending Kansas Wesleyan (B.A. Biology, 1958), he studied botany (M.A. University of Kansas, 1960) and genetics (Ph.D. North Carolina State University, 1967). He was a professor of biology at Kansas Wesleyan and later established the Environmental Studies program at California State University, Sacramento, where he became a tenured full professor until his resignation in 1976. Dr. Jackson's writings include *Rooted in the Land: Essays on Community and Place*, coedited with William Vitek, *Becoming Native to This Place* (1994), *Altars of Unhewn Stone* (1987), and *New Roots for Agriculture* (1980).

ANDREW KIMBRELL is a public interest attorney, activist, and author, and currently serves as executive director of the International Center for Technology Assessment (CTA) and the Center for Food Safety (CFS) in Washington, D.C. After working for eight years as the policy director at the Foundation for Economic Trends, Mr. Kimbrell established CTA in 1994 and CFS in 1997. Mr. Kimbrell is the author of *The Human Body Shop* and *The Masculine Mystique*, among other books and essays. He has been featured on radio and television programs across the country, has lectured at dozens of universities throughout the country, and has testified before congressional and regulatory hearings. In 1994, the *Utne Reader* named Mr. Kimbrell as one of the world's 100 leading visionaries.

RON KROESE was raised in Iowa, studied journalism, and worked for several years as a newspaper reporter and then as the press secretary for Senator James Abourezk (D-South Dakota) during the Senator's first terms. In 1982, Kroese turned his attention to rural regional affairs as founder and director of the Land Stewardship Project, a nonprofit organization promoting sustainable agriculture in the upper Midwest. From 1993 to 1997 he worked as the executive director of the National Center for Appropriate Technology in Butte, Montana. Mr. Kroese currently serves on the board of directors of the Land Stewardship Project and the Michael Fields Agricultural Institute, a nonprofit sustainable agriculture organization headquartered in East Troy, Wisconsin.

BETSY LYDON formerly served as program director of Mothers & Others for a Livable Planet. Ms. Lydon is also the coordinator to the Environmental Grantmakers Association's Sustainable Agriculture and Food Systems Funders Group, based in New York City. Additionally, she was a consumer representative to the National Organic Standards Board and is currently a board member of Just Food (N.Y.C.), the Consumer's Choice Council (D.C.) and the Organic Farming Research Foundation (CA).

JERRY MANDER is a senior fellow at the nonprofit Public Media Center in San Francisco and is the program director of the Foundation for Deep Ecology. He is a cofounder and chair of the International Forum on Globalization, an international organization of activists opposed to the global economy. He is also the author of several bestsellers, including *Four Arguments for the Elimination of Television, In the Absence of the Sacred,* and *The Case against the Global Economy.*

JASON MCKENNEY is the owner and principal grower for Purisima Greens farm in Half Moon Bay. Purisima Greens is a five-acre organic farm that operates primarily as a community supported agriculture (CSA) project and also distributes to farmers' markets, restaurants, and retail stores in the Bay Area. Before starting Purisima Greens, Mr. McKenney worked on two other organic farms—a working-educational farm in Rhode Island and one supplying produce to Bay Area restaurants, located in San Gregorio, California. He has nearly ten years of farming and teaching experience and holds a B.S. in environmental science and evolutionary biology from Brown University.

JOSEPH MENDELSON III is legal director for the International Center for Technology Assessment (CTA) and the Center for Food Safety (CFS). His career includes significant litigation, public advocacy, and environmental grassroots organizing. Before joining CTA in 1995, Mr. Mendelson worked as a staff attorney with the Foundation on Economic Trends and directed the Friends of the Earth's stratospheric ozone protection project. He has written numerous articles for environmental, general, and legal journals, including *The Ecologist, Boston College Environmental Affairs Law Review, Environmental Law Reporter,* and the *Utne Reader.* He has also appeared in numerous media outlets.

MONICA MOORE is codirector of Pesticide Action Network (PAN) North America. She has worked on pesticide issues since 1980, including cofounding PAN International in 1982 and PAN North America Regional Center in 1984. Ms. Moore oversees all PAN North America's programs and represents PAN North America to PAN International. Her own program interests include accelerating the reduction of pesticide use and increasing organic and sustainable agriculture in her home state of California. She serves as an advisor to many organizations and holds an M.S. from the University of California at Berkeley's College of Natural Resources.

GARY NABHAN, PH.D., is director of the Center for Sustainable Environments, Northern Arizona University, and cofounder of the Migratory Pollinators Project at the Arizona-Sonora Desert Museum. He is coauthor of *The Forgotten Pollinators* (Island Press), and has written 12 other books, including *Coming Home to Eat: The Sensual Pleasures* and *Global Politics of Local Food* (Norton).

JOAN IVERSON NASSAUER, FASLA, is a professor of landscape architecture in the School of Natural Resources and Environment at the University of Michigan. Her work focuses on understanding what local people value about their landscapes and on using their values to make ecological design and planning successful over the long term. She works in rural landscape management—including countryside protection and ecologically appropriate growth strategies, and technical guidelines for conservation planning—in addition to urban ecological design—retrofitting the city to improve ecological health. Ms. Nassauer serves on numerous boards, including the advisory board of The Land Institute in Salina, Kansas, and the editorial board of *Landscape Ecology*. She is the author of dozens of papers, reports, books, and monographs, including *Placing Nature: Culture and Landscape Ecology*.

HELENA NORBERG-HODGE is the director of the International Society for Ecology and Culture (ISEC), a nonprofit organization concerned with the protection of both biological and cultural diversity, based in England. Ms. Norberg-Hodge is also director of the Ladakh Project, which since 1975 has been providing Ladakhi leaders with information about the impact of conventional development in other parts of the world while exploring more sustainable patterns of development in Ladakh itself, based on the use of local resources and indigenous knowledge. She is also the author of numerous articles and books on the subjects of localization and agriculture, including *From the Ground Up: Rethinking Industrial Agriculture* and *Ancient Futures: Learning from Ladakh*, which has been translated into more than 30 languages.

HOPE J. SHAND is the research director of the Rural Advancement Foundation International (RAFI). Headquartered in Winnipeg, Manitoba, Canada, RAFI is an international civil society organization dedicated to the conservation and use of biodiversity as the cornerstone of sustainable agriculture and world food security. Ms. Shand has written extensively on the topic of agricultural biodiversity and on the social and economic impacts of new biotechnologies. She is editor of *RAFI Communique*, author of *Human Nature: Agricultural Biodiversity and Farm-Based Food Security* (1998), and coauthor of *The Ownership of Life: When Patents and Values Clash* (1997). In 1993, Ms. Shand authored *Harvesting Nature's Diversity*, the official document on agricultural biodiversity published by the United Nations Food and Agriculture Organization.

MICHAEL SLIGH is the director of sustainable agriculture for the Rural Advancement Foundation International-USA (RAFI-USA), for which he has worked for over 16 years. His current work focuses on the promotion of sustainable and organic agriculture reforms, including development of domestic and international organic standards, monitoring and evaluation of biotechnology, and the promotion of agricultural biodiversity. Mr. Sligh was the founding chair of the USDA/National Organic Standards Board, which was responsible for the development of the U.S. Organic Standards. He also is a member of the United Nations-based FAO/WHO CODEX Alimentarius, the USDA Agricultural Biotechnology Advisory Board and is the author of *Toward Organic Integrity*, a guide to the development of U.S. organic standards.

REBECCA SPECTOR is the campaign director for the Center for Food Safety's (CFS) West Coast office outside San Francisco, where she works primarily on advocacy campaigns to ensure the mandatory safety testing and labeling of all genetically engineered foods and to protect the integrity of organic foods. Before working with CFS, Ms. Spector served as program coordinator for Mothers & Others for a Livable Planet, where she comanaged their national organic cotton campaign. With her husband, Ms. Spector is co-owner of Purisima Greens, a small-scale organic farm in Half Moon Bay, California, which operates primarily as a community supported agriculture (CSA) farm. She is also a board member of the Community Alliance with Family Farmers and holds an M.S. in Environmental Policy from the University of Michigan's School of Natural Resources and Environment.

KELLEY R. TUCKER, director of the Pesticides and Birds Campaign at the American Bird Conservancy, received her degree in social-cultural anthropology from the University of Chicago in 1986. She has worked in nonprofit fund-raising and social policy work in Chicago and as a consultant for the John D. and Catherine T. MacArthur Foundation. Ms. Tucker is a federally permitted migratory bird rehabilitator and works with birds of prey in educational programs for children. She has worked as an advocate for pesticide use reduction for several years, primarily with the Safer Pest Control Project in Chicago. She also served as senior field biologist for a study of Swainson's Hawk nesting and reproduction in southwestern Minnesota, sponsored by the University of Minnesota and The Raptor Center.

PETER WARSHALL has spent 30 years teaching, guiding, and writing on natural and cultural history. He is presently the editor of *Whole Earth*, the magazine of the *Whole Earth Catalog*. In addition to technical, peer-reviewed, and report writing, he has written for the general public since the early 1970s as an editor of the *Whole Earth Catalog* and *Coevolution Quarterly* (now *Whole Earth*). Recent essays include "Four Ways to Look at Earth" in *Earth Matters: The Earth Sciences, Philosophy, and the Claims of Community*; "Environmental Change in Aravaipa (1870-1970)," an ethnoecological study; and "The Biodiversity of Mali," among others. Dr. Warshall received his B.A. in biology with a minor in French literature and a Ph.D. in biological anthropology from Harvard University.

ALICE WATERS, award-winning chef, author, and food activist, opened Chez Panisse restaurant in Berkeley, California, in 1971. The set menu that changes daily features only the highest-quality products, only when they are in season. Over the past three decades, the restaurant has developed a network of local farmers and ranchers whose dedication to sustainable agriculture assures a steady supply of pure and fresh ingredients. Ms. Waters is also actively involved in the development of the Edible Schoolyard, an edible garden and kitchen classroom at Berkeley's Martin Luther King, Jr. Middle School. Her publications include *Chez Panisse Menu Cookbook, Chez Panisse Cooking, Chez Panisse Vegetables*, and *Chez Panisse Café Cookbook*, among others.

SELECTED REFERENCES
AND READINGS

*The following is a selected list of books and resources referenced
or utilized in the production of this book.*

Ableman, Michael. *From the Good Earth: A Celebration of Growing Food around the World.* New York: Abrams Press, 1993.

Ableman, Michael, and Cynthia Wisehart, eds. *On Good Land: The Autobiography of an Urban Farm.* San Francisco: Chronicle Books, 1998.

Altieri, Miguel. *Agroecology: The Science of Sustainable Agriculture.* Boulder: Westview Press, 1995.

_____. *Biodiversity and Pest Management in Agroecosystems.* New York: Haworth Press, 1994.

_____. *Genetic Engineering in Agriculture: The Myths, Environmental Risks, and Alternatives.* Oakland, Calif.: Food First Books, 2001.

Ashworth, Suzanne. *Seed to Seed.* Seed Savers Exchange (3076 North Winn Rd., Decorah, IA 52101), 1991.

Aspelin, Arnold. *Pesticides Industry Sales and Usage: 1994 & 1995 Market Estimates.* Washington, D.C.: U.S. Environmental Protection Agency, August 1997.

Bailey, Liberty Hyde. *The Holy Earth.* New York: Macmillan, 1905.

_____. *The Outlook to Nature.* New York: Macmillan, 1905.

Bello, Walden, and Anuradha Mittal, eds. *The Future in the Balance.* Oakland, Calif.: Food First Books, 2001.

Berry, Wendell. *Another Turn of the Crank: Essays.* Washington, D.C.: Counterpoint Press, 1996.

_____. *The Gift of Good Land.* San Francisco: North Point Press, 1981.

_____. *Life Is a Miracle: An Essay against Modern Superstition.* Washington, D.C.: Counterpoint Press, 2001.

_____. *A Place on Earth.* Washington, D.C.: Counterpoint Press, 2001.

_____. *The Unsettling of America: Culture and Agriculture.* San Francisco: Sierra Club Books, 1977.

Bickel, Gary; Steven Carlson; and Mark Nord. *Household Food Security in the United States 1995–1998: Advance Report.* Alexandria, Va.: USDA Office of Analysis, Nutrition, & Evaluation, Food and Nutrition Service, July 1999.

Bird, Elizabeth; Gordon Bultena; and John Gardner, eds. *Planting the Future: Developing an Agriculture That Sustains Land and Community.* Ames: Iowa State University Press, 1995.

Boucher, Douglas H., ed. *The Paradox of Plenty: Hunger in a Bountiful World.* Oakland, Calif.: Food First Books, 1999.

British Medical Association Board of Science and Education. *The Impact of Genetic Modification on Agriculture, Food and Health.* Interim statement. London, May 1999.

Buchmann, Stephen L., and Gary Paul Nabhan. *The Forgotten Pollinators.* Washington, D.C.: Island Press, 1996.

California Department of Pesticide Regulation. *Summary of Pesticide Use Report Data 1999.* Sacramento, September 2000.

Carroll, C. Ronald; John Vandermeer; and Peter Rosset, eds. *Agroecology.* New York: Food Products Press, 1994.

Carson, Rachel. *Silent Spring.* Boston: Houghton Mifflin, 1962.

Centers for Disease Control. *Disease Information on Foodborne Infections.* Atlanta: CDC, Division of Bacterial and Mycotic Diseases, December 2000.

Chossudovsky, Michel. "The Causes of Global Famine." *Third World Resurgence,* no. 64 (December 1995).

Colborn, T.; D. Dumanoski; and J. P. Myers. *Our Stolen Future.* New York: Dutton, 1996.

Colby, Michael. "Food Irradiation and the Lies of Industrial Food." *Food & Water Journal,* Fall/Winter 1997–98.

Consumers Union. "How Safe Is Our Produce?" *Consumer Reports,* March 1999.

Cook, Ken. *How 'Bout Them Apples? Pesticides in Children's Food Ten Years after Alar.* Report. Washington, D.C.: Environmental Working Group, February 1999.

Crouch, Martha L. *How the Terminator Terminates: An Explanation for the Non-Scientist of a Remarkable Patent for Killing Second Generation Seeds of Crop Plants.* Occasional paper. Edmonds, Wa.: Edmonds Institute, 1998.

Cummins, Ronnie, and Ben Lilliston. *Genetically Engineered Food: A Self-Defense Guide for Consumers.* New York: Marlowe, 2000.

Cushman Jr., John H. "After Silent Spring: Chemical Industry Put Spin on All It Brewed." *New York Times,* 26 March 2001.

Dodson, Calaway H., and Alwyn H. Gentry. "Flora of the Rio Palenque Science Center." *Selbyana: Journal of the Marie Selby Botanical Gardens* 4, nos. 1–6 (1978).

Duesing, Bill. *Living on the Earth: Eclectic Essays for a Sustainable and Joyful Future.* Solar Farm Education (Box 135, Stevenson, CT 06491), 1993.

Durning, Alan. *How Much Is Enough? The Consumer Society and the Future of the Earth.* Washington, D.C.: Worldwatch Institute/W. W. Norton, 1995.

Ehrenfeld, David. *The Arrogance of Humanism.* New York: Oxford University Press. 1981.

_____. *Beginning Again: People and Nature in the New Millennium.* New York: Oxford University Press, 1993.

_____. *Swimming Lessons: Keeping Afloat in the Age of Technology.* New York: Oxford University Press, 2001.

_____. *To Preserve Biodiversity: An Overview. Readings from Conservation Biology.* Cambridge, Mass.: Blackwell Science, 1995.

Ellul, Jacques. *The Technological Society.* New York: Vintage Books, 1964.

Epstein, Samuel. "Winning the War against Cancer: Are They Even Fighting It?" *Ecologist* 28, no. 2 (March/April 1998).

Fowler, Cary. *Unnatural Selection: Technology, Politics, and Plant Evolution.* Langhorne, Pa.: Gordon and Breach, 1994.

Fowler, Cary, and Pat Mooney. *Shattering: Food, Politics, and the Loss of Genetic Diversity.* Tucson: University of Arizona Press, 1990.

Fox, Michael. *Beyond Evolution: The Genetically Altered Future of Plants, Animals, the Earth and Humans.* New York: Lyons Press, 1999.

Fox, Nicols. *Spoiled: The Dangerous Truth About a Food Chain Gone Haywire.* New York: Basic Books, 1997.

Freyfogle, Eric T, ed. *The New Agrarianism: Land, Culture, and the Community of Life.* Washington, D.C.: Island Press, 2001.

Gershuny, Grace, and Joseph Smillie. *The Soul of the Soil: A Guide to Ecological Soil Management.* Davis, Calif.: agAccess, 1995.

Goldman, Lynn R. "Chemicals and Children's Environment: What We Don't Know About Risks." *Environmental Health Perspectives* 106, suppl. 13 (June 1998).

Goldschmidt, Walter. *As You Sow: Three Studies in the Social Consequences of Agribusiness.* Montclair, N.J.: Allanheld, Osmun, 1978.

Goodman, David, and Michael Watts, eds. *Globalizing Food.* New York: Routledge, 1997.

Greider, William. "The Last Farm Crisis." *Nation,* 20 November 2000.

Groh, T., and S. McFadden. *Farms of Tomorrow: Community Supported Farms, Farm Supported Communities.* Kimberton, Pa.: Biodynamic Farming and Gardening Association. 1990.

Gussow, Joan Dye. *This Organic Life: Confessions of a Suburban Homesteader.* White River Junction, Vt.: Chelsea Green, 2001.

Hanson, Victor Davis. *Fields without Dreams: Defending the Agrarian Idea.* New York: Free Press, 1996.

Hart, John Fraser. *The Land That Feeds Us.* New York: W. W. Norton, 1993.

Hawken, Paul. *The Ecology of Commerce: A Declaration of Sustainability.* New York: Harper Business, 1993.

Hightower, Jim. *If the Gods Had Meant Us to Vote, They'd Have Given Us Candidates.* New York: HarperPerennial, 2001.

———. *There's Nothing in the Middle of the Road but Yellow Stripes and Dead Armadillos.* New York: HarperCollins, 1998.

Howard, Sir Albert. *An Agricultural Testament.* London: Oxford University Press, 1940.

Hudson, Rick H.; Richard K. Tucker; and M. A. Haegele. *Handbook of Toxicity of Pesticides to Wildlife.* Resource Publication No. 153. Washington, D.C.: U.S. Department of the Interior, Fish and Wildlife Service, 1984.

Hynes, H. Patricia. *The Recurring Silent Spring.* New York: Pergamon, 1989.

Imhoff, Daniel. *Farming with the Wild: Strategies for Enhancing Biodiversity on Farms and Ranches.* Philo, Calif.: Watershed Media, 2002.

Imhoff, Daniel, with the Wild Farm Alliance. "Farming with the Wild: Agriculture and the Biodiversity Crisis," *Biodiversity* 11, no. 1 (Winter 2001).

Jackson, Dana L., and Laura Jackson, eds. *The Farm as Natural Habitat.* Washington, D.C.: Island Press, 2002.

Jackson, Wes. *Altars of Unhewn Stone: Science and the Earth.* San Francisco: North Point Press, 1987.

———. *Becoming Native to This Place.* Lexington: University Press of Kentucky, 1994.

_____. "Natural Systems Agriculture: A Radical Alternative." Paper presented at conference hosted by Professor Charles Sing, Bozeman, Montana, 6–10 October 1999.

_____. *New Roots for Agriculture*. Lincoln: University of Nebraska Press, 1980.

Jackson, Wes, and Brian Donahue. *Reclaiming the Commons: Community Farms and Forests in a New England Town*. New Haven: Yale University Press, 2001.

Jeavons, John. *How to Grow More Vegetables*. Berkeley: Ten Speed Press, 1995.

Jeyaratnam, J. "Acute Pesticide Poisoning: A Major Global Health Problem." *World Health Statistics Quarterly* 43 (1990): 139–144.

Kegley, Susan; Lars Neumeister; and Timothy Martin. *Disrupting the Balance: Ecological Impacts of Pesticides in California*. Report. San Francisco: Californians for Pesticide Reform and Pesticide Action Network North America, 1999.

Kimbrell, Andrew, and Don Davis. "Globalization and Food Scarcity." *Ecologist* 29, no. 2 (March/April 1999).

King, Franklin H. *Farmers of Forty Centuries*. Emmaus, Pa.: Rodale Press, 1973; reprint of 1911 edition.

Kluger, Jeffrey. "Anatomy of an Outbreak [of *E. coli*]." *Time*, 3 August 1998, 55.

Kneen, Brewster. *Invisible Giant: Cargill and Its Transnational Strategies*. Halifax, Nova Scotia: Fernwood Publishing, 1995.

Korten, David. *When Corporations Rule the World*. West Hartford, Conn.: Kumarian Press, 1995.

Krebs, Al. *The Corporate Reapers—The Book of Agribusiness*. Washington, D.C.: Essential Books, 1992.

Lambrecht, Bill. *Dinner at the New Gene Café: How Genetic Engineering Is Changing What We Eat, How We Live, and the Global Politics of Food*. New York: St. Martin's Press, 2001.

Lampkin, Nicolas. *Organic Farming*. Ipswich, England: Farming Press, 1990.

Lappé, Frances Moore; Joseph Collins; and Peter Rosset. *World Hunger: Twelve Myths*. New York: Grove Press, 1998.

Lappé, Marc, and Britt Bailey. *Against the Grain: Biotechnology and the Corporate Takeover of Your Food*. Monroe, Me.: Common Courage Press, 1998.

Leopold, Aldo. *For the Health of the Land: Previously Unpublished Essays and Other Writings*. Washington, D.C.: Island Press/Shearwater Books, 1999.

Liebman, J. *Rising Toxic Tide: Pesticide Use in California, 1991–1995*. Report. San Francisco: Californians for Pesticide Reform and Pesticide Action Network, 1997.

Lockeretz, William, ed. *Visions of American Agriculture*. Ames: Iowa State University Press, 1997.

Lodgson, Gene. *The Contrary Farmer*. White River Junction, Vt.: Chelsea Green Press. 1994.

_____. "Get Small or Get Out." *New Farm* (Rodale Institute, Emmaus, Pa.), July/August 1994.

Losey, John E.; Linda S. Rayor; and Maureen E. Carter. "Transgenic Pollen Harms Monarch Larvae." *Nature*, 20 May 1999.

Madden, J. Patrick. *For All Generations: Making World Agriculture More Sustainable.* Glendale, Calif.: OM Publishing, 1997.

Madgoff, Fred; John Bellamy Foster; and Frederick Buttel, eds. *Hungry for Profit: The Agribusiness Threat to Farmers, Food and the Environment.* New York: Monthly Review Press, 1999.

Mander, Jerry. *In the Absence of the Sacred: The Failure of Technology and the Survival of the Indian Nations.* San Francisco: Sierra Club Books, 1991.

Mander, Jerry, and Edward Goldsmith, eds. *The Case against the Global Economy.* San Francisco: Sierra Club Books, 1996.

Manning, Richard. *Food's Frontiers: The Next Green Revolution.* New York: North Point Press, 2000.

Mellon, Margaret, and Jane Rissler. *Now or Never: Serious New Plans to Save a Natural Pest Control.* Cambridge, Mass.: Union of Concerned Scientists, 1998.

Mendelson, Joseph. "Round-up: The World's Biggest-Selling Herbicide." *Ecologist* 28, no. 5 (September/October 1998): 273.

Mlot, Christine. "The Rise in Toxic Tides: What's behind the Ocean Blooms?" *Science News*, 27 September 1997, 202.

Mollison, Bill. *Permaculture: A Designer's Manual.* Tyalgum, New South Wales, Australia: Tagari Publications, 1988.

Moore, Michael. *Downsize This!* New York: Crown, 1996.

Moses, Marion. *Designer Poisons: How to Protect Your Health and Home from Toxic Pesticides.* San Francisco: Pesticide Education Center, 1995.

Nassauer, Joan Iverson. "Agricultural Landscapes in Harmony with Nature." In *Visions of American Agriculture*, edited by William Lockeretz, 59–73. Ames: Iowa State University Press, 1997.

_____. *Placing Nature: Culture and Landscape Ecology.* Washington, D.C.: Island Press, 1997.

National Research Council, Committee on 20. "The Role of Alternative Farming Methods in Modern Production Agriculture." 21 *Alternative Agriculture*, 9. Washington D.C.: National Academy Press, 1989.

National Research Council, Institute of Medicine. *The Use of Drugs in Food Animals: Benefits and Risks.* Washington, D.C.: National Academy Press, 1998.

Norberg-Hodge, Helena: Peter Goering; and John Page. *From the Ground Up: Rethinking Industrial Agriculture.* New York: Zed Books, 1993.

Norberg-Hodge, Helena; Todd Merrifield; and Steven Gorelick. *Bringing the Food Economy Home: The Social, Ecological and Economic Benefits of Local Food.* Devon, UK: International Society for Ecology and Culture, 2000.

Perucca, Fabien, and Gerard Pouradier. *The Rubbish on Our Plates.* London: Prion Books, 1996.

Pesticide Action Network. *Nowhere to Hide: Persistent Toxic Chemicals in the U.S. Food Supply.* Report for the Pesticide Action Network and Commonweal, March 2001. San Francisco: Pesticide Action Network, 2001.

_____. Pesticide Database. http://www.pesticideinfo.org (3 October 2001).

Pesticide Action Network and Californians for Pesticide Reform. "Hooked on Poison: Pesticide Use in California 1991–1998." San Francisco: Pesticide Action Network, 2000.

Pimentel, David, ed. *Handbook of Pest Management in Agriculture*. 2nd ed. Vols. 1–3. Boca Raton: CRC Press, 1991.

Pimentel, David, and Hugh Lehman. *The Pesticide Question: Environment, Economics, and Ethics*. New York: Chapman and Hall, 1993.

Pimentel, David, et. al. "Environmental and Economic Costs of Pesticide Use." *BioScience* 42, no.10 (1992): 750–760.

_____. "Environmental and Economic Costs of Soil Erosion and Conservation Benefits." *Science* 267 (February 1995): 1117–1123.

Pollan, Michael. *The Botany of Desire: A Plant's Eye View of the World*. New York: Random House, 2001.

Population Reference Bureau. *2000 World Population Data Sheet*. Washington, D.C.: PRB, 2000.

Postel, Sandra. *Pillar of Sand: Can the Irrigation Miracle Last?* New York: W. W. Norton, 1999.

Reeves, Margaret, et al. *Fields of Poison: California Farm Workers and Pesticides*. Report by Pesticide Action Network North America (PANNA), United Farm Workers, California Rural Legal Assistance Foundation, and Californians for Pesticide Reform, 1999.

Reisner, Marc. *Cadillac Desert: The American West and Its Disappearing Water*. New York: Penguin Books, 1986.

Repetto, Robert, and Sanjay S. Baliga. "Pesticides and the Immune System: The Public Health Risks." *Pesticide News*, no. 32 (June 1996).

Rhodes, Richard. *Deadly Feasts*. New York: Simon & Schuster, 1997.

Rifkin, Jeremy. *The Biotech Century*. New York: Penguin Putnam, 1998.

Rissler, Jane, and Margaret Mellon. *The Ecological Risks of Engineered Crops*. Boston: MIT Press, 1996.

Robbins, John. *The Food Revolution: How Your Diet Can Help Save Your Life and the World*. Berkeley: Conari Press, 2001.

Roberts, Paul. "The Sweet Hereafter." *Harper's*, November 1999.

Rosset, Peter. *The Multiple Functions and Benefits of Small Farm Agriculture*. Food First Policy Brief No. 4, prepared for "Cultivating Our Futures," the FAO/Netherlands Conference on the Multifunctional Character of Agriculture and Land, 12–17 September 1999, Maastricht, The Netherlands. Oakland, Calif.: Food First Books, 1999.

_____. "Twelve Myths about Hunger." *Institute for Food and Development Policy Backgrounder* 5, no. 3 (Summer 1998).

Rural Advancement Foundation International (RAFI). "Bioserfdom: Technology, Intellectual Property and the Erosion of Farmers' Rights in the Industrialized World." RAFI *Communique*, 30 March 1997.

Sale, Kirkpatrick. *Dwellers in the Land: The Bioregional Vision*. San Francisco: Sierra Club Books. 1985.

Schlosser, Eric. *Fast Food Nation*. New York: Houghton Mifflin, 2001.

Schumacher, E. F. *Small Is Beautiful*. London: Anchor Press, 1973.

Shand, Hope. "Gene Giants: Understanding the Life Industry." In *Redesigning*

Life? The Worldwide Challenge to Genetic Engineering, edited by Brian Tokar. New York: Zed Books, 2001.

_____. *Human Nature: Agricultural Biodiversity and Farm-Based Food Security*. Ottowa: Rural Advancement Foundation International, 1997.

Shiva, Vandana. *Biopiracy: The Plunder of Nature and Knowledge.* Cambridge, Mass.: South End Press, 1997.

_____. *Monocultures of the Mind: Perspectives on Biodiversity and Biotechnology.* New York: Zed Books, 1993.

_____. *Stolen Harvest: The Hijacking of the Global Food Supply.* Cambridge, Mass.: South End Press, 2000.

Sierra Club. *Corporate Hogs at the Public Trough: How Your Tax Dollars Help Bring Polluters into Your Neighborhood.* 1999 Sierra Club Report. San Francisco: Sierra Club, 1999.

Soley, Lawrence. *Leasing the Ivory Tower: The Corporate Takeover of Academia.* Cambridge, Mass.: South End Press, 1995.

Solomon, Gina. *Trouble on the Farm: Growing up with Pesticides in Agricultural Communities.* Report. San Francisco: Natural Resources Defense Council, 1998.

Solomon, Gina; Oladele Ogunseitan; and Jan Kirsch. *Pesticides and Human Health: A Resource for Health Care Professionals.* San Francisco: Physicians for Social Responsibility and Californians for Pesticide Reform, 2000.

Soule, Judith, and Jon Piper. *Farming in Nature's Image.* Washington, D.C.: Island Press, 1992.

Stauber, John, and Sheldon Rampton. *Mad Cow USA.* Monroe, Me.: Common Courage Press, 1997.

_____. *Toxic Sludge Is Good for You! Lies, Damn Lies and the Public Relations Industry.* Monroe, Me.: Common Courage Press, 1995.

Steiner, Rudolph. *Agriculture.* Kimberton, Pa.: Bio-dynamic Farming and Gardening Association, 1993.

Steingraber, Sandra. *Living Downstream.* New York: Vintage Books, 1998.

Strange, Marty. *Family Farming: A New Economic Vision.* San Francisco: Institute for Food and Development Policy, 1988.

Teitel, Martin, and Kimberly Wilson. *Genetically Engineered Food: Changing the Nature of Nature.* Rochester, Vt.: Park Street Press, 1999.

Unger, Douglas. *Leaving the Land.* New York: Harper & Row, 1984.

United Nations Development Programme. *United Nations Human Development Report 1999.* New York: Oxford University Press, July 1999.

United Nations Food and Agriculture Organization. *Agriculture and Food Security: Environmental Constraints.* Fact sheet prepared for the World Food Summit, Rome, Italy, 13–17 November 1996.

United Nations Food and Agriculture Organization. *State of the World's Plant Genetic Resources for Food and Agriculture.* Background document prepared for the Fourth International Technical Conference on Plant Genetic Resources, Leipzig, Germany, 17–23 June 1996.

U.S. Department of Agriculture. *America's Private Lands: A Geography of*

Hope. Washington, D.C.: USDA Natural Resources Conservation Service, 1997.

_____. *Census of Agriculture: Specified Crops by Acres Harvested for 1997, 1998, 1999*. Washington, D.C.: USDA National Agricultural Statistics Service, 1999.

_____. *Farmers Market Survey Report*. Washington, D.C.: USDA Agriculture Marketing Service, 2000.

_____. *Grain: World Markets and Trade*. Washington, D.C.: USDA Foreign Agricultural Service, 2000.

_____. *Price Support Division — 2000 National LDP Totals*. Washington, D.C.: USDA Farm Service Agency, 2001.

_____. *A Time to Act*. Report of the USDA National Commission on Small Farms. Washington, D.C.: USDA, January 1998.

_____. *U.S. Vegetable Commodity Rankings, Top Ten States and United States Based on Production*. Washington, D.C.: USDA National Agricultural Statistics Service, 1997.

U.S. Department of Agriculture, Economic Research Service. *Agricultural Chemical Usage 1999 Fruit and Nut Summary*. Washington, D.C.: USDA, July 2000.

_____. *Agricultural Chemical Usage Field Crops Summary 2000*. Washington, D.C.: USDA, 2000 and May 2001.

_____. *Cotton: Background*. Washington, D.C.: USDA, 12 December 2000.

_____. *Government Food Safety Policies*. Washington, D.C.: USDA, March 2001.

_____. *Wheat Situation and Outlook Yearbook*. Washington, D.C.: USDA, 2001.

U.S. Department of Agriculture, National Agriculture Statistics Service. *Agricultural Statistics, 1997–2002*. http://www.usda.gov/nass/.

U.S. Department of Agriculture, Office of Pest Management Policy & Pesticide Impact Assessment Program. Crop Profiles Database. http://ipmwww.ncsu.edu/opmppiap/subcrp.htm (3 October 2001).

U.S. Environmental Protection Agency, Office of Pesticide Programs. *Pesticide Industry Sales and Usage: 1996 and 1997 Market Estimates*. Washington, D.C.: U.S. EPA, November 1999.

U.S. Geological Survey. *Water Resources of the United States*. http://water.usgs.gov.

U.S. Government Accounting Office. *Food Safety: Information on Foodborne Illnesses*. Report #GAO/RCED-96-69. Washington D.C.: USGAO, May 1996.

Vandermeer, John; Vandana Shiva; and Ivette Perfecto. *Breakfast of Biodiversity*. Oakland, Calif.: Institute for Food and Development Policy, 1995.

Vogeler, Ingolf. *The Myth of the Family Farm: Agribusiness Dominance of U.S. Agriculture*. Boulder: Westview Press, 1981.

Wackernagel, Mathis, and William Rees. *Our Ecological Footprint: Reducing Human Impact on the Earth*. Gabriola Island, B.C.: New Society Publishers, 1996.

Wargo, John. *Our Children's Toxic Legacy: How Science and Law Fail to Protect Us from Pesticides*. New Haven: Yale University Press, 1998.

Welsh, Rick. *Reorganizing U.S. Agriculture: The Rise of Industrial Agriculture and Direct Marketing.* Greenbelt, Md.: Henry A. Wallace Institute for Alternative Agriculture, August 1997.

White, Gilbert. *The Natural History of Selbourne.* New York: Harper & Bros., 1841.

Wiles, Richard, and Kert Davies. *Overexposed: Organophosphate Insecticides in Children's Food.* Report. Washington, D.C.: Environmental Working Group, January 1998.

Wiles, Richard; Kert Davies; and Susan Elderkin. *A Shopper's Guide to Pesticides in Food.* Report. Washington, D.C.: Environmental Working Group, 31 August 1999.

Wilken, Elena. "Assault of the Earth." *Worldwatch* 20 (March–April 1995).

Wilson, Duff. *Fateful Harvest: The True Story of a Small Town, a Global Industry, and a Toxic Secret.* New York: HarperCollins, 2001.

Wilson, E. O. *The Diversity of Life.* Cambridge: Harvard University, Belknap Press, 1992.

Wright, Angus. *Death of Ramón González: Modern Agricultural Dilemma.* Austin: University of Texas Press, 1990.

ORGANIZATIONAL RESOURCES

The following is a partial list of nongovernmental organizations
whose work is relevant to the issues raised in this book.

Action Group on Erosion, Technology and Concentration P.O. Box 68016, RPO Osborne, Winnipeg MB R3L 2V9, Canada; tel. 204-453-5259; www.rafi.org. An international nongovernmental organization dedicated to the conservation and sustainable improvement of agricultural biodiversity, and to the socially responsible development of technologies useful to rural societies.

Alliance for Bio-Integrity 406 W. Depot Ave., Fairfield, IA 52556; tel. 641-472-5554; www.biointegrity.org. A nonprofit, nonpolitical organization dedicated to the advancement of human and environmental health through sustainable and safe technologies.

Alternative Energy Resources Organization 25 S. Ewing, Suite 214, Helena, MT 59601; tel. 406-443-7272; www.aeromt.org. A grassroots organization dedicated to promoting smart growth, family farming, and ecologically sound resource use. AERO fosters economically vital sustainable communities in Montana and throughout the Rocky Mountain West.

American Farmland Trust 1200 18th St. NW, Suite 800, Washington, DC 20036; tel. 202-331-7300 / 800-431-1499; www.farmland.org. A nationwide nonprofit organization dedicated to protecting agricultural resources. AFT works to stop the loss of productive farmland and to promote farming practices that lead to a healthy environment.

Appropriate Technology Transfer for Rural Areas P.O. Box 3657, Fayetteville, AR 72702; tel. 800-346-9140; www.attra.org. A leading information source on sustainable farming practices for farmers and agricultural extension agents.

Biodynamic Farming and Gardening Association Building 1002B, Thoreau Center, The Presidio, P.O. Box 29135, San Francisco, CA 94129; tel. 888-516-7797; www.biodynamics.com. A nonprofit organization whose mission is to foster, guide, and safeguard the biodynamic method of agriculture.

California Sustainable Agriculture Working Group P.O. Box 1599, Santa Cruz, CA 95061; tel. 831-457-2815; www.calsawg.org. A collaborative network of organizations committed to the development of sustainable agriculture and food systems in California.

Californians for Pesticide Reform 49 Powell St., San Francisco, CA 94102; tel. 415-981-3939 / 888-CPR-4880; www.igc.org/cpr. A coalition of over 150 public interest groups dedicated to protecting human health and the environment from the dangers of pesticide use.

Campaign to Label Genetically Engineered Foods P.O. Box 55699, Seattle, WA 98155; tel. 425-771-4049; www.thecampaign.org. An organization whose mission is to create a national grassroots consumer campaign for legislation requiring the labeling of genetically engineered foods in the United States.

Center for Ethics and Toxics 39120 Ocean Dr., P.O. Box 673, Gualala, CA 95445; tel. 707-884-1700; www.cetos.org. A nonprofit environmental group dedicated to protecting vulnerable and susceptible populations by providing educational information on the risks of exposure to potentially hazardous toxic substances and infectious agents, and by acting directly to encourage new policies designed to reduce toxic risks.

Center for Food Safety 660 Pennsylvania Ave. SE, Suite 302, Washington, DC 20003; tel. 202-547-9359; www.centerforfoodsafety.org; www.foodsafetynow.org. A public interest and environmental advocacy organization that utilizes legal actions, policy initiatives, grassroots organizing, and public education to curtail our current industrial agricultural production system and promote sustainable agriculture alternatives. Current CFS goals include maintaining the integrity of organic foods and ensuring the testing and labeling of genetically engineered foods.

Center for Rural Affairs 101 S. Tallman St., P.O. Box 406, Walthill, NE 68067; tel. 402-846-5428; www.cfra.org. An organization working to build communities that stand for social justice, economic opportunity, and environmental stewardship. CRA encourages people to accept both personal and social responsibility for creating such communities and provides opportunities for people to participate in decisions that shape the quality of their lives and the futures of their communities.

Center for Urban Agriculture at Fairview Gardens 598 N. Fairview Ave., Goleta, CA 93117; tel. 805-967-7369; www.fairviewgardens.org. An organization whose mission is to preserve the agricultural heritage of a 100-year-old farm; provide the local community with fresh, chemical-free produce; demonstrate the economic viability of sustainable agricultural methods for small farm operations; research and interpret the relationship between food, land, and community well-being; and nurture the human spirit through educational programs and outreach.

Citizens for Health P.O. Box 2260, Boulder, CO 80306; tel. 800-357-2211; www.citizens.org. A nonprofit grassroots consumer advocacy group that champions public policies empowering individuals to make informed health choices.

Clean Water Network 1200 New York Ave. NW, Suite 400, Washington, DC 20005; tel. 202-289-2395; www.cwn.org. An alliance of more than 1,000 organizations that endorse CWN's platform paper, the *National Agenda for Clean Water*, which outlines the need for strong clean water safeguards to protect human health and the environment.

Commonweal P.O. Box 316, Bolinas, CA 94924; tel. 415-868-0970; www.commonweal.org. A small, 25-year-old health and environmental research institute. Commonweal's principal focuses are people with cancer and the health professionals who work with people with life-threatening illnesses; children and young adults with learning and social difficulties and the childcare professionals who work with them; and the global search for a healthy and sustainable future.

Community Alliance with Family Farmers P.O. Box 363, Davis, CA 95617; tel. 530-756-8518; www.caff.org. A nonprofit member-activist organization dedicated to building a movement of rural and urban people who foster family-scale agriculture that cares for the land, sustains local economies, and promotes social justice.

Community Farm Alliance 624 Shelby St., Frankfort, KY 40601; tel. 502-223-3655; www.communityfarmalliance.com. A statewide grassroots organization of persons committed to family-scale farming as the most efficient and sustainable method of producing the best-quality food while protecting the environment and strengthening rural community life.

Community Food Security Coalition P.O. Box 209, Venice, CA 90294; tel. 310-822-5410; www.foodsecurity.org. An organization whose mission is to bring about lasting social change by promoting community-based solutions to hunger, poor nutrition, and the globalization of the food system.

Consumer Policy Institute 225 Brunswick Ave., Toronto, Ontario M5S 2M6, Canada; tel. 416-964-9223; www.c-p-i.org. A division of the Energy Probe Research Foundation, a watch group on government spending and monopolies working to prevent consumer abuse by promoting economic, social, and environmental well-being.

Consumer's Choice Council 2000 P St. NW, Suite 540, Washington, DC 20036; tel. 202-785-1950; www.consumerscouncil.org. A nonprofit association of 60 environmental, consumer, and human rights organizations from 25 different countries, dedicated to protecting the environment and promoting human rights and basic labor standards through ecolabeling. CCC works to ensure that consumers in the United States and around the world have the information they need to purchase products that are produced in more environmentally sustainable and socially just ways.

Consumers Union 101 Truman Ave., Yonkers, NY 10703; tel. 914-378-2000; www.consumer.org. A nonprofit organization whose mission is to test products, inform the public, and protect consumers. CU publishes *Consumer Reports* magazine, which provides informative and educational materials developed by CU's advocacy offices on a variety of consumer issues.

Corporate Agribusiness Research Project P.O. Box 2201, Everett, WA 98203; tel. 425-258-5345; www.ea1.com/CARP. An organization whose goal is to increase public understanding of corporate agribusiness through awareness, education, and action, and to advocate the importance of building alternative, democratically controlled food systems. CARP publishes the *Agribusiness Examiner*, a weekly e-mail newsletter, and the *Agbiz Tiller Online*.

Council for Responsible Genetics 5 Upland Rd., Suite 3, Cambridge, MA 02140; tel. 617-868-0870; www.gene-watch.org. A national nonprofit organization of scientists, environmentalists, public health advocates, physicians, lawyers, and other concerned citizens. CRG encourages informed public debate about the social, ethical, and environmental implications of new genetic technologies; advocates for socially responsible use of these technologies; and publishes *Genewatch* magazine.

David Suzuki Foundation 2211 W. 4th Ave., Suite 219, Vancouver, BC V6K 4S2, Canada; tel. 604-732-4228; www.davidsuzuki.org. An organization whose goal is to study the underlying structures and systems that cause environmental crises and then to work to bring about fundamental change. The David Suzuki Foundation engages in research, application, education, and advocacy.

Earth Island Institute 300 Broadway, Suite 28, San Francisco, CA 94133; tel. 415-788-3666; www.earthisland.org. An organization founded by environmentalist David R. Brower to develop and support projects that counteract threats to the biological and cultural diversity that sustain the environment. Through education and activism, these projects promote the conservation, preservation, and restoration of the Earth.

Earthjustice Legal Defense Fund 180 Montgomery St., Suite 1400, San Francisco, CA 94104; tel. 415-627-6700; www.earthjustice.org. A nonprofit law firm representing public interest clients without charge. Earthjustice works through the courts to safeguard public lands, national forests, parks, and wilderness areas; to reduce air and water pollution; to prevent toxic contamination; to preserve endangered species and wildlife habitat; and to achieve environmental justice.

EarthSave International 1509 Seabright Ave., Suite B1, Santa Cruz, CA 95062; tel. 800-362-3648 / 831-423-0293; www.earthsave.org. A global organization promoting food choices that are healthy for people and the planet. ESI supplies information, support, and practical programs.

Ecological Farming Association 406 Main St., Suite 313, Watsonville, CA 95076; tel. 831-763-2111; www.csa-efc.org. A nonprofit educational organization that promotes ecologically sound agriculture. EFA holds events to bring people together from all over the world to share ideas and experiences in producing healthful food from a healthy Earth.

Edmonds Institute 20319 92nd Ave. W, Edmonds, WA 98020; tel. 425-775-5383; www.edmonds-institute.org. A nonprofit public interest organization dedicated to education about environment, technology, and intellectual property rights.

Educational Concerns for Hunger Organization 17391 Durrance Rd., North Fort Myers, FL 33917; tel. 941-543-3246; www.echonet.org. A religious organization focusing mainly on tropical subsistence agriculture and offering publications of interest to small-scale farmers and urban gardeners. ECHO publishes the *ECHO News* quarterly and *ECHO Development Notes* and offers an online bookstore, a tropical video series, and a tropical crops seed list. Internships are available.

Environmental Defense 257 Park Ave. S, New York, NY 10010; tel. 212-505-2100; www.environmentaldefense.org. A national nonprofit organization with more than 300,000 members. Environmental Defense is dedicated to protecting the environmental rights of all people, including future generations. Among these rights are clean air; clean water; healthy, nourishing food; and a flourishing ecosystem.

Environmental Working Group 1718 Connecticut Ave. NW, Suite 600, Washington, DC 20009; tel. 202-667-6982; www.ewg.org. A leading content provider for public interest groups and concerned citizens campaigning to protect the environment. Drawing on its original analyses of government and other data, EWG produces hundreds of headline-making reports each year.

Evangelical Lutheran Church in America 87656 W. Higgins Rd., Chicago, IL 60631; tel. 800-638-3522; www.elca.org. A national organization of Lutheran churches. The Minnesota ELCA bishop addresses Minnesota's farm crisis in a statement available at www.elca.org/do/bishopstate.html.

Farm Aid 11 Ward St., Suite 200, Somerville MA 02143; tel. 800-FARM-AID / 617-354-2922; www.farmaid.org. A national organization whose mission is to provide assistance to poor and needy families in rural farming communities. Farm Aid conducts a yearly musical concert to draw attention to the needs of such families and to raise funds to relieve those needs. It brings together the common interests of family farmers, consumers, and people who care about the environment with the goal of keeping family farmers on their land and restoring a strong family farm system of agriculture.

Farm Labor Organizing Committee 1221 Broadway St., Toledo, OH 43609; tel. 419-243-3456; www.iupui.edu/~floc/home.html. A union dedicated to improving conditions for migrant and seasonal farm workers in the Midwest.

Food Alliance 1829 NE Alberta, Suite 5, Portland, OR 97211: tel. 503-493-1066; www.thefoodalliance.org. A nonprofit coalition of farmers, consumers, scientists, grocers, processors, distributors, farmworker representatives, and environmentalists dedicated to promoting expanded use of sustainable agriculture practices.

Food & Water 389 Route 215, Walden, VT 05873; tel. 802-563-3300; www.foodandwater.org. A national nonprofit advocacy organization working to combat the industrialization of culture and agriculture. The organization publishes the quarterly *Food & Water Journal*, dedicated to education, agitation, and inspiration.

Food First / Institute for Food & Development Policy 398 60th St., Oakland, CA 94618; tel. 510-654-4400; www.foodfirst.org. A member-supported nonprofit people's think tank and education-for-action center whose work highlights root causes and value-based solutions to hunger and poverty around the world, with a commitment to establishing food as a fundamental human right. Food First participates in activist coalitions and furnishes clearly written and carefully researched analyses, arguments, and action plans for people who want to help change the world.

Foundation on Economic Trends 1660 L St. NW, Suite 216, Washington, DC 20036; tel. 202-466-2823; www.biotechcentury.org. A nonprofit organization whose mission is to examine emerging trends in science and technology and their impacts on the environment, economy, culture, and society.

Friends of the Earth 1025 Vermont Ave. NW, Suite 300, Washington, DC 20005; tel. 202-783-7400/800-843-8687; www.foe.org. A national environmental organization dedicated to preserving the health and diversity of the planet for future generations. As the largest international environmental network in the world, with affiliates in 63 countries, FOE empowers citizens to have an influential voice in decisions affecting their environment.

Greenpeace USA 702 H St. NW, Suite 300, Washington, DC 20001; tel. 202-462-1177/800-326-0959; www.greenpeaceusa.org. An independent campaigning organization that uses nonviolent, creative confrontation to expose global environmental problems and to force solutions that are essential to a green and peaceful future.

Health Care Without Harm c/o CCHW, P.O. Box 6806, Falls Church, VA 22040: tel. 703-237-2249; www.noharm.org. An organization whose mission is to transform the health care industry so it is no longer a source of environmental harm. HCWH works to eliminate pollution in health care practices without compromising safety or care.

Henry A. Wallace Center for Agricultural & Environmental Policy at Winrock International 38 Winrock Dr., Morrilton, AR 72110, tel. 501-727-5435; 1621 N. Kent St., Suite 1200, Arlington, VA 22209, tel. 703-525-9430; www.winrock.org. A nonprofit research and education organization established to encourage and facilitate the adoption of low-cost, resource-conserving, environmentally sound, and economically viable farming systems. Winrock International works with people around the world to increase economic opportunity, sustain natural resources, and protect the environment.

Humane Society of the United States — Sustainable Agriculture Program 2100 L St. NW, Washington, DC 20037; tel. 202-452-1100; www.hsus.org. An animal protection organization whose mission is to create a humane and sustainable world for all animals, including people. Through International Partners for Sustainable Agriculture, HSUS seeks to provide opportunities for international communication among sustainable farmers and activists, especially on issues that arise in the United Nations and other international organizations, treaties, or conventions.

Illinois Stewardship Alliance P.O. Box 648, Rochester, IL 62563; tel. 217-498-9707; http://todggg.tripod.com/Web-docs/ISA.htm. An alliance linking traditional agricultural organizations, environmental groups, and other citizen and religious groups around a concern for the long-term sustainability of agriculture and rural communities. ISA addresses the environmental quality of the food system and promotes environmentally sound farming practices through newsletters, field days, workshops, and on-farm research projects.

Independent Organic Inspectors Association P.O. Box 6, Broadus, MT 59317; tel. 406-436-2031; www.ioia.net. A nonprofit, professional association of organic farm, livestock, and process inspectors dedicated to verification of organic production practices.

Institute for Agriculture and Trade Policy 2105 First Ave. S, Minneapolis, MN 55404; tel. 612-870-0453; www.iatp.org. An organization dedicated to promoting resilient family farms, rural communities, and ecosystems around the world through research, education, science, technology, and advocacy.

Institute for Social Ecology 1118 Maple Hill Rd., Plainfield, VT 05667; tel. 802-454-8493; www.social-ecology.org. An organization involved in research, publishing, and activist projects, such as biotechnology and regional food system design. ISE offers a B.A. degree program, intensive summer programs, workshops, lecture series, internship opportunities, and a speakers bureau.

International Center for Technology Assessment 660 Pennsylvania Ave. SE, Suite 302, Washington, DC 20003; tel. 202-542-9359; www.icta.org. A nonprofit, nonpartisan organization committed to providing the public with full assessments and analyses of technological impacts on society. CTA voices the public interest in issues ranging from sustainable agriculture and biotechnology to transportation, globalization, and intellectual property.

International Forum on Food and Agriculture Thoreau Center for Sustainability, 1009 General Kennedy Ave., Suite 2, San Francisco, CA 94129; tel. 415-561-7650; www.ifg.org/IFA/ifa.html. A program of the International Forum on Globalization whose mission is to articulate the full range of consequences of the rapid global conversion to industrial agriculture. IFA works to develop international cooperative strategies to counter this dangerous trend and to clearly articulate successful alternative models.

International Society for Ecology and Culture Foxhole, Dartington, Devon TQ9 6EB, UK; tel. +44-1803-868-650; www.isec.org.uk. A nonprofit organization concerned with the protection of biological and cultural diversity. ISEC challenges economic globalization and conventional notions of "progress" to promote localization. Its emphasis is on education for action: moving beyond single issues to look at the more fundamental influences that shape our lives. ISEC activities include books, reports, conferences, and films; local, national, and international networking; community initiatives; and campaigning.

Kansas Rural Center 304 Pratt St., P.O. Box 133, Whiting, KS 66552; tel. 785-873-3431; www.kansasruralcenter.org. A private, nonprofit organization that promotes the long-term health of the land and its people through education, research and advocacy. KRC cultivates grassroots support for public policies that encourage family farming and stewardship of soil and water.

Kerr Center for Sustainable Agriculture P.O. Box 588, Poteau, OK 74953; tel. 918-647-9123; www.kerrcenter.com. A nonprofit educational foundation whose mission is to encourage a more sustainable agriculture in the state of Oklahoma and beyond. The center produces a variety of publications for use by farmers, ranchers, and others, including a free newsletter, *Field Notes*.

Land Institute 2440 E. Water Well Rd., Salina, KS 67401; tel. 785-823-5376; www.landinstitute.org. A public policy and education organization dedicated to research on natural systems agriculture. The Land Institute seeks to develop an agriculture that will save the soil from being lost or poisoned while promoting a community life at once prosperous and enduring.

Land Stewardship Project 2200 Fourth St., White Bear Lake, MN 55110; tel. 651-653-0618; www.landstewardshipproject.org. A private nonprofit organization whose mission is to foster an ethic of stewardship for farmland, promote sustainable agriculture, and develop sustainable communities. LSP houses the Farmland Steward Center and publishes a quarterly newsletter, *Land Stewardship*, as well as videos and booklet series for farmers considering transition to low-input farming.

League of Conservation Voters 1920 L St. NW, Suite 800, Washington, DC 20036; tel. 202-785-8683; www.lcv.org. A national environmental organization dedicated to educating citizens about the environmental voting records of members of Congress. LCV works to create a Congress more responsive to the environmental concerns of the public.

Leopold Center for Sustainable Agriculture Iowa State University, 209 Curtiss Hall, Ames, IA 50011; tel. 515-294-3711; www.ag.iastate.edu/centers/leopold. An organization whose mission is to identify and reduce the negative impacts of agriculture on natural resources and rural communities; to develop profitable farming systems that conserve natural resources; and to work with ISU Extension and other groups to inform the public of new research findings.

Michael Fields Agricultural Institute W2493 County Rd. ES, East Troy, WI 53120; tel. 262-642-3303; www.mfai.org. A nonprofit education and research organization committed to promoting resource conserving, ecologically sustainable, and economically viable food and farming systems. A newsletter and publications list are available on request.

Michigan Agricultural Stewardship Association 605 N. Birch, Kalkaska, MI 49646; tel. 231-258-3305; www.sustainable-ag.org. An organization whose mission is to research and disseminate information on agricultural systems that are economically feasible, agronomically sound, and environmentally safe. MASA sponsors on-farm demonstrations and research plots comparing conventional and alternative methods and publishes the monthly *Michigan's Farm and Country Journal* for its members.

Midwest Sustainable Agriculture Working Group c/o NCRLC, 4625 Beaver Ave., Des Moines, IA 50310; tel. 515-270-2634; msawg@aol.com. A collaborative network of organizations committed to the development of sustainable agriculture and food systems in the Midwest.

Missouri Rural Crisis Center 1108 Rangeline St., Columbia, MO 65201; tel. 573-449-1336; morural@coin.org. A statewide nonprofit organization that works to empower farmers and other rural families. MRCC's mission is to preserve family farms; to promote stewardship of the land and environmental integrity; and to strive for economic and social justice by building unity and mutual understanding among diverse groups, both rural and urban.

Mothers for Natural Law P.O. Box 1177, Fairfield, IA 52556; tel. 641-472-2499; www.safe-food.org. An organization dedicated to working with industry and consumers to create financially viable, environmentally responsible solutions to the challenges of genetically engineered foods. MNL spearheads a national public awareness campaign on the dangers of genetically engineered foods and an initiative to secure rigorous premarket safety testing and a mandatory moratorium on these foods.

National Campaign for Sustainable Agriculture P.O. Box 396, Pine Bush, NY 12566; tel. 845-744-8448; www.sustainableagriculture.net. A nationwide coalition of farmers, environmentalists, and consumer advocates focusing on federal policies, land grant university priorities, and marketing systems. The campaign is dedicated to educating the public on the importance of a sustainable food and agriculture system that is economically viable, environmentally sound, socially just, and humane.

National Catholic Rural Life Conference 4625 Beaver Ave., Des Moines, IA 50310; tel. 515-270-2634; www.ncrlc.com. A national Catholic organization whose mission is to promote a living community in which every person is valued, the Earth is carefully stewarded, the poor are fed, and community life is nourished by public and private deeds. NCRLC urges public action on rural life and environmental issues.

National Coalition against the Misuse of Pesticides 701 E St. SE, Suite 200, Washington, DC 20003; tel. 202-543-5450; www.beyondpesticides.org. A national network committed to pesticide safety and the adoption of alternative pest management strategies that reduce or eliminate dependencies on toxic chemicals.

National Education Center for Agricultural Safety 10250 Sundown Rd., Peosta, IA 52068; tel. 319-557-0354 / 888-844-6322; www.nsc.org/necas.htm. An organization whose mission is to reduce the level of preventable illnesses, injuries, and deaths among farmers, ranchers, their families, and their employees.

National Environmental Trust 1200 18th St. NW, Fifth Floor, Washington DC 20036; tel. 202-887-8800; www.environet.org. A nonprofit, nonpartisan membership group whose mission is to inform citizens about environmental problems and how they affect health and quality of life. Current NET campaigns include global warming, genetic engineering, clean air, and children's environmental health.

National Family Farm Coalition 110 Maryland Ave. NE, Suite 307, Washington, D.C. 20002; tel. 202-543-5675; www.nffc.net. A national link for grassroots organizations working on family farm issues. NFFC brings together farmers and others to organize national projects focused on preserving and strengthening family farms. It strongly opposes the vertical integration of agriculture and serves as a network for groups opposing corporate agriculture.

Native Seeds / SEARCH 526 N. 4th Ave., Tucson AZ 85705; tel. 520-622-5561; www.nativeseeds.org. A nonprofit organization that works to conserve the traditional crops, seeds, and farming methods that have sustained native peoples throughout the southwestern United States and northern Mexico. NS/S promotes the use of these ancient crops and their wild relatives by gathering, safeguarding, and distributing their seeds while sharing benefits with traditional communities and preserving knowledge about their uses.

Natural Resources Defense Council 40 W. 20th St., New York, NY 10011; tel. 212-727-2700; www.nrdc.org. A nationwide organization whose purpose is to protect the planet's wildlife and wild places and to ensure a safe and healthy environment for all living things through law, science, and the support of its more than 400,000 members.

New York Sustainable Agriculture Working Group 121 N. Fitzhugh St., Rochester, NY 14614; tel. 716-232-1520; www.smallfarm.org/nesawg/neswag.html. A consortium of farm, farmworker, environmental, faith, consumer, and antipoverty groups.

Northeast Sustainable Agriculture Working Group P.O. Box 608, Belchertown, MA 01007; tel. 413-323-4531; www.smallfarm.org/nesawg/

nesawg.html. A collaborative network of organizations committed to the development of sustainable agriculture and food systems in the West.

Northern Plains Sustainable Agriculture Society 9824 79th St. SE, Fullerton, ND 58441; tel. 701-883-4304; www.npsas.org. A grassroots educational organization committed to the development of a sustainable society through the promotion of ecologically and socially sound food production and distribution in the Northern Plains. NPSAS publishes a quarterly newsletter and a selection of farm booklets and poetry. It organizes an annual winter conference, a summer symposium, and farm tours on sustainable agriculture practices.

Northwest Coalition for Alternatives to Pesticides P.O. Box 1393, Eugene OR 97440; tel. 541-344-5044; www.pesticide.org. An organization dedicated to keeping the public informed about pesticide hazards and alternatives, and to increasing the adoption of alternatives to pesticides in agriculture. NCAP works to protect people and the environment by advancing healthy solutions to pest problems.

Occidental Arts and Ecology Center 15290 Coleman Valley Rd., Occidental, CA 95465; tel. 707-874-1557; www.oaec.org. A nonprofit educational center and biodiversity focused farm whose programs seek innovative and practical solutions to the pressing environmental, economic, and social challenges of our day. OAEC focuses on research, demonstration, and popular education in sustainable living practices and in developing grassroots activist strategies and campaigns for positive social change.

Ohio Ecological Food & Farm Association P.O. Box 82234, Columbus, OH 43202; tel. 614-421-2022; www.oeffa.org. A grassroots coalition of food producers and consumers supporting and promoting a healthful, ecological, accountable, and permanent agriculture.

Organic Consumers Association 6101 Cliff Estate Rd., Little Marais, MN 55614; tel. 218-226-416; www.purefood.org. A public interest organization dedicated to building a healthy, safe, and sustainable system of food production and consumption. OCA utilizes public education, media work, direct action, grassroots lobbying, consumer boycotts, and litigation to achieve its three basic goals: a global moratorium on genetically engineered foods and crops; a phase-out of industrial agriculture; and at least 30 percent organic production in U.S. agriculture by 2010.

Organic Farmers Marketing Association P.O. Box 2407, Fairfield, IA 52556; tel. 515-472-3272; www.iquest.net/ofma. An organization whose purpose is to assist organic farmers in marketing, communication, and public advocacy, and to bring together organic farmers, consumers, and supporters of organic farming from all over the world. OFMA publishes *The Organic Organizer* to aid in creating new marketing options and offers a list of private and state certifiers, plus other publications and services.

Organic Farming Research Foundation P.O. Box 440, Santa Cruz, CA 95061; tel. 831-426-6606; www.ofrf.org. A nonprofit organization whose mission is to sponsor research related to organic farming practices; to disseminate research results to organic farmers and growers interested in adopting organic production systems; and to educate the public and decision makers about organic farming issues.

Pennsylvania Association for Sustainable Agriculture 114 W. Main St., P.O. Box 419, Millheim, PA 16854; tel. 814-349-9856; www.pasafarming.org. A nonprofit organization working to improve the economic and social prosperity of Pennsylvania food and agriculture. PASA creates networks and markets to strengthen the ties between concerned consumers and family farmers. It publishes the *PASA Passages* newsletter and sponsors a yearly February "Farming for the Future" conference.

Pesticide Action Network North America 49 Powell St., Suite 500, San Francisco, CA 94102; tel. 415-981-1771; www.panna.org. An international coalition of public interest organizations and civil society groups and individuals that advocate adoption of ecologically sound, socially just practices to replace pesticide use.

Pesticide Watch 3486 Mission St., San Francisco, CA 94110; tel. 415-206-9185; www.pesticidewatch.org. An organization dedicated to fighting dangerous pesticide use in California communities. PW provides communities with the tools they need to protect themselves and the environment from the hazards of pesticides by offering general information about pesticides and alternatives; assistance for organizing and strategy in campaigns; connections to other grassroots groups; and referrals to legal and technical experts.

Pesticides and Birds Campaign 1834 Jefferson Place NW, Washington, DC 20036; tel. 202-452-1535; www.abcbirds.org/pesticides/pesticideindex.htm. A campaign established by the American Bird Conservancy, a nonprofit organization dedicated to the conservation of wild birds and their habitats in the Americas. The campaign's mission is to reduce wild birds' risk of exposure to pesticides proven to have lethal and sublethal effects when used according to law and accepted practice.

Program on Corporations, Law and Democracy P.O. Box 246, South Yarmouth, MA; tel. 508-398-1145; www.poclad.org. An organization that instigates democratic conversation and actions that contest the authority of corporations to govern. POCLAD publishes the quarterly publication *By What Authority*, as well as *Defying Corporations, Defining Democracy* and *Building Unions*. POCLAD also leads activist strategy sessions across the United States.

Public Citizen / Global Trade Watch 1600 20th St. NW, Washington, DC 20009; tel. 202-588-1000; www.tradewatch.org. A national nonprofit organization whose mission is to educate the American public about the impact of international trade and economic globalization on jobs, the environment, public health and safety, and democratic accountability. Global Trade Watch publishes reports, including *Down on the Farm: NAFTA's Seven-Years War on Farmers and Ranchers in the U.S., Canada and Mexico.*

Research Foundation for Science, Technology and Ecology A-60 Hauz Khas, New Delhi, India 110016; tel. +91-11-696-8077; www.vshiva.net. An organization whose mission is to conserve biodiversity and to protect people from threats to their livelihood and environment by centralized systems of monoculture in forestry, agriculture, and fisheries.

Rodale Institute 611 Seigfriedale Rd., Kutztown, PA 19530; tel. 610-683-1400; www.rodaleinstitute.org. An organization working with people worldwide to achieve a regenerative food system that renews environmental and human health.

Rural Advancement Foundation International USA P.O. Box 640, Pittsboro, NC 27312; tel. 919-542-1396; www.rafiusa.org. An organization dedicated to community, equity, and diversity in agriculture. Although focusing on North Carolina and the southeastern United States, RAFI-USA also works nationally and internationally to promote sustainable agriculture; to strengthen family farms and rural communities; to protect the diversity of plants, animals, and people in agriculture; and to ensure responsible use of new technologies.

Rural Coalition/Coalición Rural 1411 K St. NW, Suite 901, Washington, DC 20005; tel. 202-628-7160; www.ruralco.org. An alliance of over 70 regionally and culturally diverse organizations working to build a just and more sustainable food system that brings fair returns to minority and other small farmers and rural communities; that establishes just and fair working conditions for farm workers; that protects the environment; and that brings safe and healthy food to customers.

Rural Vermont 15 Barre St., Montpelier, VT 05602; tel. 802-223-7222; www.efne.org/members/rural.html. A nonprofit organization committed to supporting a strong rural economy that is environmentally sound and economically just. Rural Vermont is involved in community education, grassroots organizing, and advocacy concerning farm and rural issues. It builds coalitions between farmers and nonfarmers to broaden awareness of, and action on, rural affairs.

Seed Savers Exchange 3076 North Winn Road., Decorah, IA 52101; www.seedsavers.org. A nationwide nonprofit membership organization dedicated to promoting preservation of genetic diversity by saving old-time food crops from extinction. SSE provides a seed exchange network, a seed catalog, and other publications.

Sierra Club 85 Second St., San Francisco, CA 94105; tel. 415-977-5500; www.sierraclub.org. A grassroots environmental organization with more than 700,000 members. Sierra Club's mission is to explore, enjoy, and protect the wild places of the Earth; to practice and promote responsible use of the Earth's ecosystems and resources; to educate and enlist humanity to protect and restore the quality of the natural and human environment; and to use all lawful means to carry out these objectives.

Southern Sustainable Agriculture Working Group P.O. Box 324, Elkins, AR 72727; tel. 501-587-0888; www.sustainableagriculture.net/ssawg.htm. A network of approximately 50 member organizations working for more sustainable agriculture in 13 southern states. Southern SAWG assists family farmers and farm communities to prosper in a healthy environment by helping to remove technical, institutional, and economic barriers to sustainability.

Sustainable Agriculture Coalition 110 Maryland Ave. NE, Suite 211, Washington, DC 20002; tel. 202-547-5754. The lobbying arm of the Midwest Sustainable Agricultural Working Group, representing the interests of farms, rural communities, environmental, religious, and consumer interests. SAC's mission is to help fashion a system of agriculture that is economically profitable, environmentally sound, family farm based, and socially just.

Sustainable Cotton Project 6176 Old Olive Hwy., Oroville, CA 95966; tel. 530-589-2686; www.sustainablecotton.org. An organization fostering shared information among farmers, manufacturers, and consumers to pioneer markets for certified organically grown cotton.

Union of Concerned Scientists 2 Brattle Sq., Cambridge, MA 02238; tel. 617-547-5552; www.ucsusa.org. An alliance of 50,000 committed citizens and leading scientists who aim to augment rigorous scientific research with public education and citizen advocacy to help build a cleaner, healthier environment and safer world. UCS studies risks and benefits of the various applications of genetic engineering and supports sustainable alternatives.

United Farm Workers P.O. Box 62, Keene, CA 93531; tel. 661-822-5571; www.ufw.org. An organization working to advance economic and social conditions in farmworker and Latino communities. UFW is an outgrowth of the National Farm Workers Association, founded by Cesar Chavez.

United Methodist Church General Board of Church and Society, 100 Maryland Ave. NW, Suite 212, Washington, DC 20002; tel. 202-488-5645; www.umc.org/abouttheumc/policy/social/o-agriculture.htm. A religious organization advocating a sustainable agricultural system that will maintain and support the natural fertility of agricultural soil, promote the diversity of flora and fauna, and adapt to regional conditions and structures — a system in which agricultural animals are treated humanely and in which their living conditions are as close to natural systems as possible. UMC aspires to an effective agricultural system in which plant, livestock, and poultry production maintains the natural ecological cycles, conserves energy, and reduces chemical input to a minimum.

United Plant Savers P.O. Box 98, East Barre, VT 05649; tel. 802-496-7053; www.plantsavers.org. A grassroots membership organization whose mission is to protect native medicinal plants of the United States and Canada and their native habitat and to ensure an abundant renewable supply of medicinal plants for generations to come. UPS publishes a semiannual newsletter, offers opportunities to receive free native plants and seeds, and sponsors community planting projects.

U.S. Public Interest Research Group 218 D St. SE, Washington, DC 20003; tel. 202-546-9707; www.uspirg.org. A national public interest watchdog organization. U.S. PIRG's mission is to uncover dangers to the public health and well-being and to fight to end them through investigative research, media exposés, grassroots organizing, advocacy, and litigation.

Western Organization of Resource Councils 110 Maryland Ave. NE, Suite 307, Washington, DC 20002; tel. 202-547-7040; www.worc.org. An association of state organizations united to advance the vision of a democratic, sustainable, and just society through collective action focusing on agriculture, energy, and the environment.

Western Sustainable Agriculture Working Group 3040 Continental Dr., Butte, MT 59702; tel. 406-494-8636; www.westernsawg.org. A collaborative network of 43 nonprofit private and publicly affiliated organizations committed to the development of sustainable agriculture and food systems in the West.

Worldwatch Institute, 1776 Massachusetts Ave. NW, Washington, D.C. 20036; tel. 202-452-1999; www.worldwatch.org. A nonprofit public policy research organization dedicated to informing policy makers and the public about emerging global problems and trends, and the complex links between the world economy and its environmental support systems.

ADDITIONAL RESOURCES

The following is a partial list of web sites offering additional links relating to sustainable agriculture.

Eco-labeling programs Consumer's Union; www.eco-labels.org.

Educational and training opportunities in sustainable agriculture (1) On-farm internships and apprenticeships in the United States — list maintained by Appropriate Technology Transfer for Rural Areas (ATTRA); www.attra.org/attra-rl/intern.html. (2) Internships available at U.S. and international institutions and organizations, and at farms outside the United States — list maintained by the Alternative Farming Systems Information Center; www.nal.usda.gov/afsic/AFSIC_pubs/edtr11.htm.

Farmers' markets and community supported agriculture farms (CSAs) Local Harvest; www.localharvest.com.

Federal programs for sustainable agriculture Building Better Rural Places; http://attra.ncat.org/guide/index.htm.

Local watershed organizations For a list, e-mail cleanwaternt@igc.org.

Organic certifiers Organic Certifiers Directory — list maintained by the Organic Farming Research Foundation; http://ofrf.org/publications/certifier.html.

Grateful acknowledgement is made to the following for permission to reprint copyrighted material. Portions of "The Whole Horse" and "Hope" originally appeared as an article titled "Back to the Land" in *The Amicus Journal* (Winter 1999) and "The Whole Horse" in *Resurgence* (May/June 1998, Issue 188), ©1998 Wendell Berry. "Agricultural Landscapes in Harmony with Nature" adapted from *Visions of American Agriculture*, edited by William Lockeretz, Iowa State University Press, ©1997 Joan Iverson Nassauer. "Global Monoculture" is a reprint of "Break Up the Monoculture" which originally appeared in the July 15, 1996 issue of *The Nation*, ©1996 Helena Norberg-Hodge. "Farming in Nature's Image" adapted from *New Roots for Agriculture* by Wes Jackson, University of Nebraska Press, ©1985 Wes Jackson. "Hard Times for Diversity" from *Beginning Again: People and Nature in the New Millennium* by David Ehrenfeld, © 1993 Oxford University Press, Inc., reprinted by permission of Oxford University Press, Inc. and from *Biodiversity*, edited by E.O. Wilson, ©1988 by the National Academy of Sciences, reprinted by permission of the National Academy Press. "Machine Logic" from *Ecoforestry: The Art and Science of Sustainable Forest Use*, edited by Alan Drengson and Duncan Taylor, ©1997 New Society Publishers, reprinted by permission of New Society Publishers. "The Impossible Race" is a reprint of "Tropical Deforestation and the Fallacies of Agricultural Hope" from *Ethics and Agriculture: An Anthology on Current Issues in World Context*, edited by Charles V. Blatz, University of Idaho Press, ©1991 University of Idaho Press. "Tilth and Technology" originally appeared as "Celebrating Soil—Mother of All Things" in *Whole Earth* (Spring 1999, No. 96), © 1999 Peter Warshall. "Our Forgotten Pollinators" adapted from *The Forgotten Pollinators* by Stephen L. Buchmann and Gary Paul Nabhan, ©1996 Stephen L. Buchmann and Gary Paul Nabhan, reprinted by permission of Island Press/Shearwater Books. "Can Agriculture and Biodiversity Coexist?" originally appeared in *Wild Earth* (Vol. 8, No. 3), ©1998 Catherine Badgley. "Uncle Ben" is excerpted from *There's Nothing in the Middle of the Road but Yellow Stripes and Dead Armadillos* by Jim Hightower, ©1997 Jim Hightower, reprinted by permission of HarperCollins Publishers, Inc.

INDEX